Advance Praise for *Understanding th*

"Alisa Belzer and Brian Dashew have assembled an ⟨
ing. This edited text brings together established and emerging
multiple perspectives on learners, the individual and social context of learning, and
the key processes and approaches for adult learning. This text should be required in
every graduate program and professional development activity that prepares practitioners and scholars of adult learning."—*Ronald M. Cervero, Professor and Deputy
Director, Center for Health Professions Education, Uniformed Services University of the
Health Sciences*

"Adult education is a rich and diverse field of study that includes not only formal
training and development, but also self-directed learning, community action, learning that occurs in social settings as well as the classroom, and much, much more.
It is above all learner-centered that respects the intellect and capacity every adult
brings to their community. *Understanding the Adult Learner* eloquently captures this
richness and diversity, meeting the needs of those who are new to our field as well as
being a valuable resource to seasoned scholars and practitioners. Although this book
has many strengths, I see its greatest strength in how it bridges theory to practice,
and practice to theory. It is a book that is a worthy addition to one's library."—*Jeff
Zacharakis, Professor, Kansas State University*

"Belzer and Dashew's *Understanding the Adult Learner: Perspectives and Practices* is an
exceptional book that explores many facets of adult learning and development theories, bridging the theory-to-practice gap in an accessible and readable way. In each
chapter, authors focus on the purposes of adult education through distinct theoretical
lenses, providing insightful reflections and discussions of learning and development
theories, adult learners in diverse contexts, and actions adult educators can take to
support them on their learning journeys. This volume is an essential addition to
the field and should be required reading for all adult education scholars, graduate
students, and practitioners."—*Catherine A. Hansman, Emeritus Professor of Adult
Learning and Development, Cleveland State University*

"This comprehensive volume offers emerging scholars and practitioners in adult education insights into a wide variety of theoretical perspectives. The book is highly
readable and loaded with practice-based ideas informed by theory. The authors are
theorists and educators with extensive expertise in their areas of scholarship. Readers
are encouraged to explore and consider the theories from a critically reflective perspective with regard to the learning context and positionality of the learners."—*Randee
Lipson Lawrence, Professor Emeritus, Adult Education, National Louis University;
Adjunct Professor, Teachers College, Columbia University*

"This book is compelling in its grasp of the 21st-century issues and challenges facing the field of adult and continuing education. Drawing upon the insights of many iconic authors and their impactful theoretical and practical literary contributions that have shaped our research and practice for over 30 years, this text is indispensable for developing professionals seeking to understand the depth and breadth of the field."—*Larry Martin*, *Professor Emeritus, University of Wisconsin, Milwaukee*

"This book makes a significant contribution to the study and practice of adult education as it brings together a collection of foundational theories, perspectives, and concepts that will enhance teaching and learning in the profession. A major strength of the book is its translational approach where in each chapter, content experts present theories and concepts followed by ideas for practical pedagogical implications. Kudos to the editors for the design! Centralizing the theories and concepts of adult learning and development in one book will aid emerging scholars in making informed decisions about appropriate literature within which to frame their investigations. This will be a seminal book, particularly for its translational approach to bridging research, teaching, and learning."—*Mary V. Alfred*, *Professor Emeritus, Texas A&M University*

UNDERSTANDING THE ADULT LEARNER

UNDERSTANDING THE ADULT LEARNER

Perspectives and Practices

Edited by Alisa Belzer and Brian Dashew

Foreword by Hal Beder

Routledge
Taylor & Francis Group

NEW YORK AND LONDON

First published in 2023 by Stylus Publishing, LLC.

Published in 2023 by Routledge
605 Third Avenue, New York, NY 10017
4 Park Square, Milton Park, Abingdon, Oxon OX14 4RN

Routledge is an imprint of the Taylor & Francis Group, an informa business.

Library of Congress Cataloging-in-Publication-Data

Names: Belzer, Alisa, editor. | Dashew, Brian, editor.
Title: Understanding the adult learner : perspectives and practices / edited by Alisa Belzer
    and Brian Dashew ; foreword by Hal Beder.
Description: First edition. | Sterling, Virginia : Stylus Publishing, LLC, [2023] | Includes
    bibliographical references and index.
Identifiers: LCCN 2023009657
    ISBN 9781642672329 (cloth : acid-free paper) | ISBN 9781642672336
    (paperback : acid-free paper)
Subjects: LCSH: Adult education. | Adult education teachers--Training
of. Classification: LCC LC5215 .U38 2023
    DDC 374--dc23/eng/20230308
LC record available at https://lccn.loc.gov/2023009657

ISBN: 9781642672329 (hbk)
ISBN: 9781642672336 (pbk)
ISBN: 9781003448471 (ebk)

DOI: 10.4324/9781003448471

CONTENTS

FOREWORD   vii
  Hal Beder

ACKNOWLEDGMENTS   xi

PART ONE: SETTING THE STAGE

1   FOUNDATIONAL CONCEPTS AND COMMITMENTS FOR
    ADULT LEARNING   3
     Alisa Belzer and Brian Dashew

2   CREATING INCLUSIVE LEARNING SPACES FOR A DIVERSE WORLD
    The Womanist Perspective   21
     Vanessa Sheared

3   THE DEMOCRATIC IMPULSE IN ADULT EDUCATION   39
     Stephen Brookfield

PART TWO: INTERNAL INFLUENCES AND THE LEARNER

4   MOTIVATING ADULT LEARNERS   59
     David A. Bergin, Christi A. Bergin, and Sarah L. Prewett

5   MINDING THE BRAIN
    The Emotional Foundations of Adult Learning   79
     Kathleen Taylor and Catherine Marienau

6   THE ROLE OF EMOTION-LADEN EXPERIENCES IN SELF-FORMATION   99
     John Dirkx and Steven Schlegel

7   ADULT DEVELOPMENT
    Robert Kegan's Constructive–Developmental Theory   117
     Deborah Helsing

PART THREE: ADULT LEARNING PROCESSES AND APPROACHES

8   STRUCTURED SILENCES IN ADULT LEARNING THEORY   137
    Edith Gnanadass and Lisa R. Merriweather

9   ANDRAGOGY
    The Philosophy Behind the Practice   157
    Ralf St. Clair

10 SELF-DIRECTED LEARNING
    A 21st-Century Imperative   173
    Ralph G. Brockett

11 EXPERIENTIAL LEARNING
    Defining Parameters, Contextual Foundations, and Influential Contributions   193
    Colin Beard

12 TRANSFORMATIVE LEARNING
    Evolving Theory for Understanding Change   213
    Chad Hoggan and Elizabeth Kasl

13 DIGITAL LEARNING AND THE PROMISE OF CONNECTIVISM FOR
    ADULT EDUCATION   235
    Rita Kop

PART FOUR: CONCLUSIONS

14 INSTRUCTIONAL DESIGN
    Applying Principles of Adult Education   255
    Brian Dashew and Diane Gayeski

15 NEXT STEPS
    Interrogating and Using Theory   275
    Alisa Belzer and Brian Dashew

    EDITORS AND CONTRIBUTORS   285

    INDEX   291

When most people think of education, they think of elementary, secondary, and postsecondary education. These forms of education are prevalent in discussions of policy. They are also highlighted in the media and are evident in our tax and tuition bills. As will become clear as you read this book, however, adult educators look at education more broadly. From an adult education perspective, education is all around us. If you went to a museum, you might not know that an adult educator, also known as a curator, organized the exhibits for educational impact. If you looked up a recipe on the internet, you probably would not realize that an adult educator, known as a chef, developed the recipe so you could follow it without mistakes. When adults purposely learn something, they are engaging in adult education; when adults convey knowledge and skills to other adults, they are adult educators. Yet it is also true that many adult educators neither identify with the role nor consider it their occupation.

In contrast to the myriad adults who function as adult educators unwittingly, there are some who do identify themselves as adult educators and consider adult education to be their profession. These individuals comprise the professional core of adult education as a field of study and practice. This book is an important source for helping them learn what they need to know to be maximally effective. But it is also important for those nonformal adult educators who expand and extend this field of practice—curators and chefs, but also coaches, managers, master gardeners, registered dieticians, community advocates, and more.

Perhaps the most influential book about adult education ever written is Malcolm Knowles's *The Modern Practice of Adult Education* (chapter 9 discusses Knowles's concepts in depth). Knowles is important because he strived to answer the question "How is adult education different from education for children and adolescents?" After all, if adult education is not different, why study it? However, he argued that there are important differences that gave rise to the term *andragogy*, defined as the "art and science" of teaching adults. In doing so, Knowles provided adult educators with an identity that had previously been weak at best.

There are at least three characteristics of adult education that influence what adult educators need to know and how they will function: (a) the adult condition, (b) adults as voluntary learners, and (c) nonhierarchical organization.

The Adult Condition

Many people assume that adult education is like the elementary–secondary and higher education they have experienced, the only difference being that the students are older. However, in reality adult education differs markedly because adult learners are markedly different from learners at earlier stages of life. While the primary role of children and adolescents is student, adults have many important roles, none of which are typically student, including parent, worker, and citizen. Adult education is a secondary, enabling role. For adults, meeting the demands of their adult roles is often a major motivation for participating in adult education. As St. Clair notes in chapter 9 of this volume, adult education helps adults build the knowledge and skills they need to deal with the problems adulthood poses.

As a result of these differences, some forms of education are typically adult, transformative education (chapter 12) and self-directed learning (chapter 10) being examples. Adult education also often has a social mission, as exemplified in chapters on democracy (chapter 3) and inclusive learning (chapter 2). This book also addresses the conditions of adulthood that shape and influence the way that learning takes place—shaping factors such as the adult brain (chapter 5), adult motivation (chapter 4), and the role of emotions in learning (chapter 6).

Voluntary Learners

While children are required to participate in elementary and secondary education, participation in adult education is largely voluntary. Adults participate to meet their needs and wants, to solve life-imposed problems, for enjoyment, or out of just plain curiosity. Even when adults are required to participate, their cognitive and affective engagement with learning may be largely up to the individual. The implication of voluntary participation is that unless adult educators can understand adults' reasons for participation and respond with relevant programming, learners will not participate, and there would be no adult education. Much of the theory that undergirds adult education is directly or indirectly based on understanding participation. We need to understand how adults learn, so we can create programs that help them learn. We need also to understand the problems posed by adulthood, so that we can facilitate problem resolution. This text addresses the various ways that learning and adulthood are framed in this field and invites the reader to explore the implications of these different frameworks on the development of adult education programs.

Nonhierarchical Organization

Elementary, secondary, and higher education systems are organized in a hierarchical fashion. The basic organizational unit, which is generally age related, is a grade or a year, as in higher education. It is assumed that teachers and other experts are the knowers; students are the receivers of their knowledge. Based on tests, teachers assign grades and grades determine whether students move forward on the hierarchical ladder. Knowledge content is cumulative and becomes more complex and specialized as students progress. For those who are enrolled in these systems, student is generally the primary life role.

Although there are exceptions, as with some adult-oriented college degree programs, most adult education is nonhierarchical and varies in duration, from a 10-minute segment on YouTube on how to plant a tree to a lengthy journey through the Great Courses. As Brockett explains in chapter 10, for example, self-directed learning is a predominant form of adult education and is by nature nonhierarchical. Not being locked into a hierarchical system, adult educators can adapt quickly to new needs as they arise.

About This Volume

Professional adult educators lack many of the identifying symbols that other professionals have, such as white coats, clerical collars, or judges' black robes; instead, our most important professional marker is a body of knowledge. An essential resource for conveying that body of knowledge are the professional books that describe and interpret the knowledge base. Professional books provide commonality of knowledge across many contexts of adult education practice and, in doing so, are important in molding our identity as adult educators.

Since Knowles, there have been many excellent professional books that have become classics. By *classic* I mean books that have been adopted by most graduate programs as required reading and, as such, are known to almost everyone with a graduate degree in adult education. Most are written by a single author or coauthors. By and large, they summarize, explain, and interpret theory and what is known from research in adult education and related fields, research that has been conducted by others who are experts in a particular area. This book is different. Each chapter is written by experts on its specific topic. Thus, the authors offer a depth of knowledge and perspective that is different from what is offered by texts that try to cover a broad swath of information on many topics but are written by a single or multiple authors with general adult education expertise. The contrast means that each chapter has a depth and vitality that are sometimes missing from many other professional books.

Another aspect of this book that is different is the diversity of subject matter: "inclusive learning," "the brain," "emotion," "instructional design," and so forth. This is no accident because the book reflects what adult education actually is. Adult education varies widely in form and duration. It addresses a wide range of social and individual needs. Although it is not as visible as traditional forms of education, it is more widespread. Moreover, it is absolutely necessary for the health of the social order.

For both its depth and breadth, this book will be an essential resource for adult educators new to the field and a meaningful reference for those with more experience.

Hal Beder
Emeritus Professor, Rutgers University

ACKNOWLEDGMENTS

In expressing our gratitude to the following individuals, we hope that they can understand the importance of their contributions to our lives and our work, within and beyond their express contributions to this project.

We first wish to thank the scholars who contributed chapters to this text. The ambitious aim of our book was to have the voices that shaped key theories and frameworks in adult education speak about the constructs they helped to define. That meant that we were reliant on our authors to say "yes" and we are so grateful that they did. The authors in this book had the herculean task of contributing to an edited volume that also needed to hold together as a cohesive textbook. Their contributions did not end when the chapter was submitted; instead, these authors engaged with us over nearly 2 years of collaboration and discussion to create this final text. We are so appreciative that they saw value in this project and this process, and we thank them for their care, passion, collegiality, and knowledge. We also greatly appreciate their patience and perseverance through the unusually arduous revision process. While we are most immediately thankful for their contributions to the text, we also thank them for their larger contributions to this field. Because we have had the good fortune to both study and practice adult education, we recognize the roles they have each played in defining and building our field. We thank them for engaging with us, informing us, and challenging us. For their contributions to this project and for all they do for the field of adult education, they have made us better educators and better learners.

At Rutgers University's Graduate School of Education, we have both been lucky enough to teach the *Understanding the Adult Learner* course that informed the design of this text. We owe enormous thanks to the students in the Adult and Continuing Education graduate program who have taken this class, and whose class discussions, questions, and responses to assignments have pushed us to re-examine the foundational theories of our field and encouraged us to take on this text. They have taught us so much about the connections between theory and practice, about the role that identity and culture play in how theory is enacted, and about how the global context informs the way we think about adult learners and learning. We hope that they can see evidence of the impact they have had on us throughout this text.

We are grateful, as well, to David Brightman from Stylus Publishing for believing in the vision for this book. David became our champion of this vision, keeping us on track and reminding us what we were attempting to build. This book was written in 2020 and 2021, and the world around us led to delays and challenged some of the priorities we had for this text. David worked with us through all of this and always encouraged us to prioritize getting the book right over getting the book done. In so many different ways, this final product would not have been possible without him.

Closer to home, we want to thank our families. We are sure that this book was the topic of far more dinners out, walks with the dogs, and weekend car rides than people in our orbit might have anticipated. Brian wants to thank Brad for being his perennial champion and for his patience and support during the creation of this book. Alisa thanks Jon for exactly the same things along with him offering his sense of humor whenever it was most needed.

Lastly, we thank all of you for reading this book. We have tried to infuse this text with calls to action for our readers about how we can all be more engaged and just adult educators. We hope this book both guides and inspires you in the work that you do, and we look forward to the contributions of future generations to our collective understanding of adult learners.

PART ONE

Setting the Stage

FOUNDATIONAL CONCEPTS AND COMMITMENTS FOR ADULT LEARNING

Alisa Belzer and Brian Dashew

Marketing professionals dressed in business casual rushed through the hotel hallways, looking to find the location of the next concurrent session they would attend at the annual conference. Many had chosen to come to the conference, but some were "volunteered" to participate by their employer. They knew they would be listening to a presentation on a topic they had chosen and hoped they would have time to ask questions and pick up hand-outs before they rushed off to the next session.

Teachers and school administrators trickled into a university building after a long day of work. They were attending a required course in their doctoral program. If this week was like every other week, the professor would lead them in a discussion on the readings, asking them to analyze and critique them and then think about how they apply to their own practices. They would leave the classroom several hours later, only to return the following week, their midterm paper completed and concerns multiplying about the qualifying exam that was coming up.

At 7:30 at night, adults began to arrive at the restaurant where they would participate in a 2-hour cooking class. They had chosen to participate because they wanted to learn how to cook dishes in an unfamiliar cuisine. Working together, they prepared the meal while the instructor circulated, making suggestions and demonstrating techniques. After the meal was prepared, the class sat down to enjoy the meal.

At the city museum of art, adults shuffled past paintings in the special show on display there for a few months. Some wore headphones and listened to a curator explain the history and artistic features of the works; others glanced at signage in the galleries; and some simply walked through, taking in the great works of art.

An employee and her supervisor met to discuss her performance over the preceding year. They identified strengths and challenges, successes and defeats. The supervisor offered some suggestions, and they concluded by identifying a performance plan for the next year.

Leadership and uniformed officers from a city's police force gathered at a community center with community members for a monthly series of discussion circles. They shared their feelings and experiences with community-based policing practices to raise awareness and ease tensions between the police department and the citizens it serves.

These brief descriptions of adult learners in different contexts help set the stage for this book. They convey that adults seek out learning for very different reasons in very different contexts. The chapters were written to support adult educators' development in responding to this rich array. There is no single way to be an adult learner, and so it should not be surprising that there is no single way to be an adult educator. However, we believe that all educators must demonstrate a commitment to meeting adult learners where they are. They should help them move forward not only with new content knowledge, information, and skills but also with new ways of making meaning and seeing themselves, their role, and the world. Thus, adult educators need to be expert in their content area and understand how to use adult learning theories to convey it. They should also understand the different ways in which adults learn and have a genuine interest in knowing who their learners are, including their hopes and dreams; experiences, goals, and interests; identities as racialized, ethnic, gendered, classed individuals; and cognitive, affective, and logistical supports and barriers. This volume introduces many theories and concepts that can help adult educators do this effectively. Although they generate implications for practice, perhaps more importantly, they offer a lens through which to plan, design, implement, and interpret practice that is responsive to the diversity of adult learners. No one theory is generally sufficient—substantively or culturally—to do this in every context. How and when to draw on them require adult educators to engage in ongoing reflection and analysis.

As an introduction to this book, we begin this chapter with the adult learner. We explore the question of what defines an adult learner as adult and then reflect on the ways in which adulthood shapes the learner, the learning needs, and the learning context. We also provide an overview of learning theories considered foundational to the adult learning theories and concepts that are explored in this volume. Along with this, we describe some key commitments in the field that impact teaching and learning opportunities in adult education. We then conclude with a description of contexts for learning and an overview of how the subsequent chapters are organized.

Defining the Adult in Adult Education

Several chapters in this book are dedicated to understanding how adults are distinct from children—including emotional, cognitive, motivational, and developmental differences. Because of these distinctions, as well as the experiences and responsibilities adult learners bring to the classroom (e.g., work and family), adult education is grounded in the belief that educational approaches should be different from those for children. In recognition of these distinctions, we begin our focus on adult learners by asking what it means to be an adult; what does "adult" mean in the term "adult learner"?

Chronological age may seem like a logical place to start in defining adulthood. Yet, for many, choosing a specific threshold age is difficult, even arbitrary. In fact, Ross-Gordon et al. (2016) made clear that age is an insufficient delineation. Despite the long effort to concisely and concretely define adults as a specific learner population, the term can be viewed through a number of different lenses, including legal, religious, biological, cognitive, social and cultural expectations, and self-perception (Ross-Gordon et al., 2016). Delineations of adulthood have shifted across time and differ by country and culture around the world. When it comes to social and cultural determinants of adulthood, we look, for example, toward what is considered an acceptable age for marriage, parenthood, and the start of careers as well as expectations related to financial independence and responsibilities; understandings of these are highly variable across cultures and societies. When it comes to self-perception, adulthood arrives when individuals identify themselves as such, and this often occurs when new (adult) roles and responsibilities are assumed. By stating that adults are "those whose age, social roles and self-perception define them as adults" (p. 8), Merriam and Brockett (2007) drove home the ambiguity and relativity of the term. This implies that adulthood is relative, variable, and ambiguous. It also points to the danger of generalizing about the nature of adulthood and its effect on adult learning.

Many students enrolled in our master's degree program in adult and continuing education and who work in higher education ask if undergraduates should be considered adults. Through some lenses (e.g., legal), traditional-aged college students (aged 17–22) in the United States are adults because most have reached the age of legal majority; they can vote and serve in the military. Yet, few have taken up social roles and responsibilities that many associate with adulthood, including more or less permanent employment, marriage, parenthood, or leadership responsibilities. It is true that some traditional-aged college students are parents or, increasingly, must work full time to support themselves. However, many institutions of higher education have a separate adult undergraduate student category, often designated as "nontraditional"; typically the threshold for this category is 25. This seems to imply that there is a difference between 17- to 22-year-olds and older college students, regardless of legal definitions or roles they have taken up. While some may consider undergraduates to be adults, others might say they are at the doorway of adulthood rather than having crossed its threshold. We can see that chronological age plays a role in defining adulthood but is not the only marker.

Exploring where the threshold of adulthood sits is a question we return to annually with our students. We always start our master's level course on adult learning by discussing definitions of adulthood. First, we draw on our own and each other's experiences by asking our students to respond to the question "When did you first feel like you were an adult?" Typically, they select events such as the birth of a first child, caring for an elderly relative who had previously cared for them, becoming financially independent, getting life insurance, or buying a house. As our class discussions seek to identify themes across these events, we note that these transitions mean undertaking increased responsibilities for the needs of others, gaining emotional or financial self-reliance and independence, forging new roles and relationships, and deepening awareness of self in relation to others. Additionally, students often see their arrival into adulthood as an ongoing journey rather than a single point in time. The progress toward it is uneven and can be specific to the domains of family, work, and community, where they feel more adult in one than another and more at some times than others. They also suggest that their self-perception of adulthood is recurrently challenged, suggesting when they thought they had reached adulthood a subsequent event—a first job, the death of a parent, a divorce—led them to define a new event as the true transition to adulthood. By comparing experiences with classmates it becomes clear that adulthood is a concept that is socially constructed and specific to time, place, and culture. It is obvious that there is no one definition of the term, and yet our students all recognize that there is an undeniable difference between adulthood as they experience it and their childhood and adolescence. It is often these differences, rather than any particular age, that impel adults to pursue adult education in the first place. As Ross-Gordon et al. (2016) explained,

> While chronological age represents the literal number of years one has lived, biological or functional age (physical condition), psychological (developmental maturity), and social age (perception of roles and expectations at any given point in life) are different measures of age that may significantly impact an adult's desire for and ability to pursue learning. (p. 14)

Responding to the Diversity of Learners

The ambiguity of culturally and self-defined definitions of adulthood suggests that individuals seek adult education at many different stages of life, thus adding one dimension of diversity to the population that participates in adult education. Purposes of and contexts for learning create another kind of diversity. As the vignettes at the beginning of this chapter illustrate, adult education occurs not only in places we might naturally consider, such as classrooms on college campuses and meeting rooms at corporate headquarters, but also in restaurants, museums, and community spaces. It could also happen in many other contexts, including on the sidewalk, along the trail, in the car or the living room, in a doctor's or dentist's office or a massage or acupuncture studio, at the gym or the playing field. This means that adult learners, depending on the type of learning they are engaged in, might be there in any number of identities, including student, parent, patient, employee, volunteer, friend, or tourist.

Research on learning has also helped us understand important differences among learners. Some differences are due to preferences, such as variance in preferences for auditory, visual, or kinesthetic learning. Others are due to innate capacities. For example, Howard Gardner (1983) conceptualized "multiple intelligences," including linguistic, musical, logical–mathematical, spatial, and interpersonal, recognizing that we all have different innate strengths in how we function cognitively. Others have made clear that difference emerges because of inequitable opportunities to learn (Shores et al., 2020) due, for example, to poverty and systemic racism. But learners are diverse in many other ways as well. These domains include racial or ethnic identity, gender, sexual orientation, developmental level, and physical and intellectual ability. They are also diverse in terms of goals, motivations, purposes, intended outcomes, and expectations regarding time commitments for learning.

Thus, adult educators must learn to build on the affordances of working collaboratively in a setting composed of learners who are diverse along multiple dimensions. However, from our experience teaching adult education graduate students, we know that sometimes their response, when presented with one type of diversity or another, is to think that they should assess each learner and then develop individualized instructional plans to respond. While it is clearly important to assess learning needs, developing an individualized approach is often unrealistic or inappropriate. Instead, the goal should be to frame diversity as a rich resource, and working to support all learners in a growth-oriented context takes advantage of the benefits of learning collaboratively across differences. In contrast to the isolation of individualized instruction, interaction among diverse learners can be generative, intellectually stimulating, and emotionally supportive. Additionally, learning to work collaboratively and collegially is a key 21st-century skill in just about every work context imaginable; this should be modeled and supported in the adult learning context.

Many of the chapters in this book elaborate on what this diversity looks like, why it is an asset and important for learning, and how best to capitalize on and be responsive to the wide range of learners adult educators encounter. Here, we offer several strategies that apply across adult learning theories and concepts and will resonate with those that you will read about in this book:

- Build a sense of community and commitment within the group such that learners feel responsible for each other, safe to share experiences, and heard.
- Provide instructional resources from authors who are diverse in as many ways as possible. It is important that learners see themselves in the materials they encounter; it is also important that they see authors with identities that are different from their own.
- Give instructional choices that are responsive to differences represented in the learner population. For example, vary choices by learner interests and goals, cognitive or developmental levels, and identities.

- Engage learners in shaping the learning context so that their voices, experiences, and needs are elevated and integrated into the work.
- Acknowledge, highlight, leverage, and value the diversity that is present in the context.

A Brief Overview of Learning Theories

An important starting point for any text on adult education is the foundational knowledge that research on learning in general (i.e., not specific to adults) has provided. Learning theories help us understand "how learning occurs as well as being suggestive as to how such an explanation translates into practices" (Merriam & Bierema, 2014, p. 25). While it might seem a straightforward task to define learning, understandings of what it includes are diverse (Barron et al., 2015). Early learning researchers, as shall be discussed in the following sections, thought of it as observable changes in behavior not due to physical change, changes in motivation, or other contextual factors not related to actual efforts to learn. Definitions within this realm do not focus on the cognitive processes that support these changes. Barron et al. (2015) offered an interesting contrast in their very modern definition that is so general it can even include machine learning: "a structured updating of system properties based on the processing of new information" (p. 405). This definition may barely sound like a description of human learning, but it does reflect current understanding of what happens in the brain when humans learn. American psychologist Robert Gagne (1985) provided a definition that reflects a more descriptive understanding of learning that focuses on outcomes, not just processes. He said it is a "change in human disposition or capability that persists over a period of time and is not simply ascribable to processes of growth" (p. 2). Other definitions focus on the acquisition of new knowledge or understanding (Pritchard, 2002). This suggests a more comprehensive and holistic examination of learning theory—as opposed to strict adherence to a single approach—is most helpful for practitioners. What follows is a brief overview of behaviorism, cognitivism and constructivism, and social learning, all general learning theories that are applicable across the life span and that also intersect with specific adult learning theories.

Behaviorism

Research on learning was first systematically and scientifically pursued in the late 19th century. This work gave rise to the first important modern theory of learning, behaviorism. Behaviorism focuses on changes in the individual that can be observed (National Research Council, 2000). The early research on behaviorism ignored the mental processes that we now understand are engaged in learning. Early research focused on what is known as *classical conditioning*, which looks at the relationship between a stimulus and a response. Although the American psychologist John B. Watson may have coined the term *behaviorism*, many people are more familiar with the work of Russian psychologist Ivan Pavlov, who is famous for training dogs to salivate at the sound of a bell, a behavior elicited through the stimulus of a reward. Later behaviorist researchers, perhaps most famously American psychologist B.F. Skinner, worked on *operant conditioning*, which focused on reinforcing or extinguishing existing behavior using rewards or punishments.

Behaviorism is associated with learning that centers on concrete and specific externally articulated performance standards, competencies, and learning outcomes that are observable and measurable. Although the learner must play an active role in engaging with reinforcements in operant conditioning, behavioral learning is generally highly orchestrated by the teacher or trainer. The characteristics of behavioristic learning approaches include repetition, drill, rote learning, feedback, and incentives. Behaviorism has been critiqued as rigid, rote learning without understanding or meaning making, which can actually suppress motivation (Pritchard, 2002; Stewart, 2012). Yet, versions of it are still commonly employed in adult settings in which the goal is to get learners to consistently and predictably enact a set of behaviors. Examples of this can be seen in trainings on topics ranging from food safety, to the use of purchasing software platforms, to pilot takeoff and landing procedures.

Cognitivism and Constructivism

Researchers gradually began to understand the importance of the mental processes that are engaged during learning and began to develop ways to study these. This development was grounded in the assumption that humans actively seek information to meet their goals. By the 1950s, researchers' focus shifted from observable processes to the internal, invisible elements of learning that take place in the brain. This gave rise to the field of study known as *cognitive science*, which focuses on the role of mental processes such as understanding, reasoning, meaning making, memory, and problem solving. Jean Piaget, the Swiss psychologist known for his pioneering work on child development, was one of the most highly influential early cognitive scientists. He found that the brain develops frameworks and conceptual networks—known as *schema*—as children grow and accrue knowledge and experience. Piaget asserted that when individuals encounter new information, it either gets added on to, elaborates, or reinforces existing knowledge organized around a schema (accommodation) or actually alters or restructures the schema (assimilation). He and other researchers came to understand that this process involves active construction of understanding and meaning. This contributed to the development of the theory of constructivism, which recognizes that learning is a process of "active mental work" (Woolfok, 1993, cited in Pritchard, 2002, p. 20).

While Piaget viewed this process as neutral, we now understand that individuals filter new experience through the lens of prior experiences that are shaped by culture, identity, and many other external and internal factors. Thus learners build on "prior knowledge, skills, beliefs, and concepts that significantly influence what they notice about the environment and how they organize and interpret it. This, in turn, affects their abilities to remember, reason, solve problems, and acquire new knowledge" (National Research Council, 2000, p. 10). Clearly this understanding of learners and learning differs markedly from behaviorism, which framed learners as receivers and reactors but not active, autonomous participants at the center of their own learning who both shape and are shaped by the micro and macro contexts in which they function.

An instructional approach that emphasizes cognitivism helps learners build schemas, activate prior knowledge, develop strategic approaches to storing and retrieving information, and reflect on and externalize their learning. Additionally, constructivist practices emphasize active learning, discovery, exploration, experimentation, hypothesis testing, project and inquiry-based learning, and self-assessment (Stewart, 2012). A more constructivist approach does not deny the importance of students gaining knowledge through interaction with experts and informational sources. Constructing meaning is grounded in these experiences. But constructivism sees learners as building on their understandings of factual knowledge and having ways to organize new information around prior experiences and existing schemas; cognitive science helps inform our understanding of how individuals retrieve and apply it. Learning (or developing more expertise and competence) comes from "a deepening of the information base and the development of a conceptual framework for that subject matter" (National Research Council, 2000, p. 16).

A key mechanism for supporting cognitive learning (including constructivist approaches) is *metacognition*. Metacognition is awareness of the mental processes of the self or knowledge of one's own cognition (Pritchard, 2002). Simply put, it is often explained as "thinking about thinking." It involves the acts of consciously planning, monitoring, and evaluating learning. This type of awareness is important to learning because it enables the learner to take control over, by being conscious about, the process. Metacognitive thinking is not necessarily automatic and thus often needs to be developed. Effective metacognitive skills are discipline specific but, overall, activities such as goal setting, planning, reflection, and progress monitoring are examples that can support this process. Metacognition has perhaps been most thoroughly investigated in relationship to effective meaning making while reading. In this activity, moment-to-moment metacognitive activities include activating prior knowledge (schema) before and during reading, predicting what will come next, and checking understanding, noting when there are breakdowns, and deploying "fix up" strategies when needed (National Research Council, 2000).

Social Learning

An important line of thought that was subsequently developed acknowledges the important role of social interaction and social context in learning. While early cognitivists focused on the internal thought processes of the individual, now we understand that these processes are supported and enhanced by contact with others. An originator of social cognitivism, Albert Bandura (1977) stated that most learning occurs as a result of modeling: "From observing others one forms an idea of how new behaviors are performed, and on later occasions this coded information serves as a guide for action" (p. 22). Lave and Wenger (1991) focused on learning in day-to-day interactions in what they called "communities of practice." Participants in these spaces have shared interests and commitments, shared language, and shared practices. *Situated learning* posits that learning occurs through observation along with gradually increasing engagement with the practices of that community within a context where more knowledgeable, competent members are carrying out its everyday tasks. Many people who learn on the job, for example, are engaging in situated learning. This type of learning is marked by authentic opportunities to learn and practice in the presence of experts within actual contexts of practice (i.e., in social settings).

The idea of *social constructivism* originated with Lev Vygotsky, a Soviet psychologist, who recognized that knowledge construction does not generally happen in isolation. Even when not physically present, the social artifacts of language and culture shape the ways in which learning occurs. More concretely, however, he identified the important role of dialogue with a more "knowledgeable other" (Vygotsky, 1978). Often, but not always, this role is taken up by teachers; their task is to help learners move forward from what they can comfortably accomplish or understand on their own by scaffolding (supporting) them as they move through the "zone of proximal development," the point of challenge just slightly beyond what learners can do independently. The scaffold includes modeling and bridging to help make connections, cues, and stimulating questions (Stewart, 2012). The emphasis in all social learning is on interaction, pointing to the importance of according all learners a "rightful presence" (Calabrese Barton & Tan, 2019) in social contexts that will support their learning. This does not necessarily occur without consciously undoing racist structures and attitudes in the learning context.

Implications for the Practice of Contemporary Learning Theories

An important summary of learning research, *How People Learn* (National Research Council, 2000), offers helpful implications for practice based on contemporary understandings of learning. Clearly, as understanding of learning has evolved, so too have ideas about effective instruction. These are complemented by brain-based research, as described in chapter 5, this volume. We now understand that practices that support active learning and sense-making through hands-on experiences are critical, as are learning environments that acknowledge and build on the knowledge and skills that learners bring. In this way, educational contexts are learner centered, offering the appropriate level of challenge. An emphasis on understanding rather than rote memorization suggests an emphasis on depth over breadth of content. Assessments in this type of learning environment should be formative (providing ongoing feedback rather than summative evaluation), which, in addition to informing teachers and learners about learning progress and problems, can inform instruction and activate learners' metacognition. Additionally, students need to feel free to take risks, ask questions, and make mistakes knowing they will get helpful feedback.

While instructors plays a central role in achieving this, it is also important that the learning context is a place of collaboration and cooperation.

Although most learning research has been done with children and the implications that emerge from that work, the principles apply equally to adults. However, "many approaches to teaching adults consistently violate principles for optimizing learning" (National Research Council, 2000, pp. 26–27). Not only should adult educators do better to apply what is known about learning processes in general, but adult education researchers and theorists argue that adult learners also need approaches that are specific to them as adults. The emergence of adult learning theories, especially in the second half of the 20th century, has been an effort to address this. Presumably, the differences between adult and younger learners are, at least in part, due to the quality and quantity of experience from which adults have to draw, and are influenced by, in the learning setting. In addition, their roles and responsibilities likely help shape their motivations for learning, their interests, and the time and energy they have to devote to learning. In the adult learning theories and concepts described in this text, we believe that there is much that affirms the implications for practice previously described, but also elaborate and add on to them in ways that are specific to meeting the needs of adults.

Contexts for Adult Education

We now turn from a focus on the learner and learning to a focus on the contexts for learning. Many may think of learning as an activity that takes place primarily in schools and universities. As indicated by the vignettes at the beginning of this chapter, however, it is clear that adult education can have different kinds of sponsors and durations and draw on different kinds of educational resources. In other words, adult education includes a wide variety of contexts and purposes for learning. It is common in the adult education literature to see these contexts divided into three broad categories: formal, informal, and nonformal education (Coombs et al., 1973). These categories can serve as a helpful organizing framework for understanding the types of contexts where adult learners are.

In this framework, *formal learning* includes any systematic, institutional, hierarchically organized educational system organized for the purpose of academic, professional, and technical training. Formal learning settings include schools, colleges and universities, and vocational training programs offered within community colleges. They confer degrees and formally recognized professional certificates. *Nonformal learning* includes any organized, structured learning activity that takes place outside of formal learning contexts. The learning approach may be structured and organized, but nonformal learning tends to be more flexible than formal learning. This includes apprenticeship programs, continuing professional education and professional conferences and seminars, library- or museum-based education, or volunteer training, for example, to become an adult literacy tutor. Finally, *informal learning* is the kind of lifelong learning that happens organically as we go about our day-to-day lives. If there is an educator role, it is not formally recognized and could include a neighbor, friend, or family member. It is not necessarily planned, and learning engagement may not even be conscious. Informal learning can take place in stores, museums, on nature trails, or when surfing the Web. Our students have found it useful to think about informal learning in the workplace as what you might get from the conversations that take place in the breakroom or kitchen—the "water cooler chat." It is important to note that learning contexts may overlap in terms of these categories; the lines between them are somewhat porous (Fordham, 2020).

Adult education contexts are established by such micro dimensions as purpose and place, but they are also shaped by the macro level. In other words, what is going on in the world around us plays a role. As we write this, the economy and its impact on the labor market, climate change, a global pandemic, a threatened presidential election, and the so-called racial reckoning that was sharpened by the murders of George Floyd and Breonna Taylor in the late spring of 2020 have had an impact on the purposes for learning and the tone and content of talk in adult education classes. For example, the precarity of a labor market shaped increasingly by a gig economy has altered the kinds of preparation for work required and the desire for continuing education training that adults seek out. The pandemic forced many to reconsider their work situations and has led to the "great resignation"; this has encouraged adults to seek out new learning opportunities in response as they explore kinds of work. The pandemic has also pointed out the importance of scientific literacy and the capacity to evaluate research findings. Many have been sent rushing off to their computers to teach themselves about viruses and vaccines. A tumultuous presidency and disputes over voting results have suggested the need to counter misinformation through adult education. And a growing understanding of systemic racism has pointed to the importance of centering diverse voices and experiences that have led to a great deal of learning, relearning, and unlearning of U.S. racial history.

Adult educators, then, have the task of meeting learners where they are in a wide range of physical, intellectual, and emotional places. They clearly are not just professors in graduate courses or trainers in the training room. Additionally, they are supervisors or coworkers, community organizers, speakers at a protest, clergy, legislators, nurses and doctors and community health workers, immigrant advocates, environmentalists, friends, and neighbors. The list of possible roles in which adult educators may function, when thought of expansively, is long. Anyone who is leading change efforts involving adults or helping adults learn, change, grow, and develop is an adult educator, regardless of whether the setting is formal, nonformal, or informal.

Foundational Commitments in Adult Education

As much as adult educators should be guided by what we know about how people learn, they are also guided in their practices by some specific commitments that shape their practice. There is no consensus on what these are, but there are at least three that we think many adult educators share: that adults always have the potential to grow, develop, change, and even transform; that adult education can contribute to increasing democracy, social justice, and equity; and that reflection is a key activity in accomplishing these as well as a whole range of learning approaches described in this book. These commitments are captured in two theories described in this section—humanism and critical pedagogy—and one practice. These commitments are not the only commitments that adult educators have, and they are not necessarily shared by all adult educators. Adult educators are just as diverse as adult learners, and adult education is a big tent with regard to whom it serves, in what contexts, and for what purposes. These will influence educator beliefs and practices as well, but reflection, the potential to self-actualize, and the ways in which learning can help adults understand and act on injustice are important starting points for many adult educators.

Humanism

The assumption that adults can continue to grow and change is informed by the theory of *humanism*. Originated by American psychologist Abraham Maslow in the early 1900s, it was a response to behaviorism and sought to identify what it is that makes us human, distinctive from other biological beings that simply respond to stimuli (Stewart, 2012). He argued that humans are motivated, once their basic needs are met, by a desire to reach their highest potential (which he called *self-actualization*), not just to fulfill biological needs, as the behaviorists believed (Maslow, 1954). Inherent here is the optimistic assumption that there is a basic tendency of humans to want to become their best selves. Maslow's ideas were amplified by Carl Rogers, an American psychologist who evolved his client-centered therapeutic approach to a learner-centered educational approach. Here, it is assumed that learners should play a key role in shaping and evaluating their learning, grounded in their needs, experiences, and assets. Thus, the hallmarks of a humanistic approach are that learners have choices and control over learning which is in response to their felt concerns, which focuses on the whole person (emotions and intellect), and which places a high value on their self-evaluation. The role of the educator is to facilitate learning by fostering engagement and spurring inquiry. Additionally, it suggests the importance of teaching from a place of care for the individual in which learners feel they belong. These principles are threaded throughout the theories and concepts that are discussed in this text. Here adult education, regardless of its explicit purpose (e.g., to increase knowledge and skills), also implicitly focuses on the individual's personal growth.

Critical Pedagogy

In addition to personal growth, another key belief that is foundational to adult education is its potential to promote democratic principles and increase equity and social justice. This is accomplished, first and foremost, by its very existence. In other words, by enabling adults to learn more, understand more, and be able to do more, adult education broadens "learning opportunities . . . and access to those not served [well] by established educational venues; in particular, the invisible, disenfranchised, or neglected groups of society in adult populations" (Ross-Gordon et al., 2016, p. 109). The assumption here is that many adults missed opportunities to learn when they were younger due to poverty, structural racism, or other barriers. When opportunities to learn in adulthood are offered, individuals can then participate more fully in civic life and overcome inequalities. Additionally, some see that an explicit purpose of adult education is to educate for participation in democratic processes.

Critical pedagogy is an important theoretical and practical thread aligned with this commitment. Here, curriculum is designed with educating for understanding, analyzing, and acting on social structures that promote the many forms of oppression in the forefront. One of the best known practitioners and writers on this aspect of the field is Brazilian educator Paulo Friere. His book *Pedagogy of the Oppressed* (1970) is considered one of the most influential texts shaping the notion of critical adult pedagogy. In it, he described an approach he developed to teach literacy to peasants in Brazil. He explained that educators must eschew the "banking model" of teaching, which centers on transmission of knowledge from teacher to student and indoctrinates them to accept an inequitable and unjust status quo. In this approach, learners are assumed to be empty of ideas and understanding and receptive to receiving "deposits" of knowledge. They are expected to memorize and repeat what they have been taught. He argued that, instead, education is inherently political and the teacher's role is to support the development of a critical consciousness in which learners are able to reflect on, analyze, and act against oppression through a problem-posing approach. Through facilitated dialogue around codifications or artifacts of their day-to-day lives, learners can come to see that economic problems exist because of structural inequalities (oppression) and then work collectively to develop actions to undo them. Although he did not do his work in the United States, he has been highly influential there and around the world. Embedded in his approach was the idea that learners may need help to understand oppression and collective dialogue to identify actions to overcome it. This makes the role of the adult educator one of facilitator and animator—not teacher—who joins in as an equal in building a community of learners who can both reflect on and act to address inequality

These ideas gave rise to and enhanced the importance of the relationship between adult education and social movements, including those struggling for economic justice, a sustainable environment, worker rights, sexual rights, and gender equality. Even when the intent is less radical, adult education often focuses on both individual and community improvement, with progressive goals underlying these efforts (Ross-Gordon et al., 2016). Regardless of the philosophical underpinning of the various purposes of adult education, some of the characteristics of Freire's (1970) problem-solving approach have been carried into or are echoed in what is considered by many to be the essentials of effective adult education practice. Decentralization of authority and the challenging of prevailing ideology have been significant through-lines in the history of adult education, from the founding of the Chautauqua Institute in the 1870s to the Highlander Folk School in the 1930s, from Citizenship Schools during the 1960s to the Massive Open Online Course movement of the 2010s (see chapter 13 for more information on the MOOC movement). As adult education has become a more common field of practice in higher education, workplace learning, community education, and within less formal learning contexts, these values have remained foundational to work with adult learners. For this reason, these programs often include efforts to make the educator–learner relationship as egalitarian as possi-ble, creating a context in which collaboration and cooperation are valued and learning activities build on learner experiences and encourage reflection and critical analysis.

Reflection

Reflection is critical to both humanistic and critical pedagogy approaches. Clearly, constructivism suggests that reflection is also key to making meaning, and metacog-nition is also a kind of reflection. Additionally, it is an essential activity that sup-ports self-directed (chapter 10, this volume), experiential (chapter 11, this volume), and transformational learning (chapter 12, this volume), all of which are described in depth in later chapters. Reflection is also a part of informal learning while adults do day-to-day activities where they may engage in reflection-in-action, in the moment-to-moment decisions made while carrying out a task, or reflection-on-action, when thinking about practices after the fact (Schön, 1983), both examples of situated learning as previously discussed. It is clear from the many ways in which reflection is embedded in learning that it may be instigated by adult educators or by adult learners.

Reflection can play several important roles in learning. Taylor and Marienau (2016) suggested that it creates "a bridge between tacit and explicit aspects of know-ing" (p. 87). Kolb (1984) asserted that it plays a role in transforming experience into learning. It can also help learners consider applications of new learning. Reflection is also needed to critically analyze and assess assumptions about how we should behave, our worldview, and how we explain causalities (Brookfield, 2012; Mezirow, 2000). Reflection is also critical to making decisions about learning, including selecting goals, assessing progress, and identifying needed resources and process. Reflection can focus both on rational thought and sense-making and on feelings and bodily responses.

An important practice to encourage reflection is simply pausing and inviting learners to engage in reflection on what has happened, what they make of it, and how it applies to their professional and/or personal lives. This could be done in quiet contemplation or visualization, by journaling, or through the use of drawing or media. However, learners may need specific prompts and supports to make good use of these moments. They may also benefit and grow in their ability to reflect by having the opportunity to share their thoughts and hear from others who are also tasked with reflection around shared learning experiences. Many people may think of reflection as a personal, internal process. However, Mezirow (2000) argued that social interaction and discourse encourages individuals to reflect on their most closely held beliefs. When reflective discourse is based on trust and empathy, Mezirow said, learners can hear and try on other perspectives and search for a synthesis and reframing of new ideas. It is important to recognize that what an adult learner makes of experiences through reflection is going to be highly autonomous and individualized. An educator can provide content, experiences, activities, and resources and then can encourage reflection, but the learner has complete autonomy over the meaning making that occurs as a result of reflection.

Overview of the Book

The book is organized into four parts. Part One includes three chapters that provide a frame for the subsequent chapters: this introductory chapter; chapter 2, which focuses on the diversity of adult education learners and what it means to be an adult educator who puts an emphasis on establishing the rightful presence (Calabrese Barton & Tan, 2019) for all who come into the learning space; and chapter 3, which focuses on the democratic ideals that undergird many threads of adult education. The emphasis in these chapters is on elevating learner voices and experiences in the classroom as well as critically analyzing the systems and structures that have led to unequal opportunities for those voices to be heard and for learning. We feel this is the right place to start because it puts learners in the center of their own learning, making them coauthors and collaborators with adult educators in meeting their learning needs.

While Part One focuses on the contexts for adult learning, Part Two looks at how internal characteristics of the learner can both facilitate and inhibit learning and how these factors differentiate and point to the uniqueness of learners. Seeing learners through this lens can help adult educators see them in more vivid detail and elevate their needs and experiences in ways that can substantively inform practice. Chapter 4 focuses on motivation to learn and how it can be enhanced to increase participation and engagement; in particular, goal theory and the comprehensive self-determination theory of motivation are discussed. Chapter 5 describes brain research and how the adult brain responds to learning experiences. Beyond cognitive processes, Chapter 6 considers the less rational aspects of adult learning by acknowledging the important role that emotion plays in learning and the development of the self. Finally, chapter 7 acknowledges that development can influence why and how adults learn and hones in on Robert Kegan's constructive developmental theory as one among many which we believe is helpfully explanatory and applicable to adult learning.

Part Three focuses on instructional approaches, within the parameters of a range of adult learning contexts that are designed to meet the needs of adults given their diverse identities and developmental, cognitive, and emotional profiles. This part begins with a chapter (chapter 8) that considers the theory base of adult education through the lens of structured silences. This is an important backdrop for the exploration of adult learning theories discussed in this section of the book. We encourage you to use this chapter as guidance for your own reflections on the subsequent chapters and on our field. The chapters in this part then turn to the four canonical and most commonly described adult learning approaches: andragogy, self-directed learning, experiential learning, and transformative learning. Although these theories have been part of the adult learning literature for decades, and have seen their share of critique and evolution, we believe they represent important foundational knowledge for adult educators. The part concludes with a chapter (chapter 13) on adult learning in the digital age with a focus on connectivism. It discusses the new affordances of digital technology for learning at the same time that it raises important questions about the role of the educator in our times when adults can and do learn almost anything on their own.

The final part, Part Four, synthesizes across parts and chapters, acknowledging the ways in which the contexts for learning, the learner, and the instructional approaches that have been explored by theorists and researchers influence and shape the learning opportunities for adults. First, we offer a chapter (chapter 14) on instructional design, one of the central activities in which the adult educator can enact the theories and concepts described in this book. And finally, in our concluding chapter (chapter 15), we point to the essential role of reflection in the uptake and use of theory in the day-to-day realities of practice. First, reflection is essential to critically assess theory for what it offers and what and whom it leaves out. Reflection is also important in deciding the ways in which theory will be used. This chapter is meant to both model and encourage the interrogation and use of theory as a way of participating in its necessary evolution.

For each chapter in this text, we invited authors with a history of leading scholarship in the specific topic being covered. Rather than try to comprehensively cover each theory, we asked them to take a deeper dive into one or only a very few theorists or researchers they felt are illustrative of themes and debates on each topic, choosing depth over breadth. In most chapters, the authors describe the theory and its central proponent and then trace its critiques and how it has evolved. We believe this supports greater understanding, but we are also aware that many choices had to be made about what to leave out in order to maintain focus. Therefore, we offer key seminal and supplemental text suggestions at the end of each chapter. We believe that this helps create a balance between depth and breadth that the interested reader can pursue.

We hope that this text will help you discover and develop a path as an adult educator that is not so much about the perfect way to teach but rather ways to meet learners where they are, to help them learn through your facilitating guidance, and to support their growth and development. We believe that this process is a mutually beneficial journey; when adult learners and adult educators collaborate, build on experiences, analyze and reflect, listen, and connect, everyone learns.

References

Bandura, A. (1977). *Social learning theory*. Prentice Hall.

Barron, A. B., Hebets, E. A., Cleland, T. A., Fitzpatrick, C. L., Hauber, M. E., & Stevens, J. R. (2015). Embracing multiple definitions of learning. *Trends in Neurosciences, 38*(7), 405–407. https://doi.org/10.1016/j.tins.2015.04.008

Brookfield, S. (2012). *Teaching for critical thinking: Tools and techniques to help students question their assumptions*. Jossey-Bass.

Calabrese Barton, A., & Tan, E. (2019). Designing for rightful presence in STEM: The role of making present practices. *The Journal of the Learning Sciences, 28*(4–5), 616–658. https//:doi.org/10.1080/10508406.2019.1591411

Coombs, P., Prosser, R., & Ahmed, M. (1973). *New paths to learning*. International Council for Educational Development.

Fordham, P. (2020, May 19). *Informal, non-formal and formal education programmes*.infed. org. https://infed.org/mobi/informal-non-formal-and-formal-education-programmes/

Freire, P. (1970). *Pedagogy of the oppressed*. Seabury Press.

Gagne, R. M. (1985). *The conditions of learning* (4th ed.). Holt, Rinehart and Winston.

Gardner, H. (1983). *Frames of mind: The theory of multiple intelligences*. Basic Books.

Kolb, D. A. (1984). *Experiential learning: Experience as the source of learning and development*. Prentice Hall.

Lave, J., & Wenger, E. (1991). *Situated learning: Legitimate peripheral participation*. Cambridge University Press.

Maslow, A. H. (1954). *Motivation and personality*. Harper & Row.

Merriam, S. B., & Bierema, L. L. (2014). *Adult learning: Linking theory and practice*. Jossey-Bass.

Merriam, S. B., & Brockett, R. G. (2007). *The profession and practice of adult education: An introduction*. Jossey-Bass.

Mezirow, J. (2000). *Learning as transformation: Critical perspectives on a theory in progress*. Jossey-Bass.

National Research Council. (2000). *How people learn: Brain, mind, experience, and school: Expanded edition*. National Academies Press. https://doi.org/10.17226/9853

Pritchard, A. (2002). *Ways of learning: Learning theories and learning styles in the classroom* (2nd ed.). Routledge.

Ross-Gordon, J. M., Rose, A. D., & Kasworm, C. E. (2016). *Foundations of adult and continuing education*. Jossey-Bass.

Schön, D. A. (1983). *The reflective practitioner: How professionals think in action*. Basic Books.

Shores, K., Kim, H. E., & Still, M. (2020). Categorical inequality in black and white: Linking disproportionality across multiple educational outcomes. *American Educational Research Journal, 57*(5), 2089–2131. https://doi.org/10.3102/0002831219900128

Stewart, M. (2012). Understanding learning: Theories and critique. In L. Hunt & D. Chalmers (Eds.), *University teaching in focus* (pp. 3–20). Routledge.

Taylor, K., & Marienau, C. (2016). *Facilitating learning with the adult brain in mind: A conceptual and practical guide*. Wiley.

Vygotsky, L. S. (1978). *Interaction between learning and development*. Harvard University Press.

2

CREATING INCLUSIVE LEARNING SPACES FOR A DIVERSE WORLD

The Womanist Perspective

Vanessa Sheared

Teaching is as much an art, as it is a science.

The science of teaching refers to a set of structures and acts that we employ, guided by a set of principles and methods that we believe will lead us to a specific end. In adult education, the science of teaching is resonant in the attempts of Knowles (1984) to provide a "systematic framework of assumptions, principals, and strategies" (p. 7) and in our further attempts to integrate our growing knowledge of biological and social sciences into comprehensive and universal models for teaching and learning.

Many of the ideas presented in subsequent chapters of this book focus on theories and concepts that are specific to meeting the needs of adult learners. The differences between learning in childhood and learning in adulthood presented here are primarily related to developmental, cultural, behavioral, and/or experiential differences. We might see these differences as pointing the way to a science of teaching adults, and that may lead us to assume that there is a single, homogenous adult learner. However, this perspective of a single archetype for adulthood fails to account for what makes each adult unique: factors such as race, gender, sexual orientation, culture, history, and politics as well as others that impact how we interact with each other in the "inclusive and diverse" classroom, workshop, training, or professional development setting.

This is where I believe the art of teaching must factor in. If teaching is at least in part an art, then one needs to look beyond specified unilateral ways to meet the needs of learners. Recognizing the uniqueness of individuals is key to this because it impels educators to explore and raise up the beauty and relevance of both individual and collective responses in the learning context.

So, what do educators need to do to develop the art of teaching? How does an intentional focus on individual diversity challenge an educator's assumptions about themselves and their learners and how they operate with one another in formal and informal learning contexts?

The purpose of this chapter is to introduce the concept of polyrhythmic realities and to propose a way for educators to think about and engage in the enterprise of teaching and learning that engages not only the science but also the art of doing so. As a construct, *polyrhythmic realities* was born out of my search to give voice to the multiple and intersecting points of realities that impact the teaching and learning experience. Our polyrhythmic realities are the intersection of our multiple and varied authentic lived experiences, which include race; gender; sexual orientation; class; religion; language; and political, historical, and sociocultural factors that make up our identity or positionality (Sheared et al., 2010; Sissel & Sheared, 2001).

The assumption is that who we are is born out of these polyrhythms and that they ultimately have an impact on who learners are and how educators should engage them across the array of ways in which they are diverse.

Throughout this chapter I will examine what it means to teach and learn. I will consider how our polyrhythmic realities—and our ability to recognize those realities in service of being our authentic selves—affect an educator's behaviors and abilities to create spaces that will include both the learners' and educators' lived experiences and ways of knowing. It is through a recognition and understanding of our multiple and varied realities that the teaching and learning environment becomes more inclusive.

Giving Voice

An important place to begin any discussion of learning contexts is to recognize that knowledge is *socially constructed. Constructivism* assumes that individuals create (construct) meaning of their world, largely by the act of filtering it through their own lived experience. Constructivists assert that the act of creating meaning is an essential human activity; Kegan (1980) highlighted that the term "human being" is in fact a verb and that the very act of "*human* being is *meaning making*" (p. 374).

Although traditional constructivism has highlighted the individual's role in this process, *social constructivism* recognizes the impact that social context has on the individual's meaning making. This means that each individual's positionality helps define the lens through which they make meaning from a learning experience. Closely related to this is a recognition that through their interaction in the learning context, each individual's perspective—and the experiences that define these perspectives—can be recognized by others in the learning community. This engagement is therefore essential to other learners developing a more holistic, diverse understanding. In other words, the positionality of each member of the community must be recognized as critical to the interpretation and meaning making of all other members of the community. Because social constructivism recognizes the way in which the positionality of each member of a learning community impacts the learning of every other participant, it represents a shift in the role of the educator, from being an authority over content to being the facilitator of a diverse community of individuals who not only cocreate but begin to "coauthor" (document) this new knowledge, so that it becomes a part of the group's discourse. The documentation of shared knowledge enables learners to critique and advance their own understanding of information, knowledge, and experiences as it attempts to give voice and create inclusive learning environments (Sheared et al., 2010).

This assumption of coauthorship is based in part on the belief that both the educator and the learner bring a wealth of knowledge and experiences to the educational context and that there is collaborative responsibility for assessing and interpreting the meaning and relevance of the information they seek to share and learn. In other words, all members of a learning community—educators and learners alike—must play a mutually beneficial role in contributing to each other's growth. For this reason, I refocus attention away from more traditional interpretations of educator and learner roles and focus instead on the dual roles of educator–learner and learner–educator as both leave the space having learned or gained a better appreciation and understanding of the lens of our polyrhythmic realities within a diverse and inclusive learning context. Rather than seeing themselves as responsible for simply providing information to learners, adult educators operating within a social constructivist paradigm recognize that it is their job to seek information and greater understanding about their learners and how their experiences inform the ways in which they make meaning from the information. Both educator and participants evolve together in a search for truth and meaning, unveiling the possibilities garnered through reading, engaging, dialoguing, applying, and evaluating how useful the information, knowledge, and skills are to self, family, career, community, profession, and/or service.

I have called this collaborative, evolutionary teaching approach *giving voice*. The focus on giving voice seeks to undo the manner in which the traditional educator–learner paradigm has silenced voices, however unintentionally, and it recognizes that we must acknowledge the different ways in which reality is interpreted within a learning community. Giving voice allows us all—learners and educators—to engage and disengage with our polyrhythmic realities and the polyrhythmic realities of others. The roots of this theory are explored in the following section.

Before I begin describing the theoretical foundations of giving voice, I think it is important to reflect upon and include my sense of how the multiple and varied ways of knowing and being have impacted my own interpretation of the world around me. I must ask myself, "Who am I?"

I enter this space, as a Black female educator, mother, daughter, grandma, sister, womanist, sistah . . . and the list goes on.

At first glance you might ask why it matters how I name myself. I do this because naming is the first step toward recognizing who you are and the ways in which identity impacts what and how you teach. As a Black woman, I acknowledge and recognize that there is something unique about me, yet I am connected to others like me. And as you answer the question "Who am I?" you will begin to recognize that your responses reflect the multiple and vast experiences you have had and deepen your understanding about how these experiences impact what you do in your classroom. How you see yourself impacts and shapes your journey as an educator–facilitator, and impacts the theories, philosophies, and methods employed in your classroom. The intent here is not to suggest that you have to shed your identity in order to become an effective adult educator; rather, it is to acknowledge the ways in which your experiences shape how you think and what you say and will do to create an inclusive learning space. You will also notice that inviting your learners to ask "Who am I?" will help them understand how their identities influence their learning. It can also open spaces for sharing and talking with those who are different from them.

In some ways, these invitations are natural for adult educators. The adult education theory base and our professional knowledge point to the importance of recognizing that a learner's age, career pathway or job type, and educational experiences (e.g., high school, bachelor's, master's, doctoral degree) are all factors that contribute to shaping their authentic lived experience and who they are as learners. At the same time, it is often quite difficult for adult educators to act on this knowledge and to give voice to the multiplicity of perspectives present in a learning environment. And while you may not focus initially on this, it is something that you might quickly think about after a difficult encounter with a learner who challenges your perspective or your role, expresses resistance to learning in some way, or expresses privilege in a way that is oblivious or hurtful to others.

For me, this happened the day that my department chair called me into his office to let me know that a White male learner told him that I always talked about race in the class, and this made him uncomfortable. While it is true that I talked about the assumptions that guide my role as an educator and that I think should guide their role as learners, along with the theoretical perspective—*womanist*—that supports my own work, I had never said that it was a position that learners had to incorporate into their toolbox. In fact, I asked them to explore and reflect on their assumptions as well as the theories in which those assumptions may have been grounded. So, upon hearing this learner's complaint, I did a check in with all the learners to see how they felt about and what they understood the references to race and theories used in the class. They shared their thoughts, and it became the first step toward dialoguing about how our authentic lived experiences impact how we make and assess meaning.

As a novice educator at the time, my own reflections on this episode led me to discover my authentic lived experiences and their impact on my teaching. They also encouraged me to examine theories and perspectives that informed the development of my teaching philosophy. While these theories resonated with me because of my own answers to the question "Who am I?" they were also helpful in centering the polyrhythmic realities of all learners. From the examination of these theories, I could begin to really teach and lead from the mind and the heart and to connect with the lived experiences of others. Simultaneously, I could now more effectively help learners make meaning out of, critically reflect upon, and ultimately support their growth in the ways in which they understand, think, and behave. In this chapter, I will explore the frameworks that enabled me to reflect on my own polyrhythmic realities, and I will share the process I went through with my students, so that you can incorporate it into your own practice as an adult educator.

Frameworks for Centering Identity

Perhaps because they were theories I examined in answering the question of "Who am I?" the concept of giving voice emerged from the lenses of the Afrocentricity and Black feminist/womanist paradigm (here, the terms "Black feminist," "African-centered feminist," and "womanist" are used interchangeably). This section describes these theoretical perspectives. These frameworks were selected because they offer historical and cultural lenses, as well as processes for creating inclusive learning environments or classrooms, or spaces (Davis, 2006; Gay, 2010; Guy, 1999; Hayes & Colin, 1994; Hayes & Flannery, 2000; Merriam & Brockett, 1997; Palmer, 1998; Sheared et al., 2010; Sissel & Sheared, 2001; Tisdell, 1995; Wlodkowski & Ginsberg, 1995), and because they allow us to acknowledge the multiple and varied polyrhythmic realities (Sheared, 1994, 1999) of all learners.

Centering and Creating Knowledge for Greater Understanding: From Mis-Education to Africentrism

In 1933, Carter G. Woodson, known as the father of Black History month in the United States, wrote the seminal book *The Mis-Education of the Negro*. In this book he posited that

> The thought of the inferiority of the Negro is drilled into him in almost every class he enters and in almost every book he studies. If he happens to leave school after he masters the fundamentals, before he finishes high school or reaches college, he will naturally escape some of this bias and may recover in time to be of service to his people. . . . To handicap a learner by teaching him that his black face is a curse and that his struggle to change his condition is hopeless is the worst sort of lynching. It kills one's aspirations. (p. 2)

For many, this book set the stage for gaining a better understanding of how Blacks in America had been, and all too often continue to be, viewed by European Americans and others throughout the world. What we learn from Woodson is that while our educational institutions are supposed to provide knowledge, skills, and information equally and equitably to everyone, often for Blacks—and it is now recognized this is also true for Native Americans, Latinx, women, and other racially marginalized groups—this has not been the case. Instead, we find that the knowledge and experiences of these individuals have been negated or eliminated from both American and global histories, because these histories have been written or authored through a predominantly Eurocentric White male lens. In *The Mis-Education of the Negro*, Woodson explores how the negation of Black lives and Black histories being abbreviated or told inaccurately led not only to Black bodies being lynched but also to Black minds being lynched within schools through devaluation and marginalization. It also ultimately leads to systemic racial oppression. As Woodson (1933) concluded, "There would be no lynching if it did not start in the classroom" (p. 2).

Woodson (1933) argued that a myth about Black individuals' inability to learn takes shape, persists, and is perpetuated not only in our schools but, more importantly in all institutional settings, leading to the systematization of "-isms." This myth has led to who and how people participate or are allowed to participate in our schools and in other work/life spaces and institutions. Given the great role that education has played in shaping our minds, thoughts, and behaviors, educators who seek to create inclusive spaces must first recognize the role that education has played or can play in changing how we live, work, and operate in society.

Therefore, in addition to assessing our roles and what we teach in inclusive classroom environments, we must recognize and acknowledge the importance of debunking the myths and reject the premises upon which the myths were started. Like Woodson, for instance, Herskovits (1943), Du Bois (1903), Turner (1949), Colin (1992), and other African American educators, sociologists, and linguists stress that when educators recognize and understand the value of incorporating race, culture, and experiences into the curriculum and content there is a greater likelihood that the his/herstories of Blacks in particular—and, I would surmise, the stories of all students—are less likely to be eliminated or distorted. This points to the importance of selecting instructional materials and resources that enhance learning opportunities for all within the classroom; I will discuss this in greater detail later in the chapter.

While Woodson, Du Bois, and others provide us with fundamental knowledge about how schooling has led to the miseducation of Blacks in America, during the latter part of the 20th century, Molefe Asante, Wade Nobles, and other African-centered scholars defined and developed an academic and political framework that respected the uniqueness and importance of African American contributions in America. Asante (1998) introduced the term "Afrocentricity" into our lexicon and provided many scholars with a historical and theoretical framework and foundation to ground our research and practices. He defined Afrocentricity as

> the belief in the centrality of Africans in postmodern history. It is our history, our mythology, our creative motif, and our ethos exemplifying our collective will. On the bases of our story, we build upon the work of our ancestors who gave signs toward our humanizing function. (p. 6)

The Womanist Perspective

While the work of African-centered scholars offered us a way of centering Africans in America and beyond, African American women recognized that their voices were all too often silenced, not only by African-centered scholars speaking from a set of histories that are viewed predominantly through the lens of a generalized African American experience but also by feminist scholars speaking from a set of experiences grounded in predominantly White women's experiences. This led to Black women having to juxtapose their realities with those of either White women, White men, or, oftentimes, Black men. The former perspective tended to focus on the gender, racial, political, historical, and global differences between White women and Black and White men and did not focus explicitly on the experience of Black women. All too often, African American women's worldview was framed as what Wallace (1990) referred to as the "other of the other." The womanist perspective attempts to give voice to the experiences of Black women as being distinct and yet interconnected to the multiple and varied realities of their lives (Collins, 1990, 1991, 1996; hooks, 1984, 1995; King, 1990; Sheared, 1992, 1999; Wallace, 1990). It is a worldview that acknowledges and situates Black women's experiences within history and discourses in, across, and throughout the African diaspora as well as within their varied cultural, geopolitical, and social contexts. African American womanist scholars have developed a framework that includes both a Black feminist perspective and an African-centered perspective.

In *In Search of Our Mothers' Gardens* (1994), Walker explored the essence of Black women's ways of knowing and being. Through her description of her mother and Black women who have come before her, Walker described the essence of how Black women come to know, experience, and speak about their lives. In 1984, she coined the term *womanist* to capture this perspective and way of knowing. Walker asserted that "womanist" is a commitment to the survival and wholeness of entire peoples—men and women—and urged the "valorization of women's works in all their varieties and multitudes" (p. 70). Like Walker, hooks (1994) explored the ways in which knowledge is produced and held by those in power. These and other Black feminists created a theoretical paradigm shift to address the experiences of Black women; specifically, Walker (1984), Collins (1990), and hooks (1994) posited frameworks that outline a way of knowing, an epistemological (knowledge) shift that centers the lived experiences of Black women in the discourse and an axiological (values) shift that assumes women should have agency and control over their stories and their lives. Collins offered an Africanist analysis of Black experience that not only respects the connectivity of our experiences as Blacks in America but also expanded the definition to highlight the importance of examining the stories of both Black men and women across the diaspora. She noted that there is a shared Afrocentric value system that permeated

> the family structure, religious institutions, culture and community life of Blacks in varying parts of Africa, the Caribbean, South America, and North America. This consciousness permeates the shared history of people of African descent through the framework of a distinctive Afrocentric epistemology. (p. 308)

She went on to describe this shared consciousness and history to situate the African American womanist and African American womanhood perspective into an Afrocentric feminist epistemology. She concluded, "The significance of an Afrocentric feminist epistemology may lie in its enrichment of our understanding of how subordinate groups create knowledge that enables them to resist oppression" (p. 309).

Collins drew a distinction between *knowledge* (what people think they know) and *wisdom* (the world perspectives needed to assess the quality and applicability of knowledge), noting that "this distinction between knowledge and wisdom, and the use of experience as the cutting edge dividing them, has been key to Black women's survival" (Collins, 1989, p. 759). In examining this distinction she identified two epistemological (meaning making) and two axiological (ethical) assumptions. She first suggested that individuals make meaning out of the world through *concrete experiences* (visual and actual things one does) and that they then assess and validate this meaning using *dialogue* with others. From the axiological perspective, individuals learn how to value and find worth in others through what Collins described as *an ethic of caring*, which focuses on the uniqueness of the individual, and an *ethic of personal accountability*, which demonstrates how the individual is held accountable for their actions, words, and deeds. Centering Black women's experiences allows us to tell our stories, separate and apart from White women and Black men.

These four assumptions are the premise upon which giving voice in an inclusive and diverse classroom is grounded. Because adopting these assumptions requires educators to consider how learners' perspectives shape the way information is shared and valued in the learning environment, the teacher must adopt a shared perspective as teacher–learner. In practice, the teacher–learner begins by assessing and determining the ways one's experiences shape or impact the lens through which knowledge and information are viewed, interpreted, and communicated within the classroom. The goal of the teacher–learner is to come to an understanding born out of one's ability to listen, respect, appreciate, and understand how our authentic lived experiences impact how they and their learners speak and act within the learning environment. According to Sheared (1999),

> [This] method involves an acknowledgment of a way of knowing that is not grounded in western linear traditions. Africentric [womanist] epistemology attempts to provide a medium through which one's interpretation of behavior and thought is grounded in the history, culture, economics, race, gender, language, sexual orientation, and religion of those involved in the [classroom] . . . it is the intersection of these positions or realities that ultimately affects the way a person interprets, speaks, and reads the word and the world. (p. 40)

The Intersection of Perspectives and a Defining Proposition

To create an inclusive learning environment, it is important to know, understand, and appreciate one's history and place or positionality ("Who am I?") in the world. So, as a womanist educator, it was important for me to understand both the African-centered

(Colin, 2000) and African-centered feminist perspective. The importance of knowing one's history and understanding one's place in the world is an important place for teachers and students to begin. More often than not, knowing this highlights the fact that if individuals do not know how to center their own histories, they, like their stories, will be marginalized. In the context of learning interactions, to have one's authentic lived experience marginalized or silenced leads to negation of the self—not only from classroom discourse but also from the curriculum as well as from the sociocultural and geopolitical landscape. However,

> While both Africentric and feminist scholars discuss the silencing of voices and marginalization. . . . Africentric scholars and feminist scholars fail to address both gender and race as a unifying whole. . . . As a result, the black woman's voice, as well as other marginalized voices, has been silenced. . . . Thus the black women's issues become secondary to the dominant discourse on race, gender and class. (Sheared, 1994, p. 29)

It is critical to an understanding of this chapter to explain that while the African-centered, womanist framework can provide a way to value and understand African Americans, and African American women in particular, it also can provide *any* educator, as Asante (1998) noted, with tools to develop classroom spaces that value and respect the uniqueness and contributions of all learners simultaneously. In addition to reflecting upon the way of knowing that is grounded in an examination of one's historical, sociocultural, and political contexts as found in the womanist perspective, there are other theoretical perspectives (e.g., social constructivism, perspective transformation, feminist, critical theory, critical race theory, multiculturalism) that provide additional insights and focus on creating a diverse and inclusive learning space.

The concept of polyrhythmic realities in adult education discourse can help educators begin to recognize and understand how their lived experiences impact a learning community's perceptions of learner positionality and the educator's practice as educator–learner in each context. Giving voice may require a paradigm shift—a shift in thinking, doing, and communicating in the educational context. It requires an examination of the ways in which the educator comes to know, believe, and behave, and it should ultimately impact interactions among learners and between learners and educators. Through this examination we can begin to move from an "I" to a "we." We can learn to value each other's ways of knowing and being. In so doing, we can begin to create the type of spaces that are inclusive and respectful and that value each other's perspectives. Giving voice will influence the ways in which all members of a learning community learn, interpret, and use knowledge, information, and skills and impact personal, professional, and social lives across a multitude of settings. The remainder of this chapter is dedicated to an exploration of how this model can be put into practice.

Building Inclusive Spaces for Learning

Learners and educators communicate through a cultural lens that is grounded in our polyrhythmic realities. We have all been taught within the P/K–16 educational system that there is an acceptable form and structure to communication. Yet this "normative" communication style may not align with the polyrhythmic realities of all students. While many learners of color have learned to code-switch to communicate in this expected way, educators in general still rely on traditional patterns and styles of communication. To build inclusive spaces for learning, educators need to recognize and understand the ways in which communication styles impact how they, as well as learners, view intellect and abilities of learners' written and verbal skills, knowledge, and abilities, especially when they vary from mainstream patterns.

To better understand the significance of communication, I offer the examples described by Collins (1990, 1991), Barkley-Brown (1990), and hooks (1994), who each introduced communication styles used by members of the African diaspora that are also used within other marginalized communities (to varying degrees). Barkley-Brown adopted the term "polyrhythmic" to describe a pattern of quilting performed by African Americans to tell their story and "gumbo yaya" as a way of communicating and talking among women. Together, they are a form of talking and finishing one another's sentences or, as it has been described by some, as "everybody talking at once." The amazing thing is that even though multiple people may be talking at once, everyone in the group understands what is being said because of their common set of experiences. Collins also explained this style of talking and communicating as being related to "call and response." In this type of interaction, someone calls out something that everyone acknowledges because of their shared understanding; the members of the group generally respond in the affirmative. This is most recognizable in Black churches, when the minister calls out (or preaches) and the congregation responds with an "Amen." Understanding how these styles evoke particular emotional and cognitive responses—and incorporating these new patterns into educational practice—is one way to build inclusive learning spaces in which all voices are heard and recognized.

Barkley-Brown (1990) used the term "polyrhythmic structures" in her analysis of what one needs to consider when teaching African American women's history. Embedded in the notion that one can adopt an African-centered, womanist framework without necessarily needing to be African American or a woman, Sheared (1994) used the term "polyrhythmic realities" to refer to our multiple and varied points of reality (i.e., the intersection of race, gender, class, and subsequently language history, political, social, and cultural factors). "Giving voice to one's polyrhythmic realities has become the aim of those who seek to engage in critically reflective dialogue . . . on the proposition that all knowledge is grounded in a social, political and economic context" (Sheared, 1994, pp. 31–32).

As noted, giving voice may require a shift in one's epistemological and axiological perspective. The shift in paradigm occurs through the incorporation of several practices: (a) reflecting on polyrhythmic realities; (b) encouraging learners to reflect on their polyrhythmic realities, and finding common threads of understanding within the learning community; (c) fostering dialogue that embraces the epistemological and axiological perspectives needed for giving voice and establishing a hub of learning and change; and (d) identifying resources and materials that support the lived experiences of learners.

Reflecting on Polyrhythmic Realities

While the creation of an inclusive learning environment presupposes respect and understanding of the authentic lived experiences of all, it is made stronger when educators examine their own assumptions and worldview before asking learners to do so.

In this section, I introduce processes that will help educators critically reflect upon their identity in ways that will help them create more inclusive learning environments.

The polyrhythmic reality chart depicted in Figure 2.1 can be a helpful starting point for engaging in this exercise. Take a few moments to look over the diagram. Under each category, note how you would describe yourself. For example, how would you label yourself under gender or language? Once all categories on the diagram have been addressed, add others as needed. Although this type of self-exploration may be difficult or uncomfortable for some, I propose that it is far easier than it may appear at first. Really, it is as simple as reflecting on a series of life events and considering how these factors impact "who I am in the here and now" and "current understandings of who I am now." As suggested by Collins (1989, 1990, 1991), lived experience and dialogue are central to our efforts to challenge

Figure 2.1. Polyrhythmic reality chart.

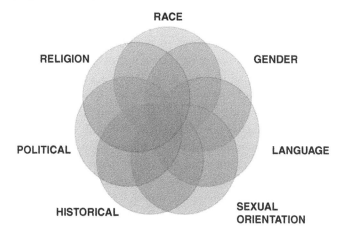

prevailing knowledge structures. It is also through understanding the impact of our own polyrhythmic realities that we can begin to give voice to the realities of others. As Apps (1996) described, educators must take stock of their own lived experiences and the assumptions they hold and then assess and determine why creating positive learning environments or workspaces is important before they can connect fully to their learners.

Both the teacher and learner should spend time thinking about this and begin to develop a basic understanding of how one's philosophical standpoint or assumptions, as well as knowing one's history (story) and understanding one's place in the world, is important. The importance of this may be unclear now, but once you spend time reflecting it becomes more evident and noted in how you as teacher or student engage in the classroom and with the information that is being shared.

Connecting: Finding a Common Thread of Understanding

To give voice (Sheared, 1994, 1999; Sheared et al., 2000, 2010), one must focus on providing learners with opportunities to engage in a process of uncovering and discovering along with the educator, so that all participants can become cocreators of knowledge and information. The challenge is to find ways for both teacher and learner to practice an ethic of care and responsibility that privileges the sharing, acknowledgment, and discussion of experience through dialogues; the building of connections, and the enhancement of understanding within the learning space. These connections are made because our race, gender, native language, and other sociocultural, historical, and political factors all have an impact on the collaborative construction of knowledge in the learning context. And if these factors matter, they should be made visible. In other words, you will see my color, you will see my gender, or recognize my right to name what I want to be called; every member of the group will need to recognize that I matter; and I will need to recognize that every other member of the group also matters. We can connect when we care and understand that all voices and experiences in the learning space should and must be factored into how the curriculum is developed, enacted, and evaluated.

Creating opportunities for learners to connect with each other and with the educator should occur at the start of each class session. All too often we do this once and then wonder why difficulties crop up later in the course. Sheared et al. (2010) provided some tools in *The Handbook on Race and Education* to help guide the conversations and identified some tools that people can use to help facilitate the discussion, recognizing that it should complement, not replace, the content.

One activity that I recommend prior to engaging in class discussion is to have learners complete their own polyrhythmic reality chart. Then, have them sit with another learner to discuss their descriptions. Next, ask them to identify the common threads of experiences or differences noted. Create a list that includes common threads and differences. This is where participants will start to uncover and discover themselves but also find ways to connect with others in the class.

By reflecting on questions about polyrhythmic realities, reaching deep into your heart, and having conversations that focus on similarities as well as differences, "we" can begin to recognize, respect, and see each other as unique and authentic selves. In other words, through this type of activity common threads of understanding can be found that may not have occurred had there been no dialogue of this kind. This then frees learners to learn, to grow, and to change the way one thinks, interprets, and acts in the world (Freire, 1970).

Recognizing the Importance of Dialogue

It is through dialogue that we come to understand others' ways of knowing. Engaging in dialogue opens the possibilities of mindfully respecting, acknowledging, and appreciating the ways in which all participants' polyrhythmic realities impact the learning environment. Making space, giving voice, and acknowledging our multiple and varied realities in the learning space allows us to grow and develop, to share and to gain knowledge and skills to support our personal, professional, and social goals.

As Sissel and Sheared (2001) observed,

> Given that we are living in an age in which information is moving at the rate of 115,000 baud (bits per second), via the computer and internet, the types and forms and substances of the dialogues in which we engage begin to take on new meanings. (p. 335)

This has only become truer since then, as social media has permeated every aspect of modern life. As educators, we need not only to create opportunities for face-to-face dialogue but also to think about ways to assist our learners with discovering and uncovering the uniqueness of all and to help each other learn in these new media.

It is also critical for us to establish spaces in which people can engage in what Sheared et al. (2010) called "the sometimes very difficult conversations about race and racism that can lead to improved relationships among men and women of all races, languages, religions, sexual orientations, class, and other groups" (p. 355). Creating inclusive learning spaces enables educators–teachers and learners–educators to grapple with, interpret, or make meaning out of course content, which leads to the cocreation/coauthorship of knowledge, experiences, and skills.

Identifying Appropriate Resources and Materials

There is a significant body of literature (Colin, 1992; Davis, 2006; Gay, 2010; hooks, 1994; Sheared, 1994, 1999; Sheared et al., 2000, 2010; Thomas, 2014; Tisdell, 1995; Wlodkowski & Ginsberg, 1995) on the importance of utilizing curriculum and reading or resource materials that are relevant and culturally grounded in learners' identities. This can help learners and educators make meaningful connections in the classroom. Some might think that the choice of resources should be driven solely by the content. However, educators seeking to develop inclusive classrooms and give voice to their learners' experiences and understandings and to select meaningful resources to aid learners with meaning making must first examine the ways in which their own authentic lived experiences impact the resources and materials they elect to use in support of the information or content. This is the challenge that many formal educators experience in an uncritical inclusion of "the cannon" without questioning whether the classics are truly representative of the polyrhythmic realities of all learners or if they represent only the academic tradition and experiences of the educator. In preparation for creating a more diverse classroom environment it is important to address the extent to which their own lived experiences—and the selection of materials that such experience prompts—might contribute to negating or enhancing the authentic lived experiences of learners.

Educators should include elements of their learners' and their own personal experiences and ways of knowing in the class. Therefore, it is important to seek out materials that focus on multicultural, Africentric, bilingual, feminist, perspective transformation, critical race theory, and social emotional learning perspectives within the curriculum. When learners enter a learning environment it is important for them to feel a sense of belonging, a connection with the educator and with the information that is being shared. Learners should be able to see themselves as being authors of their world. What better way to see and be able to do this than to see reflections of themselves, their history, and their culture in the texts they read? If they see it, they can then believe in the power they have to become authors (i.e., decision makers, owners of and responsible for telling their own stories and experiences) of their own world and their learning as well. Learners who are authors take on responsibility for what is learned; they are not just bystanders or subjects in the learning context.

Bringing It Together: Creating a Hub for Learning

The ultimate goal of reflecting on polyrhythmic realities, finding a common thread, fostering dialogue, and identifying appropriate instructional resources is to create a classroom context that is a hub for learning and change—a space in which learners commune with one another, see and celebrate each other's successes, challenge each other with respect, and learn to see each other for who they are and how they connect with the work to make meaning out of the content as well as their experiences with each other. When learners have voice, they have agency and autonomy; they learn not only to trust themselves but also to trust the other learners in the class. For example, after introducing learners to the concept of giving voice and using dialogue focused on challenging and supporting each other's ways of knowing, I attended a conference toward the end of the term. Unfortunately, my flight was delayed, and I was unable to get a message to the campus to inform the learners that I would not be there at the start of the class. I was able to make it, rather late; to my amazement, rather than leaving, the learners decided to hold class and to take responsibility for facilitating and providing resources for each other as warranted. They indeed had created their own community—a hub and space where they could give voice to their shared authentic lived experiences.

Conclusion

In our efforts to develop culturally relevant and inclusive classrooms it is important to accept the premise that teaching is an art (as well as a science) and that there are personal identity factors that influence how educators and learners interpret and operate within the learning environment. It is also important to acknowledge that there are no silver bullets or any one single method that will work in all contexts and with all learners. A degree of comfort with ambiguity that often comes in thinking of teaching as an art is helpful; even what and how information is taught once examined in the ways suggested in this chapter will be impacted. The hope is that the ideas that were shared here will lead to discovering and understanding how the assumptions educators begin with will influence how they engage all learners.

Researchers have learned that to uncover and discover new information and knowledge, and to make meaning out of experiences (see chapter 11 of this volume for more information about experiential learning), it is important to examine one's assumptions and develop and pose questions. In this way, we can acquire a deeper and better understanding of that which we seek to learn or change. So, instructors, educators, or facilitators should do the same. How educators enter and use a space will often determine the experiences they and their learners will have.

Educators can either create a space for engaging learners or stifle their potential for growth, development, and change. They can create a space that is individualistic, competitive, and exclusionary or become an inclusive and diverse collective hub for learning because positive possibilities have been created not just for some individuals, but in collaboration with others, for all learners. Creating inclusive learning spaces for diverse learners provides important opportunities not only to change our own beliefs and behaviors but also to lead us to understand and communicate better with those whose lived experiences are different.

The goal of the educator, then, is to recognize and understand our polyrhythmic realities in relationship to those of our learners, as well as the corresponding polyrhythmic realities among learners. In so doing, we begin to examine and then to create new or alternative ways of thinking, behaving, and communicating, first in the classroom and ultimately within everyday contexts.

The more comfortable educators become with the ambiguity that is created by giving voice to learners as well as themselves, the more that creating inclusive learning spaces becomes a canvas for creativity, a place in which the multiple and varied (polyrhythmic realities) voices, stories, and perspectives can be heard, respected, challenged, and developed, together. An inclusive classroom becomes a site for learning content as well as for generating opportunities for individuals from diverse backgrounds to learn to respect and understand the ways in which our polyrhythmic realities impact how we think, behave, and communicate within the classroom as well as in other institutional and cultural settings. It is through this lens of understanding that educators and learners begin to create positive social and systemic changes within and beyond the classroom environment.

References

Apps, J. W. (1996). *Teaching from the heart*. Krieger.

Asante, M. (1998). *The Afrocentric idea*. Temple University Press.

Barkley-Brown, E. (1990). African American women's quilting: A framework for conceptualizing and teaching African American women's history. In M. Malson, E. Mudimbe-Boyi, J. O'Barr, & M. Wyer (Eds.), *Black women in America: Social science perspectives* (pp. 9–18). University of Chicago Press.

Colin, S. A. J., III. (1992). *Culturally grounded programs* [Unpublished manuscript]. North Carolina State University.

Colin, S. A. J., III. (2000). Marcus Garvey: Africentric adult education for self-reliance. In E. Peterson (Ed.), *Freedom road: Adult education for African Americans* (pp. 41–65). Krieger.

Collins, P. H. (1989). The social construction of Black feminist thought. *Signs, 14*(4), 745–773. https://doi.org/10.1086/494543

Collins, P. H. (1990). The social construction of Black feminist thought. In M. Malson, E. Mudimbe-Boyi, J. O'Barr, & M. Wyer (Eds.), *Black women in America: Social science perspectives* (pp. 297–326). University of Chicago Press.

Collins, P. H. (1991). *Black feminist thought*. Routledge.

Collins, P. H. (1996). What's in a name? Womanism, Black feminism, and beyond. *The Black Scholar, 26*(1), 9–17. https://doi.org/10.1080/00064246.1996.11430765

Davis, B. M. (2006). *How to teach learners who don't look like you: Culturally relevant teaching strategies*. Corwin Press.

Du Bois, W. E. B. (1903). *The souls of Black folks: Essays and sketches*. A. C. McClurg.

Freire, P. (1970). *Pedagogy of the oppressed*. Bloomsbury.

Gay, G. (2010). *Culturally responsive teaching: Theory, research, and practice* (2nd ed.). Educators College.

Guy, T. C. (Ed.). (1999). *Providing Culturally Relevant Adult Education: A Challenge for the Twenty-First Century* (New Directions for Adult and Continuing Education, no. 82). Jossey-Bass.

Hayes, E., & Colin, S. A. J., III (Eds.). (1994). *Confronting Racism and Sexism in Adult Education* (New Directions for Adult and Continuing Education, no. 61). Jossey-Bass.

Hayes, E., & Flannery, D. D. (with Brooks, A. K., Tisdell, E. J., & Hugo, J. M.). (2000). *Women as learners: The significance of gender in learning*. Jossey-Bass.

Herskovits, M. J. (1943). Education and cultural dynamics. *American Journal of Society, 48*(6), 737–749. https://doi.org/10.1086/219271

hooks, b. (1994). *Teaching to transgress: Education as the practice of freedom*. Routledge.

hooks, b. (1995). *Killing rage, ending racism*. Henry Holt.

Kegan, R. (1980). Making meaning: The constructive–developmental approach to persons and practice. *The Personal and Guidance Journal, 58*(5), 373–380. https://doi .org/10.1002/j.2164-4918.1980.tb00416.x

King, D. K. (1990). Multiple jeopardy, multiple consciousness. The context of Black feminist ideology. In M. Malsom, E. Mudimbe-Boyi, J. O'Barr, & M. Wyer (Eds.), *Black women in America: Social science perspectives* (pp. 265–296). University of Chicago Press.

Knowles, M. S. (1984). *Andragogy in action: Applying modern principles of adult learning.* Jossey-Bass.

Merriam, S. B., & Brockett, R. G. (1997). *The profession and practice of adult education.* Jossey-Bass.

Palmer, P. (1998). *The courage to teach: Exploring the inner landscape of an educator's life.* Jossey-Bass.

Sheared, V. (1992). *From welfare to edfare, African American women and the elusive quest for self-determination: A critical analysis of the JOBS plan* (Publication No. 9230723) [Doctoral dissertation, Northern Illinois University]. Proquest Dissertations and Theses Global. https:// www.proquest.com/docview/303996451?pq-origsite=gscholar&fromopenview=true

Sheared, V. (1994). Giving voice: An inclusive model of instruction—A womanist perspective. In E. Hayes & S. A. J. Colin III (Eds.), *Confronting Racism and Sexism in Adult Continuing Education* (New Directions for Adult and Continuing Education, no. 61, pp. 27–37). Jossey-Bass. https://doi.org/10.1002/ace.36719946105

Sheared, V. (1999). Giving voice: Inclusion of African American learners' polyrhythmic realities in adult basic education. In T. Guy (Ed.), *Providing Culturally Relevant Adult Education: A Challenge for the Twenty First Century* (New Directions for Adult and Continuing Education, no. 82, pp. 33–48). Jossey-Bass. https://doi.org/10.1002/ace.8203

Sheared, V., Johnson-Bailey, J., Colin, S. A. J., III, Peterson, E., Brookfield, S. D., & Associates. (2010). *The handbook on race and education, A resource for dialogue on racism.* Jossey-Bass.

Sheared, V., McCabe, J., & Umeki, D. (2000). Adult literacy and welfare reform: Marginalization, voice, and control. *Education and Urban Society, 32*(2), 167–187. https://doi .org/10.1177/0013124500322002

Sissel, P. A., & Sheared, V. (2001). *Making space: Merging theory and practice in adult education.* Bergin and Garvey.

Thomas, C. (Ed.). (2014). *Inclusive Teaching: Presence in the Classroom* (New Directions for Teaching and Learning, no. 140). Wiley.

Tisdell, E. J. (1995). *Creating inclusive adult learning environments: Insights from multicultural education and feminist pedagogy* (Information Series No. 361). Ohio State University: ERIC Clearinghouse on Adult, Career & Vocational Education.

Turner, L. W. (1949). *Africanisms in the Gullah dialect.* University of Chicago Press.

Walker, A. (1984). *In search of our mothers' gardens.* Harcourt Brace Jovanovich.

Walker, A. (1994). In search of our mothers' gardens. In A. Mitchell (Ed.), *Within the circle: An anthology of African American literary criticism form the Harlem Renaissance to the present* (pp. 401–409). Duke University Press.

Wallace, M. (1990), Variations on negation and the heresy of Black feminist creativity. In H. Gates (Ed.), *Reading Black, reading feminist: A critical anthology* (pp. 52–67). Meridian Books.

Wlodkowski, R. J., & Ginsberg, M. B. (1995). *Diversity and motivation: Culturally responsive teaching.* Jossey-Bass.

Woodson, C. G. (1933). *The mis-education of the Negro.* Associated Publishers.

Editors' Key Seminal and Supplemental Text Suggestions

Guy, T. C. (1999). Culture as context for adult education: The need for culturally relevant adult education. In T. C. Guy (Ed.), *Providing Culturally Relevant Adult Education: A Challenge for the Twenty-First Century* (New Directions for Adult and Continuing Education, no. 82, pp. 5–18). Jossey-Bass. https://doi.org/10.1002/ace.8201

Isaac, S. E. P., & Merriweather, L. R. (2021). Preparing adult educators for racial justice. In M. V. Alfred & E. P. Isaac-Savage (Eds.), *The Black Lives Matter Movement: Implications for Anti-Racist Adult Education* (New Directions for Adult and Continuing Education, no. 170, pp. 109–118). Jossey-Bass. https://doi.org/10.1002/ace.20430

Lund, C. L. (2010). The nature of white privilege in the teaching and training of adults. In C. L. Lund & S. A. J. Collin III (Eds.), *White Privilege and Racisim: Perceptions and Actions* (New Directions for Adult and Continuing Education, no. 125, pp. 15–25). Jossey-Bass. https://doi.org/10.1002/ace.359

Manglitz, E., Guy, T. C., & Merriweather, L. R. (2014). Knowledge and emotions in cross-racial dialogues. *Adult Learning, 25*(3), 111–118. https://doi.org/10.1177/104515951434193

McIntosh, P. (1989, July/August). White privilege: Unpacking the invisible knapsack. *Peace and Freedom*, pp. 10–12. https://psychology.umbc.edu/wp-content/uploads/sites/57/2016/10/White-Privilege_McIntosh-1989.pdf

3

THE DEMOCRATIC IMPULSE
IN ADULT EDUCATION

Stephen Brookfield

This chapter reviews one of the strongest intellectual and practical influences on the field of adult education in the United States. This is the notion that adult education has an important role to play in building a democratic society by teaching democratic habits of participation. By extension, this means that adult education practices themselves should conform to democratic principles. Throughout much of the 20th century this was the grand political project of adult education in the United States. Essentially the field was viewed as the guarantor of liberal democracy. If adults were educated to think critically about public affairs, so the argument went, then they would be able to exercise a productive skepticism regarding the self-serving machinations of politicians. A well-educated citizenry would be resistant to propaganda and demagoguery. For example, the rise of fascism as had happened in Germany and Italy during the 1930s would be countered by critically alert citizens who would see through the hysteria of mass patriotic rallies and the racist propaganda. In this project there was a privileging of rationality and evidence-based reasoning. If people were provided with the relevant facts and information pertinent to an issue or situation, they would be able to see through politically motivated lies and obfuscation and come to their own independent, critically informed judgments. Democracy would thus be preserved.

As we move into the third decade of the 21st century it is remarkable to reflect on this project. The belief in objective facts, first challenged by postmodernism's late 20th-century critique of the grand narrative of democratic progress, has devolved into a widespread refusal to accept what were previously viewed as authoritative sources of information. The neoconservative project to delegitimize the institutions of the state, dismantle civil society, and call into question the credibility of the mainstream media has been remarkably successful. Warnings of external interference in elections from U.S. government intelligence agencies have been portrayed as partisan and unreliable interference from the deep state. Reports from scientists regarding climate change or the threat of a worldwide pandemic are disregarded as hoaxes.

It is salutary therefore to remind ourselves of the democratic impulse that has traditionally informed the practice of adult education in the United States. This impulse took many forms. Most adult education scholars acknowledge the progressive humanism of John Dewey (1916) and Eduard Lindeman (1926) in the early

20th century. Moreover, from 1952 to 1968 the Center for the Study of Liberal Education for Adults investigated the connections between liberal education and democratic health. Adult education has been entwined with the growth of the labor movement and the clarification of education's role in building a socialist society (Schied, 1993). It also played a central role in the civil rights movement for racial equality (Horton, 2003).

As the 21st century dawned, feminist pedagogy (English & Irving, 2015; Mojab & Carpenter, 2020), popular education (Kane, 2001; Wiggins, 2011), and adult education's role in insurgent social movements (Holst, 2002) became prominent in the scholarship of the field. Adult educators across the world examined how its traditional democratic practices could now be recast as revolutionary efforts by ordinary people to wrest control from dominant interests and ideologies (Allman, 2000; Brookfield & Holst, 2010; Coben, 1998; Mayo, 1998).

But adult educators have not just advocated for the field's place in a broader social and political movement. There has also developed a corresponding interest in methods and practices that both promoted democracy and enabled these revolutionary movements. If adult education was so connected to the democratic impulse, how did this translate into matters of instruction? What would an adult education classroom look like if it were informed by these revolutionary efforts? Was it even possible to teach and learn in a democratic manner within the confines of formal educational institutions? How could curricula be negotiated democratically when some people know more than others and teachers have spent a career studying a specific content area? Could power; status; and cultural, racial, and economic imbalances that existed amongst participants outside the classroom be mitigated inside it? Under what conditions could the person designated as teacher, instructor, leader, or facilitator exercise legitimate authority? In a democratic environment, would it be more appropriate to designate teachers as catalysts, animateurs, or colearners, and how would those different designations affect how the class was run? What would power and authority look like in a properly organized democratic learning environment?

Over the years, multiple responses have been offered to these questions. Influenced by the writing of Paulo Freire (1970), some have seen adult education as a process of cocreating curricula and knowledge. Malcolm Knowles's (1970) outline of andragogy emphasized practices of self-directed learning that allowed adults to exercise their own innate desire to take control over their learning (Knowles, 1975). The work of the Highlander Folk School encouraged circles of activists to examine their experiences critically and collaboratively (Preskill, 2020), a model that has been particularly influential to adult educators working in social movements and grassroots settings. For a while, learning contracts were a highly popular tool to allow learners to exercise democratic control over their learning (Caffarella & Caffarella, 1986). In hierarchical organizations the nature of democratic process has received much attention (Avila et al., 2000; Lindeman, 1951; Ramdeholl et al., 2011). More recently, social media back channels, such as backchannelchat.com, have been lauded for their inherently democratic nature although, as Careless (2015) pointed out, the owners of social media platforms privilege profit over the exposure of lies and manipulation.

What has become clear through the evolution of these efforts is that defining democracy is prerequisite for understanding its use in an educational context.

How Is Democracy Defined?

In 1973, English philosopher of adult education Harold Wiltshire identified how certain terms in the lexicon of adult education function as premature ultimates. A *premature ultimate* is a phrase or term that, once invoked, carries such weight and reverence that it stops critical analysis in its tracks. Premature ultimates are "assumptions or concepts which have a spurious finality and which therefore silence questions which need to be raised and block off routes of inquiry which it would be profitable to follow" (Wiltshire, 1973, p. 26).

Democracy is one of the most powerful premature ultimates in adult education. To say one practices democratic adult education, or that one's classroom functions democratically, is to convey a sense that one is on the side of adult education's angels, doing good things in the field in an inherently unimpeachable way. Critical scrutiny of what that practice looks like or how it is experienced differently by those involved is often brushed aside. The analysis of the contradiction of extending democracy in a power-ridden, hierarchical institution is only occasionally broached (Ramdeholl et al., 2011). For the purposes of this chapter the democratic process within adult education is considered to exhibit three core elements.

Democracy as an Ongoing Conversation

First, those involved in democratic practice are engaged in a continuous, ever-widening conversation about how to organize their affairs. In terms of classroom process this means that curriculum, teaching practices, and evaluative procedures are a matter of constant negotiation. To be properly democratic this conversation must be as inclusive and wide ranging as possible, involving widely different groups and perspectives. Those involved should be able to make decisions based on full knowledge of the situations in which they find themselves, full awareness of the range of different possible courses of action, and the best information about the potential consequences of their decisions.

In Habermas's (1996) terms, democratic action is best facilitated by an ideal speech situation that allows all participants full access to all relevant information pertaining to the issues discussed. Mezirow (1990) used this element of Habermas's work to develop his theory of transformative learning, and it informs his conviction that adult educators need to ally themselves with social movements that seek to secure people's full access to the knowledge that affects how they might live. This is a contemporary reincarnation of Lindeman's (1945a) earlier assertion that "all successful adult education groups sooner or later become social action groups" (p. 12).

As those involved make decisions about adult educational purposes and practices these decisions draw their democratic legitimacy from the fact that all fully informed stakeholders have been involved in the conversation leading to it. However, how specific decisions are arrived at varies according to who has the greatest stake in it. This is the argument of Albert's (2004, 2006) work on participatory economics or parecon. In parecon the chief decision makers involved in a particular action are those who are most affected by that decision. Teaching democratically according to this notion focuses on creating conversational forms that are as inclusive as possible and fighting any vested interests concerned to block access to relevant information. When an organization or structure seeks to privatize knowledge and keep it the province of professionals this also inspires adult educators to fight to make this information democratically available.

Democracy as Economic Equity

Second, democracy is an economic arrangement. Democracy is not just a political form involving voting procedures and structures of representation, but an economic one requiring the abolition of vast disparities in wealth, the equalization of income, and the placing of all forms of resources under common control. This is why democracy and socialism are often argued as being intertwined (Brookfield & Holst, 2010). Important elements of democracy include many of the things that FDR called for in his 1944 State of the Union Address, sometimes called the Second Bill of Rights (Sunstein, 2006). These include the right to good education, a decent job and liveable wage, adequate food and clothing, acceptable medical care, and some protection from the ravages of old age.

In adult educational terms this economic dimension to democracy raises all sorts of questions, particularly regarding access. In fee-paying institutions an undemocratic form of stratification serves to exclude many who wish to learn. In informal and community-based education settings that do not charge a fee, access is still limited by other economic and logistical factors, such as availability of child care and transportation, or the need for prospective participants to work multiple jobs because of low minimum wages. Online adult education is of course subject to a digital divide in which participation is a function of technological access, which itself is often a function of personal wealth. So the democratic principle that all who wish to participate should be allowed to do so unfettered by economic constraints means that most of what is described as adult education in the United States would be deemed undemocratic.

One of the best articulations of this idea in adult education is W.E.B. Du Bois's *Basic American Negro Creed* (Du Bois, 1971), which was part of a work commissioned by an offshoot of the American Association for Adult Education and then not published (Guy & Brookfield, 2009). Adult education, according to Du Bois (2017), entails working to further the interests of organizations, groups, and movements that are trying to establish cooperative economic forms. Du Bois's creed linked the advancement of African Americans, and the abolition of racism, to socialism. The sixth element of his creed states baldly "We believe in the ultimate triumph of some form of Socialism the world over; that is, common ownership and control of the means of production and equality of income" (p. 321). This equalizing of work and wealth is urged as "the beginning of the rise of the Negro race in this land and the world over, in power, learning, and accomplishment" (p. 321). This equalization is to be achieved through taxation and through "vesting the ultimate power of the state in the hands of the workers" (p. 321), a situation that will be accompanied by the working class demanding their "proportionate share in administration and public expenditure" (p. 322). Du Bois ended the creed with an expansive appeal to people of all races to join in fighting white supremacy and creating socialism. In his words, "to this vision of work, organization and service, we welcome [people] of all colors so long as their basic subscription to this basic creed is sincere and proven by their deeds" (p. 322).

Democracy as a Struggle Against Ideological Manipulation

The third element in an understanding of democracy is that it is a struggle against ideologies that exclude disenfranchised groups from full and equal participation in social life. These ideologies would be those of white supremacy, class superiority, patriarchy, homophobia, ableism, and so on. Western industrial societies like the United States purport to be completely open democracies in which all have equal opportunity to flourish, yet they are actually highly unequal societies in which economic inequity, racism, and class discrimination are empirical realities. The way this state of affairs is reproduced as seeming to be normal, natural, and inevitable (thereby heading off potential challenges to the system) is through the dissemination of dominant ideologies. This means that democracy can only flourish if these ideologies are challenged and then replaced. So from this third perspective, adult education involves subverting and destroying elements of dominant ideology.

Frameworks of Democratic Practice in Adult Education

In this section I explore four major democratic frameworks in the adult education field. Each of these frameworks has slightly different emphases regarding how democracy is best practiced. Although many activities and approaches are common to all four traditions, I will emphasize practices that are predominant in each of these frameworks.

Experiential Democracy

The first strand in adult educational theory I wish to explore is experiential democracy, which emphasizes the primacy of adult learners' experiences. The importance of working with adults' experiences is at the heart of many lionized practices in the field, but I will focus on three: Malcolm Knowles's concept of andragogy (Knowles, 1970, 1984), the work of the Highlander Folk School (Horton, 1990, 2003), and Paulo Freire's problem-posing education originating in South America (Freire, 1970). Knowles's work developed in mainstream U.S. contexts, primarily at the YMCAs in Boston and Chicago; Horton developed his methodology in the context of union organizing and the civil rights struggle; and Freire worked with rural peasantry. Yet all three emphasized the primacy of adults' experiences as the dominant construct in adult educational work.

Knowles's concept of andragogy stressed that adult learning was typically in response to needs that sprung from adults' daily circumstances and the particular life problems they faced. He argued that adults' motivation to learn came from an inner determination of what was most important to them, so their learning had to be relevant for them. Only if people diagnosed their own learning needs would they demonstrate a true commitment to learning. Knowles's work was preceded by Lindeman's use of the term *andragogy* in a text on *Education Through Experience* (Anderson & Lindeman, 1927) and his view of adult education as "a cooperative venture in nonauthoritarian, informal learning the chief purpose of which is to discover the meaning of experience" (Lindeman, 1925, p. 3).

The Highlander Folk School was founded as an experiment in what is now called popular education (Kane, 2001; Wiggins, 2011). It sought to gather activists together from across the South to brainstorm ways to deal with the problems constraining their communities (Preskill, 2020). Highlander's approach was based on the democratic sharing and collaborative analysis of participants' experiences. The intent was to create a democratic format in which everybody had an equal opportunity to share insights gained from their own experiences as they contemplated how to work through problems they shared.

The cofounder and director of Highlander, Myles Horton, believed it was crucial to value the experience of every person since in his view people had the answers to their problems locked inside them. The purpose of education was to help them unlock these answers by getting them to analyze their experiences critically. Highlander workshops were discussion based, with facilitators asking questions designed to prompt people to share responses based solely on their experiences. In their book *We Make the Road by Walking* (Horton & Freire, 1990) Horton and the Brazilian popular educator Paulo Freire keep returning to the importance of working with people's experiences.

The adult education strain of experiential democracy has been influential in the field ever since Lindeman and Dewey's work. One of its clearest connections is to the explosion of interest in the last several decades in reflective practice and critical reflection (Brookfield, 2017; Mezirow & Associates, 1990). The idea of analyzing experience is now enshrined as a part of professional preparation in a number of fields, including education, health care, social work, counseling psychology, and management (Beres & Fook, 2020; Fook & Gardner, 2007, 2013). Many institutions and organizations mandate reflective portfolios where the analysis of experience is assessed according to criteria centrally drafted by an oversight body (Bradbury et al., 2010). Those engaged in organizing and teaching courses, workshops, and seminars on reflective practice and critical reflection typically use a variant of dialogic methodology asking participants to disclose particular professional critical incidents that are then discussed by group members. Alternatively, case studies, scenarios, and simulations are deployed that are then collaboratively analyzed.

Experientially inclined democratic practices include working in teams of colleagues and cofacilitators in which team members give each other constant feedback regarding how they interpret events that happen to them. Sometimes this feedback happens in the middle of an event as a quick debriefing between colleagues. Sometimes it happens via a more structured critical conversation protocol where colleagues sit down and try to unearth assumptions each team member holds and pose alternative ways of seeing situations all experience (Brookfield, 2017). As an example, the circle of voices exercise gives equal time to each person and requires participants to listen carefully and respond to comments already made (Brookfield & Preskill, 2016). Experiential democracy also places a strong emphasis on educators constantly collecting data from participants on how they are experiencing learning. This information is then used to make decisions regarding what to do next. One example of this is the Critical Incident Questionnaire (Jacobs, 2015; Keefer, 2009), in which participants anonymously respond to questions about moments and actions that are helpful to them as learners or that inhibit their progress. These are reviewed by the educator, who prepares a report that is shared with learners. A conversation then ensues where the whole group discusses what next steps to take that would best facilitate learning.

Democracy as Self-Directed Control

A second influential framework places the exercise of self-directed control at the heart of democratic practice. Given the widely held cultural belief that anyone can be anything if they put their minds to it, it is unsurprising that the idea of adult educators encouraging and supporting learners in whatever learning efforts they choose to conduct has been widely accepted. This kind of practice sits well alongside the democratic idea that people should have the ultimate control over what they decide to do.

An emphasis on privileging learner control is embedded in the work of many of the major adult education thinkers already cited, such as Lindeman, Knowles, Horton, and Freire. In U.S. adult education self-directed learning is probably most associated with Knowles (1975) and the andragogical tenet that learners must always be in control of their own learning.

The way in which self-directed learning is framed within andragogy emphasizes the notion of individual choice, of a learner deciding to study whatever is of greatest relevance to him or her. An andragogically framed self-directed learner is seen as one who makes free and uncoerced choices from amongst a smorgasbord of enticing possibilities. The choices such a learner makes are held to reflect her desire to realize the strivings, dreams, and aspirations that lie at the core of her identity. However, this notion of there being an identifiable, differentiated "self" that chooses what and how to learn has been notably criticized by critical and postmodern adult educators who argue that so-called core identities are nothing more than the result of contextual factors (Kilgore, 2002). This perspective claims that identity is malleable and queries whether supporting the exercise of self-directed control should be so influential.

Notwithstanding this criticism, there is something intrinsically freeing and empowering to many adult education practitioners and theorists about the idea of self-direction. People understand that embedded in the idea is some strain of resistance that sets learners in opposition to powerful interests and institutional attempts to mandate how and what people should learn. So self-directed learning has a distinctively political edge that fits squarely into the tradition of democratic practice.

Adult educators who see their role as being to support learners to exercise their own control invariably become engaged in two democratic political projects. The first is ensuring that what are conceived of as acceptable and appropriate learning activities and processes are not constrained by experts or authorities. This means challenging the power of gatekeepers to prescribe what they think others should learn. The second is helping learners gain access to the resources necessary to them successfully completing learning. Each of these adult educational tasks is essentially political in nature.

The most consistent element in the majority of definitions of self-direction is the importance of the learner's exercising control over all educational decisions. The goals of a learning effort, the resources to be used, the methods that will work best for the learner, and the criteria for determining learning all rest in the learner's hands. This emphasis on control is of course central to notions of democratic adult education. For example, when talking about his work at Highlander Myles Horton (1990) stressed that "if you want to have the students control the whole process, as far as you can get them to control it, then you can never, at any point, take it out of their hands" (p. 152).

Self-direction as an organizing concept for adult education therefore calls to mind some powerful political associations. It implies a democratic commitment to shifting to learners as much control as possible for conceptualizing, designing, conducting, and evaluating their learning and for deciding how resources are to be used to further these processes. Thought of politically, self-direction can be seen as part of a populist democratic tradition that holds that people's definitions of what is important to them should frame and instruct governments' actions, and not the other way round. This is why the idea of self-direction is so anathema to advocates of a core or national curriculum and why it is opposed so vehemently by those who see education as a process of induction into cultural literacy.

Self-directed learning is also institutionally and politically inconvenient to those who promote educational blueprints, devise intelligence measures, and administer psychological tests and profiles that attempt to control the learning of others. As Horton (1990) stressed, emphasizing people's right to self-direction invests a certain trust in their wisdom, in their capacity to make wise choices and take wise actions. Advocating that people should be in control of their own learning is based on the belief that if people had a chance to give voice to what most moves and hurts them they would soon show that they were only too well aware of the real nature of their problems and of ways to deal with these.

Adult educators working with an ethic of self-direction are likely to face pushback over their desire to help learners gain access to all relevant information and resources they need. If important information is held back or kept secret from learners then educators' responsibility is to help locate all appropriate resources to help learners conduct their projects. Educators have to fight those in administrative power who decide that certain knowledge or skills are undesirable, inappropriate, or subversive. A desire to explore an alternative political ideology is meaningless if books exploring that ideology have been removed from the public library because of their "unsuitability," or if they have never been ordered in the first place.

And what if the resources that learners need are priced exorbitantly? If learners need access to specific equipment for a self-directed effort they have planned, and are then told by those controlling such equipment that it is unavailable for reasons of cost or others' prior claims, self-direction is clearly impeded. Adults initiating a self-directed learning project that challenges the informational hegemony of a professional group may find that medical and legal experts place insurmountable barriers in their path in an effort to prevent a challenge to their credibility. For example, a desire to learn about holistic health practices or to explore natural healing remedies may be blocked by the pharmaceutically dependent medical establishment. In such a case the adult educator is surely enjoined to fight against the establishment that controls equipment and information. So exercising self-direction can be inherently politicizing as learners and educators become aware of the differential distribution of resources necessary to conduct their self-directed efforts.

Democracy as the practice of self-directed learner control takes many forms. One practice that features heavily in practices derived from Knowles's (1975) work is the generation of *learning contracts* (Caffarella & Caffarella, 1986). Here learners and teachers negotiate contracts regarding what is to be learned and how success should be determined. In his work with working-class adults, Ira Shor (2002) drew on Paulo Freire's ideas to explore how students could set the agenda for learning by proposing problems and situations from their everyday lives that could form the focus of classroom study. One example of this was students' requests to examine the different items for sale in the college cafeteria. In his book on critical teaching for everyday life, Shor (1987) described how he built a module on hamburgers that focused on food production, safety inspection standards, and the economics of profitability.

Democracy as Dialogue

Perhaps the most enduring strain of theorizing that has influenced adult education methodology is the belief that adults learn best in dialogic settings that are arranged democratically to give all an equal chance to contribute and have their voice be heard. In revealing and celebrating the multiplicity of perspectives possible, discussion at its best is believed to exemplify the democratic process. All participants in a democratic discussion have the opportunity to voice a strongly felt view and the obligation to devote every ounce of their attention to each speaker's words. When a classroom is viewed as an analog of democracy everyone has the right to express themselves and the responsibility to create spaces that encourage even the most reluctant speaker to participate.

In Dewey's (1916) view, discussion and democracy are inseparable because both have the same root purpose—to nurture and promote human growth. By "growth" Dewey meant the development of an ever-increasing capacity for learning and an appreciation of and sensitivity to learning undertaken by others. For him democracy and discussion implied a process of giving and taking, speaking and listening, describing and witnessing, all of which help to expand horizons and foster mutual understanding. Discussion is one of the best ways to nurture growth because it is premised on the idea that only through collaboration and cooperation with others can we be exposed to new points of view. By giving the floor to as many different participants as possible, a collective wisdom emerges that would have been impossible for any of the participants to achieve on their own.

This Deweyan-inspired approach was evident in Lindeman's early classic *The Meaning of Adult Education* (1926), where Lindeman declared the model for adult education to be

> small groups of aspiring adults who begin to learn by confronting pertinent situations; desire to keep their minds fresh and vigorous; who dig down into the reservoirs of their experience before resorting to texts and secondary facts; who are led in the discussion by teachers who are also seekers of wisdom and not oracles; this constitutes the setting for adult education, the modern quest for life's meaning. (p. 7)

As Lindeman's work developed he made increasingly explicit the links he saw between the practice of discussion and the preservation of democracy. His 1930 entry in the *Encyclopedia of Social Sciences* stated that "If there is anything distinctive about method in adult education, it is derived from the growing use of discussion" (Lindeman, 1930, p. 465) and affirmed the "discussion method has come to be the accepted learning process for large numbers of adult classes" (p. 465). As World War II ended he linked world peace to participation in discussion: "If we genuinely want understanding and a good peace, we must quickly bring into existence an adult education movement which springs from the grass roots of American life" (Lindeman, 1945b, p. 23). This movement would be based on neighborhood discussion groups that were "essential for democratic life" (p. 23) by combating propaganda and developing adults' critical capacity to hold leaders accountable. At the end of his career he published a piece on democratic discussion and the people's voice (Lindeman, 1951) in which he outlined how democracy was learned via participation in discussion.

This dialogic approach is also at the heart of more radical adult education approaches associated with Freire and Horton. Dialogic circles are central to popular education methodology (Kane, 2001; Wiggins, 2011), participatory research approaches (Avila et al., 2000; Cammarato & Fine, 2008), and feminist pedagogy (English & Irving, 2015), all important elements in contemporary adult education. In adult education classrooms, at adult education conferences, and in the literature of adult teaching methods discussion is the privileged methodology, largely because of its connection to notions of democratic participation and equity. We hear and read of the need to ensure everyone participates, that all voices are heard, and that all contributions are important. To say one is committed to democratic discussion is to earn the adult education Good Housekeeping seal of approval. And to incorporate some kind of discussion methodology is the starting point for the vast majority of adult educators as they think about program planning and instructional design.

One well-known example of discussion practices that purport to exemplify this democratic ideal are the culture circles Paulo Freire used in his work to teach literacy to peasants (Souto-Manning, 2010). In culture circles literacy is taught via participants generating themes that represent the dominant concerns in their lives. As these generative themes emerge people identify the problems within each theme that prevent them from reaching their potential. For example, a generative theme might be the need to grow enough food to support a family and sell the surplus in markets for a meager income. A problem in doing this might be obtaining water to irrigate the crops. Through what Freire called "problem posing" the difficulty of finding irrigation is analyzed in terms of who benefits, and who is harmed by, this situation. This in turn leads to identifying landowner practices of charging high amounts for well-irrigated land that is rented only to prosperous farmers.

David Bohm's (1996) work on dialogue has also been influential in adult education through the notion of *Bohmian dialogues* (Brookfield & Preskill, 2016). A Bohmian dialogue follows certain ground rules. People are encouraged to stay silent unless they have something consequential to share. There are to be no winners or losers, and nobody should attempt to convert anyone else to another point of view. The point of the dialogue is purely to understand the radically different perspectives people bring to a problem.

Within adult education the circular response activity first proposed by Eduard Lindeman (1926) has had an enduring effect. In a circular response discussion there is an initial round of sharing in which each person in the circle has the chance to speak uninterrupted. However, as the conversation moves around the circle the ground rule is that each contributor must strive to have her or his comments refer back to, or build on, the preceding speaker's contribution. This way the 12th person in a discussion group does not have 12 minutes to prepare what she wishes to say because her comments will be framed by what the person before her has just disclosed.

Democracy as Decentering Power

The final strain of adult education thinking around democracy concerns the need, as far as possible, to equalize power differences in the adult classroom. Here we can look to the work of Mary Parker Follett, whose *Creative Experience* (1924) introduced the notion of *power-with* decision-making processes as opposed to *power-over* management. Power-with mechanisms were designed to help people to create and wield power together by joining each individual's strengths and experiences with others. Such mechanisms required the fullest possible participation of people. The more that each person contributed something of herself or himself to the group, the more likely it was that the group as a whole would benefit and thus become more empowered. Follett's notion of power-with is the germ of the current understanding of empowerment and of the notion that empowerment's meaning is fully realized in groups of people working together for change.

Follett (1924) challenged the readers of *Creative Experience* to find common ground, to create new ideas in common, to build more comprehensive and representative syntheses. This was possible, she warned, only if sufficient time was taken to air those differences and to evolve the power that grows from genuine collaboration and mutual respect. Through the "slower process of education" (p. 190) a more constructive power-with situation is created in which each person adds his or her power to the community, thereby empowering all. Follett's analysis constitutes an early analysis of how democracy can be realized even in an increasingly diverse and fractured society. It also prefigures Ella Baker's (1972) fostering of collective leadership and Myles Horton's (1990) oft-quoted distinction between organizing (which sometimes required fast action without consultation of community members) and education (which always took more time than planned and could not be foreshortened).

Follett (1924) reminded her contemporaries that in highly complex and participatory democratic environments people are continually creating, recreating, and cocreating themselves. Hence, "I never react to you but to you-plus-me; or to be more accurate, it is I-plus-you reacting to you-plus-me" (p. 62). By this she meant we are constantly influencing each other in a mutual and cumulative process of relating. The democratic implication of this is the need for people in a democratic group to be open to being changed and to accept the possibility of being "recreated" and "cocreated" with those around them. For Follett the integrating and synthesizing of differences of opinion that result from healthy democratic conversations are progressive in that they reflect the growth of the group as a whole and the individuals who constitute it. In the interplay of group discussion "I can only free you and you me. This is the essence, the meaning, of all relation" (p. 130). This reciprocal calling forth of one from the other was the raison d'être of democracy; a living, breathing project model of democratic liberation.

Contemporary adult educational work on the need for greater racial and cultural diversity and the importance of confronting white supremacy (Sheared et al., 2010) builds on Follett's potion of power with mechanisms of decision making. Antiracist education foregrounds the need for people to be in dialogue with each other along with the willingness to take others' perspectives as seriously as one's own. Whites who believe themselves to be color blind and living in a postracial world have to engage in perspective taking (Mezirow, 1990) whereby they explore a completely different reality of the daily presence of white supremacy. Adult educators documenting how they teach against color blindness (Yanow, 2019), build working alliances with students (Cavalieri et al., 2019), create the conditions for racial dialogues (Merriweather et al., 2019), and help students uncover their positionality (Ramdeholl & Jones, 2019) all emphasize the need to decenter the racially based power imbalances that adult learners bring into classrooms and other settings for learning. Educators need to set up conversational protocols and visual exercises with ground rules that require active listening and viewing, particularly when perspectives are shared that are highly illuminating and critical of white supremacy (Brookfield, 2020a, 2020b).

The democratic tradition of deliberately decentering power in adult education does not mean that facilitators always stand aside and let learners run the show in whatever organic way the class develops. In some cases, educators will need to be highly interventionist. They will have to insist on marginalized viewpoints and authorities taking center stage. They will have to run sessions in ways that prevent the usual extroverted suspects from dominating. They will have to create exercises in which second-language learners and those intimidated by academe find ways to express their opinions and showcase their thinking.

Multiple examples of attempts to democratize classrooms are evident in the literature. Shor's (1996) detailed analysis of decentering power in one specific semester-long course described his use of what he called an "after-hours group" to help him run the class. This group comprised volunteer students who provided him with detailed feedback they had gathered from their peers about what was, and was not, working for them as learners. Based on this feedback Shor was able to make significant alterations as the course proceeded.

In an analysis of a doctoral program designed to introduce greater democracy in higher adult education, Avila et al. (2000), Heaney (2010), and Ramdeholl et al. (2011) all described how students in the program engaged in shared governance. At each weekend meeting of the class, time was allotted for students to meet on their own to generate feedback, express criticisms, and propose curricular and other changes. Students would then hold a session with faculty to present their criticisms, reactions, and suggestions. Faculty and students would then negotiate to reach a consensus all could live with.

My own work contains a number of suggestions for democratizing classroom participation. One is the use of an exercise called Chalk Talk (Smith, 2009). Here a question of concern to a group is posted on a large blank surface (blackboard, whiteboard, or wall of newsprint). Participants are told to stay silent for 5 to 10 minutes as they write or draw responses to the question. As people notice comments that are similar or contradictory they draw lines to connect these. Others answer questions that have been posted. New dialogue threads emerge as people respond to one particular comment. At the end of 10 minutes the group has silently produced a graphic on the diverse ways they respond to a question of concern, and this graphic is then used to guide the group's subsequent conversations on actions it can take.

Conclusion

In this chapter I have tried both to outline the ways that democratic ideas have shaped contemporary adult education practices and to extend the notion of democracy beyond strictly majority rule. I have also discussed some of the ways that educators can embody this extended definition and promote democratic ideals. Democratic process is not merely a matter of polling people and going with the most widely held opinion. It is not just finding out what the majority of learners wish to study and then arranging a curriculum based on those responses. It is instead an ever-widening conversation requiring the widest possible range of voices and experiences. It honors participants' control but also works diligently to stop existing ideologies and power structures from simply reproducing themselves. Democratic process needs adult educators who are prepared to intervene and exercise their authority to ensure that multiple voices, cultural traditions, and different ways of learning are deliberately introduced. In a world riven with structural power imbalances, framed by dominant ideologies of capitalism, white supremacy ,and patriarchy, and bedeviled by the denial of facts and the dismissal of research, science, and empirical reality, democracy will need to be fought for.

References

Albert, M. (2004). *Parecon: Life after capitalism*. Verso.

Albert, M. (2006). *Realizing hope: Life beyond capitalism*. ZED Books.

Allman, P. (2000). *Revolutionary social transformation: Democratic hopes, political possibilities and critical education*. Bergin and Garvey.

Anderson, M., & Lindeman, E. C. (1927). *Education through experience*. Workers Education Bureau of America.

Avila, E. B., Caron, T., Anderson Flanagan, P., Frer, D., Heaney, T., Hyland, N., Kerstein, S., Kowalski, C., & Rinaldi, E. (2000). Learning democracy/democratizing learning: Participatory graduate education. In P. Campbell & B. Burnaby (Eds.), *Participatory practices in adult education* (pp. 221–236). Erlbaum.

Baker, E. (1972). Developing community leadership. In G. Lerner (Ed.), *Black_women in white America: A documentary history* (pp. 345–352). Vintage.

Beres, L., & Fook, J. (Eds.). (2020). *Learning critical reflection: Experiences of the transformative learning process*. Routledge.

Bohm, D. (1996). *On dialogue*. Routledge.

Bradbury, H., Frost, N., Kilminster, S., & Zukas, M. (Eds.). (2010). *Beyond reflective practice: New approaches to professional lifelong learning*. Routledge.

Brookfield, S. D. (2017). *Becoming a critically reflective teacher*. Jossey-Bass.

Brookfield, S. D. (2020a). Uncovering white supremacy. In G. Yancy (Ed.), *Educating for critical consciousness* (pp. 1–17). Routledge.

Brookfield, S. D. (2020b). Using a pedagogy of narrative disclosure to uncover white supremacy. In A. Mandell & E. Michelson (Eds.), *Adult Education in the Age of Trump and Brexit* (New Directions for Adult and Continuing Education, no. 165, pp. 9–19). Jossey-Bass. https://doi.org/10.1002/ace.20364

Brookfield, S. D., & Holst, J. D. (2010). *Radicalizing learning: Adult education for a just world.* Jossey-Bass.

Brookfield, S. D., & Preskill, S. J. (2016). *The discussion book: 50 great ways to get people talking.* Jossey-Bass.

Caffarella, R. S., & Caffarella, E. P. (1986). Self-directedness and learning contracts in adult education. *Adult Education Quarterly, 36*(5), 226–234. https://doi.org/10.1177/0001848186036004004

Cammarato, J., & Fine, M. (Eds.). (2008). *Revolutionizing education: Youth participatory research in motion.* Routledge.

Careless, E. J. (2015). Social media for justice in adult education: A critical theoretical framework. *Journal of Teaching and Learning, 10*(1), 13–26. https://doi.org/10.22329/JTL.V10I1.3972

Cavalieri, C. E., French, B. H., & Renninger, S. M. (2019). Developing working alliances with students. In S. D. Brookfield & Associates, *Teaching race: Helping students unmask and challenge racism* (pp. 151–170). Jossey-Bass.

Coben, D. (1998). *Radical heroes: Gramsci, Freire and the politics of adult education.* Garland.

Dewey, J. (1916). *Democracy and education: An introduction to the philosophy of education.* Macmillan.

Du Bois, W. E. B. (1971). *Dusk of dawn: An essay toward an autobiography of a race concept.* Schocken Books.

English, L .M., & Irving, C. J. (2015). *Feminism in community: Adult education for transformation.* Sense.

Follett, M. P. (1924). *Creative experience.* Longmans, Green.

Fook, J., & Gardner, F. (2007). *Practicing critical reflection: A resource handbook.* Open University Press.

Fook, J., & Gardner, F. (Eds.). (2013). *Critical reflection in context: Applications in health care and social work.* Routledge.

Freire, P. (1970). *Pedagogy of the oppressed.* Continuum.

Guy, T. C., & Brookfield, S. D. (2009). W. E. B. Du Bois' basic American Negro creed and the associates in Negro folk education: A case study of repressive tolerance in the censorship of radical black discourse on adult education. *Adult Education Quarterly, 60*(1), 65–76. https://doi.org/10.1177/0741713609336108

Habermas, J. (1996). *Between facts and norms: Contributions to a discourse theory of democracy.* MIT Press.

Heaney, T. (2010). Democracy, shared governance, and the university. In D. Ramdeholl, T. Giordani, T. Heaney, & W. Yanow (Eds.), *The Struggle for Democracy in Adult Education* (New Directions for Adult and Continuing Education, no. 128, pp. 69–79). Jossey-Bass. https://doi.org/10.1002/ace.392

Holst, J. D. (2002). *Social movements, civil society, and radical adult education.* Bergin and Garvey.

Horton, M. (1990). *The long haul: An autobiography.* Doubleday.

Horton, M. (2003). *The Myles Horton reader: Education for social change.* University of Tennessee Press.

Horton, M., & Freire, P. (1990). *We make the road by walking: Conversations on education and social change.* Temple University Press.

Jacobs, M. A. (2015). By their pupils they'll be taught: Using Critical Incident Questionnaire as feedback. *Journal of Invitational Theory, 21,* 9–22. https://doi.org/10.26522/jitp.v21i.3512

Kane, L. (2001). *Popular education and social change in Latin America*. Latin America Bureau.

Keefer, J. M. (2009). The Critical Incident Questionnaire (CIQ): From research to practice and back again. In *Adult education research conference proceedings* (pp. 177–182). New Prairie Press. https://newprairiepress.org/aerc/2009/papers/31/

Kilgore, D. (2002). Critical and postmodern perspectives on adult learning. In S. B. Merriam (Ed.), *The New Update on Adult Learning Theory* (New Directions for Adult and Continuing Education, no. 89, pp. 53–62). Jossey-Bass. https://doi.org/10.1002/ace.8

Knowles, M. S. (1970). *The modern practice of adult education: Andragogy versus pedagogy*. Association Press.

Knowles, M. S. (1975). *Self-directed learning: A guide for learners and teachers*. Association Press.

Knowles, M. S. (1984). *Andragogy in action: Applying modern principles of adult learning*. Jossey-Bass.

Lindeman, E. C. (1925). *What is adult education?* [Unpublished manuscript]. Butler Library Lindeman Archive, Columbia University.

Lindeman, E. C. (1926). *The meaning of adult education*. New Republic.

Lindeman, E. C. (1930). Adult education. In E. R. A. Seligman & A. S. Johnson (Eds.), *Encyclopedia of social sciences* (pp. 460–472). Macmillan.

Lindeman, E. C. (1945a). The sociology of adult education. *Journal of Educational Sociology*, *19*(1), 4–13. https://doi.org/10.2307/2263073

Lindeman, E. C. (1945b). World peace through adult education. *The Nation's Schools*, *35*(3), 15–29.

Lindeman, E. C. (1951, Winter). Voice of the concurring people: An appeal on behalf of democratic discussion. *University of Kansas City Review*, 129–135.

Mayo, P. (1998). *Gramsci, Freire and adult education: Possibilities for transformative action*. ZED Books.

Merriweather, L. R., Guy, T., & Manglitz, E. (2019). Creating the conditions for racial dialogues. In S. D. Brookfield & Associates, *Teaching race: How to help students unmask and challenge racism* (pp. 131–150). Jossey-Bass.

Mezirow, J. (1990). *Transformative dimensions of adult learning*. Jossey-Bass.

Mezirow, J., & Associates. (1990). *Fostering critical reflection in adulthood: A guide to transformative and emancipatory learning*. Jossey-Bass.

Mojab, S., & Carpenter, S. (2020). Marxist–feminist pedagogies of fascism and anti-fascism. In A. Mandell & E. Michelson (Eds.), *Adult Learning in the Age of Trump and Brexit* (New Directions for Adult and Continuing Education, no. 165, pp. 129–141). Jossey-Bass. https://doi.org/10.1002/ace.20373

Preskill, S. J. (2020). *In pursuit of the ought to be: Myles Horton and the movement for popular education*. University of California Press.

Ramdeholl, D., Giordani, T., Heaney, T., & Yanow, W. (Eds.). (2011). *The Struggle for Democracy in Adult Education* (New Directions for Adult and Continuing Education, no. 128). Jossey-Bass.

Ramdeholl, D., & Jones, J. (2019). *Helping students uncover positionality*. In S. D. Brookfield & Associates, *Teaching race: Helping students unmask and challenge racism* (pp. 233–252). Jossey-Bass.

Schied, F. (1993). *Learning in social context: Workers and adult education in nineteenth century Chicago*. Learning and Educational Studies Press.

Sheared, V., Johnson-Bailey, J., Colin, S. A. J., Petersen, E., & Brookfield, S. D. (Eds.). (2010). *The handbook of race and adult education: A resource for dialog on racism.* Jossey-Bass.

Shor, I. (1987). *Critical teaching for everyday life.* University of Chicago Press.

Shor, I. (1996). *When students have power: Negotiating authority in a critical pedagogy.* University of Chicago Press.

Shor, I. (2002). *Empowering education: Critical teaching for social change.* University of Chicago Press.

Smith, H. (2009). The Foxfire approach to student and community interaction. In L. Shumow (Ed.), *Promising practices for family and community involvement during high school* (pp. 89–103). Information Age.

Souto-Manning, M. (2010). *Freire, teaching and learning: Culture circles across contexts.* Lang.

Sunstein, C. (2006). *The second Bill of Rights: FDR's unfinished revolution and why we need it more than ever.* Perseus Books.

Wiggins, N. (2011). Critical pedagogy and popular education: Towards a unity of theory and practice. *Studies in the Education of Adults, 43*(1), 34–49. https://doi.org/10.1080/02660830.2011.11661602

Wiltshire, H. (1973). The concepts of learning and need in adult education. *Studies in Adult Education, 5*(1), 26–30. https://doi.org/10.1080/02660830.1973.11730701

Yanow, W. (2019). *Teaching against color blindness.* In S. D. Brookfield & Associates, *Teaching race: Helping students unmask and challenge racism* (pp. 213–232). Jossey-Bass.

Editors' Key Seminal and Supplemental Text Suggestions

Brookfield, S. D. (2001). A political analysis of discussion groups: Can the circle be unbroken? In R. M. Cervero, A. L. Wilson, & Associates (Eds.), *Power in practice: Adult education and the struggle for knowledge and power in society* (pp. 206–225). Jossey-Bass.

Brookfield, S. D. (2005). *The power of critical theory: Liberating adult learning and teaching.* Jossey-Bass.

- Chapter 3: Challenging Ideology
- Chapter 4: Contesting Hegemony
- Chapter 5: Unmasking Power

Brookfield, S. D. (2012). *Teaching for critical thinking: Tools and techniques to help students question their assumptions.* Jossey-Bass.

- Chapter 5: Developing Critical Complexity: Intermediate and Advanced Protocols
- Chapter 8: Making Discussions Critical

Freire. P. (2007). *Pedagogy of the oppressed: 30th anniversary edition.* Continuum.

- Chapter 2
- Chapter 3

PART TWO

Internal Influences and the Learner

4

MOTIVATING ADULT LEARNERS

David A. Bergin, Christi A. Bergin, and Sarah L. Prewett

Prior to becoming knowledgeable about motivation, one of us (David) was tasked with helping Silicon Valley departments at IBM and Hewlett-Packard provide training to their engineers on topics such as problem solving, CMOS integrated chips, and UNIX. David contacted experts who might be willing to teach the courses, such as George Pólya, (1945) author of *How to Solve It*; Walter Gong, coauthor of a book on problem solving in physics (Shockley & Gong, 1966); and experts in UNIX and CMOS. David and his colleagues then put together workshops that, in retrospect, could have been better if they had been designed in light of the motivation principles that are presented in this chapter. *Motivation* refers to an internal process that directs behavior toward goals.

The purpose of this chapter is to discuss motivation concepts applied to adult learning. Adults learn in many settings—at work, in museums, and in traditional educational settings—and for many reasons, including to pursue hobbies, self-directed projects, and language learning. It is important to address motivation in these varied contexts because motivation consistently predicts adult performance and engagement (Cerasoli et al., 2014; Van Iddekinge et al., 2017). In this chapter, we discuss concepts of adult motivation and how to guide, support, and reinforce adult learners' motivation.

Many theories of motivation apply to adult learners, but in this chapter we focus primarily on three theories that are robustly supported by research and that adult educators will find effective and practical to implement: goal theory, self-efficacy theory, and self-determination theory (SDT). Although these theories are distinct, there are some overlapping and similar concepts among them that we highlight throughout the chapter. We begin with goal theory because goals provide the direction for motivated behavior. We follow with self-efficacy because it is foundational to setting goals. Finally, we discuss SDT because it is a comprehensive theory that brings together multiple components of motivation.

Goal Theory

A *goal* is an intention to achieve future valued outcomes. Research consistently shows that goals affect motivation and performance (Locke & Latham, 2002). In the next sections, we focus on three aspects of goals that are important in learning settings: (a) sources of goals, (b) influence of achievement goals, and (c) how to set goals.

Goal Sources

Goals relevant to adult learning are influenced by various sources. One influence is the network of people with whom one interacts, which can support or thwart goals (D. A. Bergin, 2016; Westaby et al., 2014). In a supporting example, a young woman had a goal to become a specialized welder. Her uncle, an engineer, supported and guided her through schooling and getting her first job. In a thwarting example, one of us (Christi) was asked by a medical school to investigate why some students dropped out of medical school. She found that sometimes family members demanded that the student drop out, get a "real job," and help support the extended family rather than stay in school for 8 years. In addition to family members, instructors, as we point out in the "Implications for Practice" section of this chapter, are part of learners' social networks and can play an important role in supporting goals.

Demographics also influence goals. For example, gender and ethnicity influence learner goals through stereotypes that help explain why there are fewer women and students of color in STEM fields (Ceci, 2018; Eccles, 2009). Age influences goals because undergraduate education usually follows soon after high school. People who do not pursue higher education until later may experience disadvantages or barriers. Another demographic influence on goals is social class. For example, high-income young adults are encouraged to aspire to high-status education and careers and are more likely to have the means to pursue them (Binder & Abel, 2018; Schleef, 2000).

Achievement Goals

Achievement goal theory is a dominant perspective on goals in learning settings. It asserts that there are two major types of goals in learning settings: (a) mastery goals, or learning in order to gain understanding, and (b) performance goals, or learning in order to perform better than others (Anderman & Wolters, 2006). For example, learners in formal courses might be motivated to learn the material so that they can use it in their jobs (mastery) or in order to achieve a high grade (performance). Both groups could be highly motivated to learn, but for qualitatively different reasons.

These two major goal types have approach and avoidance manifestations, resulting in four types of achievement goals: mastery approach, mastery avoidance, performance approach, and performance avoidance. Because mastery avoidance goals show measurement problems (Hulleman et al., 2010), we will focus on the three-goal model, also termed the *trichotomous goal model*. A *mastery approach* goal refers to striving to learn and master material. A *performance approach* goal refers to striving to do better than others (Hulleman et al., 2010; while there are other approaches to defining performance approach goals, we will use this one because it seems to be most common). A *performance avoidance* goal refers to striving to avoid appearing unable and doing worse than others. Learners tend to engage in different cognitive activities depending on which of these three types of goals they hold.

A learner holding a mastery approach goal may report high self-efficacy, experience interest, and use deep learning strategies. A learner holding a performance approach goal may experience interest and use deep learning strategies, but less so than the mastery goal learner. A learner holding a performance avoidance goal may avoid difficult tasks, experience anxiety, and have low interest (Hulleman et al., 2010; Ikeda et al., 2021; Senko et al., 2011).

Performance approach and mastery approach goals facilitate achievement, though with some inconsistency, while performance avoidance goals undermine achievement with considerable consistency (Hulleman et al., 2010; Van Yperen et al., 2014). Mastery approach goals should generally be emphasized in learning settings because compared with performance approach goals they are linked with desirable outcomes such as deep learning strategies, persistence, effort, self-efficacy, positive affect, interest, and general well-being (Grant & Dweck, 2003; Harackiewicz et al., 2008; Kaplan & Maehr, 2007).

Readers might wonder why we do not recommend fostering competition in order to activate performance approach goals. Research consistently shows no relationship between competition and achievement (Murayama & Elliot, 2012). According to Murayama and Elliot (2012), this is because invoking competition can activate both approach and avoidance goals. When instructors emphasize competition among learners they cannot control exactly how learners respond. Competition provokes learners to adopt performance goals that could be approach, especially for those who have high ability or high efficacy, or could be avoidance, especially for those who have low ability or low efficacy (D. A. Bergin, 1995). Learners with avoidance goals are likely to experience less learning, lower motivation, and higher anxiety. For this reason, we recommend encouraging mastery approach goals in learning settings in order to facilitate learning for all.

Goal Setting

Research over many years has shown that goal setting has a robust positive effect on motivation and performance (Hattie, 2009; Locke & Latham, 2002, 2006; Morisano, 2013). Goal setting in educational contexts can include broad goals, like achieving high grades; specific goals, like learning a particular data analysis skill; and assignment-level goals, like including at least three pieces of evidence to support each assertion in an essay. Goals affect performance by directing attention and action, mobilizing energy, and prolonging effort and persistence (Locke & Latham, 2006).

Research has identified aspects of goal setting that make goals more, or less, effective; namely, effective goals are specific, dividable into subgoals, and appropriately challenging (Locke & Latham, 2002). In contrast, ambiguous goals, such as "do your best," function about the same as not setting goals at all. Specific components of effective goal setting are displayed in Table 4.1 and discussed in the following sections. Table 4.1 gives examples for a worker who has lost her job and is taking a job search skill development course.

TABLE 4.1
Effective Goal Setting

Effective goal attributes	Description	Example
Specific	It is clear when the goal has been achieved.	I want to get a new job.
Distal goal is divided into subgoals	Small, proximal steps scaffold the learner toward the distal goal. The subgoals should be sequential with feedback.	Each day I will examine all the job leads on websites "A" and "B." I will make eight contacts per day.
Challenging	Goals are appropriately challenging, that is, slightly beyond the person's current ability level, but not too difficult.	Job seeking is inherently challenging, but may be more so if seeking a "stretch" job. Making eight contacts per day may be challenging but doable.
Involves feedback	A coach, teacher, expert, peer, or recording device (e.g., video) provides feedback on goal progress and strategies for improvement.	My manager friend will give me feedback on my resume, cover letters, and on a mock interview. I will keep a spreadsheet of contacts.
Highly committed	Learners are so committed to achieving the goal that they are willing to give up competing activities.	I will give up my fantasy football league in order to free up time for job seeking.
Plan to overcome barriers	Learners devise strategies for self-regulation and plans to overcome stumbling blocks.	I will probably be tempted to slack off during the upcoming holiday, so I will tell my family in advance that I need uninterrupted time every day from 7–9 a.m.

Note. Effective goal setting. Relevant works include the following: D. A. Bergin and Prewett (2020), Gollwitzer and Oettingen (2012), and Locke and Latham (2002, 2006).

Specificity

It is relatively easy to think of specific goals for activities like getting a job or running (e.g., "I will achieve a 10-minute mile"). However, generating specific goals for activities such as learning a new language, using an accounting system, getting physically fit, or appreciating Shakespeare are more challenging because what constitutes proficiency is less concrete. For some domains, specific goals can be framed in terms of time (e.g., "I will study at least 30 minutes per day") and output (e.g., "I will write at least 500 words per day").

Subgoals

Proximal subgoals help learners make better progress toward larger, distal goals. For example, someone might take a community course on home gardening in order to achieve a distal goal to produce vegetables to feed the family. Proximal subgoals might include *get information about soil composition and best plants for this climate by January 15, buy seeds and relevant supplies by March 15, prepare soil and plant seeds by April 30.*

Challenge

Performance tends to rise when learners set goals that are challenging but realistically achievable with effort. For an introvert, making eight prospective job contacts per day might be quite challenging, but others might find it less challenging and set a higher subgoal.

Feedback

Feedback is information provided by a person or some other mechanism regarding one's performance (Hattie & Timperley, 2007). Feedback regarding progress toward goals helps learners know where to focus effort. Feedback can come from others, such as a coach or an instructor who describes discrepancies between desired performance and actual performance. Feedback from self-monitoring techniques such as charts and checklists helps learners independently check their progress toward goal achievement. Feedback can also be a natural consequence of behavior, such as getting a job interview, producing plants that grow, and hitting a golf ball that sails toward the hole.

Goal Commitment

Achieving challenging goals takes effort. Learners are not likely to achieve goals unless they are committed to the toil required. Learners are more likely to commit to goals if they view the goals as important and attainable (Locke & Latham, 2002). However, when a learner has multiple goals, one goal can pull resources away from another goal (Kruglanski et al., 2002). For example, a learner might have a goal to get into medical school and a conflicting goal to work on becoming a great artist (Boudreaux & Ozer, 2013); each goal requires time that must be taken away from one goal in pursuit of the other. When goals conflict, whether the learner pursues one goal or the other depends on the relative commitment to each goal.

Plan to Overcome Barriers

The most successful goal-setters identify strategies for overcoming barriers and difficulties (Gollwitzer & Sheeran, 2006) because distractions and stumbling blocks may arise that undermine progress toward goals. Learners should anticipate obstacles (e.g., interruptions while studying or rain interfering with a planned run) and create a contingency "if–then" plan. For example, "If I feel lost in a section of my statistics course, I will read relevant sections in two additional textbooks, and I will attend tutoring sessions."

Implications for Practice

Adult educators are part of the social network of learners that can influence the types of goals they have and their goal setting strategies. The types of achievement goals a learner establishes may be the result of relatively stable individual differences (traits) or due to situational influences. Instructors can foster mastery approach goals using the following guidelines:

> *Provide interesting tasks.* Learners are more likely to engage in efforts to mas-
> ter the content when they perceive that learning tasks are interesting
> and meaningful (D. A. Bergin, 1999, 2016; Renninger & Hidi, 2011;
> Turner et al., 2011).
>
> *Recognize effort and progress.* Recognize and comment on learners' persis-
> tence, diligence, and strategy use, all of which are components of
> achieving mastery goals.
>
> *Avoid social comparison that pits learners against each other (Dweck, 1986).*
> Instructors can influence learner achievement goals by emphasizing
> learning new skills and trying hard versus emphasizing competitive goals
> such as who is best (Bardach et al., 2020). For example, do not publicly
> display a learner's scores or denigrate one learner compared to another
> ("Llami is our most productive . . ."). Avoiding social comparison also
> supports a growth mindset, discussed next.
>
> *Promote a growth mindset (Dweck & Yeager, 2019).* Dweck (1986) observed
> that learners' beliefs about their abilities are linked with achievement
> goals. Learners who have a fixed mindset—they believe that ability is
> relatively fixed and unchangeable—tend to adopt performance goals
> and thoughts like "I am not good at math, and that will never change."
> They are highly sensitive to comparison with others and the possibil-
> ity of negative judgments about their ability. They fear failure and see
> setbacks as threatening. In contrast, learners who have a growth mind-
> set believe that ability can be developed through effort, time, and effec-
> tive strategies and tend to adopt mastery goals and thoughts like "I am
> not good at math, but if I practice I will be." They like challenges and
> have less fear of failure because they believe that they learn from fail-
> ure. Although adult educators can influence mindsets (Blackwell et al.,
> 2007; Paunesku et al., 2015; Sarrasin et al., 2018), it can be difficult
> because adults have spent many years confirming their beliefs about
> themselves as learners. Adult educators can help by teaching that learn-
> ing changes the brain by forming new connections and that effective
> effort over time can result in increased competence.

In addition to fostering mastery goals, adult educators may increase learners' motivation by guiding them in effective goal setting through the following practices:

Provide explicit instruction for effective goal setting. Do not assume learners know how to set goals; they may need instruction with feedback about the quality of their goals and plans for implementation. They may need help, for example, setting specific learning goals and making sure they are measurable without being trivial. They may also need scaffolding to help them break down large, distal goals into smaller, proximal subgoals. For example, the goal of completing a course paper can be broken into steps such as separately submitting a topic statement, an outline, at least six relevant references with annotations, and so forth. Table 4.1 can be used to guide learners through the goal setting process.

Help learners set their own appropriately challenging goals. Instructors should use their experience and insight to help learners set goals that are challenging, but not too challenging. One way to increase goal commitment is by having learners set their own goals, but instructors, coaches, and supervisors can use their expertise to persuade learners that challenging goals are important and attainable and to help set the appropriate level of challenge.

Regularly monitor progress. Learners may need help and encouragement to track their progress toward their goals. For example, instructors can teach how to create a progress chart.

Self-Efficacy

Self-efficacy refers to individuals' beliefs in their capacity to control their functioning and environment. It is their perceptions of their own competence (Bandura, 1997) to *do things* (e.g., "Can I solve these calculus problems?") and to *control cognitions* (e.g., "Can I keep myself from worrying when I do math problems in front of the class?"). Self-efficacy is domain specific and is not a general trait (Bandura, 2012). Domains can be fairly broad, such as academic efficacy or sports efficacy, or they can be more limited, for example, efficacy for writing or efficacy for hitting a baseball. Adult learners might have high efficacy for some academic domains, like mathematics or science, but low efficacy for other domains, like art and literature.

Self-efficacy influences motivation to learn because adult learners are not likely to take on challenging or effortful learning goals and tasks if they feel incompetent or unable to develop competence. When learners with high self-efficacy encounter barriers or failure, they are likely to develop strategies for overcoming them. They may interpret their failure as the result of external factors such as low-quality instruction or bad luck rather than their own incompetence. Learners with high academic efficacy who do poorly on an exam or botch a procedure are less likely to quit; instead, they look for the next opportunity to show what they can do. In contrast, learners with low self-efficacy avoid challenging goals and tasks and quit after a failure because they view additional effort as fruitless. Self-efficacy is more likely to grow in situations that emphasize mastery goals and growth mindset.

Self-efficacy predicts goal commitment. Because learners with greater self-efficacy are more likely to persevere through challenges, they are then more likely to achieve their goal, and these effects have longevity. In a longitudinal study of young adults, higher levels of efficacy predicted goal commitment 6 years later (Dietrich et al., 2013). People will not commit to goals that they do not believe they can achieve. Instead, they may avoid effort and engage in self-handicapping strategies to protect their feelings of self-worth. In other words, because they fear that if they try hard and fail they will feel incompetent, they tend to experience performance avoidance goals and do not try hard. Self-handicapping behaviors include procrastination and claiming illness or anxiety as explanations in the event of poor performance. Not surprisingly, self-handicapping predicts lower achievement (Schwinger et al., 2014).

How does self-efficacy develop? Research describes four influences (Bandura, 1997). *Mastery experience*, or previous success, is usually the most powerful of these. After a learning experience, people interpret their experience and assess their capability to replicate successes and improve upon failures. The more successes they have, the greater the self-efficacy they develop.

A second influence on self-efficacy is observing others' successes and failures. Individuals use such *vicarious experiences* to assess their own probability of success or failure. Peer models are particularly effective. In this case, it is as though learners say to themselves, "If that person who is similar to me can do it, I can do it." Coping models are also particularly effective; coping models show how to cope with and overcome difficulty. For example, an instructor who quickly and expertly models how to solve an equation does little to boost learners' math efficacy compared to a coping model who shows how a novice might go down dead-end paths, discover errors, and then recover to solve the equation.

A third influence is *persuasion*, which occurs when other people express confidence in learners' capabilities. Persuasion is usually most powerful coming from an expert. If a novice fellow student tells a learner they are good at finishing concrete, they are less likely to believe it compared to the critical instructor who says the same thing.

The fourth influence on self-efficacy is *physiological states*, such as anxiety and fatigue. When learners face a task, they can suddenly experience fear or anxiety that undermines their efficacy and causes lower performance. Consider someone who is cold-called in class; they may have felt prepared but suddenly feel high anxiety and related physiological responses, like a rapid heart rate.

Implications for Practice

Instructors can influence adult learners' self-efficacy in at least four ways that parallel the sources of self-efficacy. First, they should foster mastery experience by providing high-quality instruction with appropriate scaffolding so that most learners experience success by accomplishing appropriately challenging tasks. For example, an instructional coach increased K–12 teachers' self-efficacy for using technology in their classrooms by introducing the use of one app at a time and having them practice using it in a few lessons before introducing the next one.

Second, instructors can provide vicarious experience through models, especially peer models, who show or describe their own struggles that led to increased competence and success. Models can be live or virtual, described in print or displayed in video. For example, some colleges organize events specifically to provide models to women who are considering going back to school. At such an event, a master's student who returned to school said,

> It opens the door to a lot of women who, like myself, probably thought they never could go back to school. I thought it would be great to have this event so they could hear other women, and their stories, of how they did it. (King, 2017, para. 24)

However, some learners might not notice that models' experiences are similar to their own in a domain; effective instructors point out relevant aspects of a model's experience so that learners see commonalities between their own and the model's and thus enhance their efficacy for the domain.

Third, instructors can use persuasion and tell learners that they are capable, or enlist credible significant others to do so. For example, a university women's cross-country coach whose team won the 2021 NCAA title said that her high school coach gave her an encouraging note before a meet. It enhanced her belief in herself so strongly that now she gives handwritten notes to each athlete before each meet (Kuzma, 2019).

Finally, instructors can structure learning environments to avoid negative physiological states, like anxiety. For example, they can avoid time limits (Hill & Wigfield, 1984) or help learners reinterpret anxiety as "excitement" rather than "fear" (Brooks, 2014).

Self-efficacy is related to the third theory we will discuss—SDT—because both include a focus on competence. SDT is a comprehensive theory that brings together multiple components of motivation. Like goal theory and self-efficacy, it is robustly supported by research, and adult educators will find it effective and practical to implement.

Self-Determination Theory (SDT)

SDT asserts that humans are inherently curious and active and grow within social contexts (Ryan & Deci, 2017). According to SDT, human motivation is based on needs that are innate and universal. Humans have at least three needs that, when satisfied, provide a basis for motivation and thriving (Deci & Ryan, 2000, 2002). These needs are autonomy, relatedness, and competence. *Autonomy* refers to the perception that one's behavior arises from one's own needs and desires and is not primarily the result of external forces like threats, incentives, or internalized guilt. *Relatedness*, also called *belongingness*, refers to the perception that one belongs to a group and feels emotional relatedness with others. *Competence* refers to the perception that one can influence the environment and successfully pursue desired outcomes.

Learners' intrinsic motivation, the desire to pursue a goal or activity because one wants to, not because of external forces, is greater when these three needs—autonomy, relatedness, and competence—are satisfied. Conversely, when people feel controlled, incompetent, or uncared for they are less likely to experience motivation, especially intrinsic motivation. When intrinsically motivated, one wants to pursue an activity for its own sake and the satisfaction that comes from the activity itself, not because it will result in other positive outcomes.

In this section we focus on autonomy and relatedness because the perception of competence conceptually overlaps with self-efficacy, which was previously discussed. Autonomy is the need that has been most studied by SDT researchers. A fundamental premise of SDT is that greater perceptions of autonomy lead to greater intrinsic motivation. SDT researchers recognize that "socialized life is not all fun and games" (Ryan & Deci, 2017, p. 179). Much behavior is not intrinsically interesting and is extrinsically motivated, that is, motivated to achieve an outcome separate from the activity itself, such as to achieve approval or rewards. SDT describes how internalization occurs so that behavior that was entirely controlled externally, such as through rewards and threats, can become integrated into the self. "Internalization reflects the processes through which extrinsic behaviors become an established aspect of people's minds and motives" (Ryan & Deci, 2017, p. 180). Thus, behavior can be autonomous because it is chosen by the self but not intrinsically motivated because it is not intrinsically interesting. For example, an adult learner might choose to take a course in order to move up a pay grade, not because they love the course material and would choose to learn it on their own. Learning the course material would involve a low level of autonomy and would not be intrinsically motivated. In contrast, an adult learner might choose to take a course on the history of racism and oppression because of an integration of values of fairness and antiracism into the self. This represents a higher level of autonomy and would be closer to intrinsic motivation. SDT proposes that behavior can be on a continuum from externally controlled via threats and rewards, to autonomous (controlled by the self) but not intrinsic, to autonomous and intrinsic. SDT also proposes that behavior that is fully externally controlled is likely to be of the lowest quality, and behavior that is fully autonomous is likely to be of the highest quality.

Most adult learning falls in this category of autonomous but not intrinsic. For example, Ryan and Deci (2017) pointed to this distinction when explaining reasons an individual might study for a class. An individual who says they study "so I won't fall behind in reaching my personal goals" has given a reason that is autonomous, but not intrinsic. An intrinsic rationale is "Because I find it interesting and fun to study"

(p. 192). Thus, an adult may autonomously choose to learn accounting practices for their small business because the learning is extrinsically instrumental for career success rather than because it is interesting and fun to learn. In the following sections, we discuss how an instructor can shift motivation toward the autonomous end of the continuum.

Autonomy overlaps with aspects of goal setting and achievement goals that were discussed earlier. Adult learners should autonomously set their own appropriately challenging goals, with scaffolding based on the instructor's knowledge and experience. When learners are given autonomy in choosing goals they are more likely to set desirable mastery goals, which foster intrinsic motivation.

The third need in SDT, relatedness, refers to the need to feel a connection with others. In other words, humans have a need to form meaningful interpersonal relationships (Baumeister & Leary, 1995). In adult learning settings, relatedness can occur between instructor and learner and among learners. Instructor–learner relations are a key part of fostering learners' sense of relatedness (C. Bergin & Bergin, 2009; Hagenauer & Volet, 2014). Wlodkowski and Ginsberg (2017) illustrated the important relationship between relatedness and motivation when they suggested "Ask any group of adults about their motivation in a course where they felt excluded. Their answers are searing" (p. 89). While learning environments, such as classrooms and internships, may not result in enduring, close relationships, they can cultivate the feeling of being a member of the learning group, and this can have strong motivation dividends.

Most research on instructor–learner relationships has been done with K–12 children, and it has consistently shown positive correlations between teacher–student relationships and student motivation and learning outcomes (C. Bergin & Bergin, 2009; Robinson et al., 2019). Like research with younger students, research with college students finds that when students feel connections with peers and faculty, they tend to have higher academic achievement (Pascarella et al., 2004; Robinson et al., 2019). Presumably, the same is true in adult learning contexts.

It is important to recognize that there is often a racial divide such that learners of color may feel less relatedness in formal learning settings, especially when their instructors do not look like them or when they are the only person of color in the group. This may be due to experiencing low expectations, overt racist comments, and lack of respect (Harper et al., 2018). International students may feel lack of relatedness due to social isolation and lack of social support (Lee & Rice, 2007). On the other hand, research also finds that when underrepresented students, such as women in STEM majors in college, do feel relatedness, they are more likely to complete the program (Hilts et al., 2018). Thus, instructors should be particularly sensitive to perceptions of relatedness among underrepresented learners.

Implications for Practice

In order to support motivation, instructors should consider ways to support learners' needs for autonomy, competence, and relatedness in order to increase learners' motivation. We discussed how to foster feelings of competence, or self-efficacy, earlier in the chapter. Therefore, we focus here on fostering autonomy and then relatedness.

Unfortunately, research suggests that instructors often behave in ways that undermine learner autonomy. For example, Reeve (2009) identified three actions that fail to consider this learner need: "(a) adopt only the teacher's perspective; (b) intrude into students' thoughts, feelings, or actions; and (c) pressure students to think, feel, or behave in particular ways" (p. 160). For example, instructors may insist there is only one way to grow heritage tomatoes, cast a flyline, or do a math problem. Of course, instructors may suggest an ideal method, but they should not neglect the learner's perspective. At the same time, research cautions against instructors abdicating their role as expert. Some instructors want to be the "guide on the side" instead of the "sage on the stage." Such instructors may engage constructivist approaches in which they are not the final authority, lecturing is avoided, learner discussion and collaboration are assumed to result in effective learning, and topics arise from learners. Some adult learners object to a strong constructivist approach, however. They feel they are not getting the expert instruction for which they sacrificed time and money. Culture may also be a factor in learner preferences and expectations. For example, learners from some cultures may expect courses to be instructor led and focused on knowledge transmission rather than knowledge construction (Campbell & Li, 2007; Marlina, 2009). In one study that illustrates this, Chinese graduate students at Australian universities objected to constructivist online instruction because they felt that fellow learners lacked authority and that instructors were passive and invisible (Chen & Bennett, 2012). Thus, instructors may need to balance didactic and constructivist approaches based on their learners' perspectives.

Instructors can support learner autonomy using the following guidelines:

Adopt the learner's perspective. Welcome learners' thoughts, feelings, and actions. If there is a "best" way, provide a rationale (Ryan & Deci, 2017).

Be flexible. Chinese nurses reported that flexibility was a key reason why they liked e-learning for continuing education (Xing et al., 2020).

Respond to learners' interests. Instructors can enhance interest by providing hands-on activities, social interaction, and novelty (D. A. Bergin, 1999, 2016). Novel and unexpected activities tend to be interesting as long as they are not too complex or hard to understand (Silvia, 2006, 2008). Choose topics that are neither mundane nor well understood by learners. People tend to be interested in things for which they have some background knowledge but for which there are still unknowns. This fuels continued interest.

Respond to learners' goals. Learners are likely to be more interested in topics that are relevant to achieving their goals (Harackiewicz et al., 2016; Shechter et al., 2011). Therefore, it is important to help adult learners make their own goals explicit and understand how course content is congruent with them. For example, an instructor of Master Naturalists (an education program for adults who volunteer to provide education on natural resource topics) might help learners see how being a Master Naturalist can achieve goals such as improving the environment, helping others experience nature, and being in nature.

Use utility-value interventions. "Utility-value interventions" ask learners to write brief essays about how course content might be useful in their lives or to write letters to others describing course relevance to their specific situation (Hulleman & Harackiewicz, 2021). Such interventions are practical even in large courses. The interventions can lead to increased interest and performance as learners make their own connections between their personal goals and course content. Such interventions are often more effective if learners write these types of essays two or three times rather than once. Utility-value interventions tend to be particularly effective for first-generation college students and underrepresented minority students (Hulleman & Harackiewicz, 2021).

It is also important that instructors foster relatedness with and among adult learners. Motivation increases when learners feel part of a group in which participants care about and help each other succeed. A soldier in U.S. Army Ranger School explained this well: "If you love your squad and care for them the way you would your family, you will do well, because they are doing well" (Bardenwerper, 2020, p. 79). Instructors convey caring by following guidelines already listed—by helping learners develop greater self-efficacy, supporting autonomy, and promoting goals that match their interests and core values. In addition, instructors can foster relatedness by following these guidelines:

Get to know each other. Know all learners' names and encourage them to know each other's names. Have them share something about each other—interests, families, background—to foster personal connections. Fostering relatedness can be challenging in some environments, such as asynchronous online courses in which learners proceed at their own pace, because learners may perceive peer support as absent (Chen & Bennett, 2012). Wlodkowski and Ginsberg (2017) suggested using collaborative learning, creating an inviting and inclusive syllabus, and acknowledging learners' varied backgrounds as a way to enhance connectedness in online or face-to-face contexts.

Be appropriately warm and caring. Listen, give advice, and acknowledge learners' expressions of negative affect. Behavior as simple as looking at people and smiling reduces their feelings of disconnection, whereas being ignored, even by strangers, increases feelings of disconnection (Wesselmann et al., 2012). Part of caring means providing high-quality instruction, responding to learner questions, and making instruction interesting (Wentzel, 1997).

Avoid microaggressions. Microaggressions are subtle messages that communicate bias or prejudice; they are often unintentional and subconscious (Sue et al., 2007). Examples might include an instructor complimenting learners from a different background on their articulateness. Not including course material generated by people of color can seem to ignore the racial identity of learners of color. International learners might be treated as invisible and unimportant in classroom discussions (Kim & Kim, 2010). Have high expectations for all learners. Inform yourself about possible microaggressions, and go out of your way to avoid them.

Conclusion

Adult learners are often excited to engage in new learning because they want to learn what you are teaching. They may also be anxious and fearful. Adult educators can create a learning environment that is motivating by fostering mastery approach goals; promoting high-quality goal setting; increasing self-efficacy; and supporting competence, autonomy, and relatedness needs. These are mutually supportive and interrelated strategies. Designing learning experiences around these strategies by using the implications for practice outlined in this chapter will activate and increase learners' motivation.

References

Anderman, E., & Wolters, C. (2006). Goals, values, and affect: Influences on student motivation. In P. Alexander & P. Winne (Eds.), *Handbook of educational psychology* (2nd ed., pp. 369–389). Erlbaum.

Bandura, A. (1997). *Self-efficacy: The exercise of control.* Freeman.

Bandura, A. (2012). On the functional properties of perceived self-efficacy revisited. *Journal of Management, 38*(1), 9–44. https://doi.org/10.1177/0149206311410606

Bardach, L., Oczlon, S., Pietschnig, J., & Lüftenegger, M. (2020). Has achievement goal theory been right? A meta-analysis of the relation between goal structures and personal achievement goals. *Journal of Educational Psychology, 112*(6), 1197–1220. https://doi .org/10.1037/edu0000419

Bardenwerper, W. (2020, May). A layer of grit: Army Ranger school is a laboratory of human endurance. *Outside,* 72–81. https://www.outsideonline.com/outdoor-adventure/exploration-survival/army-ranger-school/

Baumeister, R. F., & Leary, M. R. (1995). The need to belong: Desire for interpersonal attachments as a fundamental human motivation. *Psychological Bulletin, 117,* 497–529. https:// doi.org/10.1037/0033-2909.117.3.497

Bergin, C., & Bergin, D. A. (2009). Attachment in the classroom. *Educational Psychology Review, 21,* 141–170. https://doi.org/10.1007/s10648-009-9104-0

Bergin, D. A. (1995). Effects of a mastery versus competitive motivation situation on learning. *Journal of Experimental Education, 63,* 303–314. https://doi.org/10.1080/ 00220973.1995.9943466

Bergin, D. A. (1999). Influences on classroom interest. *Educational Psychologist*, *34*(2), 87–98. https://doi.org/10.1207/s15326985ep3402_2

Bergin, D. A. (2016). Social influences on interest. *Educational Psychologist*, *51*(1), 7–22. https://doi.org/10.1080/00461520.2015.1133306

Bergin, D. A., & Prewett, S. (2020). Goal concepts for understanding and improving the performance of students with learning disabilities. In A. Martin, R. Sperling, & K. Newton (Eds.), *Handbook of educational psychology and students with special needs* (pp. 315–338). Routledge.

Binder, A. J., & Abel, A. R. (2018). Symbolically maintained inequality: How Harvard and Stanford students construct boundaries among elite universities. *Sociology of Education*, *92*(1), 41–58. https://doi.org/10.1177/0038040718821073

Blackwell, L. S., Trzesniewski, K. H., & Dweck, C. S. (2007). Implicit theories of intelligence predict achievement across an adolescent transition: A longitudinal study and an intervention. *Child Development*, *78*(1), 246–263. https://doi.org/10.1111/j.1467-8624.2007.00995.x

Boudreaux, M. J., & Ozer, D. J. (2013). Goal conflict, goal striving, and psychological well-being. *Motivation and Emotion*, *37*(3), 433–443. https://doi.org/10.1007/s11031-012-9333-2

Brooks, A. W. (2014). Get excited: Reappraising pre-performance anxiety as excitement. *Journal of Experimental Psychology: General*, *143*(3), 1144–1158. https://doi.org/10.1037/a0035325

Campbell, J., & Li, M. (2007). Asian students' voices: An empirical study of Asian students' learning experiences at a New Zealand university. *Journal of Studies in International Education*, *12*(4), 375–396. https://doi.org/10.1177/1028315307299422

Ceci, S. J. (2018). Women in academic science: Experimental findings from hiring studies. *Educational Psychologist*, *53*(1), 22–41. https://doi.org/10.1080/00461520.2017.1396462

Cerasoli, C. P., Nicklin, J. M., & Ford, M. T. (2014). Intrinsic motivation and extrinsic incentives jointly predict performance: A 40-year meta-analysis. *Psychological Bulletin*, *140*(4), 980–1008. https://doi.org/10.1037/a0035661

Chen, R., & Bennett, S. (2012). When Chinese learners meet constructivist pedagogy online. *Higher Education*, *64*(5), 677–691. https://doi.org/10.1007/s10734-012-9520-9

Deci, E. L., & Ryan, R. M. (2000). The "what" and "why" of goal pursuits: Human needs and the self-determination of behavior. *Psychological Inquiry*, *11*(4), 227–268. https://doi.org/10.1207/S15327965PLI1104_01

Deci, E. L., & Ryan, R. M. (Eds.). (2002). *Handbook of self-determination research*. University of Rochester Press.

Dietrich, J., Shulman, S., & Nurmi, J.-E. (2013). Goal pursuit in young adulthood: The role of personality and motivation in goal appraisal trajectories across 6 years. *Journal of Research in Personality*, *47*(6), 728–737. https://doi.org/10.1016/j.jrp.2013.06.004

Dweck, C. S. (1986). Motivational processes affecting learning. *American Psychologist*, *41*(10), 1040–1048. https://doi.org/10.1037/0003-066X.41.10.1040

Dweck, C. S., & Yeager, D. S. (2019). Mindsets: A view from two eras. *Perspectives on Psychological Science*, *14*(3), 481–496. https://doi.org/10.1177/1745691618804166

Eccles, J. (2009). Who am I and what am I going to do with my life? Personal and collective identities as motivators of action. *Educational Psychologist*, *44*(2), 78–89. https://doi.org/10.1080/00461520902832368

Gollwitzer, P. M., & Oettingen, G. (2012). Goal pursuit. In R. M. Ryan (Ed.), *The Oxford handbook of human motivation* (pp. 208–231). Oxford University Press.

Gollwitzer, P. M., & Sheeran, P. (2006). Implementation intentions and goal achievement: A meta-analysis of effects and processes. In M. P. Zanna (Ed.), *Advances in experimental social psychology* (Vol. 38, pp. 69–119). Elsevier. https://doi.org/10.1016/S0065-2601(06)38002-1

Grant, H., & Dweck, C. S. (2003). Clarifying achievement goals and their impact. *Journal of Personality and Social Psychology, 85*(3), 541–553. https://doi.org/10.1037/0022-3514.85.3.541

Hagenauer, G., & Volet, S. E. (2014). Teacher–student relationship at university: An important yet under-researched field. *Oxford Review of Education, 40*(3), 370–388. https://doi.org/10.1080/03054985.2014.921613

Harackiewicz, J. M., Durik, A. M., Barron, K. E., Linnenbrink-Garcia, L., & Tauer, J. M. (2008). The role of achievement goals in the development of interest: Reciprocal relations between achievement goals, interest, and performance. *Journal of Educational Psychology, 100*(1), 105–122. https://doi.org/10.1037/0022-0663.100.1.105

Harackiewicz, J. M., Smith, J. L., & Priniski, S. J. (2016). Interest matters: The importance of promoting interest in education. *Policy Insights from the Behavioral and Brain Sciences, 3*(2), 220–227. https://doi.org/10.1177/2372732216655542

Harper, S. R., Smith, E. J., & Davis, C. (2018). A critical race case analysis of Black undergraduate student success at an urban university. *Urban Education, 53*(1), 3–25. https://doi.org/10.1177/0042085916668956

Hattie, J. (2009). *Visible learning: A synthesis of over 800 meta-analyses relating to achievement.* Routledge.

Hattie, J., & Timperley, H. (2007). The power of feedback. *Review of Educational Research, 77*(1), 81–112. https://doi.org/10.3102/003465430298487

Hill, K. T., & Wigfield, A. (1984). Test anxiety: A major educational problem and what can be done about it. *The Elementary School Journal, 85*(1), 105–126. https://doi.org/10.1086/461395

Hilts, A., Part, R., & Bernacki, M. L. (2018). The roles of social influences on student competence, relatedness, achievement, and retention in STEM. *Science Education, 102*(4), 744–770. https://doi.org/10.1002/sce.21449

Hulleman, C. S., & Harackiewicz, J. M. (2021). The utility-value intervention. In G. Walton & A. Crum (Eds.), *Handbook of wise interventions* (pp. 100–125). Guilford Press.

Hulleman, C. S., Schrager, S. M., Bodmann, S. M., & Harackiewicz, J. M. (2010). A meta-analytic review of achievement goal measures: Different labels for the same constructs or different constructs with similar labels? *Psychological Bulletin, 136*(3), 422–449. https://doi.org/10.1037/a0018947

Ikeda, K., Kakinuma, K., Jiang, J., & Tanaka, A. (2021). Achievement goals affect memory encoding. *Contemporary Educational Psychology, 65*, 101945. https://doi.org/10.1016/j.cedpsych.2021.101945

Kaplan, A., & Maehr, M. L. (2007). The contributions and prospects of goal orientation theory. *Educational Psychology Review, 19*(2), 141–184. https://doi.org/10.1007/s10648-006-9012-5

Kim, S., & Kim, R. (2010). Microaggressions experienced by international students attending U.S. institutions of higher education. In D. W. Sue (Ed.), *Microaggressions and marginality: Manifestation, dynamics, and impact* (pp. 171–191). Wiley.

King, L. E. (2017, October 6). *Women who returned to college are inspiring others*. https://www.bostonglobe.com/metro/regionals/north/2017/10/06/women-who-returned-college-are-inspiring-others/ljsVspyqHd6ffw26qNErWO/story.html

Kruglanski, A., Shah, J., Fishbach, A., Friedman, R., Chun, W., & Sleeth-Kepper, D. (2002). A theory of goal systems. In M. P. Zanna (Ed.), *Advances in experimental social psychology* (Vol. 34, pp. 331–378). Academic Press.

Kuzma, C. (2019, December 11). *8 unusual things Diljeet Taylor does that make her a top NCAA coach*. https://www.runnersworld.com/health-injuries/a30191488/why-diljeet-taylor-is-a-top-ncaa-coach/

Lee, J. J., & Rice, C. (2007). Welcome to America? International student perceptions of discrimination. *Higher Education, 53*(3), 381–409. https://doi.org/10.1007/s10734-005-4508-3

Locke, E. A., & Latham, G. P. (2002). Building a practically useful theory of goal setting and task motivation: A 35-year odyssey. *American Psychologist, 57*(9), 705–717. https://doi.org/10.1037/0003-066X.57.9.705

Locke, E. A., & Latham, G. P. (2006). New directions in goal-setting theory. *Current Directions in Psychological Science, 15*, 265–268. https://doi.org/10.1111/j.1467-8721.2006.00449.x

Marlina, R. (2009). "I don't talk or I decide not to talk? Is it my culture?"—International students' experiences of tutorial participation. *International Journal of Educational Research, 48*(4), 235–244. https://doi.org/10.1016/j.ijer.2009.11.001

Morisano, D. (2013). Goal setting in the academic arena. In E. A. Locke & G. P. Latham (Eds.), *New developments in goal setting and task performance* (pp. 495–506). Routledge.

Murayama, K., & Elliot, A. J. (2012). The competition–performance relation: A meta-analytic review and test of the opposing processes model of competition and performance. *Psychological Bulletin, 138*(6), 1035–1070. https://doi.org/10.1037/a0028324

Pascarella, E. T., Pierson, C. T., & Wolniak, G. C. (2004). First-generation college students: Additional evidence on college experiences and outcomes. *Journal of Higher Education, 75*(3), 249–284. https://doi.org/10.1353/jhe.2004.0016

Paunesku, D., Walton, G. M., Romero, C., Smith, E. N., Yeager, D. S., & Dweck, C. S. (2015). Mind-set interventions are a scalable treatment for academic underachievement. *Psychological Science, 26*(6), 784–793. https://doi.org/10.1177/0956797615571017

Pólya, G. (1945). *How to solve it*. Princeton University Press.

Reeve, J. (2009). Why teachers adopt a controlling motivating style toward students and how they can become more autonomy supportive. *Educational Psychologist, 44*(3), 159–175. https://doi.org/10.1080/00461520903028990

Renninger, K. A., & Hidi, S. (2011). Revisiting the conceptualization, measurement, and generation of interest. *Educational Psychologist, 46*(3), 168–184. https://doi.org/10.1080/00461520.2011.587723

Robinson, C. D., Scott, W., & Gottfried, M. A. (2019). Taking it to the next level: A field experiment to improve instructor–student relationships in college. *AERA Open, 5*(1). https://doi.org/10.1177/2332858419839707

Ryan, R. M., & Deci, E. L. (2017). *Self-determination theory: Basic psychological needs in motivation, development, and wellness*. Guilford Press.

Sarrasin, J. B., Nenciovici, L., Foisy, L., Allaire-Duquette, G., Riopel, M., & Masson, S. (2018). Effects of teaching the concept of neuroplasticity to induce a growth mindset on motivation, achievement, and brain activity: A meta-analysis. *Trends in Neuroscience and Education, 12*, 22–31. https://doi.org/10.1016/j.tine.2018.07.003

Schleef, D. (2000). "That's a good question!" Exploring motivations for law and business school choice. *Sociology of Education, 73*(3), 155–174. https://doi.org/10.2307/2673214

Schwinger, M., Wirthwein, L., Lemmer, G., & Steinmayr, R. (2014). Academic self-handicapping and achievement: A meta-analysis. *Journal of Educational Psychology, 106*(3), 744–761. https://doi.org/10.1037/a0035832

Senko, C., Hulleman, C. S., & Harackiewicz, J. M. (2011). Achievement goal theory at the crossroads: Old controversies, current challenges, and new directions. *Educational Psychologist, 46*(1), 26–47. https://doi.org/10.1080/00461520.2011.538646

Shechter, O. G., Durik, A. M., Miyamoto, Y., & Harackiewicz, J. M. (2011). The role of utility value in achievement behavior: The importance of culture. *Personality and Social Psychology Bulletin, 37*(3), 303–317. https://doi.org/10.1177/0146167210396380

Shockley, W., & Gong, W. A. (1966). *Mechanics*. Charles E. Merrill.

Silvia, P. J. (2006). *Exploring the psychology of interest*. Oxford University Press.

Silvia, P. J. (2008). Interest—The curious emotion. *Current Directions in Psychological Science, 17*(1), 57–60. https://doi.org/10.1111/j.1467-8721.2008.00548.x

Sue, D. W., Capodilupo, C. M., Torino, G. C., Bucceri, J. M., Holder, A. M. B., Nadal, K. L., & Esquilin, M. (2007). Racial microaggressions in everyday life: Implications for clinical practice. *American Psychologist, 62*(4), 271–286. https://doi.org/10.1037/0003-066X.62.4.271

Turner, J. C., Warzon, K. B., & Christensen, A. (2011). Motivating mathematics learning. *American Educational Research Journal, 48*(3), 718–762. https://doi.org/10.3102/0002831210385103

Van Iddekinge, C. H., Aguinis, H., Mackey, J. D., & DeOrtentiis, P. S. (2017). A meta-analysis of the interactive, additive, and relative effects of cognitive ability and motivation on performance. *Journal of Management, 44*(1), 249–279. https://doi.org/10.1177/0149206317702220

Van Yperen, N. W., Blaga, M., & Postmes, T. (2014). A meta-analysis of self-reported achievement goals and nonself-report performance across three achievement domains (work, sports, and education). *PLOS ONE, 9*(4), e93594. https://doi.org/10.1371/journal.pone.0093594

Wentzel, K. R. (1997). Student motivation in middle school: The role of perceived pedagogical caring. *Journal of Educational Psychology, 89*(3), 411–419.

Wesselmann, E. D., Cardoso, F. D., Slater, S., & Williams, K. D. (2012). To be looked at as though air: Civil attention matters. *Psychological Science, 23*(2), 166–168. https://doi.org/10.1177/0956797611427921

Westaby, J. D., Pfaff, D. L., & Redding, N. (2014). Psychology and social networks: A dynamic network theory perspective. *American Psychologist, 69*(3), 269–284. https://doi.org/10.1037/a0036106

Wlodkowski, R., & Ginsberg, M. (2017). *Enhancing adult motivation to learn* (4th ed.). Jossey-Bass.

Xing, W., Ao, L., Xiao, H., & Liang, L. (2020). Chinese nurses' preferences for and attitudes about e-learning in continuing education: A correlational study. *The Journal of Continuing Education in Nursing, 51*(2), 87–96. https://doi.org/10.3928/00220124-20200115-08

Authors' Additional Resource Suggestions

Ames, C. (1992). Classrooms: Goals, structures, and student motivation. *Journal of Educational Psychology, 84*, 261–271. https://doi.org/10.1037/0022-0663.84.3.261

Dweck, C. S. (2006). *Mindset: The new psychology of success.* Random House.

Locke, E. A., & Latham, G. P. (2013). *New developments in goal setting and task performance.* Routledge.

Usher, E. L. (2016). Personal capability beliefs. In L. Corno & E. Anderman (Eds.), *Handbook of educational psychology* (3rd ed., pp. 146–159). Routledge.

Vansteenkiste, M., Aelterman, N., De Muynck, G.-J., Haerens, L., Patall, E., & Reeve, J. (2018). Fostering personal meaning and self-relevance: A self-determination theory perspective on internalization. *Journal of Experimental Education, 86*(1), 30–49. https://doi.org/10.1080/00220973.2017.1381067

Editors' Key Seminal and Supplemental Text Suggestions

Ginsburg, M. B., & Wlodkowski, R. J. (2021). Motivation. In T. S. Rocco, S. C. Smith, R. C. Mizzi, L. R. Merriweather, & J. D Hawley (Eds.), *The handbook of adult and continuing education* (pp. 91–99). Stylus.

Kaplan, A. (2008). Achievement motivation. In E. Anderman & L. H. Anderman (Eds.), *Psychology of classroom learning: An encyclopedia* (Vol. 1, pp. 13–17). MacMillan Reference.

Kaplan, A. (2008). Intrinsic and extrinsic motivation. In E. Anderman & L. H. Anderman (Eds.), *Psychology of classroom learning: An encyclopedia* (Vol. 1, pp. 513–517). MacMillan Reference.

Ryan, R. M., & Deci, E. L. (2000). Self-determination theory and facilitation of intrinsic motivation, social development, and well-being. *American Psychologist, 55*(1), 68–78. https://doi.org/10.1037/0003-066X.55.1.68

5

MINDING THE BRAIN

The Emotional Foundations of Adult Learning

Kathleen Taylor and Catherine Marienau

When cognitive science held sway in the last half of the 20th century, research on the role of emotions in learning was relegated to the margins. Even so, educators in varied postsecondary programs designed for adult learners consistently observed:

> Regardless of each [adult's] history, returning to school often brings out feelings of inadequacy—for some, a feeling close to terror—about meeting the challenges of academic life . . . "I have such anxiety about returning to school—I am sure I cannot make it." (Taylor & Marienau, 1995, p. 38)

Recently, as Howard Gardner described in his introduction to Immordino-Yang's (2016) *Emotions, Learning, and the Brain*, cognitive science has made major advances by recognizing the primacy of emotions in thinking and decision making. What is now called *affective neuroscience* details the integral role of emotions in learning and offers innovative approaches for teaching and learning.

To explore these implications, we begin with a brief overview of how prehistoric brain development, molded by survival-driven emotions, still directs modern brain function. This is metaphorically explained in terms of the *anxious* and *curious* brain. We then describe how early cognitive science understood the brain as an organ of information processing, often likened, erroneously, it turns out, to the computer as a model for human cognition. We also note how Descartes's assertion that body and mind were separate informed Western philosophical thinking for 400 years. These perspectives contributed to limiting research in emotions and embodied learning for much of the last half of the 20th century. We then show how neuroscience, especially Damasio's studies of patients with damaged brains, revived the crucial role of emotions in cognition and learning. Finally, we illuminate how current contributions of affective neuroscience—the science of emotion—and John Heron's model of facilitating learning can inform adult educators' practice across formal, informal, and nonformal settings.

Brain Basics and Emotion

The brain's prime directive is to help us survive and function. To thrive, all organisms must maintain homeostasis by continually rebalancing the body's biochemical changes within specified ranges. Our one-celled ancestors responded to variations in temperature, light, and chemical constituents of the surround by moving toward beneficial environments and away from harmful ones.

According to neuroscientist Antonio Damasio (1999), the primitive capacity to evaluate internal and external changes, in order to maintain homeostasis, is the precursor of a nervous system directed by a brain. Our modern brain constantly regulates and responds to critical, interconnected aspects of the internal milieu, such as hormones, neural excitation and suppression, electrochemical signaling, and so on, by moving toward or away.

Neuroscience has only recently determined that emotions are crucial to this process. "The biological 'purpose' of emotions is clear. . . . [They] are . . . part and parcel of the machinery with which organisms regulate survival. . . . At their most basic, emotions are part of homeostatic regulation" (Damasio, 1999, p. 54). Immordino-Yang (2016) elaborated:

> The brain has evolved . . . to cope with the problem of reading the body's condition and responding accordingly, and it begins doing so via the machinery of emotion. This coping shows up in simple ways in simple organisms and in remarkably rich ways as brains get more complex. In the brains of higher animals and people, the richness is such that they can perceive the world through sensory processing and control their behavior. (p. 35)

In the human brain, memory is also essential to this achievement. Contrary to common assumptions, memory is neither a discrete thing nor does it occupy a particular place in the brain. It is a process that begins with a stimulus to which the body responds. We fail to notice most short-term stimuli; others pass a threshold of attention to establish long-term memories that include body-state responses. Every time we "remember," we actually reconstruct countless neural traces of associated prior experiences affected by both our attentiveness and the intensity of emotions connected to each experience (Taylor & Marienau, 2016). Though each memory appears to us as a whole, intact representation of a given moment in time, it is pieced together from innumerable traces of body-states (i.e., emotions) that the brain's associative process connects to different aspects of the original experience. Stronger emotional associations affect both the character of the connections and the likelihood of future recall. Family members often discover this when they compare sincerely described memories of shared experiences that vary dramatically in content and emotional intensity.

Attention and emotion are also factors in motivation. Motivation—from *movere,* to set in motion—directs our behavior to move toward or away. As Ratey

(2001) explained: "Motivation . . . ties emotion to action" (p. 247). It also determines how much attention and energy our brain is willing to give to the internal and external stimuli that it perceives. For our survival-directed brains, the motivation to move away is dominant, as expressed in *negativity bias*. To survive long enough to reproduce, hominids had to be on constant alert for danger. A competing tribe or hungry predator needed to catch them off guard only once to eliminate their contribution to the gene pool. Those whose brains developed a hyperdefensive stance were more likely to become our ancestors. Thus, our modern brain is wired to be seven times more likely to make a negative assessment than one that is positive.

Anxious and Curious Brain

To better understand the role of emotions in meaning making, we use *anxious* and *curious* to represent the activity of the embodied learning system known as brain. The metaphor of *anxious brain* describes the predominant response to threat or uncertainty. Survival impulses early hominid brains developed in the primeval savannah, when circumstances demanded instant reaction—eat or be eaten, flee, fight, or freeze—still motivate the modern brain. Our brains react immediately to perceived threat. The anxious brain seeks to avoid anything unexpected or unfamiliar because uncertainty indicates an existential threat. For the prehistoric brain, not knowing, or being wrong, often meant annihilation; in today's world, primitive parts of our modern brains still find an illusion of safety by clinging to existing expectations and beliefs (Taylor & Marienau, 2016).

Adult educators may observe the anxious brain in their work with learners experiencing the unexpected and unfamiliar, as seen in a learner whose immediate reaction is "No way I can do *that*!" Another expresses frustration at an open-ended task: "Why won't you just tell me what to do and how to do it?!" A corporate manager, perhaps back in school to burnish her credentials, remarks "I already know how to solve the problem in this case study; after all, I manage teams just like that." For many adults, the urgent question often appears to be "Did I get an A?" When evidence of such anxiety-directed brains goes unattended, learning is likely to be impeded. Moreover, educators unfamiliar with the origins of these brain-based anxieties may interpret such responses as resistance.

Fortunately, our survival does not rely solely on anxiety-related responses. Our primitive forebears also developed a *curious brain* that seeks to move toward, to engage actively and creatively with their surroundings. It is drawn to a broader perspective, to know more and see things differently, to consider possibilities beyond the immediate. In making new meaning of experiences, a curious brain elaborates and reconstructs established neural patterns. It does this despite the additional energy required to do this and to overcome the implicit risk of not knowing. When it solves a problem, it rewards itself with feel-good hormones (Taylor & Marienau, 2016).

When the curious brain is engaged, adult learners tend to ask for stretch assignments on new topics. They risk trying on perspectives that challenge their existing assumptions and beliefs. They seek feedback in order to revise their work and deepen their learning. As do all adult learners, they also have anxious moments; however, they are able—especially with support—to direct some of that anxious energy toward achieving their learning goals.

These two states of mind—anxious and curious—are not simply the inverse of one another. Decreasing anxiety does not, of itself, engender curiosity, nor does increasing curiosity eliminate anxiety. The interconnected anatomical system of the brain is always actively working with both potentials. We discuss these body–brain connections, especially with regard to emotions and learning, in the next sections.

From Cognitive to Affective Neuroscience

The field of cognitive science emerged in the second half of the 20th century partly in response to the limitations of the positivist behavioral paradigm that had occupied much of the first half. Behaviorism had insisted on observable, measurable data, such as interactions between environments and behaviors (commonly referred to as *stimulus–response*), in order to predict and control causes and effects. States of mind were defined as unobservable and therefore deemed unverifiable "mentalist" interpretations and not proper subjects of research. As it relates to learning, the behaviorist approach rejected the importance of what happened in the mind—how meaning and knowledge are constructed—as unobservable and unknowable.

Cognitive science offered a new paradigm for understanding the brain: information processing, which explored what behaviorism had dismissed as happening inside the "black box" of the mind.

> Information processing focuses on following information from the environment through the various cognitive processes that lead to perceptions, memories, thoughts, and behaviors . . . [thus] seeing the human mind as a complex type of computer engaged in a set of processes that could be specified and modeled. (Hyman, 2014, p. xvi)

Cognitive science offered tools and methods to track and examine mental organization and processing. While behaviorism had focused on controlling environments to achieve desired outcomes, as determined by whoever did the controlling, cognitive science emphasized individuals' determination to seek, select, and manipulate information to achieve their own chosen ends. Because of this, fields as diverse as computer science and artificial intelligence, philosophy of mind, experimental psychology, and linguistics all found commonalities in perceiving the brain as an organ of computational processes and symbol manipulation.

Despite this, it became evident over successive decades that the focus on information processing across disciplines had also sharply limited emotions as a subject of research. Rather than explore the positive potential of emotion, studies of emotion tended to concentrate on neurological deformity, damage, disease, or symptoms of psychological disturbance (Ellsworth & Scherer, 2003).

The Cartesian Shade

In *Descartes' Error* (1994/2005), neuroscientist Antonio Damasio traced widely held assumptions about thinking and emotion—including those affecting how emotions were studied in neuroscience and cognitive science—to Descartes's insistence on the primacy of rationality (mind) over sensation (body). Mind was associated with soul and therefore separate from and superior to base animal spirits associated with body. Cartesian mind–body dualism profoundly influenced the Western cultural narrative for 4 centuries, including, until recently, brain science.

> Throughout most of the twentieth century, emotion was not trusted in the laboratory. Emotion was too subjective, it was said. Emotion was too elusive and vague. Emotion was at the opposite end from reason, easily the finest human ability, and reasoning was presumed to be entirely independent from emotion. . . . In the end, not only was emotion not rational, even studying it was probably not rational. (Damasio, 1999, p. 39)

Neuroscience now finds that, far from being separate, "mind is probably not conceivable without some sort of *embodiment*. . . . Images of body-state are in the background, usually unattended but ready to spring forward" (Damasio, 1994/2005, p. 234). Thus, the anatomical system called brain is a *body–brain*, as it directs and responds to every other embodied system concerned with memory or cognition. Nevertheless, current definitions of *mind* still tend to emphasize capacity for intellect, consciousness, and reason, whereas *brain* is often defined as an organ of the body that enables and coordinates various physical and intellectual functions. It is as if mind is the creative architect and brain is merely the contractor. Damasio identified Descartes's fundamental error as "the separation of the most refined operations of mind from the structure and operation of a biological organism" (p. 250).

The body–brain connection, refined over eons of human development, plays a crucial role in survival because it integrates two avenues of information. The "structure and operation of a biological organism" is direct physical experience in the moment, via a sensory portal (sound, sight, touch, smell, taste). "The most refined operation of mind" involves what the body has experienced at other times. This combination—"What is happening now?" and "How is this moment similar to some other moment?" (Damasio, 1994/2005, p. 250)—makes possible deeper understanding and problem solving, including future projection. Descartes could not have known that what he ultimately experienced as thinking is in fact the end result of a process that the body–brain initially engages via symbolic, metaphorical images (Lakoff & Johnson, 2003).

"Cognition is embodied," Kahneman (2011) stated unequivocally: "You think with your body, not just your brain" (p. 51). Though the process is invisible to the thinker, between initial experience and ultimate awareness the embodied brain organizes, connects, and reconstructs a lifetime of analogical memory traces, including associated body-states, to arrive at what we eventually experience as thought. As David Gelertner (1994), a leading figure in artificial intelligence, observed, people have to stop thinking they can separate the emotional from the rational: "Emotions are not . . . an additional cognitive bonus, [they] are *fundamental* to thought" (p. 47).

Emotions are essential contributors to what for centuries was considered the apex of disembodied human expression: rationality. Rather than what Descartes believed was the confusing evidence of a misleading body, Damasio (1994/2005) observed that impulses to move away and move toward, or "pain and pleasure, . . . control the development of social decision-making strategies" (p. 262).

The Case of Elliot

As Damasio (1994/2005) initially documented with his patient Elliot, later confirmed by other cases, emotion plays a crucial role in meaningful cognition. Elliot recovered from tumor-excising brain surgery with all his cognitive faculties intact. He could recall previously learned facts and describe details of presurgery experiences with enough clarity to demonstrate no memory impairment. Tests of his thinking ability revealed he was as smart as he had ever been, which was above average. But his life rapidly changed for the worse. He soon divorced, quickly remarried, then divorced again. His economic life was disrupted by unacceptable work performance leading to multiple dismissals, followed by rash and ultimately bankrupting involvement in poorly planned business schemes. Yet in multiple laboratory tests— of problem-solving, awareness of social consequences, ethical dilemmas, and moral reasoning—he demonstrated either no impairment or superior results.

This apparent contradiction was resolved only after researchers compared the demands of tests taken under lab conditions to application in real life situations. The tests required reasoning through problems, constructing various possible responses, and imagining what those results implied—but they did not require actively committing to a particular choice. Given Elliot's demonstrated abilities to gather, categorize, and retrieve linguistic, factual information, the difficulty seemed to occur at a later step in the brain's process—when it shifted from organizing perception to creating and applying meaning.

Further study revealed that surgical removal of tissue around the tumor affected the processing of embodied signals arising from the limbic system, the so-called *emotional brain*. "Elliot's predicament [w]as *to know but not to feel*" (original emphasis, Damasio, 1994/2005, p. 45). Absent the fundamental emotion-directed impulse to move toward or move away, Elliot could not apply his superior cognitive abilities to in-the-world decision making and appropriate action.

The Neuroscience of Emotion

Damasio (1999) further outlined the specific roles emotions and feelings play in learning and cognition: "Emotions and feelings of emotion, respectively, are the beginning and end of a progression . . . cycles of emotion followed by feelings that become known and beget new emotions" (pp. 42–43). To appreciate how this understanding may affect adult educators' practice, we sketch out the underlying neuroscience.

Though the terms *emotions* and *feelings* are interchangeable in common conversation, they have different meanings to a neuroscientist. In what follows, we observe Damasio's distinctions: *Emotion* describes unconscious changes in body-states that direct the brain to move toward and move away to support life-sustaining homeostasis. *Feelings* emerge when we become conscious of those embodied changes.

At the neural level, emotions are electrochemical responses essential to survival. They provoke what the social sciences describe as *primary emotions*, such as disgust, happiness, and fear—visibly evident in everyday interactions. They also figure in background emotions, such as the inner sense of being "down" or "up." All emotions are part of life regulation: "Emotions [in all their forms] are inseparable from the idea of reward and punishment, of pleasure or pain, *of approach or withdrawal* [emphasis added], of personal advantage and disadvantage" (Damasio, 1999, p. 55). To understand the implications of emotions and feelings, we trace Damasio's definitions, depicted in Figure 5.1.

Figure 5.1. Emotion–feeling cycle.

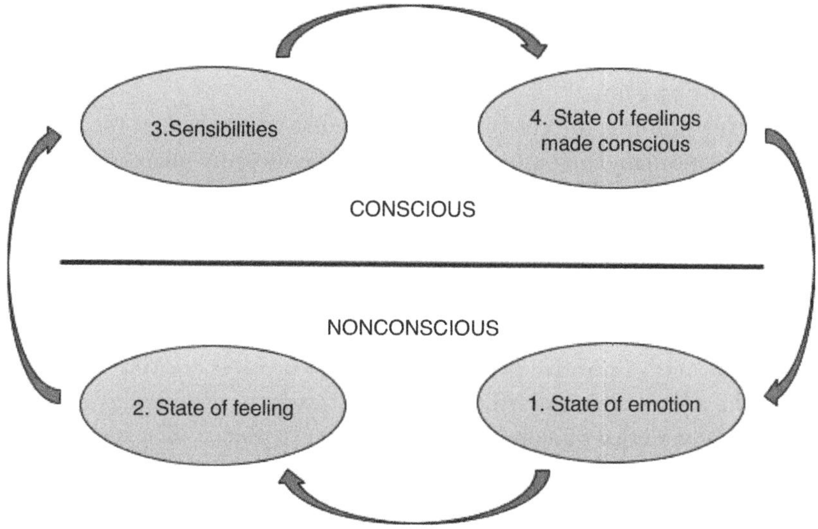

Note. Adapted from Damasio (1999).

A state of emotion occurs when the brain initiates homeostatic adjustments in response to changes in the body's internal or external environment. Each individual's life history also contributes to emotions as the brain compares the current moment to memory traces of earlier moments. Since the brain interprets every circumstance in terms of survival, "virtually every object or situation in our experience" also plays a role (Damasio, 1999, p. 58).

Consider the toddler who takes an inconsequential tumble. Left alone for a moment, and not experiencing pain or physical injury, she may simply pick herself up and continue what she was doing. But if her parents suddenly scoop her up in alarm as if something dreadful happened, her change in body-state will be more in line with a life-threatening experience. Repetition of similar emotion-laden experiences can create patterns that affect an adult's responses to stress throughout the life span, even, perhaps, to the announcement of an unexpected test.

Emotional changes originate in earlier anatomical structures than the prefrontal cortex. The brain continually records these fluctuations and, as new experiences (and their associated body-states) occur, they also alter the existing emotional balance. "The result of these coordinated and neural commands is a global change in the state of the organism" (Damasio, 1999, p. 67). We remain unaware of these responses even as hormones and other neurotransmitters affect interconnected anatomical systems, including the brain itself.

If these associations motivate toward or away, we are in *a state of feeling*. This still-unconscious stage in the emotion continuum accounts for intuitions and gut feelings. Such feeling states may guide wise behavior—or unwise bias—based on our history of prior associated experiences; this also explains our often-mysterious initial reactions to encountering people about whom we know little to nothing.

It also accounts for *priming*, as described by Kahneman (2011) in *Thinking Fast and Slow*. Though anyone who stops to think realizes that $6.99 is inconsequentially different from $7.00 (or $699,999 from $700,000), the unconscious tendency is to move toward the bargain.

To observe priming in real time, ask someone where Kenya (or Uganda, or Ghana, etc.) is located. Then ask them to name the most frequent opposing colors in a game of chess. Finally, ask them to name an animal. You are far more likely to get "Zebra" than if you initially asked them merely to name an animal. Having first alerted the brain to *things-African* and *things-black-and-white*, you enhanced the likelihood that the animal named will reflect those characteristics (Buonomano, 2011). This aspect of how the brain categorizes and connects memory traces may offer adult educators a positive pedagogical tool. It involves creating a context that will nudge the adult's brain toward the deep satisfaction of discovering—rather than being told—the intended outcomes of the learning experience. The positive emotion associated with that achievement is likely to enhance learning.

Though he emphasizes its importance, Damasio (2010) did not name the moment when a state of feeling becomes a *state of feeling made conscious*: "Emotional feelings are mostly perceptions of what *our bodies do* during the emoting, *along with* our perceptions of *our state of mind* during that same period of time [emphasis added]" (p. 110). This happens when lack of awareness of biophysical responses shifts to concurrent awareness. To underscore the significance of this almost imperceptible change, we identify it as *sensibility.*

Sensibility may be so subtle as to be barely noticed, such as a change in our mood. If, however, we do not then pause to focus our attention, these sensations can pass without ever reaching full consciousness. In environments that include many forms of distraction and sensory overload, and little expectation for reflection, this omission can mean a lost opportunity to understand the deeper implications of the experience. By contrast, Heron's (1992) model, which we examine in the "Affective Neuroscience and Adult Learning" section, takes special note of this learning potential.

If sensibilities become too intense to escape your own notice (or perhaps someone who noticed a subtle change in your body language or tone asks, "How do you feel?"), we may try to identify what has become a *state of feeling made conscious* by finding words for an elusive body-state. For example: "It's like I'm walking through a dense fog," or "My heart is going to jump out of my chest," or "I'm all goosebumps." As noted earlier, each individual's history of neural associations will determine the underlying meanings of such revelations. Even so, it is not a stretch to suggest the first might indicate a sense of impediment or confusion, the second may be joy or anticipation, the third may be fear or positive excitement. In any case, a doorway has been opened to exploration of emotion-laden, preconscious associations that, according to Heron (1992, 1999), are essential to more meaningful understanding of the experience.

Not coincidentally, cliché descriptions of emotions are often body-based metaphors: "blood boiling" for anger, "heartbroken" for sadness, "hair standing on end" for fear, "knot in the stomach" for anxiety, "butterflies in the stomach" for anticipation. Such expressions are also commonly cross-cultural, because emotion is a universally physical (embodied) reaction (Geary, 2012).

Damasio (1999) verified that the system we call brain functions as a body–brain. "Both the brain and the body proper are largely and profoundly affected by the set of [emotional] commands" that trigger responses in both brain sites and the body (p. 68). Though the earliest patterns of hominid brain development focused on the emotions of survival, over eons, as more brain energy turned toward thinking, metabolic efficiency led to coopting many of the same neural pathways. Recent research on the emotional brain confirms this: "It is literally neurologically impossible to engage complex thoughts or make meaningful decisions without emotions" because the neural processes that support emotion and cognition are inextricably intertwined (Immordino-Yang, 2016, p. 18).

Though still a developing field, in the past 2 decades discoveries in affective neuroscience have been applied in social neuroscience (Dolan, 2002), moral decision making (Horberg et al., 2011), and early education (Immordino-Yang & Damasio, 2007). This has led to a broader redefinition of, and more wide-ranging research within the field of, cognitive science. Affective neuroscience also offers adult educators evidence that mind—and all that term represents relative to cognition's many triumphs—is a crowning achievement of the body–brain, inseparable in thinking, feeling, and behaving. Thus, deeper learning, and learning that lasts, may be enhanced by intentional focus on how the body–brain functions.

Affective Neuroscience and Adult Learning

Although the world of learning and knowing has historically emphasized concepts; logical relations; and explicit, declarative expression grounded in evidence, affective neuroscience now states unequivocally, "We feel, therefore we learn" (Damasio & Immordino-Yang, 2007, p. 3). Referring to the growing body of research on the inseparability of cognition and emotion, as exemplified in cases such as Elliot's, Damasio and Immordino-Yang explained:

> Without the ability to adequately access the guiding intuitions that accrue through emotional learning and social feedback, decision making and rational thought become compromised, as did learning from their mistakes and successes. . . . Their emotions are dissociated from their rational thought, resulting in compromised reason, decision making, and learning. (p. 5)

In exploring how emotions may inform adult learning practices, we highlight the work of John Heron, often absent from discussions of theorists of adult learning. Of note, however, is Kasl and Yorks's (2012) appreciative treatment of Heron's work as "enhancing possibilities for transformation" (p. 504). His philosophical and psychological approaches to facilitation are also congruent with recent discoveries in affective neuroscience.

How Heron's Model Embodies Affective Neuroscience

For humanistic psychologist John Heron (1992), the purpose of adult learning is the development of the whole person toward their fullest positive potential. This requires upending the model, developed in ancient Greece (Descartes's dualist philosophy is the most influential modern example), of intellectual development as the supreme objective of [a person], along with exalting reason that can "control and regulate emotion and the passion" (p. 12).

In briefly describing Heron's approach to facilitating learning, we focus on his attention to affect—a key aspect of his model—and how this may be of value to adult educators. We also note that many of his insights, which preceded Damasio's discoveries on the foundational role of emotions in meaningful learning, accord with affective neuroscience. At times, Heron uses the terms *affect*, *emotions*, and *feelings* differently than Damasio. We follow Damasio's usage.

Heron's Up-Hierarchy

Conventional facilitation focuses on conscious cognitive processes and explicit verbal and descriptive expressions of learning (Taylor & Marienau, 2016). By contrast, Heron required targeted attention to emotions before they are consciously known. In typical learning sequences, a topic is presented and explained, adults think about and discuss what they heard or read, and finally look for applications. This approximates Kolb's (1984, 2015) well-known experiential learning model: experience, reflection, conceptualization, application. Though Kolb did identify feelings as an element of experience, he failed to address the underlying embodied emotions. His learning sequence is firmly planted in verbal, cognitive awareness. In Heron's view, such approaches ignore the inescapable affective foundation of learning (Damasio would also criticize the lack of attention to emotions).

The structure of Heron's (1992, 1999) model, the up-hierarchy (Figure 5.2), immediately signals a paradigm shift. Rather than the traditional hierarchy, in which higher positions control and, in effect, rule those below, the up-hierarchy "works from below upwards, like a tree with roots, a trunk, branches and fruit . . . [with] the higher branching and flowering out of, and bearing the fruit of, the lower" (1999, p. 46). In this pyramid-shaped design, the lowest and broadest level is the ground of everything that follows.

This foundation is experiential, affective, and imaginal, and it aligns with elements of Damasio's state of emotion and state of feeling. Similarly, sensibilities and state of feeling made conscious mark the dawning of affective awareness. The next

Figure 5.2. Heron's up-hierarchy.

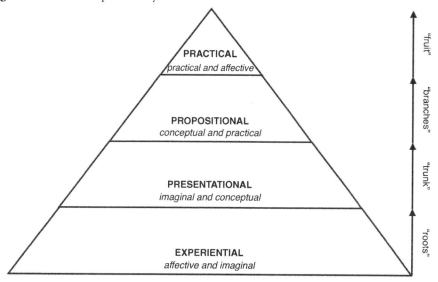

Note. Adapted from Heron (1999) and Paxton (2003).

movement in Heron's model is toward the threshold where the unconscious and imaginal may emerge into consciousness. Notably, the *presentational mode*, which manifests in imaginal, symbolic, metaphorical, and largely nonverbal expression, is the instrument of that emergence.

Means of Symbolic, Imaginal Expression

Heron (1999) offered specific guidance on how to access the wealth of tacit, emotion-related associations that experience stimulates. Rather than move briskly from "having" an experience to intellectualizing its meaning, his model first nurtures these newly stirring feelings so richly endowed with associations not available to the conscious mind. If instead, the brain is immediately encouraged to start "thinking," it will rely on readily available neural patterns rather than spend additional energy trying to explore what is as yet unexpressed. To avert this loss, *presentational knowing* encourages this embryonic awareness to speak in its own symbolic, imaginal voice before moving on to explicit conceptualization.

Heron (1992) explained, "Images are packed with meaning *prior to any explicit formulation of this meaning in verbal and conceptual* [emphasis added] terms" (p. 138). Damasio (1999) appeared to echo this: "The simplest form in which the wordless knowledge emerges mentally is the feeling of knowing" (p. 26). In presentational knowing, adults are guided to notice and then express these wordless feelings in the only appropriate language—symbolic and imaginal—because "subsequent linguistic translation and manipulation may distort and misrepresent it" (Damasio, 1999, p. 139). Nonverbal modalities for communicating the feeling of knowing include the visual and plastic arts, music, and dance. There is also a place for the expressive verbal arts (though care must be taken to avoid "performing" in place of presenting one's own emergent feelings); these include

> all forms of myth, fable, allegory, story and drama, all of which require the use of language, and all of which involve the telling of a story. Storytelling is one of the two great linguistic kinds of presentational knowledge, the other being poetry. (Damasio, 1999, p. 167)

In short, symbolic, imaginal expression—often, though not always, nonverbal—represents an aspect of the learning process validated by affective neuroscience but historically ignored by cognitive-focused facilitation methods.

Implications for Practice: Symbolize Before Verbalize

Based on Heron, and because in the embodied brain, symbolic precedes cognitive, our motto is "Symbolize, then verbalize!" With this in mind, we revisit two activities we constructed before we realized that Heron's model and affective neuroscience could more fully inform our own practice: Crowded Brain and Evocative Images.

The Crowded Brain

Consciously or not, adults experience anxiety in new learning environments. "New situation, new people, new facilitator, new material: *yikes! tigers may be ahead!*" (Taylor & Marienau, 2016, p. 91). Adults also have more upbeat feelings but, given the brain's negativity bias, these may pale compared with their insecurity about what awaits them. In addition, aside from concerns focused specifically on their educational journey, adults have complex lives they can't leave behind at the door to the classroom. Unfortunately, as Dirkx (2001) noted,

> Adult educators refer to personal or emotional issues adults bring to the educational settings as "baggage" or "barriers" to learning. . . . If and when such issues *are* acknowledged by educators, it is often to provide opportunities for learners to "vent" and "get it off their chests" so they can get back to the "business of learning." (p. 67)

The overarching purpose of the Crowded Brain activity is to help adults acknowledge and work with their underlying anxieties about learning, rather than ignore or diminish them. The arc of the activity is to first bring to awareness memories that negatively affected their beliefs about themselves as learners and "describe" the experience symbolically; then, within the safety of an empathic environment, to actively engage their reawakened feelings; and, finally, to forge new neural connections by foregrounding positive feelings.

We use this activity near the start of sessions with adult learners. This description is not prescriptive; our bracketed comments provide additional pointers to how it typically unfolds and choices we make.

> First we ask [perhaps in a way that telegraphs "We know this is an odd question"] "How many people are in this room?" [Slightly nervous laughter may erupt as people count. This is fine; laughter lowers anxiety.]
>
> Our playful follow-up piques curiosity: "What if I told you the room is more crowded than it seems?" We then ask them to think back to a vivid experience, whether in school or the family, of voices that told them, in unflattering terms, how to regard themselves as learners. [In working with hundreds of learners over decades, we have found everyone has such experiences seared into their memories, no matter how successful they may have become professionally and educationally.]
>
> When they have identified an occasion, we gently prompt them to silently relive it, such as: "What was the circumstance, who said what, and how did that make you feel?" [The room tends to go still as people's body language and facial expressions speak volumes about their memories.]
>
> Before any discussion, we provide paper and writing materials (crayons, colored pens, markers are good; a simple pen/pencil will do). We ask that they quickly sketch what they felt about the situation and whoever

was involved, and that they not use any words in the sketch [explaining that visualizing involves a different part of the brain than verbalizing. Also, by immediately emphasizing "This is not art," "There's no time for a finished piece of work," and "No one will have to show their sketch," we address the anxiety that the word "draw" can create.]

We invite people to share what they depicted. [Though most adults willingly describe their feelings, memories, and sketches, we sometimes break the ice with our own crudely drawn sketches and a brief recounting of an experience of our feeling belittled as learners. Sharing for a minute, more or less, is usually enough for each person to let their own feelings sink in and realize how those early messages still echo. Others usually murmur empathically; the group as a whole appears to experience both greater self-realization and deepening connection to one another.]

After everyone has been heard [sometimes including spontaneous mutual acknowledgment] we encourage each of them, as adults in the here-and-now, to actively reject the negative message and perhaps the messenger. [For example, they may forcefully crumple up the sketch and eject it into a trash can. They can name and emphatically contradict—aloud to the whole group—whoever once belittled or diminished them. Using their bodies actively—throwing away the sketch, yelling at the individual—helps to create an alternative neural pattern to the hurtful memory of being denigrated as a learner. This is enhanced by the experience of commiseration and community. If we then ask, "How did that feel?", people often report an unexpected sense of relief and empowerment.]

After a pause to anchor that feeling, we repeat the exercise, this time focused on a positive experience of being validated as learners, again briefly exploring the feelings, voices, and participants. [If they are using crayons or colored pencils, the images are often brighter and more colorful. The group's energy becomes more playful and upbeat. On the rare occasions when someone cannot recall a validation, we provide it. For example, we might point out how their presence as a learner has caught our attention; we find that others tend to spontaneously chime in.]

Though the Crowded Brain activity works as a stand-alone experience, if the group reconvenes with us over time it may be revisited and used at intervals. It can be effective when learners seem to have hit a snag, perhaps because old anxieties have been reawakened. It may also be used prophylactically, before problems are evident, to access positive energy and remind (re-mind) them of feelings of agency and empowerment. This simple, effective, emotion-based activity does not require deep familiarity with Heron's (1999) approach. It also affirms adult educators who intuitively include emotion-based approaches in their practices.

Evocative Images

Although early split-brain research proved to be oversimplified, as both hemispheres consistently work together, there are meaningful differences in how each approaches the task of meaning making (Tompkins et al., 2008). The left hemisphere is the primary location for semantic processing and responds more quickly to such prompts than does the right. However, the right hemisphere engages preferentially with visual input and symbolic language (Gainotti, 2014).

But when an adult is directed to verbally describe their response to a visual (or other symbolic) experience, the left hemisphere immediately engages and preempts slower right hemisphere processing (McGilchrist, 2009/2019). Deeper meanings are unexplored as the brain reverts to established semantic networks. By contrast, Heron's (1992, 1999) presentational knowing explicitly draws on the symbolic, imaginal precursors of cognition, thus accessing this emotion-based reservoir before semantic processing takes over and limits what may emerge.

The Evocative Images activity has various applications. It is especially effective with a newly constituted group about to begin work on an endeavor or with an ongoing group that may have hit a creative lull. Rather than revisiting an internal experience, as was the case with Crowded Brain, participants respond to an external stimulus—in this case, visual images.

Typically, we use images gathered from print sources, such as magazines. For online delivery, we compile virtual images. To avoid evoking semantic association, we leave out images with prominent words or well-known people. We also omit images that appear to have ready-made connections to the focus topic, such as pictures of classrooms when the focus is learning. Some examples of general purpose images include nature, animals, geography, design, and people in ambiguous attitudes or settings, as well as abstract illustrations.

We make the images available for selection on a large table or in a virtual folder. (We provide many more images than the number of participants.) Participants are asked to pick one quickly and intuitively, not because they see the makings of a storyline. We say, "Choose an image that grabs you." Rather than look for one that makes sense, we encourage learners to "go with your gut"—perhaps to look for something pleasing or intriguing.

Until the final debrief, the following activities take place in small groups. We advise, in advance, that the process may feel counterintuitive (brains want to move immediately to storytelling) and ask them to "stay with us" as best they can.

> They first take turns sharing their images and describing the feelings it evoked, focusing on details that caught their attention. It is fine if others ask to hear more about these reactions, but we caution them to avoid interpreting what those details might "mean."
>
> After this individual sharing, we suggest they discuss as a group anything that seems to stand out, such as similarities or differences in their individual reactions. They may also further explore whether there are any

overarching symbolic/abstract connections (e.g., freedom, toil, exploration, collaboration). Only then do we ask them to consider any aspect of their reactions or discussion, thus far, that might shed light on the topic they had in focus at the outset of the activity.

Each small group then briefly presents their highlights to the large group. Participants usually uncover perspectives about themselves or the issue at hand that can be a springboard to further learning. For example, students newly embarked on a master's degree in adult learning observed: "I have deeper appreciation for the hurdles that adult learners face," "I was not aware that I hold some unflattering judgments about older students," "I need to become more patient in allowing time for people to reflect," and "I need to see myself as an adult learner too." Participants may also find that even when the immediate outcome is not especially compelling, meaningful echoes of the activity continue to reveal themselves over time.

Referring to his use of *imaginal method*, Dirkx (2001) noted that through awareness of

> the images behind our emotions and feelings . . . we learn to participate with them in a more conscious manner. Entering into a conscious dialogue with these images creates the opportunity for deeper meaning and more satisfying relationships with our world. (p. 69)

Where we differ from Dirkx's Jungian-inspired approach is the speed with which we move from the emotional experience to verbalization. His guidance engages the learner in a cognitive appraisal, asking:

> What do these emotions feel like, remind me of? What other times have I felt this way, experienced, these emotions? . . . As we elaborate these feelings and these emotions, *the nature of the image behind them may begin to emerge* [emphasis added]. (p. 69)

We choose to follow Heron, and thus we focus first on capturing the emotional nature of the image symbolically, before moving to self-questioning that foregrounds semantic expression; we *symbolize, then verbalize!*

Affective Neuroscience and Human Flourishing

Heron (1992) framed the meaning and purpose of higher education, including tertiary, adult, and continuing professional development, through the lens of the learner as a whole person: "Learning is extended from its traditional restriction to the theoretical and applied intellect, into the domains of body awareness, emotions and attitudes, interpersonal relations, social and political processes, psychic and spiritual awareness" (p. 4). Thus, the answer to "What is learning for?" extends beyond mastery of content or skills. It embraces the development of core values that prioritize human flourishing.

Heron (1992) also defined the affective mode as "the absolute mark of personhood" (p. 94) and contrasted this with education that exalts reason and the knowledge it generates. The cognition-centered, emotion-suppressing origins of Western culture is, in Heron's view, a major factor in exploitation and control at every level of society: children by adults; women by men; workers by management; citizens by the state; and, in global terms, the pillaging of underdeveloped nations and planetary resources. In each case, those who have power maintain it by ignoring and denying what emotional awareness would otherwise inhibit, thus countering human flourishing.

Affective neuroscience not only identifies the inextricable relationship between learning and emotion but also reassures us that "The more educators come to understand the nature of the relationship between emotion and cognition, the better they may be able to leverage this relationship in the design of learning environments" (Immordino-Yang & Damasio, 2007, p. 9).

As part of this design, adult educators may wish to more fully embrace complexity and ambiguity. As practitioners, we can pay attention to and take note of our own affect, feelings, and emotions that arise in relation not only to what we read and study, but also in our interactions with others and with ourselves. Affective neuroscience deems emotion as essential to making meaning, especially the kind of deep or transformative learning needed in global times.

References

Buonomano, D. (2011). *Brain bugs: How the brain's flaws shape our lives*. W. W. Norton.

Damasio, A. (1999). *The feeling of what happens: Body and emotion in the making of consciousness*. Harcourt Brace.

Damasio, A. (2005). *Descartes' error: Emotion, reason, and the human brain*. Penguin. (Original work published 1994)

Damasio, A. (2010). *Self comes to mind: Constructing the conscious brain*. Pantheon/Random House.

Damasio, A., & Immordino-Yang, M. H. (2007). We feel, therefore we learn: The relevance of affective and social neuroscience to education. *Brain, Mind and Education, 1*(1), 3–10. Wiley. https://doi.org/10.1111/j.1751-228X.2007.00004.x

Dirkx, J. (2001). The power of feelings: Emotion, imagination, and the construction of meaning. In S. B. Merriam (Ed.), *The New Update on Adult Learning Theory* (New Directions for Adult and Continuing Education, no. 89, pp. 63–72). Jossey-Bass. https://doi.org/10.1002/ace.9

Dolan, R. J. (2002, November 8). Emotion, cognition, and behavior. *Science, 298*(5596), 1191–1194. https://doi.org/10.1126/science.1076358

Ellsworth, P. C., & Scherer, K. R. (2003). Appraisal processes in emotion. In R. J. Davidson, K. R. Scherer, & H. H. Goldsmith (Eds.), *Handbook of affective sciences* (pp. 572–595). Oxford University Press.

Gainotti, G. (2014). Why are the right and left hemisphere conceptual representations different?. *Behavioural Neurology, 2014*, 603134. https://doi.org/10.1155/2014/603134

Geary, J. (2012). *I is an other: The secret life of metaphor and how it shapes the way we see the world.* HarperCollins.

Gelertner, D. (1994). *The muse in the machine.* Free Press.

Heron, J. (1992). *Feeling and personhood: Psychology in another key.* SAGE.

Heron, J. (1999). *The complete facilitator's handbook.* Kogan Page.

Horberg, E., Oveis, C., & Keltner, D. (2011). Emotions as moral amplifiers: An appraisal tendency approach to the influences of distinct emotions upon moral judgment. *Education Review, 3*(3), 237–244. https://doi.org/10.1177/1754073911402384

Hyman, I. (2014). The rallying cry for the cognitive revolutions. In U. Neisser (Ed.), *Cognitive psychology: Classic edition* (pp. xv–xix). Psychology Press.

Immordino-Yang, M. H. (2016). *Emotions, learning, and the brain: Exploring the educational implications of affective neuroscience.* W. W. Norton.

Immordino-Yang, M. H., & Damasio, A. R. (2007). We feel therefore we learn: The relevance of affective and social neuroscience to education. *Mind, Brain and Education, 1*(1), 3–10. https://doi.org/10.1111/j.1751-228X.2007.00004.x

Kahneman. D. (2011). *Thinking fast and slow.* Farrar, Straus, and Giroux.

Kasl, E., & Yorks, L. (2012). Learning to be what we know: The pivotal role of presentational knowing in transformative learning. In E. Taylor, P. Cranton, & Associates (Eds.), *The handbook of transformative learning: Theory, research, and practice* (pp. 503–519). Jossey-Bass.

Kolb, D. (1984). *Experiential learning: Experience as the source of learning and development.* Prentice-Hall.

Kolb, D. (2015). *Experiential learning: Experience as the source of learning and development* (2nd ed.). Pearson Education.

Lakoff, G., & Johnson, M. (2003). *Metaphors we live by.* University of Chicago Press.

McGilchrist, I. (2019). *The master and the emissary: The divided brain and the making of the Western world.* Yale University Press. (Original work published 2009)

Paxton, D. (2003). *Facilitating transformation of white consciousness among European-American people: A case study of cooperative inquiry* [Doctoral dissertation, California Institute of Integral Studies]. Dissertation Abstracts International, 64(01), 297A. (UMI No. AAT3078796)

Ratey, J. J. (2001). *A user's guide to the brain.* Vintage Books.

Taylor, K., & Marienau, C. (Eds.). (1995). *Learning Environments for Women's Adult Development: Bridges Toward Change* (New Directions for Adult and Continuing Education, no. 65). Jossey-Bass.

Taylor, K., & Marienau, C. (2016). *Facilitating learning with the adult brain in mind: A conceptual and practical guide.* Wiley.

Tompkins, C. A., Scharp, V. L., Meigh, K. M., & Fassbinder, W. (2008). Coarse coding and discourse comprehension in adults with right hemisphere brain damage. *Aphasiology, 22*(2), 204–223. https://doi.org/10.1080/02687030601125019

Authors' Additional Resource Suggestions

Asma, S., & Gabriel, R. (2019). *The emotional mind: The affective roots of culture and cognition.* Harvard University Press.

Bresciani, M. L. (Ed.). (2016). *The neuroscience of learning and development.* Stylus.

Dirkx, J. (2008). The meaning and role of emotions in adult learning. In J. M. Dirkx (Ed.), *Adult Learning and the Emotional Self* (New Directions for Adult and Continuing Education, no. 120, pp. 7–18). Jossey-Bass. https://doi.org/10.1002/ace.311

Genter, D., Holyoak, K. J., & Kokinov, B. N. (2001). *The analogical mind: Perspectives from cognitive science.* MIT Press.

Greene, J. D. (2013). *Moral tribes: Emotion, reason, and the gap between us and them.* Penguin.

Johnson, S., & Taylor, K. (Eds.). (2006). *The Neuroscience of Adult Learning* (New Directions for Adult and Continuing Education, no. 110). Jossey-Bass.

Kegan, R. (1994). *In over our heads: The mental demands of modern life.* Harvard University Press.

Lieberman, M. D. (2013). *Social: Why our brains are wired to connect.* Crown.

Merriam, S., & Baumgartner, L. (2020). *Learning in adulthood: A comprehensive guide* (4th ed.). Jossey-Bass.

Mezirow, J. (1991). *Transformative dimensions of adult learning.* Jossey-Bass.

Mezirow, J. (2009). Transformative learning theory. In, J. Mezirow, E. Taylor, & Associates (Eds.), *Transformative learning in practice* (pp. 18–31). Jossey-Bass.

Varela, F. J., Thompson, E., & Rosch, E. (1991). *The embodied mind: Cognitive science and human experience.* MIT Press.

Editors' Key Seminal and Supplemental Text Suggestions

Damasio, A. (2003). *Looking for Spinoza: Joy, sorrow, and the feeling brain.* Harcourt Books.

Taylor, K., & Marienau, C. (2016). *Facilitating learning with the adult brain in mind.* Jossey-Bass.

- Chapter 1: Brain Basics
- Chapter 2: The Learning, Changing Adult Brain
- Chapter 3: Metaphors, Embodiment, and Hemispheres
- Chapter 10: Toward Complexity and Commitment

6

THE ROLE OF EMOTION-LADEN EXPERIENCES IN SELF-FORMATION

John Dirkx and Steven Schlegel

Larry, a white adult male in his mid-20s who dropped out of high school several years ago, enrolled in an Adult Basic Education program through the local community college to study for a high school equivalency exam. At one point in his program, Larry was struggling to learn some basic math concepts. His progress was slow, and he was having a hard time concentrating and staying with his learning tasks. One day, Larry seemed particularly frustrated and upset with his lack of progress. He angrily tossed his pencil across the table and pushed back his chair. With his arms folded across his chest, and slouching back in his chair, Larry explained that he couldn't see the point of learning "this stuff," saying that it didn't have anything to do with his life. Larry said he wanted to learn something that was meaningful and relevant to his interests, like pottery.

Tina, a middle-aged, African American single mother with three children under 10, works full time as a faculty development specialist for a medical school. She is in her third year of study as a doctoral student in adult education and hopes to do medical education research after completing the program. Tina found her first 2 years difficult but managed the many demands on her time and energy. In her third year, however, she felt increasingly overwhelmed by the emphasis on shaping a research agenda. At a meeting with her advisor, on the verge of tears and visibly shaken, Tina expressed feelings of doubt about her ability to do her doctoral work and balance the other demands in her life.

These brief vignettes illustrate two important features of adult learning. First, adult learning is often emotionally laden (Dirkx, 2008; MacKeracher, 2004; Merriam & Baumgartner, 2020; Zembylas, 2007). And second, adult learning engages the self of the learner. These vignettes also force us to ask questions about the role of emotion-laden experiences in adult learning. For example, how are we to understand the meaning of the emotion-laden experiences, such as those we see in Larry and Tina's respective stories? What is their relationship, if any, to the process of meaning making and adult learning? And what is the role educators play in responding to them?

We use the term *emotion-laden experiences* to refer to those learning experiences in which powerful emotions are evoked within the learner through interaction with the subject matter, peers, the teacher, or the broader social and cultural context. Regardless of the particular adult education sector, when adults engage in meaningful and challenging learning, emotional issues and dynamics are often at or just below the surface (Brookfield, 1986; Hascher, 2010).

In this chapter, we explore the complex relationship between emotion-laden experiences and the formation of self in adult learning. We begin by exploring this relationship in the Western historical and philosophical contexts in which we have come to understand how emotion and learning intersect, acknowledging that this Eurocentric analysis is a limitation. Next, we describe a conceptual framework that we refer to as the *imaginal approach* (Johnson, 1986; Samuels, 1985). We suggest this framework can be used to interpret and make sense of self-formative processes and the emotion-laden experiences that characterize them. We conclude the chapter with a discussion of the practical implications and applications of this approach to emotion-laden experiences in adult learning.

The Self and Emotion-Laden Experiences in Adult Learning

In this chapter, we argue that meaningful adult learning engages the learner in a self-formative process and that emotion-laden experiences play a critical role in fostering and contributing to this process. We develop this argument within the context of four eras, or perspectives on the self, and the role that emotion-laden experiences play in its formation. These are the Pre-Rational, Rational, Romantic or Humanistic, and Extra-Rational eras. We use these eras to situate and more fully develop evolving understandings of self-formation and the role of emotion-laden experiences within this process. However, because these eras are in many ways intellectual constructs, they overlap, and the break between one era and the next is rarely clean or completely distinct. The key characteristics of these eras are summarized in Table 6.1 and explored in detail in the sections that follow.

Pre-Rational Era

Asking questions about who we are, where we come from, and where we are going has long been a central human preoccupation (Shealy, 2016). Fundamentally, these are critical questions about the nature of the self (Barrett et al., 2018; Elliott, 2020; Fineman, 2008; Gallagher & Shear, 1999; Kashima et al., 2002; Pekrun & Linnenbrink-Garcia, 2014; Siegel, 2005; S. E. Taylor, 1989). For centuries, philosophers and scholars contemplated the idea of the self, its formation and development (Elliott, 2020; Gallagher & Shear, 1999; Kashima et al., 2002; Siegel, 2005; S. E. Taylor, 1989), and the role of emotions in our sense of self. During the Pre-Rational

TABLE 6.1
Summary of Key Periods of the Self and Emotion in Adult Learning

Era	Construction of self	Meaning of emotion
Pre-Rational	Mystical construction, seen in religious terms	Viewed as "voices of the gods"
Rational	Understood as coming from careful, thoughtful, dispassionate analysis	Subservient to reason and a potential barrier to meaning making
Humanistic	Conceptualized in terms of inner personality and interpretation of life experience to advance self-actualization	Bound up with meaning making. Emotions may be harnessed to improve learning outcomes. Emotion and rational self are unified.
Extra-Rational	A conscious and unconscious self; unconscious self is primarily visible symbolically through emotion-laden experience, dreams, images, and creative works	Psychosocial and emotional responses are core to meaning making. Emotion and rational self are divided and fragmented.

era, expressions of the self were primarily construed in religious terms that equated it with an immortal soul (Stein, 2008) and the presence of the divine. Emotions were thought to be representative of the voices of the gods, mystically illuminating paths of deep self-understanding.

Western conceptions of knowledge and what it means to come to know one's self gradually shifted these early mystical perspectives away from a reliance on the heavens and toward an expression of the human condition. The Pre-Rational era increasingly gave way to the prominence of reason, rationality, science, and the goal of making societies better through fostering individual growth and self-knowledge. We refer to this period as the *Rational era*. Yet, this spiritual or mystical perspective on self-formation and emotion-laden experiences is also manifest later in the Humanistic and Extra-Rational eras, as well as in the Jungian and post-Jungian perspectives. We briefly return to these characteristics later when we discuss those eras in more detail.

Rational Era

During the 17th and 18th centuries, reason came to be the way we advance our understanding of human nature. Knowing one's self was understood to be achieved through careful and dispassionate discussions and analyses. Scholars of the Rational era paved the way for a deeper exploration of the meaning of the self. Arguing that self-knowledge was a critical goal of adult learning, Kapp (1833, cited in Loeng, 2017) described an inward, self-directed, reflective process. However, these inquires did not provide an understanding of the role played by experience, imagination, and emotion. Furthermore, they disregarded the role of social and cultural contexts in the process of self-formation.

While views of human nature during the Rational era often included both the head and heart, emotions were considered to be subservient to reason. They also represented a potential barrier to the development of rational thought, an enemy of reason (Scarantino, 2016), and a threat to self-knowledge and actualization of the ideal self. As viewed in the Rational era, emotions and imagination did not yet play a part in self-understanding. Descartes's well-known phrase "I think, therefore I am" represents dominant beliefs of the Rational era regarding reason and emotion, a view that still dominates in adult education practice (e.g., Mezirow, 1991). From this, adult educators often see expressions of emotion, such as those in the chapter opening vignettes, simply as natural and constructive venting after which learners are expected to return to the task at hand.

Similar to the Pre-Rational era, the Rational era contributed to a growing understanding of self-formation and emotion-laden experiences in adult learning, especially with its emphasis on reflection and self-knowledge. Yet, a growing awareness of the importance of emotions led many to critique this era in terms of the ways in which self-formation and emotion-laden experiences were conceptualized.

Humanistic Era

The Humanistic era is the first significant representation of psychology in self-formation and emotion in adult learning. While the Humanistic era represents a chronologically shorter amount of time than either the Pre-Rational or the Rational era, it offers a much deeper, richer scholarly landscape that encompasses 19th-century Romanticism, 20th-century reactions to World War II, and even contemporary 21st-century scholarship.

Shaped by the emergence of Romanticism in the latter part of the 18th century, scholars began to emphasize the importance of experience, emotion, and imagination in adult learning. The Romantic philosophers stressed that our emotions influence the ways we construe our realities. For these scholars, emotions are intimately bound up with meaning making. During the Humanistic era conceptualizations of the self became more unified, taking account of one's inner personality and life experiences and interpretations of them (Rogers, 1995). Adult learning was increasingly perceived as experience based (Fenwick, 2003), problem focused, and oriented toward immediate application (Knowles et al., 2005).

As we came to understand the role of experience in learning, our understandings of the self became intertwined with adult learning (Lange, 2015; MacKeracher, 2004; Merriam & Baumgartner, 2020; Mezirow, 1991; Tennant, 2012). For example, MacKeracher (2004) argued that adult learning experiences are deemed meaningful (or not meaningful) in relation to the self. In the absence of this relationship, they are ignored or "denied organization or given a distorted meaning because the experience seems inconsistent with the structure of the self [and threatens it]" (Kidd, 1973, cited in MacKeracher, 2004, p. 130). The experiences of Larry and Tina can be interpreted as reflecting this disconnect between their sense of self and their learning experiences.

Humanistic scholars in the 19th and early 20th centuries increasingly recognized the complexity of the self and its formation and expression, including the role of emotion in our understanding of it. These scholars stressed that emotions influence the ways we construe our realities. They are intimately bound up with the meaning making of one's experiences. This way of thinking is most evident in the visual arts, music, and literature, but it is also manifest in education.

Despite the growing recognition of the role emotions and imagination play in adult learning, the view of the self that emerged from 20th-century adult education scholars continued to be depicted as rational, conscious, and reflective (Tennant, 2012). The self was seen as adapting to the demands of one's outer realities of work, family, or personal enrichment. The sense of self emerging from the Humanistic era is holistic, autonomous, and unitary, and it continues to be reflected in much of the contemporary discourse in adult learning (Tennant, 2012).

In the early expressions of the Humanistic era, similar to the Rational tradition, emotions were regarded as dysfunctional and interfering with rational thought and the ability to adapt to the demands of one's outer reality. However, in the late 20th and early 21st centuries this view began to shift. The role of emotions was neither sidelined nor seen as negative in scholarly discussions about them; instead, substantive discussions about the role of emotions appeared in major texts on adult learning (Brookfield, 1986; MacKeracher, 2004; Merriam & Baumgartner, 2020; Merriam & Bierema, 2014; K. Taylor & Marienau, 2016). Scholars increasingly argued that emotions could be integrated into the learning process to improve outcomes. For example, Hagen and Park (2016) asserted that educators should draw on "learning materials that will elicit emotions" (p. 183) in the service of learning content. In a practitioner-oriented blog post, Meacham (2014) encouraged readers to ask themselves "what emotional response are you targeting for your learners? How do you want them to feel as they implement the new skill you are covering?" (para. 11). Similarly, MacKeracher (2004) pointed out that "at low to moderate levels, emotions can enhance or motivate learning" (p. 15). For these authors, emotion-laden experiences are valued to the extent that they contribute to the learner's ability to adapt to the demands of his or her outer reality.

Illustrative of this late 20th-century shift was the work of Daniel Goleman (1995), who was himself building on earlier work (Beldoch, 1964; Salovey & Mayer, 1990), which popularized the notion of *emotional intelligence*. He defined this as the ability to monitor one's own emotions and their interplay with the emotions of others. Goleman's work prompted increased attention on the role emotion can play in organizational life and, by extension, adult learning. Goleman created space to see emotion-laden experiences in a more expansive way; however, his work still reflected a view of emotion-laden experiences as potentially interfering with learning and thus in need of regulation.

The Extra-Rational Era

The ideas of emotion-laden experiences and their contribution to self-understanding continued to be largely framed by scholars through a rational and instrumental lens. However, this scholarship paved the way for a deeper understanding of the complexity of the self and the role of emotions in self-formation, a perspective we refer to as the *Extra-Rational*. Before elaborating on how scholars within the Extra-Rational era approached the self and emotion-laden experiences in adult learning, we first sketch some key ideas from two scholars whose work represents a kind of conceptual bridge between the Humanistic and Extra-Rational eras.

One of the scholars who has contributed to a deeper understanding of the self and emotions is Martha Nussbaum (2001). While grounded fundamentally in a rational framework, Nussbaum's work is framed in moral philosophy. She posited that emotions reveal us as vulnerable to events that we do not control. Earlier conceptions of the self grounded in the work of the 19th- and 20th-century founder of psychoanalysis, Sigmund Freud, depicted the ego as a mediator between the rational self and the emotional nature of the unconscious self. However, Nussbaum challenged the ego's dominance over our everyday affairs and its role as mediator. Instead, she argued that emotions play a relatively unique role in illuminating aspects of ourselves not readily visible through our everyday interactions. Building on her work, Donovan Plumb (2014) argued that "emotions are a form of cognition through which we can think about things that are deeply important to us but that are beyond our control" (p. 145). In contrast to the subservient role that is depicted for emotions in earlier eras, the work of Nussbaum (2001) and Plumb (2014) recognized that emotions represent a more independent aspect of the self.

While still grounded fundamentally in rational thought, the work of Nussbaum and Plumb goes beyond the technical–rational paradigms characteristic of the Rational and Humanistic eras. Scholars who take their view stress the importance of psychosocial or emotional responses as a core part of meaning-making processes in learning rather than a disruption or sign of dysfunction.

Late-20th– and early-21st–century scholars working within the Extra-Rational perspective emphasized the subconscious or unconscious aspects of adult learning (Bainbridge & West, 2012; Boyd & Myers, 1988; Hunt & West, 2009). For these scholars a central question was how conscious and unconscious aspects of adult learning influence the meaning-making processes in which adult learners engage (Fenwick, 2003; West, 2014). The Extra-Rational perspective points to an inner self, visible only symbolically through its expression in emotion-laden experiences, dreams, images, and creative or esthetic works of art (Lawrence, 2012). According to this view, the inner world of the self is dominated by struggles between the unconscious and conscious mind.

In contrast to the Rational and Humanistic eras, the Extra-Rational view of the self and emotion-laden experiences is grounded in psychodynamic thought, a body of scholarship characterized by several different theories, such as object relations theory (Greenberg & Mitchell, 1983), psychosocial theories (e.g., Erikson, 1950), and Jungian (Stein, 1998) and post-Jungian theory (Hillman, 1983; Watkins, 2000). While these theories differ in important ways and emphasize different dimensions of the adult learning context, they reflect a common idea that our way of being in the world is largely shaped and influenced by our inner worlds. This inner world reflects a self that is divided, fragmented, conflicted, and multiplistic (Clark & Dirkx, 2000), unlike holistic and unitary humanistic conceptions of the self. Behaviors and ways of interpreting and making sense of our world are largely shaped and influenced by unconscious forces not readily accessible to conscious awareness. Coming to an awareness of these forces constitutes a critical dimension of how we learn through emotion-laden experiences and foster self-formative processes.

The work of scholars in the Extra-Rational era is grounded in the belief that aspects of the self are involved in self-formation in ways that are beyond our immediate control and are not fully visible. The self and its formative processes become visible and known to us through emotion-laden experiences, such as those reflected in the opening stories of Larry and Tina. Meaningful adult learning experiences engage the self of the learner and evoke potentially powerful emotions associated with self-formation processes. How these emotion-laden experiences are interpreted, however, represents one of the ways in which the perspective we take here differs from the Rational and Humanistic approaches, and even from other Extra-Rational theories. We might interpret the emotion-laden experiences that Larry and Tina manifest as their inner selves giving voice to their souls. We might then also acknowledge that trying to learn the knowledge and skills that society requires does not connect with them on a deeper level, with their souls.

Larry's desire to do pottery reflects a creative expression he is seeking from his environment but is not getting. The fragmented image of the self is evident in Larry's desire to learn something that is meaningful to him while at the same time seeking to address the academic competencies society expects of him. Tina's experience suggests a self in which she has invested considerable psychic energy. She struggles to balance the demands of family, school, and work (each of which represents a different aspect of her self). Her strong emotions suggest it is an image that is unraveling. Their experiences represent a self engaged in differentiation, conflict, and struggle, albeit largely at an unconscious level. Possibly something formative is occurring.

Viewing self-formation from an Extra-Rational perspective "helps open ways of approaching the realm of the unconscious; our resistances to knowledge; the desire for closure and mastery that sometimes governs the educational impulse; and enigmatic tensions between learner, knowledge, and educator" (Fenwick, 2003, pp. 27–29). The Extra-Rational view of the self reflects prominent themes of the individual's relationship with both the outside world—objects of knowledge—and "the inner world of psychic energies and dilemmas relating to these objects of knowledge" (Fenwick,

2003, p. 28). For these reasons, we may be totally unaware of the motives that drive our thoughts and behaviors. Notably, scholarly work that accepts the role of the Extra-Rational remains limited; the Humanistic approach still dominates.

An Overview of the Imaginal Approach to the Self and Emotion-Laden Experiences in Adult Learning

In keeping with the emerging Extra-Rational perspective, we understand the self as both a holistic and fragmented entity that shapes, and is shaped by, social and cultural contexts in ways that are both conscious and unconscious. This view of the self reflects a sense of tension, struggle, and even contradiction (Fenwick, 2003). It is out of this experience and through the process of individuation (Stein, 2008) that the self paradoxically becomes both more fully differentiated and integrated (Clark & Dirkx, 2000); that is, different aspects of the self increasingly become differentiated and its different parts become more unified and expressed through this process.

Such a view of the self is reflected in our understandings of how it adapts to the demands of our inner and outer realities. In addressing the outer reality, the inner reality comes to be expressed, in part, through powerful unconscious emotions and emotion-laden experiences. These experiences form the foundations for what we call the *imaginal approach* to understanding adult learning and the processes of self-formation bound up with learning and development. We use the term *imaginal approach* to refer to the set of assumptions and beliefs that characterize the way in which this work is framed. Thus, the imaginal approach is the theoretical context. We use the term *imaginal method* to describe a set of strategies we use to implement the approach in adult learning contexts.

The Imaginal Approach

The imaginal approach to emotion-laden experiences is informed by all of the eras described earlier. For example, the Pre-Rational era provides a way to frame the spiritual dimension of self-formation, the Rational stresses the importance of reflection and dialogue in the self-formation processes, and the Humanistic helps to illuminate the importance of experience and the role of emotional dynamics in the learning process. However, the Extra-Rational era connects most closely with the imaginal approach.

The imaginal approach recognizes the need for learners both to address the demands of their outer realities and to engage the unconscious dimensions of emotion-laden experiences. The methods developed in the emotional intelligence literature provide a helpful set of lenses and strategies for doing so. For example, the idea of *emotion management* refers to the ability of adults to constructively handle positive and challenging emotions that arise within their learning experiences. As we have seen, however, meaningful adult learning also engages the learner's self-formative processes in deeper, more Extra-Rational processes that are beyond our conscious awareness. Thus, learners may also need to address unconscious messages they are receiving from their inner selves (through emotion-laden experiences). Rather than seeing emotion-laden experiences as dysfunctional or disruptive to the learning process, we assert that they convey a more complex and emotionally powerful way to make meaning that is grounded in our life stories and can yield deeper, more meaningful learning. By fostering self-formation from an Extra-Rational perspective, the learner is encouraged to establish a dialogue with unconscious processes and aspects of the self. The imaginal approach provides a context in which to foster this dialogue among the various selves represented by the images arising within emotion-laden experiences in adult learning.

The imaginal approach is grounded in Jungian and post-Jungian psychology (Jones et al., 2008; Samuels, 1985; Stein, 1998). The term *Jungian* refers to a psychology informed by the theory and writings of Carl Jung (Stein, 1998); *post-Jungian* refers to those who largely adhere to his core principles and assumptions but have deviated from Jung's corpus in significant ways (Hillman, 1983; Samuels, 1985; Watkins, 2000). Like many of the theorists described earlier, Jung characterized the human psyche as constituted by multiple structures, and chief among these are ego, or personal consciousness, and the unconscious. *Ego consciousness* reflects our everyday level of awareness. The *personal unconscious* refers to the personal images, memories, and experiences that are too painful to be expressed through ego consciousness. Post-Jungians (Hillman, 1983; Watkins, 2000) built on this perspective but emphasized the importance of the imagination in the expression of the human psyche. This expression is often unconscious and is manifest in the form of images and symbols. Emotion-laden experiences represent this symbolic expression of the psyche. The imaginal approach builds on the human propensity for creative storytelling to uncover and support development of the self through emotion-laden experiences.

Unlike some of his colleagues, however, Jung also argued for a third major structure, the *collective unconscious*. The collective unconscious captures the broader level of unconscious in which we all participate. And so Jung understood culture to be an expression of the collective unconscious. Jung placed strong emphasis on the role of the unconscious in understanding human behavior and development. A primary goal of adult educators working in this tradition is to help make the unconscious conscious, including aspects of both the personal and collective conscious. Their goal is to help foster this process; doing so is also the goal of the imaginal method.

A Jungian perspective contributes two important concepts to our understanding of the imaginal approach in adult learning: individuation and active imagination. *Individuation* provides a conceptual map for understanding and interpreting changes in individual and collective consciousness, emphasizing the importance of enhancing and developing human consciousness to its fullest potential (Stein, 1998, p. xiii). In other words, individuation reflects "the process or state of achieving an inner integration of disparate elements of the Self, both conscious and unconscious elements"

(Jones et al., 2008, p. 4). The journey toward consciousness also reflects a major aim of adult learning (Dirkx, 2012). Post-Jungians interpret the struggles associated with this as, in part, characteristics of the consciousness development journey, of working to make the unconscious conscious. This individuation process reflects an ongoing, lifelong process of differentiating and integrating the various parts of the self into a holistic sense of who we are, both individually and collectively.

Individuation is mediated through the *active imagination* (Chodorow, 1997). *Active imagination* refers to "a technique for eliciting and working with unconscious material. . . . It brings to conscious awareness images and feelings that serve the individuation process" (Jones et al., 2008, p. 4). What is unseen and unknown is made visible through the manifestation of emotion-laden experiences, images, symbols, or other emotional reactions to evocative objects within one's learning environment. At the individual level, these are manifest to the conscious self as dreams, symbols, personal stories or myths, and emotion-laden images evoked by the personal, social, and cultural contexts of one's situation. The imaginal approach therefore reflects an understanding of both personal and collective levels of learning and change. In engaging the imagination and narrative ways of knowing, imaginal approaches are reflected in non-Eurocentric perspectives, such as storytelling (Clark, 2010), and the oral traditions of indigenous cultures (Marovic & Machinga, 2017). These processes are also evident in dream tending, in which we elaborate the stories represented by our dreams and imagination.

The active imagination recognizes and gives voice to the myth making, or mytho-poetic, capacity of the human psyche that may be expressed within adult learning contexts (Aadlandsvik, 2009). Thus, as a way of making meaning of our learning experiences, as individuals and collectives, we tell stories to ourselves and to others about the deeper meaning of our experiences (MacAdams, 1993). How and why these stories are told is largely beyond our levels of conscious awareness. Over time, however, attention to the self can reveal their meanings. While some of these stories are or can be readily known, others are less accessible and revealed only through imaginal work.

By making our inner selves more visible, the imaginal approach encourages learners to engage in dialogue between the conscious and unconscious aspects of the self. The strong emotions Tina and Larry express can be seen as signaling to them and to their teachers that there is something more going on than just frustration with what they are being asked to learn in their programs or doubt about their ability to complete what is required of them. These experiences are saying something about their inner journeys, their personal myths. The imaginal method helps us understand the nature and meaning of these experiences, especially as they relate to individual and collective processes of self-formation.

The Imaginal Method in Practice

In this final section, we suggest ways in which adult educators can develop and facilitate learning experiences. These suggestions can help to more fully integrate emotion-laden experiences into learners' lives and thereby contribute to the realization of a more differentiated and integrated sense of self. We describe the process of facilitating the emergence and interpretation of images or figures that are revealed in the process and are at the core of emotion-laden experiences. Grounded in the concept of the active imagination and the imaginal approach discussed in the prior section, this *imaginal method* refers to specific methodological strategies that facilitate understanding and working with emotion-laden experiences in adult learning contexts. At the heart of most emotion-laden experiences are images or figures that tend to give form or shape to the experiences; this method, illustrated by the active imagination, provides a bridge from the unconscious self to the conscious self (Chodorow, 1997).

The imaginal method consists of four steps (e.g., Aizenstat, 2011; Clarkson, 2008; Johnson, 1986): Description, Association, Amplification, and Animation. It is helpful initially to think of these steps sequentially. However, they need not always follow this sequence.

Description

As learners prepare to engage and describe an emotion-laden experience, they should try to calm their minds; deep breathing or other meditation techniques may help here (Aizenstat, 2011; Chodorow, 1997; Johnson, 1986). In the Description step, learners call to mind an emotion-laden experience and seek to recognize the image that may undergird it and note everything they can observe about it. What does it feel like? What is happening in the experience? Who is involved? Is there a figure or image behind the experience? As they call this experience and any accompanying images to mind, learners should write down their observations and feelings.

Association

In the Association step, learners work to develop associations between images that arose within the emotion-laden experience and similar experiences in their life. While there is no "right" way to do this, learners should pay particular attention to, and connect with, events, ideas, or other aspects from their personal history. It is often helpful to ask, "What aspects of my history does this experience remind me of? In what life context or experience have I felt like this before?" These questions may cause the learner's mind to wander, which is a perfectly natural phenomenon. When learners become aware of this wandering, they should return to the image in their mind's eye. At the end of this reflection period they should note the narrative trajectory of experiences or relationships that arise, making special note of childhood experiences. Such observations may provide a deeper understanding of the journey the self is seeking to undertake (Aizenstat, 2011). As with the Description step, learners should write down everything they observe in this process, providing a record of how this emotion-laden experience is similar to previous experiences.

Amplification

Amplification is another aspect of the imaginal method that allows us to connect more deeply not only with our personal experiences but also with more collective experiences. In the Amplification step, learners are asked to go beyond their personal experience and feelings by asking themselves, "What figures or images in my cultural context does this emotion-laden experience remind me of? Are there figures or images from mythology, literature, theater, movies, or fairy tales that seem to resemble elements of the emotion-laden experience?" Here, learners are attempting to connect the emotion-laden experience with more universal themes. This step can involve the identification of multiple figures that cut across time and cultures.

These figures are all manifestations of the multiple selves that populate our psyche. As with the other steps, learners should journal what they learned from the processes of amplification. Aizenstat (2011) posed a guiding question for this journaling process: "How does this expanded view of the image [within the emotion-laden experience] offer insight into your present life circumstances?" (p. 23).

Animation

In the Animation step, learners take the figure or image that arose for them in the Description phase and bring it to life in the here-and-now. Learners can begin by imagining their emotion-laden experience as if it were actually in the room with them. They are encouraged to imagine it has a life of its own. As this image comes into view, learners should notice what it is doing and record these observations in their journals. Developing an implicit dialogue with one or more of the images and then documenting this dialogue is a helpful tool to deepen the meaning of the emotion-laden experience and to more clearly elaborate a sense of self.

After completing the Animation step, learners should reread their journal and reflect on the previous entries, taking note of what was going on with the image in each of the steps and what may have surprised or impressed them. In addition, learners should reflect on how the images evoked in each step affected them. They might want to ask, "What did I learn from each of these steps? How did these steps enhance intimacy with the image that arose within the emotion-laden experiences?"

The overall point of the imaginal method is to learn more about one's self and to foster the differentiation and integration of the selves that make up one's psyche. This reflects the process of individuation. It is important to remember, when enacting an imaginal approach that, regardless of specific strategies used, there is almost always more to explore than meets the eye. The techniques elaborated here are intended to help make these invisible aspects of experience more visible and understandable within the context of self-formation.

Larry's emotion-laden experience reflects considerable frustration. He is also agitated and angry that he is being asked to learn material that is meaningless to him. While he holds his teachers partially responsible for the disconnect between his interest in pottery and the learning tasks he is being asked to complete, he may also be angry with himself. Larry seems to be aware, at least dimly, of the need to balance his inner reality with the demands of his outer reality (the learning tasks assigned to him). He could use the imaginal method to explore this image in the context of his current learning environment. Doing so could provide him with the ability to see the connection between an artistic self spinning pots and a well-educated self.

Tina's emotion-laden experiences represent a mixture of powerful emotions arising from the multiple roles she is playing, including being a doctoral student. Although she entered her graduate program full of promise and excitement, she now feels as if she is being smothered by competing demands. She worries that a part of her is slipping away along with her dream of working in medical research. Like Larry, Tina is animated by a vision of herself that isn't fully realized. The imaginal method can provide her with a more fully developed sense of self that acknowledges the person, in her heart, she knows she is.

Larry and Tina both need to give voice to their inner self. Doing so will help them express a more authentic version of who they are. They can seek this expression through the emotion-laden experiences that have come to characterize their educational journeys. This inner work will involve accepting and recognizing the selves that are at the heart of their experiences. By engaging in the processes of dialogue and journaling through the imaginal method, they can foster a deeper integration between their inner and outer realities, between their needs as individuals and the demands of learning for the world of work. In each case, they would benefit from educators who act more like guides who recognize the importance of the invisible, value the powerful emotions their students bring to the learning environment, and help them navigate through them. Implementing the imaginal method can help Larry and Tina reframe their understanding of emotion-laden experience. At the time these vignettes were occurring, Larry and Tina perceived their emotions as disruptive to the learning experience. Reframing emotion-laden experiences can allow them to (re)appreciate the value of their own emotions and the role they play in the meaning-making process. This reframing may enable Larry and Tina to be less reactive in their educational and personal pursuits and allow them to more fully integrate their inner lives with the outer realities of work and school. Integrating these two aspects of their selves is vitally important if they are to be successful and engage with students, instructors, and content.

Other Approaches to the Imaginal Method

A variety of techniques that encourage reflection and expression are available within the imaginal method. Reflective approaches rely on a greater degree of conscious participation by one's ego in the imaginal method process; expressive approaches seek to bridge our conscious selves with the unconscious. Whichever approach is used, it should actively engage learners' imaginations.

Journaling reflects a key reflective technique in the imaginal method. The journaling process can take shape in several different ways (Progroff, 1992). Recording observations and experiences is a simple but important journaling activity. Free-writing can be used to further elaborate images that arise within the experience, and storytelling can provide a means to further associate and amplify the meaning of one's emotion-laden experience. Any form of journaling that helps to connect more deeply and profoundly with the emotion-laden experience is helpful.

Developing a dialogue with the images or figures that arise within emotion-laden experiences is a powerful way to deepen the meaning of one's emotion-laden experiences. This dialogue is usually mediated through writing. While the imagined dialogue may at first seem somewhat awkward, as learners further engage in the process it will begin to feel more authentic and real. For example, when I (John) was teaching a course on transformative learning, the class seemed to start out well, but after a few weeks the atmosphere in the group seemed to grow heavy and somewhat lifeless. Noting this, the learners were asked to develop a dialogue between them and their group of classmates. I asked them to give the group a name and then, using the first steps of the imaginal method, to observe the feeling in the group and to develop a written dialogue with it. The next week, the group was again feeling vital and animated. When asked about developing this dialogue, several students commented that the exercise enabled them to helpfully understand what was going on in the group. Not everyone engaged in the activity, but apparently enough did to help us deepen their experience of themselves and of the group to have an impact on the energy in the room. This process of developing a dialogue represents a bridge between reflective and expressive approaches.

Expressive approaches seek to foster a deepening of consciousness through techniques that loosen ego and allow unconscious expression through techniques such as role plays, performances, dancing, painting, and drumming. Reflection and dialogue can be important features of these activities as learners seek to communicate with themselves and with others, but performative techniques emphasize elements of expression.

Conclusion

In this chapter, we have argued that powerful emotion-laden experiences can make positive contributions to the process of fostering meaningful adult learning as they further the developmental processes of self-formation. We have argued that learning is more meaningful if and when the outer reality of the learning environment aligns with the inner reality of the learner (or at least gives it voice). The process of self-formation is furthered by engaging with emotion-laden experiences. Through the imaginal method, emotion-laden experiences can have a life of their own within the adult learning context. By providing a bridge from the unconscious to consciousness, emotion-laden experiences create a means through which we can further expand and elaborate differentiation and integration of our individual and collective psyches.

The focus of this chapter is on learners. But this perspective can be important to the professional development of adult educators as well. Attending to and working with emotion-laden experiences requires the full and authentic presence of the educator who has also experienced this process. In general, when working with emotion-laden experiences, educators should move toward and embrace the complexities and disorientations these experiences may evoke. Rather than avoiding potentially troubling aspects of learning, educators should embrace them just as they should encourage learners to do, noting what arises within the process and working within the context of what has been described in this chapter.

Educators should also pay attention to what is evoked within themselves as they continue to read about and study their respective disciplines. While we often read professionally for more instrumental purposes, it is also helpful to note powerful feelings and emotions that might arise in more technically focused writing. The imaginal method provides opportunities to learn about one's self through additional cultural sources and experiences. Adult educators should make a practice of connecting with their own emotion-laden experiences through these practices. Just as the imaginal method can help learners be more successful as they develop their selves, it can also help educators be more effective in their interactions with their students and themselves.

References

Aadlandsvik, R. (2009). In search of a lost eye: The mythopoetic dimension in pedagogy. *Phenomenology & Practice, 3*(1), 94–110. https://doi.org/10.29173/pandpr19823

Aizenstat, S. (2011). *Dream tending: Awakening to the healing power of dreams.* Spring Journal.

Bainbridge, A., & West, L. (Eds.). (2012). *Psychoanalysis and education.* Routledge.

Barrett, L. F., Lewis, M., & Haviland-Jones, J. M. (2018). *Handbook of emotions.* Guilford Press.

Beldoch, M. (1964). Sensitivity to expression of emotional meaning in three modes of communication. In J. R. Davitz & M. Beldoch (Eds.), *The communication of emotional meaning* (pp. 31–42). McGraw-Hill.

Boyd, R. D., & Myers, J. G. (1988). Transformative education. *International Journal of Lifelong Education, 7*(4), 261–284. https://doi.org/10.1080/0260137880070403

Brookfield, S. D. (1986). *Understanding and facilitating adult learning: A comprehensive analysis of principles and effective practices.* Open University Press.

Chodorow, J. (Ed.). (1997). *Jung on active imagination.* Princeton University Press.

Clark, M. C. (2010). Narrative learning: Its contents and its possibilities. In M. Rossiter & M. C. Clark (Eds.), *Narrative Perspectives on Adult Education* (New Directions for Adult and Continuing Education, no. 126, pp. 3–11). Jossey-Bass.

Clark, M. C., & Dirkx, J. (2000). Moving beyond a unitary self: A reflective dialogue. In A. L. Wilson & E. R. Hayes (Eds.), *Handbook of adult and continuing education* (pp. 101–116). Jossey-Bass. https://doi.org/10.1002/ace.367

Clarkson, A. (2008). The dialectical mind: On educating the creative imagination in elementary school. In R. A. Jones, A. Clarkson, S. Congram, & N. Stratton (Eds.), *Education and imagination: Post-Jungian perspectives* (pp. 118–141). Routledge.

Dirkx, J. (2008). The meaning and role of emotions in adult learning. In J. Dirkx (Ed.), *Adult Learning and the Emotional Self* (New Directions for Adult and Continuing Education, no. 120, pp. 7–18). Jossey-Bass. https://doi.org/10.1002/ace.311

Dirkx, J. M. (2012). Self-formation and transformative learning: A response to "Calling Trans-formative Learning Into Question: Some Mutinous Thoughts," by Michael Newman. *Adult Education Quarterly, 62*(4), 399–405. https://doi.org/10.1177/0741713612456420

Elliott, A. (2020). *Concepts of the self.* Polity Press.

Erikson, E. (1950). *Childhood and society.* W. W. Norton.

Fenwick, T. (2003). Innovation: Examining workplace learning in new enterprises. *Journal of Workplace Learning, 15*(3), 123–132. https://doi.org/10.1108/13665620310468469

Fineman, S. (2008). Whither emotion. In D. Barry & H. Hansen (Eds.), *The SAGE hand-book of new approaches in management and organization* (pp. 239–240). SAGE. https://doi.org/10.4135/9781849200394.n43

Gallagher, S., & Shear, J. (1999). *Models of the self.* Imprint Academic.

Goleman, D. (1995). *Emotional intelligence: Why it can matter more than IQ.* Bantam.

Greenberg, J., & Mitchell, S. (1983). *Object relations in psychoanalytic theory.* Harvard University Press.

Hagen, M., & Park, S. (2016). We knew it all along! Using cognitive science to explain how andragogy works. *European Journal of Training and Development, 40*(3), 171–190. https://doi.org/10.1108/ejtd-10-2015-0081

Hascher, T. (2010). Learning and emotion: Perspective for theory and research. *European Educational Research Journal, 9*(1), 13–28. https://doi.org/10.2304/eerj.2010.9.1.13

Hillman, J. (1983). *Interviews: Conversations with Laura Pozzo.* Harper & Row.

Hunt, C., & West, L. (2009). Salvaging the self in adult learning. *Studies in the Education of Adults, 41*(1), 68–82. https://doi.org/10.1080/02660830.2009.11661574

Johnson, R. (1986). *Inner work: Using dreams and active imagination for personal growth.* HarperCollins.

Jones, R. A., Clarkson, A., Congram S., & Stratton, N. (Eds.). (2008). *Education and imagi-nation.* Routledge.

Kapp, A. (1833). *Platon's erziehungslehre, asl Padagogik fur die Eizelnen und als Staatspad-agogik. Oder dessen praktische Philosophie [Plato's educational theory for the state and the individual].* Schulzische buchhandlung.

Kashima, Y., Foddy, M., & Platow, M. (Eds.). (2002). *Self and identity: Personal, social, and symbolic.* Psychology Press.

Kidd, J. R. (1973). *How adults learn.* Association Press.

Knowles, M. S., Holton, E., & Swanson, R. (2005). *Adult learning: The definitive classic in adult education and human resource development.* Elsevier.

Lange, E. (2015). Transformative learning and concepts of the self: Insights from immi-grant and intercultural journeys. *International Journal of Lifelong Education, 34*(6), 1–20. https://doi.org/10.1080/02601370.2015.1036944

Lawrence, R. L. (2012). Intuitive knowing and embodied consciousness. In R. L. Lawrence (Ed.), *Bodies of Knowledge: Embodied Learning in Adult Education* (New Directions for Adult and Continuing Education, no. 134, pp. 5–13). Jossey-Bass. https://doi.org/10.1002/ace.20011

Loeng, S. (2017). Alexander Kapp—The first known user of the andragogy concept. *Inter-national Journal of Lifelong Education, 36*(6), 629–643. https://doi.org/10.1080/026013 70.2017.1363826

MacAdams, D. P. (1993). *The stories we live by: Personal myths and the making of the self.* Morrow.

MacKeracher, D. (2004). *Making sense of adult learning.* University of Toronto Press.

Marovic, Z., & Machinga, M. M. (2017). African shamanic knowledge and transpersonal psychology: Spirits and healing in dialogue. *Journal of Transpersonal Psychology, 49*(1), 31–44.

Meacham, M. (2014, October 16). *All learning is emotional.* https://www.td.org/Publications/Blogs/Science-of-Learning-Blog/2014/10/All-Learning-Is-Emotional

Merriam, S. B., & Baumgartner, L. M. (2020). *Learning in adulthood: A comprehensive guide.* Jossey-Bass.

Merriam, S. B., & Bierema, L. (2014). *Adult learning: Linking theory and practice.* Jossey-Bass.

Mezirow, J. (1991). *Transformative dimensions of adult learning.* Jossey-Bass.

Nussbaum, M. (2004). Emotions as judgements of value and importance. In R. C. Solomon (Ed.), *Thinking about feeling: Contemporary philosophers on emotions* (p. 183–199). Oxford University Press.

Pekrun, R., & Linnenbrink-Garcia, L. (2014). *International handbook of emotions in education.* Routledge.

Plumb, D. (2014). Emotions and human concern: Adult education and the philosophical thought of Martha Nussbaum. *Studies in the Education of Adults, 46*(2), 145–162. https://doi.org/10.1080/02660830.2014.11661663

Progoff, I. (1992). *At a journal workshop: Writing to access the power of the unconscious and evoke creative ability.* Putnam.

Rogers, C. R. (1995). *On becoming a person: A therapist's view of psychotherapy.* Houghton Mifflin.

Salovey, P., & Mayer, J. D. (1990). Emotional intelligence. *Imagination, Cognition and Personality, 9*(3), 185–211. https://doi.org/10.2190/dugg-p24e-52wk-6cdg

Samuels, A. (1985). *Jung and the post-Jungians.* Routledge.

Scarantino, A. (2016). The philosophy of emotions and its impact on affective science. In L. Barrett, M. Lewis, & J. Haviland-Jones (Eds.), *Handbook of emotions* (pp. 3–48). Guilford Press.

Shealy, C. N. (2016). *Making sense of beliefs and values: Theory, research, and practice.* Springer.

Siegel, J. (2005). *The idea of the self: Thought and experience in western Europe since the seventeenth century.* Cambridge University Press.

Stein, M. (1998). *Jung's map of the soul: An introduction.* Open Court.

Stein, M. (2008). "Divinity expresses the self . . .": An investigation. *Journal of Analytical Psychology, 53*(3), 305–327. https://doi.org/10.1111/j.1468-5922.2008.00729.x

Taylor, K., & Marienau, C. (2016). *Facilitating learning with the adult brain in mind: A conceptual and practical guide.* Jossey-Bass.

Taylor, S. E. (1989). *Positive illusions: Creative self-deception and the healthy mind.* Basic Books.

Tennant, M. (2012). *The learning self: Understanding the potential for transformation.* Jossey-Bass.

Watkins, M. (2000). *Invisible guests: The development of imaginal dialogue.* Spring.

West, L. (2014). Transformative learning and the form that transforms: Towards a psychosocial theory of recognition using auto/biographical narrative research. *Journal of Transformative Education, 12*(2), 164–179. https://doi.org/10.1177/1541344614536054

Zembylas, M. (2007). Emotion ecology: The intersection of emotional knowledge and pedagogical content knowledge in teaching. *Teaching and Teacher Education, 23*(4), 355–367. https://doi.org/10.1016/j.tate.2006.12.002

Editors' Key Seminal and Supplemental Text Suggestions

Brookfield, S. D. (2006). *The skillful teacher*. Jossey-Bass.

- Chapter 4: Understanding the Tensions and Emotions of Learning
- Chapter 11: Overcoming Resistance of Learning

Leonard, T., & Willis, P. (Eds.). (2008). *Pedagogies of the imagination: Mythopoetic curriculum in educational practice*. Springer.

ADULT DEVELOPMENT

Robert Kegan's Constructive–Developmental Theory

Deborah Helsing

If we are lucky, our adulthood covers several decades, far longer than the time we spend in childhood. We may face daunting challenges and achieve thrilling successes. We may experience heartbreaking loss and also enormous love and compassion. We may face times of complete confusion and bewilderment and also experience stunning moments of clarity and insight. Making sense of all of these experiences means that the decades of our adulthood can lead us to change and grow in dramatic ways, to increase our capacities to understand our experience, our selves, and the world. Adult education settings can provide us with the types of support and challenge necessary for this growth, and theories of adult development help us chart the commonalities among our paths of growth. Despite the infinite differences among individuals, these theories illuminate notable similarities. Educators who understand these patterns and possibilities can optimally support adult learning, have insight into why learners do what they do, and in those moments of loss and confusion, point to next steps they might take in their own evolution.

The Evolution of Developmental Theories

Despite the day-to-day consistency in our personal ways of making sense, when we take a much longer view of any human's life we see that the ways individuals construct meaning do change, and that there are shared, underlying patterns to the changes. Earlier in our development, our frameworks are simpler, and as we evolve they become increasing complex.

Most adult developmental theories are grounded in the work of Jean Piaget (1952) and describe development in terms of the different underlying principles or structures that shape understanding and that change in a predictable and invariant sequence. Piaget was a Swiss biologist and psychologist whose groundbreaking work described the intellectual development of children and adolescents. Research that followed built on and extended Piaget's ideas, looking beyond pure cognition and including adulthood in their focus. For example, some of these theories focus on particular domains of the self, such as moral development (Gilligan, 1982; Kohlberg, 1981) or spiritual development (Fowler, 1981). Others focus on adult learning and higher education (Belenky et al., 1986; Magolda, 1992; Perry, 1970) and leadership (Harris & Kuhnert, 2008; Joiner & Josephs, 2007; Torbert & Associates, 2004).

Some researchers (Cook-Greuter, 1999; Kegan, 1982, 1994; Loevinger, 1976) have suggested that there is a basic coherence *across* the various domains of the self, and their models describe the evolution of the self, integrating the various domains of human experience into a larger framework. They argued that to separate the cognitive from the affective, intrapersonal, or interpersonal is to create false dichotomies. These theories all describe stages in the self's evolution, but Kegan's (1982, 1994) theory makes an important advance on the others by offering the language of subject and object, with which he identifies and explains the structures that underlie the stages, integrate the various domains of the self, and depict the deep processes involved in the evolution from one stage to the next. Kegan's theory is constructive–developmental because it honors and illustrates the patterns or frameworks we construct to actively make sense of our worlds, as well as the ways those frameworks can evolve.

Constructivism refers to the idea that humans cannot ever have an "objective" view of reality. Instead, we each construct our own versions of reality, and these versions can vary widely. Two learners who read the same article often come away with very different ideas about what the article is saying, its significance, and how to interpret it. A team of learners has a heated debate about the best way to approach a project. When asked to describe the conversation later, their descriptions suggest that completely different arguments took place. These familiar experiences demonstrate that "what *really* happened" depends on whose perspective is considered. While this does not mean that there can be no verifiable, shared facts about what happened, our interpretations will depend on which facts we pay attention to as well as what we think and feel and infer about those facts. The different perspectives or mindsets we have are not completely idiosyncratic and random. The ways we construct meaning are deeply rooted in our cultures, how we have made sense of our past experiences, our underlying beliefs about ourselves and the world, and the social identities we claim. These patterns tend to persist, at least for a time. And then they can give way to new, more complex frameworks and patterns. That is the "developmental" part of constructive–developmental theory.

Robert Kegan's Constructive–Development Theory in Depth

Robert Kegan studied under Lawrence Kohlberg and so was steeped in his theory of moral development (1981) as well as in the cognitive developmental model work of Jean Piaget, Kohlberg's predecessor. Kohlberg (1981) extended and applied Piaget's (1952) model of intellectual development to the domain of moral development, describing different stages in moral reasoning and decision making that can evolve across childhood, adolescence, and adulthood. Kegan (1982) suggested that the cognitive and moral changes their theories describe are linked by changes happening on deeper levels—in the structures or underlying principles for how individuals organize their experiences across all domains (cognitive, affective, inter-personal, and intrapersonal). His initial case study research (Kegan, 1977) was done with adult psychotherapy patients (including men and women, ages rang-ing from their 20s to their 60s and highly diverse in economic, racial, and ethnic terms) to understand their meaning-making systems rather than focusing solely on their symptoms. He also began conducting a longitudinal study of graduate learn-ers, men and women, ages 25 to 50, to further develop the theory (Kegan, 1994). This work was supported by several cross-sectional studies that included men and women, age 20s through 60s, college educated and not college educated, working class and professionals (for a summary of the samples and results of the studies see Kegan, 1994, pp. 192–195). There have since been numerous dissertations and other studies (see, e.g., Kegan et al., 2001) conducted with participants of various geographies, ethnicities, and nationalities that reinforce the validity and generaliz-ability of the theory.

The Subject–Object Relationship

The deep structures Kegan (1994) identified refer to differences in what we are "subject to" and what we can take as "object." In order to understand this concept, imagine you have spent your life sitting inside a large cardboard box. You cannot see over the walls, and so they shape and limit the ways you make sense of things. You cannot consider any information that exists outside the walls of that box. In Kegan's terms, we are "subject to" the "walls" that limit us. *Subject* refers to whatever we unquestioningly assume to be true, what we are unable to question or reflect on. We demonstrate our reliance on it in how we make sense of our experience. What we are subject to is the underlying principle we use to organize our meaning making.

Now imagine that you learn that you can stand up, raising your head up above those walls. Suddenly, you can take in all kinds of new information, and you can understand how the walls of that box have prevented you from seeing more. But you have not left the old perspective behind because you can still see everything inside the box; you have access to that familiar perspective. Even if you sit back down again, you will not be able to un-see or un-know that there is more outside the walls. You now have a different relationship to the walls of the box. They have become "object." *Object* refers to something that is separate or distinct enough from ourselves so that we can reflect on it, talk about it, call it into question, make choices about it. When you were sitting inside the box you could consider everything inside the box as object. When you stood up, you were making a *subject/object shift*. No longer subject to the walls of the cardboard box, you could see more, consider more, take more as object. And eventually, you can come to recognize that this new view has its own limits, its own walls that you can also transcend.

The cardboard box analogy is one way to begin thinking about psychological development. When we progress beyond our current stage and toward the next, it is as if we are starting to get a bird's-eye view of our prior way of making sense of things. We can take account of more. Sometimes the catalysts for these shifts are easy to pinpoint. A learner discovers an error in their teacher's thinking and suddenly questions whether teachers are always legitimate and reliable experts. A person leaves home to live in a foreign culture and begins to see their familiar home culture with new eyes.

Each stage in Kegan's developmental progression shows a step along a lifelong journey of standing up out of the cardboard boxes we were formerly sitting in, of being able to look at, reflect on, make more choices about, and take more as object. But this cardboard box analogy has its limitations. What we are subject to (in the metaphor, initially the walls of our cardboard box) are not actually things that exist outside of us. Instead, they are the frameworks we construct to make sense of ourselves and our experience. These frameworks don't tell us the surface features of a person's meaning making (what they think, feel, do, or say) but instead focus on the underlying subject/object structure that organizes their meaning making (how they determine what they do, think, or say). They show us where a person draws the psychological boundary between self and other—what psychological choices the person sees as belonging to the self (what they can take as object) and what the person cannot make choices about because that belongs outside the self (what they are subject to).

In each moment, as we interact with the world, we are all the while spending energy and engaged in a process of actively mapping our experience within our existing frameworks to develop some understanding and interpretation of those events. We are continually calling up the aspects of the frameworks that help us predict and make sense of what we are experiencing. Often, we are doing that in a way that relies on and preserves our frameworks. We select the information we can interpret with our frameworks and use those frameworks to understand what that information means. We often ignore information or interpretations that challenge our frameworks. In a mutually reinforcing cycle, our frameworks tell us how to make sense of what we experience, and then the way we make sense of those experiences bolsters our frameworks. That mutually reinforcing cycle shows why the ways we make sense tend to persist and even resist change and growth. As long as we perceive that the framework works well and allows us to think and feel and do things as we want to, we may never need to overhaul it and develop toward the next stage. When the framework no longer serves us and we do transition from one stage to the next, we retain all of the capacities of the prior stage, but they no longer govern and limit us. We include and reorganize them within a larger, overarching framework that allows us to make new choices but is itself governed and limited by new organizing principles. The four stages of adult meaning making in Kegan's theory (1982, 1994; Kegan & Lahey, 2009; Kegan et al., 2016) are the Imperial Mind, the Socializing Mind, the Self-Authoring Mind, and the Self-Transforming Mind (see Table 7.1).

Stages in Meaning-Making Development

The following sections describe the four developmental stages of adulthood as identified by constructive–developmental theory, emphasizing their relevance to adult learning. The developmental changes that are exclusively relevant to childhood

TABLE 7.1
Four Stages in Adulthood

Stage	*Subject*	*Object*
The Imperial Mind	**Cognitive**: concrete facts, information **Intrapersonal**: concrete needs, preferences, enduring dispositions **Interpersonal**: others have their own points of view (distinct from my own), consistent application of rules for all	**Capacities developed in childhood and adolescence:** perceptions, fantasy movement, impulses, sensations
The Socializing Mind	**Cognitive**: abstractions, internalized beliefs **Intrapersonal**: self-reflexive, internalized values, and identity **Interpersonal**: mutual alignment with important others	**Cognitive**: concrete facts, information **Intrapersonal**: concrete needs, preferences, enduring dispositions **Interpersonal**: others have their own points of view (distinct from my own), consistent application of rules for all
The Self-Authoring Mind	**Cognitive**: abstract systems, self-guided ideology **Intrapersonal**: self-generated and regulated identity, responsibility for own feelings/inner state **Interpersonal**: demonstrating and preserving distinctness and self-governance within relationships	**Cognitive**: abstractions, internalized beliefs **Intrapersonal**: self-reflexive, internalized values, and identity **Interpersonal**: mutual alignment with important others
The Self-Transforming Mind	**Cognitive**: transideological, dialectical **Intrapersonal**: evolution of values/identities as fundamental state **Interpersonal**: exploration of multiple identities among self and others	**Cognitive**: abstract systems, self-guided ideology **Intrapersonal**: self-generated and regulated identity, responsibility for own feelings/inner state **Interpersonal**: demonstrating and preserving distinctness and self-governance within relationships

are not described. Each description includes capacities in the cognitive or intellectual domain, ways learners understand themselves (the intrapersonal domain), and ways learners make sense of and orient to their relationships with others (the interpersonal domain). These different domains are all closely related in the self, which seeks consistency in making sense of experiences. Although people may feel like they bring different sides to themselves in different parts of their lives—in their relationships with family, in their work, in their friendships—Kegan (1994) did not find much variation in the underlying capacities people bring to make sense of these different parts of their lives.

The formal instrument for assessing developmental stages is the Subject–Object Interview (Lahey et al., 1988). The 60- to 90-minute interview requires specific training to administer and analyze. Research using this measure indicates that up to one third of the adult population in the United States has not yet fully developed socializing capacities, and one half to two thirds have not yet fully developed self-authoring capacities (Kegan, 1994). Fewer than 10% have begun to move past the Self-Authoring stage toward the Self-Transforming stage. What that means is that in any given classroom or program, there are likely to be some learners operating predominantly at the Imperial stage, some transitioning to or operating at the Socializing stage, and some transitioning to or operating at the Self-Authoring stage. Few may be operating at or transitioning to the Self-Transforming stage.

The Imperial Mind

Adult learners who make sense of the world with an Imperial Mind understand the world with a focus on the concrete, which is why Piaget (1952) referred to the intellectual capacities possible at this stage as "concrete operational." These learners understand that objects and people have persistent, clear, observable, and measurable characteristics, and the more they know about these features the more they feel they understand something. They feel a sense of mastery when they can learn and apply specific rules or concrete procedures to demonstrate their understanding. For example, in recounting a text they have read, they are able to provide a step-by-step account of all of the points made. They can understand the specific features of an object (e.g., in studying a heart—the typical size, names of various parts, path that blood takes as it flows) and can classify it as belonging to a concrete category (e.g., the category of human organs). They can practice and follow a sequential procedure to solve a math problem or perform a science experiment.

Their goals for their learning are also concrete. Immediate goals might include being able to perform a particular skill, like calculating interest or writing a resume. Concrete, longer term goals might include earning credits, earning a diploma, becoming eligible for a certain type of job, earning more money. Learners with an Imperial Mind can focus on specific and concrete actions needed to reach their goals. Because they are looking for concrete facts and skills, clear instructions and rules to follow, they tend to focus most on those aspects of an assignment ("How many pages? When is this due? What if it is late? Will this be on the test?").

These learners have also formulated a persistent sense of what type of learner they are, as well as how they feel about learning or particular types of teachers. Prior to the development of the Imperial Mind, opinions tend to be very fleeting. At one moment, a learner may feel so sad they seem inconsolable because they don't understand some classwork. Minutes later, they can feel elated if given a different task that they enjoy and can perform. They didn't see themselves as smart then, but they do now. For those with an Imperial Mind, considering themselves to be a good learner means that opinions of themselves persist across time and situations. There is also, then, the related danger that learners who define themselves in negative terms (e.g., "stupid," "hating school," "slow to learn") also persist in that view. It will take lots of specific instances of success to challenge it.

Learners operating with an Imperial Mind can see that others have their own concrete needs and interests too and consider that their relationships should be governed by rules that give each person the same treatment or resources. They expect their instructors to communicate knowledge clearly, giving them rules to follow to get the right answer. They will evaluate themselves, their teachers, their programs of study, and their learning and progress in terms of how well they meet their own concrete goals.

The capacities that those with the Imperial Mind demonstrate are obviously not exclusive to those at this stage of development. Many learners who have moved past this stage will still want and need to know factual information such as due dates and correct procedures for solving a math problem. They can continue to admire and appreciate the concrete features of their subject of study. What distinguishes learners with an Imperial Mind is that they are limited by (subject to) these understandings. As they begin to develop new, more complex capacities, they integrate the capacities of the Imperial Mind within a larger framework, the Socializing Mind.

The Socializing Mind

Adult learners who develop the capacities for making sense of the world with the Socializing Mind no longer conceive of the world as made up only of concrete objects, rules, and opinions. They can organize the concrete features of a topic of study into abstract categories. The ability to think abstractly gives them access to very useful mental functions, like generalizing, creating hypotheses, and making inferences. These are the types of tasks a good curriculum provides learners when they can identify a poem's theme, reason about "x" in math, make inferences about a speaker's intention from a political speech, and entertain hypothetical situations and determine appropriate ways to respond. They also have a more abstract understanding of their inner experiences and emotional states. Learners operating with an Imperial Mind use simpler terms to describe and define themselves, referring to their basic preferences (e.g., "I like math," "I'm good at helping others," "I hate homework"). Those operating with a Socializing Mind are able to understand and use more complex concepts like feeling conflicted, guilty, confident, optimistic, self-conscious, or insecure. These concepts connote not just a feeling but also indicate the person's attitude toward or evaluation of the feeling. To feel "optimistic about my learning" goes beyond the concrete (e.g., feeling good or happy in my learning) and indicates a more complex outlook that combines a good feeling with the idea that I expect some positive event or consequence to occur as I learn.

A learner operating at the Socializing stage can understand a procedure (e.g., creating an outline before a draft) not simply as a rule to follow that will determine their grade; instead, the Socializing learner can see that rules come about and are organized by guiding ideals and values. Creating an outline helps a writer develop greater clarity of thought and communication. To be a good learner then, is not only to follow the rules but also to understand and identify with the guiding values of a subject they are learning and of the classroom or organizational community. These learners can internalize those values so that they matter to them as much as to their teachers.

At the Socializing stage of development, learners have accepted core values of their interpersonal environment and taken them as their own. Having been raised with expectations from their family, closest friends, and surrounding culture, they have internalized these and operate according to them. In their decisions, feelings, actions, relationships, and views, they strive to stay aligned with those values that have shaped them. They have an increased capacity to be self-conscious because they focus on how others (particularly those who matter most to them) view them. If they have internalized values that align with those of the teacher and classroom community, these learners will often seek to build strong rapport with their teachers and classmates and readily feel a sense of inclusion, belonging, and loyalty that supports their learning.

When the values they have internalized conflict with others in their classroom community, those at the Socializing stage can struggle. For example, if family and friends are expecting the learner to choose a specific career, but a beloved teacher suggests a different path, they may struggle to decide whose perspective is more valid. If a Socializing learner was raised with particular religious beliefs that are challenged in course material, they will likely feel some sense of threat or confusion about how to deal with conflicting belief systems.

The Self-Authoring Mind

As learners develop self-authoring capacities, they are no longer limited by those of the Socializing stage. Cognitively, they can relate abstract concepts to each other to form a more complex theory or ideology. For example, they can propose their own views for how a society could effectively include and establish balance among ideals like "freedom," "equality," "security," and "justice." Understanding each of these concepts requires the Socializing capacity for abstract thinking. To be able to organize those abstract concepts into a larger theory that establishes a basis for prioritizing, limiting, or compromising among them requires the ability to conceive of an abstract system.

Self-authorship allows learners to make a greater range of choices about their internal lives as well, monitoring and regulating their inner feelings and states in relationship to their larger goals. There is an internal, central authority that governs all these different parts of the self. Developing capacities to self-author means learners begin to take authority for generating their own values and ideals. The socialization process involves internalizing the values and ideals of the social environment. It is a process in which we are being written upon by the external environment. As a learner develops beyond the Socializing Mind, the values and expectations of those who matter most to them and the governing principles of their social environment are not suddenly unimportant. They are just no longer ultimate and absolute. The self-authoring learner can mediate among those perspectives, evaluating them according to their own framework or identity, establishing ideological consistency and coherence.

Instead of monitoring only how a teacher (or other source of authority) views them as the measure for their self-evaluation, they can now monitor themselves in terms of how effectively they are living out their own self-selected objectives. In the face of external pressure to fall in line with what others hope or expect them to do, self-authoring learners can retain the choice to follow or resist those expectations. So, for example, the learner may consciously choose to set limits on the amount of homework they do or time they spend preparing for class if those particular activities are not of high priority to them.

Self-authoring learners can self-direct and often want their instructors to provide them with opportunities for independent thinking, to encourage them to evaluate the validity of an argument. They have developed their own larger goals or vision and can undertake projects that serve those goals. They may still carry out these plans in highly collaborative ways, and their own goals may overlap with others' (e.g., parents', teachers', or peers'). But some may prefer to work independently and show impatience or dismiss others' ideas as a way to defend their own sense of authority.

When situations or relationship don't go well, self-authoring learners can take responsibility for their part in creating the problem and in coming to a solution. Self-authorship allows them to see what things they have said and done that may have contributed to this situation and to know that they can always choose how to respond. They can choose to disappoint others' expectations in order to uphold their own. They have developed the internal authority for making the choice, and that allows them to set boundaries or limits between themselves and others.

To be clear, developing this psychological boundary does not require them to put up physical boundaries. They don't need to quit school or their jobs, file for divorce, or reject their parents. They don't need to become steely, go-it-alone types who disdain help from others. They might actually experience greater intimacy and closeness in relationships, particularly where they experience difference or disagreement. Disagreement does not immediately signal a lack of closeness or that something is wrong with the relationship. Self-authorship allows learners to see they need not share others' beliefs in order to feel close.

The Self-Transforming Mind

The development of self-transforming capacities includes those of the Socializing and Self-Authoring stages, integrating them within a larger framework that includes and is shaped by new capacities. Instead of assigning or projecting what is not consistent with a self-authored identity outside of themselves, those at the Self-Transforming stage can reject the assumption that these seemingly distinct identities are each fundamentally separate and whole. They now understand that the persistent experience of difference is evidence of a boundary they have been drawing that now unacceptably limits them from fuller understandings.

Self-transforming capacities allow individuals to identify the limits and partiality of any ideological stance, including those they have most favored. Self-authoring adults choose and regularly exercise certain frames through which they view the world and with which they establish credibility and expertise. These are often closely related to their professional choices, in becoming an economist or a lawyer, for example, as they learn and make regular use of the internal logics of these professions. Adults adopt political stances—as liberals or conservatives, as social activists or traditionalists. If these are self-authored stances, the adult will seek consistency and coherence across the stances they take and spend energy to deflect criticisms of these perspectives. In classroom discussions, it is often easy to predict what particular stances self-authored learners will adopt and defend, based on their ideological and political positions. To move beyond those capacities as a self-transforming learner is to welcome those criticisms. At this stage, adults look to challenge the central tenets of their own preferred stances and find ways to develop cross-frame perspectives that consider and capitalize on more information and perspectives, organizing them in more complex frameworks that integrate multiple ideological frameworks. What learners had seen as opposing perspectives are now included in a framework that honors and relates them, such as principles underlying liberalism and conservativism, social activism and tradition. Self-transforming learners are freer to take stances that do not fall within any one ideological framework or political party.

The learner at the Self-Transforming stage does not regard any stance or perspective as equally valid and useful. That type of relativism is characteristic of the Socializing stage and is outgrown as a learner develops a means of assessing and evaluating perspectives. In the Self-Transforming stage the learner is using that means of assessment in relationship with other means of assessment to create a more complex ability to assess (not to abandon assessment). Self-transforming capacities are also not the same as a deconstructive stance, where someone asserts that there can be no satisfactory stance or position they can take because all possibilities are limited, biased, power laden, and therefore unacceptable. Sometimes the transition toward the Self-Transforming stage involves distrust in and decentering of prior frameworks as part of the process of growth toward a more complex framework. But in moving more fully into the stage, the learner develops the capacity to recognize that any ideological stance will be limited and so build frameworks that coordinate across multiple ideologies, even among those that had formerly seemed incompatible or even contradictory. No longer limited by the internal consistency of any belief system and the drive to reinforce that system, the self-transforming adult can be open and oriented to how inconsistencies within and across belief systems fuel new learning and growth.

Self-transforming learners are no longer subject to the identities they had previously authored. Imagine a learner who has considered themselves a very competent intellectual, someone who excels at learning and demonstrates understanding of even difficult academic material. If that person is bound by self-authoring capacities, they spend energy preserving that identity. That could mean they discount others' attempts to demonstrate skill in learning, particularly if those skills reflect different definitions of what learning looks like and how to measure it. It could also mean that the learner avoids experiences that would illuminate their vulnerabilities—experiences that might reveal what they struggle to understand, where they feel incompetent and need help from others. If that same learner begins to develop self-transforming capacities, they would no longer feel threatened by being clumsy, incompetent, or naïve in any of these areas; instead, they would actually be intrigued and drawn to these experiences as they are released from fear and the pretense that they have full control over events, outcomes, and others. Now the learner is looking to evolve by embracing what they had formerly needed to exclude. Similarly, the learner who had constructed a self-authoring identity as a helper to others may come to see how that identity has limited them from embracing their own helplessness, their dependence on others. The learner who prized their own self-authoring identity as a disciplined workaholic may come to see how that identity has limited their ability to revel and lose themselves in pleasurable sensation and experience.

Self-transforming learners develop new conceptions of their relationships. There is no longer potential to feel internal threat to one's own experience of distinctness and autonomy to protect against; instead, these learners are eager to construct relationships in which they don't need to adopt and play out a consistent role (as, e.g., "a leader in the classroom," "an intellectual," or "a humanitarian"). The self-transforming learner is therefore looking for opportunities in their relationships to take on less developed identities within themselves and explore new frameworks and perspectives that can be transformative.

Transformation and Growth Cultures

Every adult learner can develop new capacities and frameworks, evolving or transforming to a new stage in their meaning making. But a person is not likely to reach the limits of their current framework for sense-making unless they have powerful and enduring experiences that demonstrate their framework is inadequate for helping them to think and feel and do the things they want to. They need to experience challenges that are both persistent and confounding, challenges that cannot be managed without undertaking the struggle to develop a more complex framework.

The term *transformation* is often connected with adult learning and can refer to many types of change. Kegan (1982, 1994) used it to refer to a particular type of change or growth, a shift in the underlying structure that shapes a person's ways of making meaning. In this view, learning is not considered transformational if it is a change in what someone knows (but not how they know). It is not considered transformational solely based on how powerful or valuable it feels to the learner or educator. When the term *transformative* is used in connection with Paulo Freire's (1981, 1989) or Jack Mezirow's (1991; Mezirow & Associates, 1990) work it refers to the development of critical understanding of the cultural context, a heightened awareness that can lead to greater political and social democratization. The process by which these changes occur shares some features of the developmental understanding of transformation in that they involve shifts of consciousness. (See chapter 12 for more information on transformative learning.) In fact, they share features of one particular shift—from the Socializing to the Self-Authoring stage—as learners demonstrate their capacity for self-directed learning, critical thinking, and reflection on imbalances of power and authority.

Kegan (1982, 1994) used the term *holding environment* or *growth culture* (Kegan et al., 2016) to refer to the ways that learning contexts can serve to nurture developmental growth. Kegan and colleagues referred to the elements of this environment as home, edge, and groove. If they are to succeed, every member of the community bears some responsibility for contributing to and participating in a growth culture. When the surrounding culture confirms an individual's way of knowing, it creates a sense of home, acknowledging and cultivating the capacities that individuals already possess and demonstrate. Learners feel that there are enough safety, trust, and care in the community to feel they can participate in honest and authentic ways. They can welcome the vulnerability necessary for growth. The community can also serve as a spur to growth when it offers experiences and information that invite learners to the edge of their meaning making, providing them with challenges that encourage them to revise their understandings and spur them to move beyond the limitations of their current ways of making sense. While everyone can feel unsettled as they encounter the difficulties and vulnerabilities in facing old, unproductive patterns, everyone can also experience the excitement and energy of development and growth. Occasions that are both supportive and challenging cannot be infrequent or irregular if all learners are to grow. The culture must also establish a groove, providing regular opportunities for practice that serve to build greater levels of support and challenge necessary to nurture and maintain the new capacities learners are building.

Critiques and Responses

Critics of adult development theory have argued that stage theories oversimplify the incredible variation of adult experience. They point out that some theories are based on limited samples that are largely Western, white, and male and so reflect biases and blind spots such as overvaluing individualism over collectivism or relational values. As a result, they challenge the idea that these theories are generalizable outside of those populations. Issues of bias are particularly concerning because developmental theories are not simply descriptive but also make normative claims. If each stage affords individuals new perspectives and capacities beyond those of prior stages, then theories of development are making value judgments that in some way privilege those adults who have evolved to higher stages and indicate the usefulness of catalyzing development.

Many of these concerns were first raised in response to Piaget's (1952) work, and the resulting debates, dialogues, and research have helped the field of developmental psychology to evolve. Kegan's emphasis on the subject–object relationship as the underlying marker of developmental change reframes these debates by clarifying the distinction between what someone focuses on and the why or how of their focus. An adult can focus on and deeply cherish relationships or tend toward a more separate, individualist orientation or (as is probably the case for most adults) display some mix of these preferences. According to Kegan (1982, 1994), our preferences can be attributed to a variety of factors, including, for example, one's personality, culture, gender orientation, and past experiences. One type of preference is not inherently more developed than another. And as we evolve, what develops isn't necessarily about what preferences we have. What matters in determining developmental stages and what evolves as we grow is how we make sense of those preferences. An individualist who has unquestioningly absorbed the individualistic expectations of their parents or surrounding culture is no more developed than the collectivist who has absorbed the expectations of their parents and surrounding culture. In Kegan's model, both are making sense of their world at the Socializing Stage. An adult who is able to reflect on their socialization and make choices aligned with an internal source of authority—whether that choice be in preference for a relational, collectivist orientation or a more separate, individualistic orientation—makes sense of the world at the Self-Authoring Stage.

Kegan was also clear that development (especially higher stage development) does not happen automatically. While some forms of human development, such as the physical changes that happen in puberty, naturally begin to unfold for the vast majority of adolescents, psychological development in adulthood depends much more on the types of challenges and forms of support experienced. The adult who grows up in an insular and homogenous community, adopting the preferred roles and belief systems of that community, may not experience many challenges to develop beyond the Socializing Stage. The adult who regularly explores perspectives and cultures that differ from their own, who welcomes feedback about their flaws or limitations both in what and how they think, is more likely to develop beyond the Socializing Stage toward and perhaps beyond the Self-Authoring Stage.

It is therefore perfectly reasonable to expect that the distribution of developmental stages in a population is going to vary across different cultures and environments. When the issue of development is not framed either as an innate process or as an individual triumph, but is seen instead as spurred by interactions between individuals and their environments, we can also reframe claims and concerns about the normative aspects of Kegan's developmental stage model. Kegan was particularly clear that these value judgments are confined to a specific claim about the complexity of an individual's meaning-making system. The relevant question then becomes, when and how does psychological complexity (i.e., stage of development) matter? When and how does the theory's normative power matter?

The relevance of developmental stage depends on the challenges an individual actually faces and is expected to face within their culture. Developmental progression can permit us to feel that we are leading lives that allow us to flourish personally and to be fully functioning, healthy, productive members of our society. Kegan's (1994) argument is that modern societies are organized according to principles that correspond with a need for adults who can function at the Self-Authoring Stage. In his book *In Over Our Heads*, he analyzed the modern expectations adults face in the major domains of life (including working, parenting, partnering, learning, as well as acting as citizens in an increasingly diverse world). He argued that these roles are sufficiently complex that they require us to develop equally complex psychological capacities if we are to be able to function effectively. For example, the heterogeneity in modern life in the United States means that most adults will regularly interact with people whose habits, viewpoints, and values are quite different from their own. If we can see these differences as assets we can further our learning, be more effective at work, and protect and defend everyone's civil rights. If we cannot look at and evaluate our own beliefs and values to see whether and where they are biased and undermine our ability to live and work with others, we extend the suffering of some groups and our society as a whole. From an equity and social justice perspective it is hard to make the case that those who have not developed those capacities should not feel challenged to do so.

It is also hard to make the case that our world is growing less complex and that there is reason to believe that the need for adults to continue to develop will wane. In our personal and work lives, many of us feel the need to do more with less, to learn new ways of communicating and producing knowledge, to outpace, or at least be able to respond to, the changes happening all around us. The myriad pressing problems we face in the 21st century—such as climate change and global pandemics—all point to the urgency of more adults developing the psychological capacities to address them using more complex interpretations and responses.

Application

An awareness of adult development can inform adult educators' practice and their expectations of learners. There are consistent and predictable ways in which learners at the same developmental position share important ways of understanding themselves, their learning, and their environment. These similarities reach across many aspects of learners' lives, including the ways they conceive of their learning experiences, their aspirations, their classrooms and teachers, the programs and institutions in which they are enrolled, and their relationships to their own and other cultures.

For example, learners operating primarily at the Imperial or Socializing Stage may be more responsive to a teacher-driven approach, while learners making meaning at the Self-Authoring Stage may prefer a learner-driven approach. A learner at the Imperial Stage can be expected to take responsibility for their learning by making sure to follow the teacher's rules and by completing assignments according to the given instructions. A learner at the Socializing or Self-Authoring Stage could also demonstrate these same types of responsibility, although they would not challenge the learner to their fullest developmental capacity. If the instructional design of a class or program favors learners at one developmental stage over those at another, there may be ways to make sure learners at other developmental stages are also engaged. Considerations of how to pace the introduction of new forms of thinking, such as self-reflection or critical inquiry, can also benefit from a developmental perspective. Program designers and teachers who are aware of the enhanced developmental capacities these goals imply can better, or more fairly, set expectations for the time it will take to help learners build these skills.

It is likely that most adult classrooms will include learners at different levels across the developmental spectrum. For teachers who aim to extend themselves to the broadest possible range of learners, a developmental perspective can serve to lend meaning to potentially puzzling differences in learner responses to the teacher's practice and presence. It may serve to build tolerance for these differences and point to possibilities for enhancing flexibility in teaching style. A teacher who can support all learners in a class, across a range of ways of knowing, can increase the chances that more learners will feel recognized and valued for the meanings they bring to their learning. Learners who are adequately and appropriately supported and challenged academically are likely to learn more and feel more competent.

Adult educators can also determine how well their programs and coursework prepares learners for the roles and careers they seek. What types of developmental challenges are inherent in these sought-after roles? For learners who do not yet possess the capacity to address the complexity of the challenges they will be facing, educators and program leaders can determine what additional forms of developmental support and challenge can be incorporated into their classes and programs. Kegan and Lahey (2009) formulated the Immunity to Change approach to support development and increase individuals' capacities. The process helps uncover the hidden commitments and assumptions that limit growth and ability to address the complex challenges we face and to develop a new relationship to those assumptions, to hold them as object. In other words, Immunity to Change is a developmental curriculum tailored to the events and conditions of an individual's life, the situations or issues where they feel most frustrated and stuck. The initial exercise—creating an Immunity to Change map—illuminates the limitations of a person's current mental frameworks in relationship to their goal for improvement. The exercises that follow provide a means to move past those limitations, creating the larger (more differentiated and integrated) frameworks that enable them to resolve their frustration, reach their stated goals, and more effectively address the complex demands they face in their lives. The increasing complexity of the demands we all face at individual, organizational, regional, and global levels means we will need more communities and cultures undertaking developmental work if we are to evolve the psychological capacities we will need to survive and thrive.

Ultimately, the ability of educators to support others' development may depend heavily on the educators' own developmental journeys. Educators who regularly invite, experience, and model transformational change in their own lives have first-hand knowledge of how to support learners' growth. Kegan et al. (2016) described the organizational conditions that best incubate adult development. In deliberately developmental organizations, characterized by regular routines, practices, and relationships, there is sufficient support and safety for everyone to actively develop in the course of their daily work. In deliberately developmental organizations all adults are working to change the behaviors that block their performance at work as well as the underlying beliefs, attitudes, or mindsets that lead to behavioral or performance weaknesses. Leaders model their own vulnerability and ongoing learning, each employee's authentic and whole self is welcome, errors are seen as opportunities to learn and grow, and conflict and disagreement are invited and explored. Making the interior life of everyone the focus for improvement spurs the development of mental complexity while simultaneously leading to greater success in realizing the organization's mission. A similar approach can be implemented in formal and informal educational contexts. As educators undertake their own developmental work, they gain greater skill and understanding in how to support the psychological capacities they and the learners need to survive and thrive in an increasingly complex world.

References

Belenky, M., Clinchy, B., Goldberger, N., & Tarule, J. (1986). *Women's ways of knowing: The development of self, mind, and voice.* Basic Books.

Cook-Greuter, S. (1999). *Postautonomous ego development: A study of its nature and measurement.* Harvard University Press.

Fowler, J. (1981). *Stages of faith: The psychology of human development and the quest for meaning.* Harper & Row.

Freire, P. (1981). *Education for critical consciousness.* Continuum.

Freire, P. (1989). *Pedagogy of the oppressed.* Continuum.

Gilligan, C. (1982). *In a different voice: Psychological theory and women's development.* Harvard University Press.

Harris, L. S., & Kuhnert, K. W. (2008). Looking through the lens of leadership: A constructive developmental approach. *Leadership & Organization Development Journal, 29*(1), 47–67. https://doi.org/10.1108/01437730810845298

Joiner, B., & Josephs, S. (2007). *Leadership agility: Five levels of mastery for anticipating and initiating change.* Wiley.

Kegan, R. G. (1977). *Ego and truth: Personality and the Piaget paradigm; a thesis exploring the usefulness of the concept of equilibration for the theory and study of personality.* Harvard University Press.

Kegan, R. (1982). *The evolving self: Problem and process in human development.* Harvard University Press.

Kegan, R. (1994). *In over our heads: The mental demands of modern life.* Harvard University Press.

Kegan, R., Broderick, M., Drago-Severson, E., Helsing, D., Popp, N., Portnow, K., & Associates. (2001). *Toward a "new pluralism" in the ABE/ESL classroom: Teaching to multiple "cultures of mind"—A constructive developmental approach.* The National Center for the Study of Adult Learning and Literacy.

Kegan, R., & Lahey, L. L. (2009). *Immunity to change: How to overcome it and unlock the potential in yourself and your organization.* Harvard Business School Press.

Kegan, R., Lahey, L. L., Miller, M. L., Fleming, A., & Helsing, D. (2016). *An everyone culture: Becoming a deliberately developmental organization.* Harvard Business Review Press.

Kohlberg, L. (1981). *The philosophy of moral development.* Harper & Row.

Lahey, L. L., Souvaine, E., Kegan, R., Goodman, R., & Felix, S. (1988). *A guide to the Subject–Object Interview: Its administration and interpretation.* Minds at Work.

Loevinger, J. (1976). *Ego development: Conceptions and theories.* Jossey-Bass.

Magolda, M. B. (1992). *Knowing and reasoning in college: Gender-related patterns in students' intellectual development.* Jossey-Bass.

Mezirow, J. (1991). *Transformative dimensions of adult learning.* Jossey-Bass.

Mezirow, J., & Associates. (1990). *Fostering critical reflection in adulthood: A guide to transformative and emancipatory learning.* Jossey-Bass.

Perry, W. (1970). *Forms of intellectual and ethical development in the college years: A scheme.* Holt, Rinehart & Winston.

Piaget, J. (1952). *The origins of intelligence in children.* International Universities Press.

Torbert, B., & Associates. (2004). *Action inquiry: The secret of timely and transforming leadership.* Berrett-Koehler.

Author's Additional Resource Suggestions

Beck, D., & Cowan, C. (1996). *Spiral dynamics: Mastering values, leadership, and change: Exploring the new science of memetics.* Blackwell.

Helsing, D. (2010). Human development. In R. A. Couto (Ed.), *Political and civic leadership: A reference handbook* (Vol. 2, pp. 678–687). SAGE.

Helsing, D. (2018). Psychological approaches for overturning an immunity to change. *Harvard Educational Review, 88*(2), 184–209. https://doi.org/10.17763/1943-5045-88.2.184

Helsing, D., Drago-Severson, E., & Kegan, R. (2004). Applying constructive–developmental theories of adult development to ABE and ESOL practices. In J. Comings, B. Garner, & C. Smith (Eds.), *Review of adult learning and literacy: Connecting research, policy, and practice* (Vol. 4, pp. 157–197). Erlbaum.

Helsing, D., Howell, A., Kegan, R., & Lahey, L. (2008). Putting the development in professional development: Understanding and overturning educational leaders' immunities to change. *Harvard Educational Review, 78*(3), 437–465. https://doi.org/10.17763/haer.78.3.888l759g1qm54660

Helsing, D., & Lahey, L. (2010). Unlocking leadership potential: Overcoming immunities to change. In K. Bunker, D. T. Hall, & K. E. Kram (Eds.), *Extraordinary leadership: Addressing the gaps in senior executive development* (pp. 69–94). Jossey-Bass.

Kegan, R., & Lahey, L. L. (2001, November). The real reason people won't change. *Harvard Business Review*, 85–92. https://hbr.org/2001/11/the-real-reason-people-wont-change

Wilber, K. (2000). *Integral psychology: Consciousness, spirit, psychology, therapy*. Shambhala.

Editors' Key Seminal and Supplemental Text Suggestions

Drago-Severson, E. (2009). *Leading adult learning*. Corwin/SAGE.

- Chapter 2: How Constructive Developmental Theory Informs the Pillar Practices

Kegan, R. (1983). *Evolving self*. Harvard University Press.

- Chapter 3: The Constitutions of the Self

Smith, M. C., & Taylor, K. (2010). Adult development. In C. E. Kasworm, A. D. Rose, & J. M. Ross-Gordon (Eds.), *Handbook of adult and continuing education* (pp. 49–58). SAGE.

PART THREE

Adult Learning Processes and Approaches

8

STRUCTURED SILENCES IN ADULT LEARNING THEORY

Edith Gnanadass and Lisa R. Merriweather

Education is often understood as a practice-oriented discipline informed by theory, though more emphasis is seemingly placed on the pragmatic aspects of practice than the theoretical (Gouthro, 2019; Tennant, 2019). According to Tennant (2019), "The emphasis is generally pragmatic . . . an eclectic understanding of how adults best learn; this may be followed by a tentative list of principles to be adopted or procedures to be employed when teaching adults" (p. 2). While our practices are what are most visible, it is our understanding of the theories that guide them and increase their effectiveness. In this chapter, we describe the criticality of theory, highlight structured silences in adult learning theory, and reimagine theory from a broader sociocultural perspective in adult education.

Criticality of Theory

Theories can be formal or informal, implicit or explicit, personal or more broadly based, informing actions both consciously and unconsciously (Gouthro, 2019). Personal theories are a compilation of ideas that arise from our experiences with the world around us, including, but not limited to, media, family and friends, experiences with phenomena, and reading, while "formal theories are theories that have evolved within particular academic disciplines and have gained credibility by their usage through the work of other scholars" (Gouthro, 2019, p. 61). Formal theories might be thought of as mainstream, accepted, and canonical. Even though theories are reductive, capturing only tiny shards of reality, they help organize our reality and determine how to best act on it. Theories and their application are therefore contextual, variable, and evolving, and they apply uniquely to people or circumstances. Theories should be understood as speaking to place, time, and people. They exist in every academic discipline, including education.

Lockey et al. (2021) stated that

> "Educational theory" is an overarching term that describes a collection of theories that explain the application, interpretation, and purpose of learning and education. . . . As such, they are important as they enable us to understand, evaluate, and improve the methods of teaching. (p. 1)

When one thinks about education theory, generally, learning as construct and activity is spotlighted. Illeris (2018) posited, "How various kinds of learning take place in the human brain and body is the basic question of learning theory" (p. 86) and demonstrated how our understanding of learning has shape-shifted with context: place, time, and people, an observation noted also by Gouthro (2019). Illeris (2018) specified,

> All learning always comprises three dimensions: the content dimension, which is usually, but not always, cognitive; the incentive dimension, which includes engagement, interest and motivation and is mainly emotional; and the interaction dimension, which is social . . . and may have many layers, ranging from the immediate situation, the local, institutional, environmental, national and other conditions to the global context in general. (p. 96)

Given this, it is difficult to understand how the relationship between theory and educational practice is not consistently recognized. However, it is not uncommon for practitioners to develop and facilitate instruction with a lack of intentionality toward theory integration (Gouthro, 2019). In part, this may be because theory is often dismissed by educators as being too far removed from the day-to-day activities and challenges involved and confronted in instruction; that is, educators may often fail to see how learning theories are involved in the everyday practical elements of teaching and learning. Another challenge is that theory language is seen as abstract, and foundational ideas may be unfamiliar, working against the more practical aims of learning, spurring resistance from learners and educators alike (Gouthro, 2019). Dismissing theory detracts from the power of practice and its potential to be grounded as theories provide the rationale and support for practices. In short, theory explains why we do what we do, why we think what we think, and why we value what we value.

Educational theory has the potential to support educators seeking to improve their practice in terms of knowledge, dispositions, and skills by providing a framework for evaluating what they do and how they do it. However, it is not always clear how educators can use theory to improve practice, make decisions, implement instruction, and increase capacity for learning as well as increase learning itself. Theory and practice become disconnected phenomena for many educators. Yet educational theories provide vehicles for asking and answering questions relative to what the educator believes about how people learn, what strategies are most effective, and what environments are most conducive to learning or, as Gouthro (2019) stated, learning theory "enables educators to understand the complexity of the teaching and learning process" (p. 60).

Our espoused theories, "those that an individual claims to follow," and theories-in-use, "those that can be inferred from action" (Argyris et al., 1985, p. 82), constrain or expand our educational approaches. What we know and what we have been exposed to relative to theories, and what theories have been promoted by virtue of their presence as useful and appropriate, provide the parameters in which we function as educators or, as Touriñán López (2020) indicated, theories have "consequences for pedagogical functions, pedagogical intervention, and pedagogical discourse" (p. 212). The idea of import for Touriñán López is the principle of signification: "Signification . . . is associated with the validity of the knowledge of education and it is defined as the *capacity to solve education problems*" (p. 212, emphasis in original). Touriñán López elaborated on this principle of signification as

> a position that assumes the complexity of the object of knowledge in education and at the same time claims for it the meaning of a practical activity, the resolution of which requires knowledge linked to practice and the theoretical consistency of the intervention. (p. 246)

Signification occurs if the theory–practice connection remains intact, is useful, and is reliable for its intended object, which is learning. An example of how signification operates can be found in the extent to which individualism is privileged in classrooms. In communalistic societies, the theory–practice connection is likely to be weak and not as useful, and hence signification may be low. Signification highlights the meaning value of the theory within practice, begging the questions, for whom and for what does a particular theory have value? It is those questions that create pathways for theories to become incorporated into the everyday lexicon of a field, resulting in theories with high meaning value for the dominant hegemonic group, becoming formalized, canonized, and mainstreamed within the field of practice.

It is our contention that the signification assigned to the formal theories of adult learning may be low for racially minoritized and other marginalized adult learners. Theories emanating from the experiences of the marginalized, the subaltern populations, are often considered niche and particularized, whereas the more accepted and widely disseminated theories are seen as having more universal signification. Because educators' practices are informed by theory, and theory is linked to signification, those for whom signification is present reap the greatest benefits from the instructional strategies and plans informed by said theory. Our concern, as we discuss in this chapter, is the failure to acknowledge theory and its influence on implementation of effective practice for all adult learners. However, that is just a small part of the challenge faced by adult educators; the larger concern is the theories themselves and their signification, resulting in sanctioning of some theories at the expense of others. When the pool of theories is shallow, so too is the pool of learners who benefit from them. When by practice some theories are considered normative, castigating by default others as alternative, messages of sanctification are sent, and structured silences are created.

Structured Silences in Adult Learning Theory

As this volume demonstrates, there is a mosaic of theories available to assist adult educators in establishing tenets for practice, each speaking to priorities that reveal themselves in particular practices: learner centered, teacher centered, and learner led (Lockey et al., 2021); and particular orientations: affective, cognitive, and social (Tennant, 2019). Belzer and Dashew, additionally, outlined three essential commitments in chapter 1: humanism—the potentiality of human beings for positive change; critical pedagogy—the potentiality to be part of the project of broad-based social justice and equity; and reflection—the potentiality of reflection as a vehicle for accomplishing adult education aims. Several elements of Lockey et al.'s (2021) practices, Tennant's (2019) orientations, and Belzer and Dashew's commitments course through the veins of many of the formalized adult education learning and development theories described in this book, theories commonly accepted as theories-in-use in adult education, theories with promise for adult education, and theories as foundational to adult education. Understanding the ways in which the commitments, and thus the adult learning theories with which they are in relationship, lean into hegemonic normativity and hegemonic signification begins the process of breaking the structured silences of adult learning theory.

Hegemonic Signification

Many adult education learning theories reflect the Grecian and Roman conception of *humanism*, a philosophy deemed foundational to Western culture (read as white, European in origin). Humanism acknowledges the centrality of self, including emotions and lived experiences, and individualism. Individualism as a value is core to humanism in its push for personal growth—the ability to reason and self-actualize. Consistent with this philosophical perspective is also the possibility for positive change often facilitated through democratic means. Prizing individualism, agency, freedom, and autonomy among other values, humanism is evident in the canonical theories of adult education: andragogy, self-directed learning, experiential learning, and transformational learning. Even in contemporary emerging adult learning theories, such as profound learning (Kroth & Carr-Chellman, 2018, 2020) and neuroplasticity (Johnson & Taylor, 2006), humanism's focus on promotion of self is present.

Commitments to reflection and critical pedagogy, as typically practiced in adult education, privilege, though not in equal measure, individualism and the individual self. Reflection often surfaces as an individual endeavor, marking the willingness and capacity of adult learners as individuals to engage, typically centering the self in service to self. And even though many critical pedagogy–informed theories draw from Freire (1970), who emphasized collective action for emancipation, adult educators often tend to characterize the task as making space for individual agency and voice. In doing so, the original intent of Freire's critical pedagogy loses the emancipatory power of the collective.

While we do not find the commitments to humanism, critical pedagogy, or reflection objectionable, or the many adult learning theories considered to be foundational and/or emerging that reflect the identified commitments, we wonder if they suggest values, both espoused and enacted, of those historically privileged and hegemonically empowered. Do they signify a particular set of values? Many adult learning theories are marked by a homogeneity that promotes normativity and exclusion in the form of centering Western, Eurocentric ideology. Since both the theories and the commitments are enshrined in a hegemonic system of values, they are both inextricably connected by those values. We do not know which came first, the commitments or the theories that reflect them, much like the chicken or the egg, but it seems clear that they are bedfellows implicated by Touriñán López's (2020) principle of signification.

Gouthro (2019) said, "Formal theories of learning may resonate with what people have experienced and fit comfortably with their perspectives or existing worldviews" (p. 66). Because of this, the meaning value of the popular and canonized theories are more easily accepted and less likely to face resistance and critique, especially if the people who experienced it and for whom it fits comfortably are white, in power, or otherwise not "othered." Theories are less often formalized or integrated when they incite resistance and negative emotions in the majoritarian population group (Gouthro, 2019). When theories are formalized, their dissemination and use are more widespread, as is their credibility. They become part of the taken-for-granted vernacular, representative of the field and values of those accepting them. They also become less malleable as they become canonized by scholars and practitioners (Gouthro, 2019), coming to represent narrowed conceptions of truth relative to learning, often lacking inclusivity while possessing hegemonic normativity.

Listening for Silence

Jansen (1989) described structured silence as "absence of critical consciousness" (p. 196), an absence resulting in "the reproduction of old patterns of power and privilege in the social distribution of knowledge" (p. 196). The silence is structured by postcolonial social and political structures such as myth making, history telling, policy formation, historically situated seats of power-wielding decision making, curriculum, and language. Structured silences suggest a need for regular engagement in self-assessment. When studying adult learning theories, one should ask what are their commitments, whom do they best represent, and whose interests are best served by them as practiced. As adult educators, we should interrogate signification of theories and listen for their silences. A first step is developing critical awareness of assumptions undergirding theories, asking what adult learning theories are considered representative of the field and what values they extol.

Critical awareness of assumptions is important in the current sociocultural context but might not be a common practice. Adult educators require theories that take into consideration the multilayered context of the "place" of adult learning—physical, geopolitical, sociopolitical, sociocultural, socioemotional, and historical—as well as the context of the "person," which includes identity markers, power and privilege, and accessibility. A critical look at the reverence for humanism as a universal, for example, reveals assumptions that contribute to structured silences. Postcolonial structures of power that manifest between people based on positionality are not developed as meaningful constructs within humanism, limiting how marginalized people and cultures have been able to inform the field. This absence in theories rooted in humanism influences how adult educators understand adult learners who may be marginalized and participating in hegemonic-driven learning systems.

Additionally, though commonly referenced terms like *diversity* and *inclusion* are interspersed throughout adult education's historical narrative, suggesting emphasis on sociocultural context, little focus is directed toward unpacking diversity in terms of equity or social justice as a core process of adult education. Diversity is understood as having a long history within adult education, but adult education has historically failed to routinely include theories that take a deep look into difference and marginality and how they matter or demand the same of formalized theories, especially in relation to pressing contemporary and historically situated issues like race and racism, gender identity and transphobia, homophobia, and xenophobia. In many cases, adult learning theories adopt the add-and-stir method for diversity, resulting in a form of structured silence. Diversity was included but did not belong within the canon; it was positioned as an afterthought, not a forethought, hunkering in the background as opposed to being showcased in the foreground. Diversity and the issues it more often obscures—equity and social justice—are not integral to andragogy, self-directed learning, transformational learning, and experiential learning.

We submit that the essence of many adult learning theories would change if the colonial predispositions that frame them were routinely named and resisted. A critical self-appraisal demonstrates how few race-based or other-based theories that often engage in naming and resisting are considered representative of the field. Little emphasis of the commonly accepted theories is aimed toward racial justice or equity, failing to speak to how different positionalities impact what an individual can do within adult education or how. Having awareness of what adult learning theories are deemed representative is an important step toward identifying structured silences.

A second step is critique and questioning of the mainstream, Western-centric, hegemonic disposition of many of the traditional and emerging adult learning theories. We should be intentional in looking for what is missing and questioning why it is absent. We offer race as an example. Few adult learning theories consider identities existing within racialized space and time. What is present to a small degree is Tennant's (2019) bifurcated taxonomy of learning theories, which either fore-grounded "the person or the social environment" (p. 4), seeing "the person as . . . largely independent of the social environment" (p. 5) or the social environment as the driver of the person. Personhood in many adult learning theories is neglected in favor of characteristics such as emotions and cognitive functions, whereas the signifi-cance of lived spaces and places is dismissed to give way to external forces. In doing so, adult learning theories stay an arm's length away from material and psychological realities of marginalized groups of Black and Brown learners, avoiding being holistic in orientation. Further, the person is almost always normative to white people, and the environment is typically generalized, with little attention paid to white suprem-acy, anti-Black racism, and systemic perpetuation of inequity. Scant consideration is evidenced to persons as marginalized beings or their level and access to privilege in the social environment. Students of adult learning theory are left to imagine how these theories extend beyond the margins of conventionality, hegemony, and pre-sumed universality. Tennant (2019) wrote,

> Education as an activity explicitly links the individual with the social. In particular, adult education is seen as a vehicle for explicitly addressing significant social issues connected to areas such as the environment, race, health, gender, class, the aged, the unemployed, and the dislocation and exploitation of migrants. (p. 6)

Yet few adult theories rise to that charge. Formalized adult learning theories tend to suffer from not-so-benign neglect wherein issues of equity and racialized social justice do not even rise to the level of being conspicuous by their absence. They tend to represent learning from an individualistic perspective, with little attention devoted to how learning occurs communally, for racially minoritized people or other people existing outside the margins. Communalism is a neglected value that offers a differ-ent cultural orientation to learning that may heighten awareness of what is missing.

A third question one should ask is, where are the sociocultural theories, race-based theories, or decolonizing theories in the field of adult education? They reside beyond the borders of canonical theories and their commitments. As a field, adult education disappointingly has missed opportunities to be more equitable of perspec-tives and to create spaces for theories informed by nonwhite, nonprivileged ideology. The existence of these theories on and beyond the margins is a structured silence.

This raises questions of how effectively adult education theories can practically engage in critical pedagogy, democratizing, or a more richly informed humanism. In chapter 1, Belzer and Dashew suggest that there has been a historical and ongo-ing practice of authorial decentralization and ideology challenging in the field, but mainstream adult learning theories do not reflect this. The majority of adult learning theories were developed by white men, begging the question, what is the state of adult education? If the roll call of formalized adult learning theories is any indication, one would be blind not to notice who and what have been included and who and what have not. Vague, ambiguous, and generalized referential overtures to equity and social justice, to racially minoritized people, to social circumstances that circumvent meaningful access and belonging, and the absence of sociocultural theories, race-based theories, or decolonizing theories ring hollow and result in these important issues being bypassed along the road of theory to practice.

Hegemonic signification is prevalent through the sanctioned mainstream adult learning theories that emanate from Western imperialistic colonial thinking. Because of this, it should come as no surprise that the most readily accepted and formalized adult learning theories fail to include subaltern framing and people groups who are relegated to the margins of society. Nor should one be surprised that a foundation built on Western imperialistic colonial thinking produces structured silences that result in critical omissions of people, cultures, and environments. While some might not be convinced of our argument, we contend that structural silences do exist and are most loudly heard by those existing within the deafening silence, whose philosophical priorities and communal experiences are inadequately attended to by the commitments and the canonized theories that encapsulate them.

We suggest the field of adult education consider how theory can be used redistributively; that is, adult theories should be constructed in ways that inherently and explicitly include provisions for equity and social justice for those inherently and implicitly left out of the discourse framed by the most popular theories of adult learning. Readers of adult learning theory should critically interrogate what philosophical commitments drive the development of theory in adult education, considering if the commitments are simply common themes. These themes reflect the hegemony of the Eurocentric canon that privileges the same conceptions of self that are embedded in humanistic philosophy and evidenced in the practices of critical pedagogy and reflection. They are not reflective of those who have different cultural and philosophical frames. Readers should also consider deeply if the theories as framed really create the space and conditions for all to experience ontological freedom, or even the most basic of human rights.

Adult Learning Theory's North Star

In order to end the structural silences, adult educators need to engage in uncomfortable conversations. Creating a more culturally pluralistic pool of adult learning theories can assist adult educators in engaging in these uncomfortable conversations with themselves and their students. Sheared and Sissel (2001) opened the gates to these conversations with their text, *Making Space*, wherein they called out the "exclusion of certain voices and knowledge bases within the adult education literature" (p. 3). And we continue to ask how and why structured silences persist and endure. We point to hegemony as implicated in its "process of continuous creation . . . [that] includes constant structuring of consciousness as well as a battle for the control of consciousness" (Sissel & Sheared, 2001, p. 4). Uncomfortable conversations therefore must include naming the postcolonial structures creating the silence and marginalized persons and their allies challenging normative power structures, asserting their right to be seen and heard, asserting their right to humanity (Gnanadass & Merriweather, 2022). Recognizing invisibility is also required within these uncomfortable conversations. As Sheared and Sissel (2001) so eloquently articulated, diverse and multiple identities must be acknowledged and valued. Furthermore, majoritarian narratives parading as universal narratives must be deconstructed. Turning earnestly and with fidelity to a wider range of theorists and a broader way of theorizing would help to reshape the narrative of adult learning theory. For instance, from a Black feminist perspective, theorization is not separate from the experiences from which it grows (hooks, 1994).

It is important to acknowledge Ross-Gordon (2017), who noted that there has been an increased presence of race in adult education scholarship since 2000. That scholarship has been framed, in many instances, with theories of race and racialization: Africentric theory (Asante, 1998), critical race theory (CRT; Delgado & Stefancic, 2017; Schueller, 2003), white privilege and whiteness studies (Manglitz, 2003), self-ethnic reflectors (Colin, 1989), Chicano cultural theory/Mestiza consciousness (Anzaldúa, 2012), anti-Black racism (Gordon, 1995), race-focused feminist theories (e.g., Collins, 2002; Hudson-Weems, 2019; Sheared, 1994), postcolonialism (Gandhi, 2019; Gnanadass, 2016; Spivak, 1994), and Indigenous decolonialization (Smith, 2012). However, that scholarship is not part of the canon of adult learning. It exists in the borderland, with a border heavily policed by hegemonic normativity, and presents in books (Sheared & Sissel, 2001; Sheared et al., 2010) or special issues (Merriweather et al., 2014; Ramdeholl, 2013) that are not mainstream nor part of the canon for the field. They are fringe and are either not present or are scantily represented in mainstream scholarship. Gnanadass and Merriweather (2020) framed these as important counterstories, observing

> Black scholars have authored powerful counter-stories, but these texts are rarely found in adult or higher education classrooms. Although these Black texts reveal, expose, resist, and counter structural racism and the individuals complicit in upholding these racist structures, they are not part of the canon. (p. 25)

Collective Signification

Adult education's past and present paint a not-so-pretty picture when texts developed in the aftermath of America's racial reckoning still fail to deal with race, equity, and social justice in demonstrable and meaningful ways. Major texts say a great deal about what the discipline values and considers important. The collective signification of theory (Touriñán López, 2020), as codified in books positioned as resources for adult education professionals, educators, and students, has incredible influence on the discourse, function, and facilitation of practice. Such signification speaks to what matters to the field, while not necessarily speaking to what matters for the people existing on the margins.

Absence, near absence, or obscuring in major texts, especially in the wake of prominent racialized events such as George Floyd's and Breonna Taylor's murders, amount to what Guy and Brookfield (2007) called *repressive tolerance*. Brookfield and Holst (2011) reasoned that

> Repressive tolerance ensures the continued marginality of minority views by placing them in close, comparative association with dominant ones. When a curriculum is widened to include dissenting and radical perspectives that are considered alongside the mainstream perspective, the minority perspectives are always overshadowed by the mainstream one . . . [whose] presence inevitably overshadows the minority ones, which will always be perceived as alternatives or others, never as the natural center to which people should turn. (p. 193)

Repressive tolerance is part of the DNA of adult education. It is part and parcel to how and which adult learning theories have been engrained as the canon, formalized within the field.

Postcolonial theory and decolonizing theory (Freire, 1970; Guy, 1996; Gnanadass & Merriweather, 2022; Hanson & Jaffe, 2020; Isaac Savage & Merriweather, 2021; Murray-Johnson et al., 2021; Ross-Gordon, 2017; Smith, 2012; Tejeda et al., 2003), while not frequently employed in adult education, disrupt the discourse of collective signification and dismantle the postcolonial structures that create the conditions for repressive tolerance and structured silences to occur. Gnanadass (2022) argued that postcolonial theory "examines the colonization of place, economy, the mind, self, and culture and argues that even though colonialism is of the past, the colonial legacy of the colonization of the mind, self, and culture is still present" (slide 5). Disruption occurs through problematizing assumptions of universality, knowledge, and history. Decolonizing theory was posited by Gnanadass and Merriweather (2022) as a project of humanization. But unlike how humanism is often described, humanization requires naming and dismantling oppression, disenfranchisement, privilege, whiteness, and power. This reimagined humanism and critical pedagogy require unlearning the taken-for-granted status quo of adult learning theory (andragogy, transformational learning, etc.), and earnestly learning other theories to inform and guide intentionality of theory selection to inform practice. In this process, adult educators would be compelled to address their complicity in anti-Black racism, and other forms of disenfranchisement, and acknowledge their role in erasure and structured silences (Gnanadass et al., 2021).

Reimagining Commitments

So, how can adult learning theories speak to learners and adult educators existing on the margins? Moreover, how can these theories help adult educators meet learner needs in the current geopolitical and sociocultural context such as those described by

Belzer and Dashew in chapter 1 as well as other pressing issues, such as the increasing violence against Asian Americans; the growing mental health crisis; the culture war against CRT and attacks on affirmative action, reproductive rights, and trans people in the United States; the war in Ukraine; the crisis in Afghanistan; environmental racism; and so on?

We as adult educators need to recognize and respond to the urgency of these challenges to the human condition and shared human project of learning, legitimizing knowledge and extending the role of adult education in our understanding of these important contemporary issues. This is an opportunity for us to use theory to engage even more directly with epistemological and ethical questions and the concerns that set us apart and unite us as educators of adults. hooks's (1994) notion of theory as a place of healing can be useful in this endeavor. However, hooks argued, and rightly so, that theory by itself "is not inherently healing, liberatory, or revolutionary. It fulfills this function only when we ask that it do so and direct our theorizing towards this end" (p. 61). Adult learning theories, canonical and emerging, do have the potential to be healing, liberatory, and/or revolutionary. It is the intentionality of the adult educator in how they think about and use these theories that directs them to these ends.

We pose these questions to adult educators—practitioners, researchers, and administrators—in all settings and formats: How can adult learning theory help us to reimagine this world and its pressing challenges? How can adult learning theories inform our teaching and learning to acknowledge difference and value it? How can adult learning theories challenge and reframe what is considered history, knowledge, and epistemological foundations while laying bare the machinations of anti-Black racism that dehumanize and degrade Black and Brown folks in service to the construction of whiteness and maintenance of white supremacy? In other words, what other commitments beyond or instead of those identified in the introductory chapter of this text are needed for adult learning theories to function as agents of decolonization, to be part of the solution aimed toward fixing, and not harming? We suggest intentionality as a broad obligation directed toward commitment to equity in all forms, emphasis on belonging as opposed to inclusion, and creation of brave spaces. These commitments are not discrete and independent of each other. Their effectiveness and strength are found in their interdependence.

To begin the work of fixing, we must be willing to name what needs fixing. A major concern that needs to be named and fixed is the whitewashing of the canon, a whitewashing that may be conscious and deliberate or may be unconscious by virtue of white supremacist signification. Overall, the canon is situated/positioned as race neutral; few of these theories were authored by persons representing the large range of racial and ethnic diversity found within our field of practice. There are many other voices—gender identity, social class, the unhoused, trans people—from which the adult education community needs to hear to broaden and deepen the scope of the taken-for-granted canon. Adult educators need to make a commitment to contributing to equity in education in their practice, research, and theorizing by recognizing critical omissions and employing critical, race-based, and decolonizing theories that can do the work of centering equity and justice. Doing so reframes the norms and reveals the assumptions that enable practices and structures that support and maintain the hegemony of white supremacist heteropatriarchal capitalism (Collins, 2002; hooks, 1995). *Heteropatriarchal capitalism* refers to our current unquestioned and taken-for-granted capitalist systems and structures that are mutually constituted and maintained by white superiority, normative heterosexuality, and gender hierarchy.

Second, there must be a commitment to belongingness, not just inclusion. Inclusion is the equivalent of pulling in a living room chair to make space at the dining room table, whereas belongingness is ensuring that the dining room table, by design, has enough seats. This also requires intentionality as we seek to dismantle spaces that historically and contemporaneously have excluded, minimized, or delegitimized multiple and intersectional perspectives and knowledges and thwarted the ability of individuals pushed and positioned at the margins to speak instead of being spoken for (Young, 2003). The intent of the canon of adult learning theories is not to dismantle racism, sexism, homophobia, transphobia, and xenophobia or to obliterate the hegemonic systems of oppression to start anew, so how can we expect them to do this work of setting conditions conducive to belongingness? Audre Lorde (2007) pointed out, "the master's tools will never dismantle the master's house" (p. 89). Like any system, it works to preserve itself through what it sanctions and promotes. Mohanty (1989) wrote 3 decades ago something that still holds true today:

> Resistance lies in self-conscious engagement with dominant, normative discourses and representations and in the active creation of oppositional analytic and cultural spaces. Resistance that is random and isolated is clearly not as effective as that which is mobilized through systemic politicized practices of teaching and learning. Uncovering and reclaiming subjugated knowledge is one way to lay claims to alternative histories. But these knowledges need to be understood and defined *pedagogically*, as questions of strategy and practice as well as of scholarship, in order to transform educational institutions radically. (p. 185)

Mohanty's suggestions represent the commitment to intentionally engage with the canon and retool it to fracture the structural silences by working toward equity and representation and infusing social justice into teaching, learning, and scholarship. This begins the construction of a dining room table designed to accommodate all, not just the privileged few.

Adult learning theories are not discrete and separate from other theories, nor do they exist in a vacuum. They build on each other from the familiar behaviorism, our go-to andragogy, the popular transformative learning, to the current focus on sociocultural and socioemotional learning. Contextualized social learning can be particularly useful in this era of the COVID-19 pandemic and the Black Lives Matter movement, offering an opportunity to place learning in the context of people's lives during the pandemic in every domain of adult education, including adult basic education, higher education, and community education. Did our canonized theories of adult learning sensitize and prepare programs, schools, or universities and their faculties and educators to do this? Reimagining the commitments of adult education as evidenced through our theories, espoused and in use, as well as reimagining the space occupied by those current theories, allows for a tapestry of theories more representative of adult learners and are necessary steps in retooling our canon.

Foundational to this reimagining is a rich and deep understanding of critical epistemology (i.e., critical ways of knowing). Gouthro (2019) lamented that much of adult education's stagnation is owed to a lack of deep engagement in theoretical and philosophical literature, particularly literature that is unfamiliar to the adult educator. Simply put, adult educators need to be exposed to a wider array of theories, and these theories need to sit alongside those already adopted and accepted as canonical theories. Currently, CRT appears as the default for those interested in a race-based theory and has gained some acceptance as useful (signification) in adult education. However, when CRT is used, it is often "theory lite," with the most challenging and threatening aspects muted. Its watershed potential is diminished, making it more palatable to the hegemonic status quo. But CRT is not the only useful theory; other theories (e.g., Africana womanism; Hudson-Weems, 2019; Sheared, 1994), self-ethnic reflectors (Colin, 1989), Chicano cultural theory/Mestiza consciousness (Anzaldúa, 2012), anti-Black racism (Gordon, 1995), Africentrism (Asante, 1998), postcolonialism (Gandhi, 2019; Gnanadass, 2016; Spivak, 1994), and Indigenous decolonialization (Smith, 2012) exist and are regularly used in disciplines outside of adult education and can act as correctives in the realm of adult learning theories. But theories that unapologetically point out the hypocrisy and degrading nature of hegemonic normativity can be threatening to dominant society as evidenced by the current culture war raging around CRT, which only seems to be gathering momentum from the right and the people/groups benefiting from white privilege. This attack on CRT is a good example of the challenge to the status quo and dominant ideology by critical theories. It can also be intimidating for instructors as they fear the loss of their jobs, their safety, and their academic freedom when doing the right thing, working toward equity and belongingness.

Expansion of the canon to include critical, race-based, and decolonizing perspectives and voices is needed to safeguard our democracy and our democratic ideals, the espoused, but not actualized, ideals and commitments of adult education. This expansion positions these theories as normative, not as other; as knowledge, not an illegitimate alternative; as applicable to the whole, not only the marginalized; and will make connection between history, knowledge, and power that is often ignored but is necessary for more complete understanding of context and understanding of why reliance on the canon is insufficient. This connection can be operationalized in our practice by turning to newly positioned perspectives for guidance, highlighting in nuanced ways the manner in which power dynamics and inequities manifest in our classrooms. In this way, we can learn with and from our learners and perhaps change the dynamics of the one-way transfer of knowledge from school to home, teacher to student, school literacy over home literacy, and recognize and value the dialectical relationship between school/home literacies and knowledges and recognize learners' funds of knowledge (González et al., 2006; Rios-Aguilar et al., 2011). This can translate into higher education and research by bringing in Black feminist and critical race methodologies when researching Black folks. Doing so would center their experiences, acknowledge their ways of knowing and meaning making as valid, and see their experience as knowledge that pivots away from studying about Black women and Black folks to learning from them (L. Menson-Furr, personal communication, April 29, 2022), a paradigmatic shift. This would make space for learners to discuss their experiences with COVID-19, Black Lives Matter, transphobia, the war in Ukraine, the suppression of voting rights, air pollution in their neighborhood, or other localized issues that might be important to them.

This shared space has the potential to function as a brave space (Arao & Clemens, 2013), the third reimagined commitment. Brave spaces, in contrast with safe spaces, facilitate honest and authentic conversations among adult educators and learners about issues of social justice, such as race and racism, that do not engender feelings of safety. Conversations around race might not feel safe for Black and Brown learners who battle anti-Black racism in their everyday lived experience, for White learners recognizing and acknowledging the benefits and privileges they reap from whiteness, for Indigenous American learners navigating their sovereignty in a country that not only stole their land and birthright but marginalizes and erases their heritage, history, and very lives. Adult learning theories that embody commitments to brave spaces provide fresh perspectives on learning, contributing to equity and belongingness. It is in opposition to deficit mindsets and practices of teaching and learning; maintenance of oppressive postcolonial structures; and support of unmerited privileges based on identities, including whiteness, maleness, and heterosexuality. Brave spaces have the capacity to invite in difference and challenges, cultivating space for learners and educators to participate in adult learning holistically with the fullness of their humanity and self. No one should fall prey to thinking along the lines of adages such as, "Leave your problems at the door and focus on learning." The notion of brave spaces turns that on its head, focusing instead on learners' problems as part of the systemic efforts to dismantle the structures creating them.

Adult learning theory's North Star will be found in theories better representing the voices of the marginalized and the subaltern that seek to disrupt and dismantle hegemonic normativity. We are convinced that a more culturally pluralistic adult learning theory canon, demonstrating a wider diversity of who and what are important, is needed to eliminate the structured silences promoting the hegemonic normativity of white privilege and white supremacy in adult learning theory. We submit that a canon committed to eschewing add-and-stir approaches and bookending alternative perspectives and theories by thoughtfully and critically curating a more culturally pluralistic field of adult learning should become the new norm. In doing so, adult education engages in the continual act of becoming a brave space where diverse people and epistemologies belong. *Becoming* acknowledges that this is an ongoing project that requires regular and consistent checking of assumptions and evaluations with a critical eye, breeding a field with theory signification that represents a broader range of perspectives, histories, knowledges, and experiences. In 2008, during President Barack Obama's historic campaign, First Lady Michelle Obama took heat for saying, "Hope is making a comeback. . . . For the first time in my adult lifetime, I am really proud of my country . . . because I think people are hungry for change" (Obama, 2008). As adult educators of color, we too want to be able to say, "We feel like hope is making a comeback," when Black and Brown learners and other marginalized learners can finally see themselves in adult learning theories and adult education makes a commitment to the same. Like Michelle Obama, we can take the heat. We are hungry for change.

References

Anzaldúa, G. (2012). *Borderlands/La frontera: The new Mestiza* (4th ed.). Aunt Lute Books.

Arao, B., & Clemens, K. (2013). From safe spaces to brave spaces: A new way to frame dialogue around diversity and social justice. In L. Landreman (Ed.), *The art of effective facilitation: Reflections from social justice educators* (pp. 135–150). Stylus.

Argyris, C., Putnam, R., & Smith, D. (1985). *Action science*. Jossey-Bass.

Asante, M. (1998). *The Afrocentric idea* (revised & expanded ed.). Temple University Press.

Brookfield, S. D., & Holst, J. D. (2011). *Radicalizing learning: Adult education for a just world*. Wiley.

Colin, S. A. J., III. (1989). Cultural literacy: Ethnocentrism versus self-ethnic reflectors. *Thresholds in Education, 15*(4), 16–19.

Collins, P. H. (2002). *Black feminist thought: Knowledge, consciousness, and the politics of empowerment*. Routledge.

Delgado, R., & Stefancic, J. (2017). *Critical race theory: An introduction* (3rd ed.). New York University Press.

Freire, P. (1970). *Pedagogy of the oppressed*. Continuum.

Gandhi, L. (2019). *Postcolonial theory: A critical introduction* (2nd ed.). Columbia University Press.

Gnanadass, E. (2016). *Perpetual outsiders?: Learning race in the south Asian American experience* [Doctoral dissertation, Pennsylvania State University]. https://etda.libraries.psu.edu/files/final_submissions/11395

Gnanadass, E. (2022, March 10). *Is postcolonial theory a useful lens for adult education?* [Paper]. Presented at the 2022 Adult Higher Education Alliance Conference [Virtual conference].

Gnanadass, E., & Merriweather, L. (2020). Troubling the discursive moment: Using Black texts for activating dialogue. In A. Mandell & E. Michelson (Eds.), *Adult Learning in the Age of Trump and Brexit* (New Directions for Adult and Continuing Education, no. 165, pp. 21–33). Jossey-Bass. https://doi.org/10.1002/ace.20365

Gnanadass, E., & Merriweather, L. (2022). Restorying COVID: Faculty and graduate students teaching and learning in crisis. In R. L. Wlodarsky & C. A. Hansman (Eds.), *The COVID-19 Pandemic and Other Ongoing Crises: Reflections, Innovations, and Adaptations* (New Directions for Adult and Continuing Education, no. 173–174, pp. 21–31). Jossey-Bass. https://doi.org/10.1002/ace.20449

Gnanadass, E., Murray-Johnson, K., & Alicia Vetter, M. (2021). Narrating the immigrant experience: Three adult educators' perspectives. *Adult Learning, 32*(1), 40–49. https://doi.org/10.1177/1045159520977708

González, N., Moll, L. C., & Amanti, C. (2006). *Funds of knowledge: Theorizing practices in households, communities, and classrooms.* Routledge.

Gordon, L. (1995). *Bad faith and antiblack racism.* Humanity Books.

Gouthro, P. (2019). Taking time to learn: The importance of theory for adult education. *Adult Education Quarterly, 69*(1), 60–76. https://doi.org/10.1177/0741713518815656

Guy, T. C. (1996, October 29). *Africentricism and adult education: Outlines of an intellectual tradition with implications for adult education* [Paper]. Annual Meeting of the American Association for Adult and Continuing Education, Charlotte, NC, United States. https://eric.ed.gov/?id=ED409457

Guy, T. C., & Brookfield, S. D. (2007, June 9). *W.E.B. Du Bois and the basic American Negro creed: The AAAE, censorship, and repressive tolerance* [Paper]. 2007 Adult Education Research Conference, Halifax, Nova Scotia, Canada. https://newprairiepress.org/aerc/2007/papers/46/

Hanson, C., & Jaffe, J. (2020). Decolonizing adult education. In T. S. Rocco, M. C. Smith, R. C. Mizzi, L. R. Merriweather, & J. D. Hawley (Eds.), *The handbook of adult and continuing education* (pp. 341–349). Stylus.

hooks, b. (1994). *Teaching to transgress: Education as the practice of freedom.* Routledge.

hooks, b. (1995). *Killing rage: Ending racism.* Henry Holt.

Hudson-Weems, C. (2019). *Africana womanism: Reclaiming ourselves* (5th ed.). Routledge.

Illeris, K. (2018). An overview of the history of learning theory. *European Journal of Education, 53*, 86–101. https://doi.org/10.1111/ejed.12265

Isaac-Savage, E. P., & Merriweather, L. R. (2021). Preparing adult educators for racial justice. In M. V. Alfred & E. P. Isaac-Savage (Eds.), *The Black Lives Matter Movement: Implications for Anti-Racist Adult Education* (New Directions for Adult and Continuing Education, no. 170, pp. 109–118). Jossey-Bass. https://doi.org/10.1002/ace.20430

Jansen, S. C. (1989). Gender and the information society: A socially structured silence. *Journal of Communication, 39*(3), 196–215. https://doi.org/10.1111/j.1460-2466.1989.tb01052.x

Johnson, S., & Taylor, K. (Eds.). (2006). *The neuroscience of adult learning.* Jossey-Bass.

Kroth, M., & Carr-Chellman, D. J. (2018). Preparing profound learners. *New Horizons in Adult Education and Human Resource Development, 30*(3), 64–71. https://doi.org/10.1002/nha3.20224

Kroth, M., & Carr-Chellman, D. J. (2020). Profound learning: An exploratory Delphi study. *International Journal of Adult Education and Technology, 11*(2), 14–23. https://doi.org/10.4018/IJAET.2020040102

Lockey, A., Conaghan, P., Bland, A., & Astin, F. (2021). Educational theory and its application to advanced life support courses: A narrative review. *Resuscitation Plus, 5*, 1–7. https://doi.org/10.1016/j.resplu.2020.100053

Lorde, A. (2007). *Sister outsider: Essays and speeches*. Crossing Press.

Manglitz, E. (2003). Challenging white privilege in adult education: A critical review of the literature. *Adult Education Quarterly, 53*(2), 119–134. https://doi.org/10.1177/0741713602238907

Merriweather, L. R., Bowman, L., & Closson, R. B. (Eds.). (2014). The pedagogy of teaching race [Special issue]. *Adult Learning, 25*(3). https://doi-org.proxy.libraries.rutgers.edu/10.1177/1045159514534392

Mohanty, C. T. (1989). On race and voice: Challenges for liberal education in the 1990s. *Cultural Critique, 14*, 179–208.

Murray-Johnson, K., Gnanadass, E., & Vetter, M. A. (2021). Where do we go from here? Immigrant scholars on race and the teaching of race. In J. Walker, G. Maestrini, & S. Smythe (Eds.), *Proceedings from the Adult Education in Global Times Conference* (pp. 567–573). University of British Columbia.

Obama, M. (2008, February 18). *Obama campaign event* [Speech audio recording]. C-Span. https://www.c-span.org/video/?204114-1/obama-campaign-event

Ramdeholl, D. (Ed.). (2013). *Decentering the Ivory Tower of Academia* (New Directions for Adult and Continuing Education, no. 139, pp. 1–95). Jossey-Bass.

Rios-Aguilar, C., Kiyama, J. M., Gravitt, M., & Moll, L. C. (2011). Funds of knowledge for the poor and forms of capital for the rich? A capital approach to examining funds of knowledge. *Theory and Research in Education, 9*(2), 163–184. https://doi.org/10.1177/1477878511409776

Ross-Gordon, J. (2017). Racing the field of adult education—Making the invisible visible. *PAACE Journal of Lifelong Learning, 26*(1), 55–76.

Schueller, M. J. (2003). Articulations of African-Americanism in South Asian postcolonial theory: Globalism, localism, and the question of race. *Cultural Critique, 55*, 35–62. https://doi.org/10.1353/cul.2003.0045

Sheared, V. (1994). Giving voice: An inclusive model of instruction—A womanist perspective. In E. Hayes & S. A. J. Colin III (Eds.), *Confronting Racism and Sexism in Adult Continuing Education* (New Directions and Adult and Continuing Education, no. 61, pp. 27–37). Jossey-Bass.

Sheared, V., Johnson-Bailey, J., Peterson, E., Colin, S. A., III, & Brookfield, S. D. (2010). *The handbook of race and adult education: A resource for dialogue on racism*. John Wiley and Sons.

Sheared, V., & Sissel, P. A. (Eds.). (2001). *Making space: Merging theory and practice in adult education*. Bergin & Garvey.

Sissel, P. A., & Sheared, V. (2001). Opening the gates: Reflections on power, hegemony, language, and the status quo. In V. Sheared & P. A. Sissel (Eds.), *Making space: Merging theory and practice in adult education* (pp. 3–14). Bergin & Garvey.

Smith, L. T. (2012). *Decolonizing methodologies: Research and indigenous peoples* (2nd ed.). Zed Books.

Spivak, G. C. (1994). Can the subaltern speak? In P. Williams & L. Chrisman (Eds.), *Colonial discourse and postcolonial theory* (pp. 66–111). Columbia University Press.

Tejeda, C., Espinoza, M., & Gutiérrez, K. (2003). Toward a decolonizing pedagogy: Social justice reconsidered. In P. Trifonas (Ed.), *Pedagogy of difference: Rethinking education for social change* (pp. 10–40). Routledge.

Tennant, M. (2019). *Psychology and adult learning: The role of theory in informing practice*. Routledge.

Touriñán López, J. M. (2020). Theory–practice relationship and common activity as focuses to solve education problems: The signification of knowledge of education does not cover the dual model. *Journal of Research in Education, 18*(3), 210–257. https://doi.org/10.35869/reined.v18i3.3265

Young, R. (2003). *Postcolonialism: A very short introduction.* Oxford University Press.

Authors' Additional Resource Suggestions

Chakrabarty, D. (2000). *Provincializing Europe: Postcolonial thought and historical difference.* Princeton University Press.

Fanon, F. (1963). *The wretched of the earth.* Grove Press.

Fanon, F. (1967). *Black skin, white masks.* Grove Press.

Guo, S., & Maitra, S. (2019). Decolonising lifelong learning in the age of transnational. *International Journal of Lifelong Education, 38*(1), 1–4. https://doi.org/10.1080/02601370.2018.1561534

Hunn, L. M. (2004). Africentric philosophy: A remedy for Eurocentric dominance. In J. A. Sandlin & R. St. Clair (Eds.), *Promoting Clinical Practice in Adult Education* (New Directions for Adult and Continuing Education, no. 102, pp. 65–74). Jossey-Bass.

Memmi, A. (1991). *The colonized and the colonizer.* Beacon Press. (Original work published 1956)

Mohanty, C. (2002). Under Western eyes' revisited: Feminist solidarity through anticapitalist struggles. *Signs, 28*(2), 499–535. https://doi.org/10.1086/342914

Mongin, O., Lempereur, N., & Schlegel, J.-L. (2006, December). What is postcolonial thinking? An interview with Achille Mbembe. *Esprit, 12*, 117–133. https://www.cairn-int.info/article-E_ESPRI_0612_0117--.htm

Mulenga, D. C. (2001). Mwalimu Julius Nyerere: A critical review of his contributions to adult education and postcolonialism. *International Journal of Lifelong Education, 20*(6), 446–470. https://doi.org/10.1080/02601370110088436

Rodney, W. (1973). *How Europe underdeveloped Africa.* Howard University Press.

Said, E. W. (1978). *Orientalism.* Routledge & Kegan Paul.

Sinha, M. (2000). How history matters: Complicating the categories of "Western" and "Non-Western" feminisms. In The Social Justice Group at the Center for Advanced Feminist Studies University of Minnesota (Ed.), *Is academic feminism dead? Theory in practice* (pp. 168–186). New York University Press.

Smith, L. T., Tuck, E., & Yang, K. W. (Eds.). (2018). *Indigenous and decolonizing studies in education.* Routledge.

Tuck, E., & Yang, K. W. (2012). Decolonization is not a metaphor. *Decolonization: Indigeneity, Education & Society, 1*(1), 1–40. https://jps.library.utoronto.ca/index.php/des/article/view/18630/15554

Editors' Key Seminal and Supplemental Text Suggestions

Arnold, C. H., Badenhorst, C., & Hoben, J. (2021). Theories on trial: Deconstructing and decolonizing higher and adult learning conceptual and theoretical frameworks. In J. Huisman & M. Tight (Eds.), *Theory and method in higher education research* (Vol. 7, pp. 1–20). Emerald.

Guy, T. C., & Merriweather, L. R. (2011, June 10–12). *Historical memory and the construction of adult education knowledge: The role of selectivity in majoritarian narratives* [Paper]. Adult Education Research Conference, Toronto, Ontario, Canada. https://newprairiepress.org/aerc/2011/papers/42

Hanson, C., & Jaffe, J. (2020). Decolonizing adult education. In T. S. Rocco, M. C. Smith, R. C. Mizzi, L. R. Merriweather & J. D. Hawley (Eds.), *The handbook of adult and continuing education* (pp. 341–349). Stylus.

Touriñán López, J. M. (2020). Theory–practice relationship and common activity as focuses to solve education problems: The signification of knowledge of education does not cover the dual model. *Journal of Research in Education,18*(3), 210–257. https://doi.org/10.35869/reined.v18i3.3265

9

ANDRAGOGY

The Philosophy Behind the Practice

Ralf St. Clair

Andragogy truly stands out among the adult education approaches of the 20th century for its reach and longevity. For educators of adults in North America, *andragogy* is a well-known term and is sometimes considered synonymous with the whole idea of educating adults. In other parts of the world it is recognized as one influential and important way to think about the education of adults, but it has never been as central in the conversation. In different contexts andragogy is seen variously as a learning theory, a philosophical commitment, a general term for teaching adults, and as a way to implicitly promote the values of mid-century American capitalism (cf. Wang & Kania-Gosche, 2010). The expansive and multidimensional nature of the term makes it challenging to summarize. Since the popularization of the concept in Malcolm Knowles's *The Modern Practice of Adult Education* (1970), the applications of andragogy have been wide and varied. An ERIC search for "andragogy" in early 2020 turned up 639 publications over the past 20 years engaging with the concept, 200 of which were in the past 5 years. There are very few notions arising from adult education with any sort of comparable impact across geographical locations and academic fields.

The aim of this chapter is to provide a strong grounding in andragogy without shying away from the complexities and controversies. The emphasis, given the potential audience for this chapter, will be placed on the North American use of the term, and the first section lays out a brief overview. Since its introduction into the lexicon of adult education around 50 years ago, the term has been the target of some critique, and the major themes of this criticism will be identified. The chapter will close by considering the potential of andragogy to continue contributing to our shared thinking around adult education and why people involved in the field in the 21st century should consider this very 20th-century concept in their thinking.

Overview

The word *andragogy* and the associated ideas first became familiar to many in the English-speaking world after Malcolm Knowles (1970) published *Modern Practice*. He continued to rework and refine the concept until his death in the late 1990s, and by his final iteration andragogy was a greatly expanded body of work containing many ideas more associated with an andragogical approach than central to it (Knowles et al., 1998). The most straightforward statement of Knowles's andragogy, and the one most clearly focused on adult education, was the 1970 version.

During the 1960s, there were considerable efforts to establish adult education as a legitimate discipline throughout North America, which received an enormous boost from the adoption in the United States of the Adult Education Act of 1966 (Parker, 1990). Malcolm Knowles was at the center of these developments and conversations. Born in 1913, he had begun working in adult education in the 1930s after completing his undergraduate degree. Knowles had an opportunity to study and reflect deeply upon the field when in the navy during World War II (Henry, 2011), and he started publishing books in and around adult education soon afterward, beginning with his master's thesis (Knowles, 1950). In 1951, he became executive director of the Adult Education Association of the USA, and by the end of the decade was an associate professor at Boston University (Smith, 2002). Knowles was an established figure in the field in the 1960s, and *Modern Practice* takes its place as one of a series of efforts, generally more aligned than not, to define a core for adult education practice and theory.

In terms of a clearly laid-out approach to adult education, one of the most striking aspects of Knowles's initial formulation was the extent to which it emphasizes the differentiation between andragogy as "the art and science of helping adults learn" (Knowles, 1970, p. 38) and pedagogy as "the art and science of teaching children" (p. 37). *Modern Practice* includes a section called "farewell to pedagogy" (p. 37), arguing that "traditional pedagogy is irrelevant to the modern requirements of both children and adults" (p. 38). The difference between "helping adults learn" and "teaching children" highlights an extremely important aspect of andragogy: Learners are viewed as self-directed individuals able to comprehend and act upon their own needs. The role of the andragogical educator heavily emphasizes facilitation of process rather than transmission of uncontestable expertise and received truth.

Ten years later, the second edition of the book changed its emphasis. While the subtitle of the earlier book (Knowles, 1970) was the slightly bellicose *Andragogy Versus Pedagogy*, the later book was subtitled *From Pedagogy to Andragogy* (Knowles, 1980). In the later volume, he states, "The models are probably most useful when seen not as dichotomous but rather as two ends of a spectrum, with a realistic assumption in a given situation falling in between the two ends" (p. 43). This may strike the contemporary reader as slightly simplistic. Current thinking is generally more comfortable with a range of models varying on several dimensions rather than lined up along a single continuum. Nonetheless, it represented a significant step back from the initial confrontational stance.

In the 1970 edition of *Modern Practice* the "emerging technology" of andragogy is laid out in 17 pages, and most of the subsequent thinking and practice is rooted in this relatively brief exposition. The starting point for Knowles's (1970) explanation is four assumptions. Knowles was always clear that these were assumptions rather than empirical findings, implicitly acknowledging that they incorporate a particular set of values about adult lives. They were:

Self-concept. Children adopt a self-concept of "learner" during their years of schooling, but adults are more likely to see themselves as "producer" or "doer." "Adults tend to resist learning under conditions that are incongruent with their self-concept as autonomous individuals" (p. 40). Adults should be treated with respect and given responsibility for their learning, even though this may produce a disorienting period as they adjust to the new role of adult learner.

Experience. Adult learners not only have more experience than children, but they also tend to view it more as part of who they are. Experience does not happen to them; it *is* them. The implication is that adults have a "deep investment in its value" (p. 44), and any educational process perceived as dismissing their experience will be seen as dismissing them.

Readiness to learn. Knowles argued that humans go through developmental stages preparing them to learn what they next need to learn throughout their lives. This is presented as both a long-cycle model, as the demands for learning change over life stages, and a shorter cycle situational model, for example, when people get a new job. Overall, the pattern reflects changing readiness to learn based on individual and societal context.

Orientation to learning. Adults, unlike children, value immediate application of what they learn. This follows from the idea adults learn in response to pressing life circumstances. People experience problems, and the point of learning is to identify and potentially implement solutions to these problems.

By Knowles's final version of andragogy (Knowles et al., 1998), two more assumptions had been added:

The need to know. It is necessary for adults to understand what benefit they will gain from learning something. At the very least, there has to be an intellectual justification for why particular knowledge will be valuable, but ideally there should be a pragmatic rationale. One of the tasks of the educator may be raising people's awareness of the need to know.

Motivation. Adults respond most strongly to internal motivators. The internal drive to learn is very powerful, though this may be set aside during adulthood due to the influence of factors such as lack of time.

These six assumptions imply a particular approach to educating adults. Knowles's work history was largely concerned with program development, so he was well placed to describe the implications of these assumptions in terms of the practical work of adult educators. He listed these implications very clearly, pulling in elements from his understanding of the sort of planning process, delivery, and environment best supporting adult learning, and presents a seven-step model for the development and delivery of an adult education program (Knowles, 1970):

- the establishment of a climate conducive to adult learning
- the creation of an organizational structure for participative planning
- the diagnosis of needs for learning
- the formulation of directions of learning (objectives)
- the development of a design of activities
- the operation of the activities
- the rediagnosis of needs for learning (p. 54)

The later versions of andragogy, not surprisingly, reflect more contemporary language and ways of thinking, for example, presenting andragogy as a "process model" (Knowles et al., 1998, p. 115). This language positions andragogy as a framework for the entire process of supporting adult learning, from discussion and mutual development of objectives, through delivery, to assessment. Other approaches, it is claimed, simply cover the transactions between the instructor and the learners, leaving the objectives, the design process, and other aspects to be established outside the instructor–learner relationship. This implies andragogy is more democratic and inclusive than these other approaches because learners have such a high level of involvement and control over the program.

The Knowlesian view of andragogy can seem strikingly North American because of its emphasis on democracy and inclusion. However, this approach to andragogy has been applied in a number of international settings, including those where cultural assumptions are quite different from North America. For example, there has been examination of the extent to which andragogical approaches can be applied to teaching and learning in China, which is widely regarded as having a set of Confucian-inspired, didactic values (Wang & Storey, 2015). It has also been influential, to some extent, across the United Kingdom and mainland Europe. Interesting examples include the establishment of a chair in andragogy at the University of Bamburg, explicitly focused on the North American approach (Reischmann, 2004), and the Cranfield University Centre for Andragogy and Academic Skills.

Application in Practice and Influences on Theory

Andragogical writing does not prescribe what educators should actually be doing in the teaching and learning process. Management of learning and teaching is not explicitly presented as a specialist skill set, and seems to be approached very often as an extension of counseling or human development work. Andragogy demonstrates strong connections with the work of midcentury psychotherapists and an especially high degree of congruence with the writing of Carl Rogers (1957). Rogers developed client-centered approaches to counseling and psychotherapy, where the counselor is expected to take a humanist stance by nonjudgmentally valuing the experience and perspectives of the client. The aspiration is to support the client to self-actualize by creating an individual model of a happy and fulfilled life. Though educational relationships are not seen as therapeutic in andragogy, there is an acceptance of learner self-actualization as the outcome of learning and a built-in expectation that the steps to that goal are transparent to learners. This parallel between andragogy and the psychological thinking of the time is important to understand because it helps explains why so much emphasis is placed on learners shaping their own learning. Put simply, educators cannot self-actualize for learners; learners have to do it for themselves.

The limited time spent on technique, therefore, is not an accidental gap in the andragogical approach but a deliberate step away from school teaching and its focus on methods. Andragogy is concerned primarily with the relationship between equal adults who have to negotiate how to work together, and from this perspective it would be inappropriate to enter into an educational setting with a preprepared toolkit of possible actions. In creating the plan together, educator and learner are recognizing and respecting the desires of the learner while building authentic relationships. For many adult educators this is not just an attractive idea, it is the central point of their vocation.

The range of contexts in which andragogy has proven useful is impressive, giving the impression of a Swiss army knife of educational thinking. Knowles developed the idea of andragogy beyond traditional adult education and moved it toward human resource development, where it has been so well received it can be considered a standard framework for corporate training. There is an accepted argument that "[human resource development] and andragogy share th[e] interest in the facilitation of adults in their learning and professional development" (Kessels, 2015, p. 16). There has been a similar application of andragogy in higher education teaching (Yoshimoto et al., 2007), and indeed in a number of other contexts where a formal argument for learner-centered education can make a contribution. Andragogy emerges in medical education, military education, adult literacy, online learning, and, perhaps ironically, school education.

While andragogy does not define the actions of the educator, it does present a linear, stepwise model of program design and delivery. Any consideration of the implications for practice begins with an expansion of these stages and what they might look like in concrete settings. The first stage, creation of a climate conducive to adult learning, builds on Knowles's assumptions by challenging the educator to think through what kind of setting and what kind of relations will recognize, for example, the adult orientation to learning. One of the keys to this step might be asking the learners what issues they hope that the shared educational experience will help to address. One aspect calling for caution is the potential to slip into a deficit framing of learners and their knowledge, with the andragogue positioned to fill in gaps and solve problems. It is more consistent with andragogical assumptions to think in terms of broadening the capabilities of learners according to their own perspectives on what would be useful than aiming to adjust learners to meet external challenges. The latter perspective is inconsistent with the fundamental humanism of andragogical approaches.

The second stage is sometimes less emphasized, though it represents one of the most explicitly democratic aspects of andragogy in practice. Knowles suggested that there is a need to create a structure for participative planning, and this structure, whether a group, a course council, or a collective approach to curriculum development, acts as the bridge between the learners and the educator. In doing so, it potentially addresses the power imbalance between educators and learners, something that Knowles saw as one of the downfalls of traditional school teaching. This participative structure is used to shape the third and fourth steps, which involve diagnosing learning needs and defining the direction learning should take. These three steps together form the heart of the andragogical approach in many ways and place the adult educator indisputably into the role of facilitator rather than content expert. The expertise of the educator is building and implementing the collaborative process, with learners foregrounded as having the experience and expertise to define and prioritize what they want to learn.

It is worth pausing to note that the role of experience may not be as straightforward as andragogy can appear to suggest. Influenced by their reading of andragogy, educators may come to think of experience as an unproblematically positive resource for learning. Experience can be drawn upon for examples and explicit connections to new material, as well as offering a way to ensure learning is relevant and motivating. This may not be the case if experience makes learning more difficult, such as when a person is convinced they cannot learn because of their school career, or if collaborative learning is a new approach for them (Smith, 2010). Based on his previous work and theoretical base of humanist psychology, Knowles generally viewed experience as a valuable resource, but in later writing his position on this point became more nuanced. Knowles et al. (1998) argued,

> But the fact of greater experience also has some potential negative effects. As we accumulate experience, we tend to develop mental habits, biases, and presuppositions that tend to cause us to close our minds to new ideas, fresh perceptions, and alternative ways of thinking. Accordingly, adult educators try to discover ways to help adults examine their habits and biases and open their minds to new approaches. (p. 66)

While this position may well be familiar to many adult educators, the recommendation is problematic. It undermines andragogy's connection to midcentury developmental psychology and seems to privilege the judgment of the educator over that of the learner. In practice, educators will come to their own position regarding this issue and how it plays out in a specific context, but it should be recognized that working with learner experience remains a thorny question in the andragogical framework.

Once objectives have been identified, the process moves into the design and operation of activities to reach those aims. Here again the educator has expertise to bring to the process, having their own experiential store of educational approaches and activities to put into the service of the collective plan. This will involve a whole range of inputs and resources, from didactic to experiential learning activities. While there may be a tendency for andragogically inspired educators to privilege group discussion as a method for learning, there is no particular support for any specific method in the andragogical framework. In andragogy, the focus of participation is the design of the program and not every single component within it, so having an expert lecturer as part of the agreed-on process would be consistent with the assumptions as long as learners and educators agreed this could be supportive of learning. The insight that learners are experts on their own learning must not be confused with the view that content-area experts are not necessary.

The final step is evaluation and rediagnosis of needs for learning. This is a highly developed and complex area in its own right and important to do well. It loops back to the original assessment of needs and the objectives set earlier in the process, and by doing so ensures a recursive, self-correcting learning plan is in place. Added benefits include helping learners to recognize the progress they have made and demonstrating the effectiveness of the participatory planning process.

The full application of an andragogical framework according to Knowles's schema is a linear, stepwise process with recursive, self-monitoring elements. It has the virtues of intuitiveness and an overarching rationality, making it understandable and usable by nonspecialists. These virtues are not always present in educational theory and underpin the influence andragogy has had in so many diverse pragmatic contexts.

Implications for Practice

On a broad level, beyond the linear program steps, andragogical thought holds important implications for practice. Perhaps the most notable is the importance of democracy in the philosophy and practice of adult education, as reflected in the need to build collaborative relationships between educators and learners. Each brings a necessary set of experiences and skills to the learning encounter, making it important to avoid any suggestion of learners as subordinate to the educator. The entire learning transaction is built upon the principle of a shared project. Not only does this apply to the actual delivery of the course, but the design of the process must also be participatory. There is a difference between inviting people to join a predesigned discussion group and inviting them to come together to decide what a discussion group might look like. Andragogical perspectives imply that the second approach is more effective and more valuable to the process of adult learning.

Andragogy also argues for viewing education and learning as a recursive process rather than a purely linear, curriculum-driven experience. The learner has an opportunity to diagnose their own learning needs, pursue appropriate resources, assess the distance they have traveled, and develop a new set of objectives. This can be seen as a radically constructivist view of learning, where the active learner not only creates their own knowledge but also defines the conditions for that creation.

These implications for practice can help explain why Knowles saw andragogy as being so different from a traditional school setting. Though he softened his position over time, initially Knowles viewed the inclusion and consultation of the learner as a fundamentally different underpinning for educational process than found in K–12 education and completely incompatible with it. It can be difficult, however, for educators to imagine what recognizing these implications in their daily work might look like, especially if they have mainly learned through formal, teacher-driven structures.

One way to illustrate these implications is through *learning contracts*, a concrete approach to adult education espoused by Knowles et al. (1998) as a way to "provide a means for negotiating a reconciliation between . . . external needs and expectations and the learner's internal needs and interests" (p. 265). One of the most interesting contexts for learning contracts is the workplace. Here, it may be very helpful if workers know how to perform a particular task or hold a specific competency, but the andragogical assumptions make it clear simply requiring people to learn something is unlikely to be effective. Authentic learning requires participation by learners and their engagement in the process, meaning that learners must understand the value of the learning and see the ways in which their experience supports it. The andragogical educator enters this situation as a facilitator who supports learners to negotiate (in both senses of the word) their learning. The starting point could be an explanation of the employer's concerns, or the employee talking about how they could broaden their skills.

When opportunities to strengthen the capabilities of the learner have been identified and agreed, they can be transformed into learning objectives. The process needed to achieve the objectives can be discussed, along with ways to demonstrate they have been accomplished. The resulting written summary is a learning contract, laying out what is to be learned, how it will be learned, and what will count as evidence that learning has occurred (Knowles et al., 1998). The learning contract serves as the reference for everybody involved in supporting the learner, making transparency and comprehensiveness essential. Throughout this process the learner has a lot of control and, if the process is done well, will see their knowledge and experience being authentically acknowledged throughout the development and implementation of the contract. Learning contracts also act as an organic and effective way to build data for program evaluation, as they can be brought together to form a record of achievement in the course.

As a concrete illustration, it is easy to imagine a class on languages where an individual wants to learn how to use conversational Mandarin, decides to watch videos on the internet and practice with the materials in the class, and then demonstrate what they learn by sharing their progress with the class. This could easily be captured in a relatively simple learning contract that would not only demonstrate the learner's growth in capability but also provide a proof point for evaluation of the learning occurring in the course.

Theoretical Influence

One remarkable point about Knowlesian andragogical perspectives is how obvious and mainstream they seem today. It can seem self-evident the process of education should be based on the sort of values andragogy promotes. The challenges inherent to the process are familiar, such as working with a group of learners with diverse objectives or managing topics unappealing to learners. The idea of the negotiation and learner-centered process appear as rarely questioned aspects of good practice. However, in understanding the significance of andragogy two things are helpful to keep in mind. First, when Knowles was writing it was not apparent what the best approach to educating adults would be. In the post–World War II era of science there was, nonetheless, confidence a universal solution could be found. When it was introduced, andragogy did not reflect a common and obvious set of values and beliefs as much as it represented an innovative and systematic response to the perceived need for a unifying framework. Second, the level of detail in Knowles's writing is considerable. When summarized in an article or a chapter, andragogy can sound rather simplistic. Engaging with the full range of writing helps to enrich and expand the idea of andragogy significantly.

Modern Practice and related publications present a remarkable statement of the initiation of a new discipline and science. However, despite the ongoing interest in andragogy, very little has been done in terms of developing the concept or building a robust theory. The vast majority of writing is reporting on the application of the andragogical approach in different situations. John Henschke, who has done a great deal to carry forward the Knowlesian legacy, has commented that

> Much of what has been published focuses only on its popularized use, reflecting either a wholesale support of Knowles's version of andragogy and the attendant excitement it generates, or a fairly straightforward debunking and dismissal for the reason of what some call Knowles's unscientific approach. (Henschke & Cooper, 2007, p. 8)

Very often, in educational research a new approach or theory is followed by a series of studies considering the evidence for the ideas and elaborating or refining them. There is a loop from experience back to the original concept, helping it to evolve and become more useful. The publication history within andragogy is distinguished by its pragmatic bent and limited engagement with the development of the framework. In other words, there is little evidence of such a loop.

While the development of andragogical theory itself has been more limited than might be hoped, there is evidence of lateral influence. For example, Candy's (1991) work on self-directed learning acknowledges the pertinence of andragogy while maintaining a distance from the specifics presented by Knowles. Candy stated:

> As people become more accustomed to, and skilled at, informed participation and choosing in these aspects of their lives, they have made increasing demands for similar power sharing in relation to their education. These demands go far beyond so-called participatory learning methods, and extend into all aspects of the educative process, from the assessment of needs through the design of programs to the evaluation of learning outcomes. (p. 33)

While the value of andragogy as a contribution to thinking around the education of adults and to ways of framing practice is hard to dispute, it has not functioned as a theoretical driver for the field of adult education. In the following section, several challenges to andragogy are discussed, and they may help to explain why the practical application of andragogy has so outstripped the theoretical influence.

Challenges to Andragogy

There have been many publications specifying challenges to andragogy, and a systematic listing of each would be both long and monotonous. The following discussion is not meant to be exhaustive regarding the commentary on andragogy but rather to highlight the most common themes. Specific authors are included illustratively to support the themes, but there are many more commentators not specifically included. It should also be acknowledged that the following discussion deals exclusively with the Knowlesian view of andragogy; any discussion involving international perspectives would be quite different. The existing analyses use a variety of approaches to ordering and collecting the critiques, but for the purposes of this discussion they can usefully be arranged in three categories.

Clarifying the Claim

Comments about the lack of clarity within andragogy emerged quite soon after first publication of the framework (Hartree, 1984; Houle, 1972). In some ways, this is an unexpected issue, since Knowles's writing style is lucid and accessible. However, the concerns manifest on a higher level, regarding the purpose and intent of andragogy. Any perspective on theory or practice must be really clear about what sort of perspective it is and what it is meant to explain, and andragogy lacks that level of clarity.

Knowles (1970) claimed andragogy should be considered as the basis for unifying the fragmented adult education field. The starting point for this claim is the view that adults and children learn differently, because if this is not true then there is no reason for a framework specific to the education of adults. In the initial discussion of the idea there was clear expression of the view that the psychological basis of education for adults, and the appropriate techniques, were not the same as those for younger people. This was watered down in later publications, and the differences between andragogy and schooling were seen as differences of educational technique. In other words, the basis for andragogy started as the need for educational science to respond to essential differences derived from the age of the learner, while in later versions the basis became one of educational philosophy. This really undermines the hope that andragogy could bridge across the field of education for adults, as the change of emphasis sets andragogy as simply one among a whole range of other philosophical approaches.

It is also not clear what the assumptions themselves represent. It is unclear whether they are *descriptive*, simply reporting what has been observed, or *normative*,

referring to the way adults should be (Hartree, 1984). There is a potential for cir-
cularity here, with adults described as having certain traits and then the traits being
used to define adults. Theoretical work in education avoids building recommenda-
tions for practice upon assumptions, and there is an expectation that explanations are
built upon a rigorous foundation.

> All of these concerns led to questions such as whether andragogy should be under-
> stood: as an initial guide to assist adult learners towards self-direction; as a process
> of learning appropriate for adults who have already attained the capacity to be self-
> directed, or as a means through which individual needs can be reconciled with insti-
> tutional or organizational demands. (Tennant, 2006, p. 14)

The scope of andragogy makes it difficult to discern the key purpose or, to put it
less formally, the question to which andragogy is the answer. It seems that the greatest impact of andragogy has been the pragmatic application of the assumptions as a
set of guiding values, but this is far more limited than the initial hopes expressed for
the framework.

Andragogy and Diversity

In the initial stages of andragogy it is apparent the approach, as well as the supporting
assumptions, were intended to be universal. This led to suggestions during the next
few decades that Knowles had developed a normative description of the perspectives
of the field in the 1960s rather than a theoretical frame for all learners. There was
concern about the way andragogical learners were not recognized as gendered, racialized, sexualized, or privileged. To some extent, this reflects the types of theory valued
when Knowles was developing andragogy, which viewed "one big explanation" as
desirable and achievable. It is important to consider whether this kind of universalist
approach is viable in adult education.

There have been some very powerful critiques of andragogy on this basis. The
approach to teaching and learning can be held to manifest a depoliticization and
individualization of the learning process, ripping it out of its social setting and psy-
chologizing it. The invisibility of culture and social justice in the model renders it
effectively apolitical, unlike transformative learning and identity-based understandings (Grace, 2001). There have been questions regarding whether andragogy can
articulate with theoretical perspectives such as Africentrism, feminism, and critical
theory (Sandlin, 2005). Writers of these critiques often approached andragogy as a
mid–20th-century idea rendered obsolete by the need for critical approaches
recognizing that all adults might not be in a position to set their own learning
goals and attain them. The individual focus of andragogy, and its concern with self-
actualization, may not reflect either the aspirations or values of people who are not
representatives of white male American culture.

To be fair to the early andragogues, the anachronistic nature of many of these
critiques should be recognized. For example, according to our current sensibility, the

use of "man" as a generic term for adults is unacceptable. At the time, however, it was not just acceptable but had a contemporary, scientific sound to it. It is more problematic that those working with andragogy over the intervening 50 years have not found ways to incorporate the notions of identity emerging over the intervening decades, even at the level of the "big three" of class, gender, and ethnicity.

Overall, it has proven difficult to peel the core of andragogical values away from the notion of the rational, self-diagnosing, individualistic actor who views increased actualization as the purpose of learning. This may underpin the value attributed to andragogy by human resource development, as these traits are very similar to an idealized and departmentalized view of the self-managing and productive worker. One constant, from the very earliest critiques, has been the suspicion that Knowles's "work . . . says what the audience wants to hear" (Hartree, 1984, p. 203) and that this emotional appeal may tend to obscure the complexities of application in a profoundly diverse world. Theoretical investigation and development within andragogy could go some way toward addressing many of these critiques.

Building an Empirical Foundation

There have been studies setting out to test the validity of andragogical assumptions and their antecedents, but they are not common. One great challenge is formulating testable hypotheses from the assumptions of an andragogical approach, and none are easily operationalized or observed. For example, the suggestion adults give a great deal of weight to their experience would need to be tested for its prima facie validity (Do they? Compared to whom?), and then the impact of this phenomenon on their learning would need to be explored (What difference does this make?). One set of authors argued unequivocally that "for andragogy to remain a fundamental focus in adult education, it must overcome the major criticism that has plagued it for the last 30 years: Finding empirical data" (Taylor & Kroth, 2009, p. 10).

There have been attempts to create instruments to assess the implementation of andragogical ideas. Such an instrument could permit instructors and educators to assess the effectiveness of their courses as well as allow researchers to identify stronger pathways to achieve outcomes (Taylor & Kroth, 2009). This is an urgent challenge for andragogy and an extremely complex one. Responding to similar needs in schooling systems has required the development of complex and expensive global testing instruments. It is interesting to note that the Program for the International Assessment of Adult Competencies, administered in a number of countries by the Organisation for Economic Cooperation and Development (2018) and the closest we have to a global adult learning survey, did permit a degree of cross-country comparison. This study concluded that

> The andragogical assumptions seem to reflect preferences that are more aligned with males, higher levels of education, and highly skilled occupations, characteristics that are not necessarily representative of adults in need of adult and continuing

education. Finally, considerable unexplained variance at both the learner and country level suggests the need to identify additional predictors in order to better understand adult learner characteristics with respect to different cultures and learner demographics. (Roessger et al., 2018, p. 13)

This conclusion underlines how much more there is to do in terms of understanding andragogy and its applications from an empirical standpoint. However, there have been good examples of research that tests propositions closely related to andragogy even if not directly derived from it. For example, one recent study looked at the distribution and economic impact of self-directedness in learning in the labor market, finding this trait to be associated with higher socioeconomic status and rewarded with higher pay (Liu et al., 2019). The value attached to self-directedness suggests there is important work to be done in exploring the connection between andragogy and social equity. Similarly, work on the life course of adults and its relationship to learner identity (Biesta et al., 2011) could shed light on the viability of the key andragogical assumptions and potentially help revive the idea of adulthood as a specific phase of human learning. Making connections between the core ideas of andragogy and the research in associated areas capable of informing its development would require a group of people committed to the concept of andragogy and determined to build an empirical foundation for the approach.

The Potential of Andragogy

The key question for any perspective on an area of human endeavor is what it allows us to see that would not otherwise be visible. This is all the more true for a body of work claiming to offer unification and coherence across a field of study and practice. Probably the first point is to acknowledge andragogy's survival. While down a little from the high point of the 1980s, many publications still appear with andragogy as their center and impetus. This is a remarkable phenomenon. It seems likely many practitioners around the world are consciously using andragogical principles every day, and many more would read Knowles with a shock of recognition regarding how well his precepts match their own assumptions and philosophy.

Adult educators of today, whether in the field or the academy (or both), have three incentives to explore andragogy and understand it. The first is simply the ubiquity of the concept. The term, and the approach to adults and to education it represents, are known in many different areas of life and work, and it has become particularly well known in professional development and vocational learning. A good working knowledge of andragogy is an essential item in the toolkit of any educator of adults, and the idea has great communicative value.

The second incentive is the flexibility of an andragogical approach. While the lack of precision is a challenge for theorization, it also offers opportunities to shape the ideas to particular circumstances or needs. There are lacunae in the presentation of andragogy, such as its assumptions about individualism and lack of criticality, yet there is no reason why an individual engaging with it could not supplement or modify practices within the andragogical values framework. For example, there remains an interesting potential for developing a fully theorized model of critical adult education aligned with andragogical commitments.

Finally, andragogy, as conceptualized by Knowles, provides a salutary reminder of the importance of adult-to-adult relationships in adult education. Andragogy points to the relationship dynamics between the people working to coconstruct learning, an aspect of practice too central and too important to overlook. Educational research has a tendency to be dominated by schooling, and while relationships are critical within schools, they take a different form. If there is a need to justify a separate discipline of adult education, the unique form of social relations can suffice. There is no need to lay out essential differences between children and adults based on psychological needs or levels of self-direction; simply recognizing that adult educators work in variable contexts with highly diverse learners is enough to justify the precepts of andragogy.

The tangles of andragogy are likely to persist; it is improbable that definitive answers to the many questions surrounding the perspective will emerge any time soon. To some extent the questions are beside the point, as they do not prevent the application of andragogical ideas in educational practice. More important, andragogy has the potential to provide a strong orientation to the values and beliefs that underpin much educational work with adults and to bring out the philosophy behind the practice.

References

Biesta, G., Field, J., Hodkinson, P., Macleod, F. J., & Goodson, I. F. (2011) *Improving learning through the lifecourse: Learning lives.* Routledge.

Candy, P. C. (1991). *Self-direction for lifelong learning: A comprehensive guide to theory and practice.* Jossey-Bass.

Grace, A. P. (2001). Using queer cultural studies to transgress adult educational space. In V. Sheared & P. A. Sissel (Eds.), *Making space: Merging theory and practice in adult education* (pp. 257–270). Bergin & Garvey.

Hartree, A. (1984). Malcolm Knowles' theory of andragogy: A critique. *International Journal of Lifelong Learning, 3*(3), 203–210. https://doi.org/10.1080/0260137840030304

Henry, G. (2011). *Malcolm Shepherd Knowles: A history of his thought.* Nova.

Henschke, J. A., & Cooper, M. K. (2007). Additions toward a thorough understanding of the international foundations of andragogy in HRD & adult education. In C. Muresanu, V. Marian, M. Albu, I. Berar, I. C. Isac, A. Negru, & S. G. Totelecan (Eds.), *Anuarul Institutului de Istorie "George Barit" din Cluj-Napoca, Series Humanistica* [2007 Yearbook of the George Barit from Cluj-Napoca Institute of History: Humanistic Series] (pp. 7–54). Editure Academiei Romane.

Houle, C. O. (1972). *The design of education.* Jossey-Bass.

Kessels, J. W. M. (2015). Andragogy. In R. Poeli, T. S. Rocco, & G. Toth (Eds.), *The Routledge companion to human resource education* (pp. 13–20). Routledge.

Knowles, M. S. (1950). *Informal adult education: A guide for administrators, leaders, and teachers.* Association Press.

Knowles, M. S. (1970). *The modern practice of adult education: Andragogy versus pedagogy.* Association Press.

Knowles, M. S. (1980). *The modern practice of adult education: From pedagogy to andragogy.* Prentice Hall.

Knowles, M. S., Holton, E. F., & Swanson, R. A. (1998). *The adult learner: The definitive classic in adult education and human resource development.* Gulf.

Liu, H., Fernandez, F., & Grotlüschen, A. (2019). Examining self-directedness and its relationships with lifelong learning and earnings for Yunnan, Vietnam, Germany and the United States. *International Journal of Educational Development, 70,* 102088. https://doi.org/10.1016/j.ijedudev.2019.102088

Organisation for Economic Cooperation and Development. (2018). *Program for international assessment of adult competencies.* http://www.oecd.org/skills/piaac/

Parker, J. T. (1990). Modeling a future for adult basic education. *Adult Learning, 1*(4), 16–18, 28. https://doi.org/10.1177/104515959000100406

Reischmann, J. (2004). *Andragogy: History, meaning, context, function.* http://www.andragogy.net/Andragogy-Internet.pdf

Roessger, K. M., Roumell, E. A., & Weese, J. (2018, December 6–7). *Testing andragogical assumptions across countries using multi-level analysis of PIAAC data* [Paper]. American Institutes for Research PIAAC Research Conference, Arlington, VA, United States.

Rogers, C. (1957). The necessary and sufficient conditions of therapeutic personality change. *Consulting Psychology, 21,* 95–103.

Sandlin, J. A. (2005). Andragogy and its discontents: An analysis of andragogy from three critical perspectives. *PAACE Journal of Lifelong Learning, 14,* 25–42.

Smith, M. K. (2002). *Malcolm Knowles, informal adult education, self-direction and andragogy.* infed.org. https://www.infed.org/thinkers/et-knowl.htm.

Smith, M. K. (2010). Andragogy. In *The encyclopedia of informal education.* https://www.infed.org/mobi/andragogy-what-is-it-and-does-it-help-thinking-about-adult-learning/

Taylor, B., & Kroth, M. (2009). Andragogy's transition into the future: Meta-analysis of andragogy and its search for a measurable instrument. *Journal of Adult Education, 38*(1), 1–11.

Tennant, M. (2006). *Psychology and adult learning* (3rd ed.). Routledge.

Wang, V. C. X., & Kania-Gosche, B. (2010). Liberating online adult teaching and learning from the lens of Marx and others. *International Journal of Technology in Teaching and Learning, 6*(2), 133–145.

Wang, V. C. X., & Storey, V. A. (2015). Andragogy and teaching English as a foreign language in China. *The Reference Librarian, 56*(4), 295–314. https://doi.org/10.1080/02763877.2015.1057680

Yoshimoto, K., Inenaga, Y., & Yamada, H. (2007). Pedagogy and andragogy in higher education: A comparison between Germany, the UK and Japan. *European Journal of Education, 42*(1), 75–98. https://doi.org/ doi:10.1111/j.1465-3435.2007.00289.x

Editors' Key Seminal and Supplemental Text Suggestions

Bowling, J., & Henschke, J. A. (2021). Pedagogy and andragogy: Intersection for learning. In T. S. Rocco, S. C. Smith, R. C. Mizzi, L. R. Merriweather, & J. D. Hawley (Eds.), *The handbook of adult and continuing education, 2020 edition* (pp. 158–167). Stylus.

Brookfield, S. D. (1986). *Understanding and facilitating adult learning: A comprehensive analysis of principles and effective practices.* Jossey-Bass.

- Chapter 5: Andragogy: Alternative interpretations and applications

Knowles, M. S., Holton, E. F., & Swanson, R. A. (1998). *The adult learner.* Butterworth-Heinemann.

- Chapter 4: A Theory of Adult Learning: Andragogy

SELF-DIRECTED LEARNING

A 21st-Century Imperative

Ralph G. Brockett

When Malcolm Knowles introduced his assumptions about what made learning in adulthood unique, he highlighted the importance of learner self-concept. He suggested that "as an individual matures, the *need* and *capacity* to be self-directing" increases (1973, p. 43). Yet while the concept of self-direction emerged as a central tenet of adult learning theory, research, and practice in the early 1970s, self-directed learning (SDL) has existed in one form or another throughout history. Its prominence in the field has made SDL one of the most frequently studied topics in adult learning. Still, the term's ubiquity has meant that it is an often confused and misleading area of study and practice. The purpose of this chapter is to introduce the concept of SDL and illustrate how it has evolved over time. It will also introduce a central organizing principle that will attempt to integrate various threads of research as a way of defining and clarifying what SDL is.

Historical Perspectives on SDL

Before moving to a definition of SDL, it might be helpful to briefly place the concept in historical context. In antiquity, the Greek philosophers Plato and Socrates were early champions of SDL. Plato, for example, believed that building capacity for self-education was the principal purpose of education. Alexander the Great, meanwhile, supposedly carried the works of Homer with him on all of his journeys and set aside time in his daily routine for self-directed study of literature and philosophy (Kulich, 1970).

Both the opportunity and need for self-education—especially in adulthood—is clear in these examples. As such, it has also become a part of current educational practice.

Gibbons et al. (1980) explored these self-education efforts in the context of what they called *continued learning*, noting that formal instructor-directed education leaves learners with hours of noninstructional time after school and decades of noninstructional time after they have completed it. Illustrating that continued learning is essential in adulthood, the authors said,

> Continued growth during those out-of-school hours and years requires continued learning—learning to master new jobs, to become better lovers, to meet life-crises,

to find new interests, to handle changes in society, to master new roles, to open new dimensions in ourselves and our relationships, and to make contributions worthy of our capacities. (p. 42)

To understand these efforts, Gibbons and his colleagues studied the biographies of prominent individuals who learned their craft without formal education beyond high school (e.g., Harry Truman, Aaron Copeland, Frank Lloyd Wright, Virginia Woolf, Malcolm X, and Amelia Earhart, among others) to identify the characteristics of individuals whose expertise was gained through continued learning and self-teaching. They found that the skills required for effective self-education, including industriousness, perseverance, and self-discipline, were distinct from those required in more traditional, formal learning (Gibbons et al., 1980). Their study suggested the presence of self-direction long before SDL was formally identified as a characteristic of learning in adulthood, a fact further emphasized by subsequent studies of self-directed learners, including the Wright Brothers and their invention of the airplane (Cavaliere, 1989), Abraham Lincoln (M. R. Brockett & Brockett, 2020), Robert Heinlein (Owenby, 1996), and John Steinbeck (R. G. Brockett, 2019). L. M. Guglielmino et al. (2004) offered further historical discussion of SDL in the United States. They identified Benjamin Franklin's Junto, mechanics institutes, the lyceum, Chautauqua, and public libraries as examples of resources that supported SDL for colonial America through the late 1800s. The formalization of SDL as an intentional area of practice and research in adult education that began to emerge in the 1970s built on these early examples.

Among the first examples of systematic research to formally introduce the study and practice of SDL was *The Adults' Learning Projects* by Allen Tough (1971/1979). Tough interviewed 66 adults about the different learning activities that they had engaged in during the past year. He asked about classes they had taken, but he also focused on their SDL projects, which he defined as "major, highly deliberative effort[s]" (p. 1) that were planned primarily by the individuals themselves. Tough found that the adults' reasons for engaging in these learning projects were "to gain new knowledge, insight, or understanding" (p. 1). He also found that participants completed an average of eight learning projects per year. Especially significant was the finding that 68% of the projects were self-planned.

Tough (1971/1979) used the metaphor of an iceberg to describe the phenomenon of SDL. Here, formal educational experiences (classes, workshops, training programs, etc.) are only the tip of the iceberg, and the vast majority of learning projects lie beneath the surface and are not as readily visible. Tough's findings were supported and affirmed by similar findings that emerged from numerous subsequent studies (e.g., R. G. Brockett & Hiemstra, 1991/2019). Given Tough's findings about the prevalence of self-planned activities among adults, it is important to understand SDL; educators can both build upon and enhance their inclinations to self-direct their learning within more structured adult education contexts.

The common implementation of SDL activities among adults in nonformal settings and the early research about the success of self-directed projects led to the emergence of SDL as a major area of research and practice. The challenge for the new area was to identify how a developing understanding of SDL in the nonformal space should and could be intentionally designed to the same effect in formal educational environments. Rather than lead to emerging clarity about what SDL is and how it works, however, this focus revealed additional questions and complexities of the practice.

Divergent Perspectives on Self-Directed Learning

There are a host of definitions for what constitutes SDL. Perhaps the most frequently cited definition was offered by Knowles (1975), who stated that

> Self-directed learning, in its broadest meaning, describes a process in which individuals take the initiative with or without the help of others, in diagnosing their learning needs, formulating learning goals, identifying resources for learning, choosing and implementing learning strategies and evaluating learning outcomes. (p. 18)

Another definition "refers to both the external characteristics of an instructional process and the internal characteristics of the learner, where the individual assumes primary responsibility for learning" (R. G. Brockett & Hiemstra, 1991/2019, p. 24). More recently, the International Society for Self-Directed Learning (2020) adopted the following definition: "Self-directed learning is an intentional learning process that is created and evaluated by the learner" (para. 4). For the purposes of this chapter, SDL can be thought of as a process in which a learner takes primary responsibility for planning, implementing, and evaluating their learning.

There is sometimes confusion about the differing terminology used in these definitions of SDL. Hiemstra (1996, 2004) has done an analysis to determine frequently used terms for SDL. He reviewed International Self-Directed Learning Symposium proceedings from 1986 to 2003 and *International Journal of Self-Directed Learning* issues from 2004 to 2018. He found that some of the terms most frequently used to refer to SDL are *self-directed learning readiness, autodidactic learning, autonomous learning, self-directed learner, self-efficacy, learning projects, self-direction in learning, self-planned, self-education,* and *self-regulation.* While this plethora of terms meaning more or less the same thing might, on the surface, not seem like a major issue, it is important to be aware of them because they have an impact on how scholars communicate with each other and with practitioners.

One such difference can be seen in the distinction between a self-directed *learner* and self-directed *learning*. This has led to a question of whether self-direction is a trait or tendency among adults, a state that develops over time as suggested in the earlier definition from Knowles, or a teaching–learning process. The challenge presented in this point of divergence leads into other questions about SDL. If SDL is a learner attribute, is it a natural tendency among adults, or is it something that grows and develops through learning? If it is a learned skill, is there a practical or philosophical rationale for why self-direction should be a goal of an adult learning program? These questions have led to different perspectives about what exactly we mean by *self-direction* and how it can be effectively leveraged or designed into an adult learning experience. A shared, comprehensive framework was necessary for making sense of these varied perspectives.

An Evolving Model of SDL: From the Personal Responsibility Orientation Model to the Person Process Context Model

As SDL became an increasingly important focus of research and practice in adult education throughout the 1980s, these contrasting perspectives and definitions of SDL led to questions about how the practices could be most effectively implemented. In an effort to address these divergent assumptions and foci, R. G. Brockett and Hiemstra (1991/2019) developed the *personal responsibility orientation (PRO) model,* a holistic conceptual model designed to reframe and integrate various interpretations of SDL. In this model, the starting point for understanding SDL is that the learner takes personal responsibility for learning. This responsibility requires a shift in both learner and learning context.

Self-direction in learning, then, consists of both characteristics of the teaching–learning transaction (e.g., planning, implementing, and evaluating learning) and characteristics of the learner (e.g., self-concept, resilience, grit, and creativity), which are psychological variables within the person. In addition, self-direction in learning takes place within a social context, which influences the learning process. This model is presented in Figure 10.1. It helped to distinguish among several elements and reduce confusion about different aspects of self-direction. It even served as a framework for the development of a widely used measure of self-direction (Stockdale, 2003; Stockdale & Brockett, 2011).

Subsequently, because some of the terminology of the PRO model was confusing, and because the role of social context was downplayed in it, Hiemstra and Brockett (2012) updated and simplified their model by introducing the *person process context (PPC) model.* In the PPC model, SDL is understood to consist of three interactive factors: (a) the individual, (b) the teaching–learning process, and (c) the social context in which learning takes place. The "ideal" SDL situation occurs when these three factors are in balance, as presented in Figure 10.2. This model strongly

Figure 10.1. The personal responsibility orientation model of self-direction in learning.

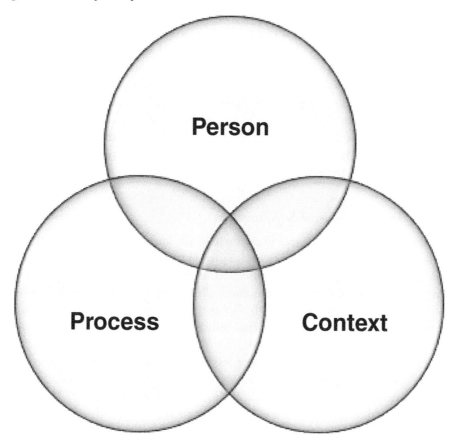

Note. Adapted from Brockett and Hiemstra (1991/2019).

Figure 10.2. The person process context model of SDL.

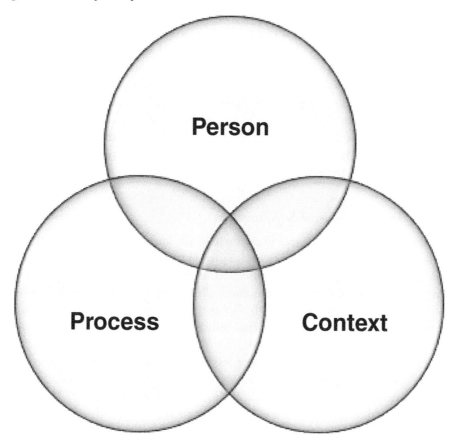

suggests that, taken alone, neither the individual, the process, nor the context can be understood as comprising SDL. It is crucial to examine all three dimensions in order to truly understand and effectively implement SDL.

For practitioners, the PPC model can be useful as it identifies three different but important aspects of SDL. As is discussed in the following section, each of the three dimensions addresses concepts and strategies for increasing self-direction in any given situation. The elements of person, process, and context will be used in the following sections to describe some of the major contributions of research and practice related to SDL.

The Person Dimension

As previously stated, the person dimension focuses on self-direction as a personal characteristic or set of characteristics present in an individual learner. These characteristics are largely, though not exclusively, psychological in focus. This emphasis is grounded in the work of Carl Rogers (1961) who stated that to be self-directing, "one chooses—and then learns from the consequences" (p. 171). Within this dimension, the essence of SDL is that those individuals who possess certain learner characteristics will display a tendency toward self-directedness as a learner.

For example, one of the most important factors related to self-directedness is *self-concept*, or how people feel about themselves as agents of their own learning. In his discussion of andragogy, Knowles (1970) stated that self-concept of the adult learner is self-directed while that of a child is more dependent. Although Knowles later acknowledged this may not be true for every adult (andragogy is a set of assumptions about adults that are not empirically demonstrated), in an early study on SDL readiness, Sabbaghian (1980) found a statistically significant relationship between self-concept and readiness for SDL. This finding underscores the idea that specific attitudes and characteristics can serve as indicators of an individual's likelihood of engaging in self-directed activities.

Assessing Tendency Toward Self-Direction

Most instruments that assess readiness for self-direction were developed primarily for research purposes, but several have also proven useful to practitioners in identifying degree or tendency toward self-direction in their learners. For example, instruments to assess readiness for asynchronous online learning might include a measure of self-concept and readiness for SDL. For the most part, research on the personal characteristics of self-directed learners has utilized one of several standardized instruments to measure the construct of SDL.

The most widely used measure of self-direction in learning was developed by L. M. Guglielmino (1977). For her doctoral dissertation, she created the Self-Directed Learning Readiness Scale (SDLRS), a 58-item Likert scale. The instrument assumes that self-direction exists as a tendency within all adults but that it exists along a continuum representing a range of individual values, attitudes, and abilities. The SDLRS provides a single readiness score for a learner that is based on alignment of questionnaire responses with a set of qualities frequently seen in highly self-directed individuals. These qualities include a degree of initiative and independence, personal responsibility, problem-solving orientation, self-discipline and curiosity, self-confidence, organization, and goal orientation (L. M. Guglielmino, 1977). It continues to be the gold standard among scales measuring SDL both in research and practice. Given the continued widespread use of the SDLRS over several decades, it is clear that the instrument has made a major contribution to SDL research.

A second early instrument designed to measure self-directedness is the Oddi Continuing Learning Inventory (OCLI). This instrument was developed to "describe the personality characteristics of self-directed continuing learners" (Oddi, 1986, p. 97). Like the Guglielmino instrument, Oddi's assessment tool uses a series of Likert-scale questions to discern an individual's tendency toward self-direction. The OCLI defines self-direction as existing across three domains. The first is *learner proactivity*, as indicated through motivation, confidence, and self-efficacy. The second domain is the *degree of cognitive openness*. Finally, Oddi's instrument explores the *degree of learner commitment* (Harvey et al., 2006).

A more recent measure of SDL was developed by Stockdale (2003). The Personal Responsibility Orientation to Self-Direction in Learning Scale (PRO-SDLS) is a 25-item scale derived from elements of R. G. Brockett and Hiemstra's (1991/2019) PRO model, discussed earlier. The scale includes four factor scores for Initiative, Control, Self-Efficacy, and Motivation. It was designed specifically for use in higher education settings.

Implications of the Personal Dimension

Although the three scales previously identified have variations in the number of items and the specific psychological dimensions explored, they all share an underlying assumption that there exists in individuals a set of psychological indicators for self-direction. It is also important to recognize that all three scale authors suggested that these psychological traits can be developed over time. This assumption has significant implications for the practice of adult educators because it suggests that self-direction itself can be developed as a learner tendency. For example, Guglielmino and Guglielmino (2004) suggested that honest self-awareness of one's readiness is itself a prerequisite for SDL; they suggested that the SDLRS—or other inventories for assessing learning style—might be appropriate first steps toward developing oneself as a self-directed learner. In chapter 4 of this volume, Bergin, Bergin, and Prewett describe strategies for improving learner self-efficacy, an indicator of self-direction in the PRO-SDLS. If such strategies as peer modeling and eliminating time limits might serve to increase learner self-efficacy, it can therefore be suggested that they may also serve to improve a learner's tendency toward self-direction.

In addition to using the scales to predict self-direction, a large number of studies have used the preceding scales, plus other measures of SDL, to correlate and predict the impact of self-directedness on various personal characteristics. A sampling of these studies include correlations between self-directedness and self-concept (Sabbaghian, 1980), life satisfaction among older adults (R. G. Brockett, 1985), positive health behaviors (Leeb, 1985), use of learning contracts (Caffarella & Caffarella, 1986), job performance (P. J. Guglielmino et al., 1987), creativity (Cox, 2002), satisfaction with an online course (Fogerson, 2005), cross-cultural adaptability (Chuprina & Durr, 2006), knowledge- and performance-based measures of success (Findley & Bulik, 2011), use of technology by students entering the workforce (Holt, 2011), information literacy (Conner, 2012), hope (Dieffenderfer, 2014), gratitude (Vess, 2015), resilience (Beeler, 2018), grit (Ruttencutter, 2018), professional development among elementary teachers (Wagner, 2018), and attitudes toward continuing education among community college students in an allied health program (Hall, 2018). In other words, these instruments may have a diagnostic value that can be useful in helping practitioners understand the level of self-directedness among their learners. This can help them design appropriate activities to enhance self-directedness or to fit existing levels of self-directedness. What is especially important for those engaged in practice with adult learners is that the presence or absence of characteristics such as those previously described are likely to have an influence on the extent to which an individual will demonstrate self-directedness and be able to participate effectively in SDL activities in a classroom context.

An emergent challenge to the personal dimension has been a recognition that some of the traits that are predictors of self-directed tendencies are valued differently within different cultures. Studies have questioned whether cultural background influences the way that learners internalize self-direction or the way that these factors influence an individual's approach to self-direction. For example, Frambach et al. (2012) studied self-direction in medical education in three locations and found that differences in how students experienced uncertainty, hierarchy, and achievement influenced their effectiveness in SDL situations. Other studies have identified differences in SDL practices based on race (Smith et al., 2013) and gender (Grover & Miller, 2014). As these dimensions of culture are similar to dimensions identified in the assessment instruments previously listed, there have been some questions about whether personal tendency toward self-direction is itself culturally determined.

This challenge has three significant implications for practice. First, if culture is a predictor of a personal readiness and tendency for self-direction, then educators in diverse, international contexts or those working with people newly immigrated to the United States must be aware of the array of comfort levels present when planning for SDL projects. In addition, this raises the question of whether other dimensions of an individual's identity may be predictors of readiness for participation in self-directed events. For example, Grover and Miller (2014) found differences in the SDL practices of men and women and suggested that these differences may emanate from differences in the ways that men and women view themselves as learners. A final implication is that these challenges reaffirm a question posed earlier in this chapter: Should SDL be a goal of teaching practice? While some have suggested that self-direction is both an ideal and a natural tendency for adults, these questions of culture suggest that these values are not universal. This particular question demonstrates an important consideration for adult educators who seek to be inclusive and culturally affirming. For more information on the complex cultural implications of adult education, please see chapter 2 of this volume.

The Process Dimension

While the personal dimension explores ways in which an individual's attributes ready them to be a self-directed learner, the process dimension is concerned with research and practice related to the structure and implementation of the teaching–learning process. Several models have been developed in order to understand the process that can be used to implement SDL.

In his classic work, *Self-Directed Learning: A Guide for Learners and Teachers,* Knowles (1975) identified seven steps involved in facilitating this type of learning approach inside or outside a formal educational setting:

- climate setting
- planning
- diagnosing needs for learning
- setting goals
- designing a learning plan
- engaging in learning activities
- evaluating learning outcomes

This model is discussed more fully in chapter 9 of this volume on the subject of andragogy. The connection between andragogy and SDL is that adults' self-directedness is one of the major assumptions Knowles (1975) made about adults and, he argued, is essential to understanding learning in adulthood. Two other teaching–learning process models with connections to SDL are discussed here; both are especially relevant to practice.

Hiemstra and Sisco (1990), in their model of individualizing instruction, identified six steps. The authors used the term *individualizing instruction* to describe a process that overlaps with elements of SDL. This model consists of (a) Preplanning Activities, (b) Creating a Positive Learning Environment, (c) Developing the Instructional Plan, (d) Learning Activity Identification, (e) Putting Learning in Action and Monitoring Progress, and (f) Evaluating Individual Learning Outcomes. Hiemstra and Sisco created a checklist that comprises several important components for each of the six steps. Clearly, there are similarities between the models presented by Knowles (1975) and Hiemstra and Sisco (1990). For example, both models emphasize the importance of establishing a climate to empower students and to give them a sense of self-efficacy and control, and both models describe shared ownership over the evaluation of learning as determined in a collaboratively defined learning plan. Interestingly, another assumption that is built into both models is that learners already possess a degree of readiness for self-direction.

Grow (1991) did not make such an assumption and suggested that a purpose of adult education was to develop learner tendency for self-direction, not to define learning projects that assume existing readiness. To address this need, he developed the *staged self-directed learning model*. In Grow's model, the learner moves through four stages that range from low to high learner self-directedness. The model begins with Stage 1, where the learner is dependent and the role of the teacher is to serve as an authority or a coach. In Stage 2, the learner demonstrates interest and begins to show a level of self-directedness. Here, the role of the teacher is to serve as a motivator or guide. Stage 3 is where the learner is involved and the teacher's role is that of a facilitator. Finally, in Stage 4, the learner is self-directed, and the role of the teacher shifts to serving as a consultant to the learner or delegating tasks based on how the learner designs the process. In Grow's model, an educator must meet the student at their stage, or the mismatch will reduce the efficacy of instruction. Through support and learner development, the educator can help the learner to move to more advanced stages of autonomy and self-direction.

An important consideration in all three of these models is that SDL is not an all-or-nothing process. Every learner falls somewhere on a continuum from low to high self-directedness (R. G. Brockett & Hiemstra, 1991/2019). When faced with a task that is unfamiliar, the learner is likely to demonstrate more dependence on the instructor for specific guidance. As the learner becomes more comfortable and familiar with content and learning processes and tasks in a given area, there is an increasing potential for self-direction. At some point, when there is significant confidence in the topic being studied, the learner may be more likely to be highly self-directed and ready to take responsibility for future learning in the area. This, however, assumes a degree of readiness for self-direction as explored in the earlier section "The Person Dimension."

While the preceding models were developed with classroom or other formal and nonformal instructional settings in mind, they can easily be adapted to assist individual learners in informal contexts outside of institutional settings. For example, in the models by Knowles (1975) and Hiemstra and Sisco (1990), learners can easily use the steps in the models to guide themselves through the process. In fact, having steps like these should help educators to more effectively facilitate SDL and learners to more effectively plan and implement their own learning projects outside of educational settings.

The Contextual Dimension

The third and final dimension of the PPC model relates to the context in which SDL takes place. Hiemstra and Brockett (2012) stated, "This encompasses the environmental and sociopolitical climate, such as culture, power, learning environment, finances, gender, learning climate, organizational policies, political milieu, race, and sexual orientation" (p. 158). This is distinct from the impact that these factors have on shaping an individual's psychological factors (personal dimension); here, these contextual factors shape our very understanding of what SDL is and of the conditions under which it can flourish.

Brookfield (1993) argued that political issues of control and power lie at the heart of SDL. From Brookfield's perspective, self-direction is neither a trait nor an instructional process; instead, it is a political act representing a learner's rejection of the repressive and hegemonic forces of more instructor-directed systems of education. By recognizing SDL as emancipatory action, Brookfield argued that true SDL can exist only when political conditions that are supportive of SDL are in place. It is therefore necessary for adult educators to recognize the political dimensions that can repress learner self-direction. These may include issues of power inherent in the instructor–student dynamic, but also macro-environmental factors, such as race, gender, and socioeconomic status, that make participation in SDL projects dangerous (socially or physically) or else logistically impossible.

Andruske (2003) offered a useful example of how social context shapes SDL. She studied SDL efforts among 23 single mothers receiving welfare benefits in British Columbia. She addressed the themes of welfare policy entitlements, education and training, employment and work skills, health, and legal rights in the SDL projects undertaken by these women. In particular, she found that the SDL projects of six of these women brought them "directly into conflict with government agents as they created oppositional actions to expert opinions and policies" (p. 16). In conclusion, Andruske stated that this study "depicts women to adult educators as political agents acting in opposition for change to regain control and power over their lives while validating women as self-directed learners seeking to fulfill needs not identified by experts" (p. 16). Andruske's work provides an apt illustration of the political milieu presented in Brookfield's (1993) work on SDL.

In a study of SDL in a rural setting, Roberson and Merriam (2005) used a qualitative study design that also demonstrated the relationship between context and SDL. They found that the study population of 10 older adults between the ages of 75 and 87 had experienced transitions in three areas—they had more time due to retirement, their family roles had changed (e.g., by becoming grandparents), and they had physical and social losses associated with later life. These transitions were the primary focus of their self-directed activities. In addition, Roberson and Merriam found that where they lived also played a role; living in a rural community was viewed as a "positive environment for learning" (p. 269).

These examples demonstrate that the context in which SDL takes place is a substantial consideration in determining the likelihood for success in learning. This means that learning context can also determine the likelihood of successful SDL. This element of the PPC model has received less attention among researchers and practitioners than the person or process dimensions. Therefore, there are many opportunities to increase understanding of the role that context plays in shaping SDL through future research and direct applications to practice. These efforts could focus on contextual factors such as cost, time, availability of learning opportunities, learning climate, culture, gender, race, sexual orientation, and political milieu.

Facilitating SDL

Earlier in the chapter, Knowles's (1973) andragogy, Hiemstra and Sisco's (1990) individualizing instruction model, and Grow's (1990) staged self-directed learning model were introduced. Together, these three models can be of use to practitioners in identifying approaches for working with self-directed learners. While understanding steps in facilitating a process is a necessary attribute, it is not sufficient. In addition, it is important to consider some of the personal qualities that are necessary in order to be an effective facilitator of SDL when it is pursued in a formal educational setting.

Elsewhere, I discussed a set of qualities that are important in order to be an effective educator (R. G. Brockett, 2015). While these qualities were discussed in terms of teaching in general, they are especially relevant to working with self-directed learners because they are personal qualities that can have a direct impact on their capacity to pursue SDL.

I discussed seven qualities using the acronym TEACHER. It is important to recognize that "facilitator" is more reflective of work with self-directed learners than the more traditional "teacher." So I encourage you to focus on the actual qualities rather than the acronym. These qualities are Trust, Empathy, Authenticity, Confidence, Humility, Enthusiasm, and Respect.

Trust "is essential in building a climate conducive to successful learning" (R. G. Brockett, 2015, p. 10). Trust is a two-way street that involves both the learner and the instructor. In the case of SDL, learners must trust that they can pursue their learning activities without fear or intimidation. Second, the instructor must trust the learner to be open to new experiences and capable of pursuing them. Finally, trust involves a willingness to trust the process. Sometimes, both facilitators and learners will have to possess a tolerance for ambiguity in a given SDL situation. In other words, things may not always run smoothly. However, by trusting the process it is possible to work through these rough patches and get back on track to a productive process.

Empathy is an important skill in nearly any human interaction, but it is of particular importance in teaching–learning interactions. Basically, "empathy involves connecting with another person and having a special understanding of what the person is going through, while still retaining a certain degree of detachment" (R. G. Brockett, 2015, p. 11). In other words, an empathic facilitator can understand what it might be like to be in the learner's shoes while at the same time maintaining a certain professional distance from the learner's personal situation in order to more fully understand the learner. In the context of SDL, empathy is needed to help students define personal learning goals and to facilitate their attainment of those goals within a given learning context.

Authenticity, quite simply, is being oneself. Another word for authenticity is *genuineness*. In working with self-directed learners, it is important for instructors to show a human side. Within the coaching relationship established in the learner–facilitator dynamic of SDL, authenticity is critical for promoting learner reflection and self-management. An authentic facilitator is not afraid to reveal oneself to learners and let them see the real person.

The next two qualities go hand in hand. It is important that a facilitator demonstrate a degree of *confidence*, both relative to the content and in one's ability to help adults learn that content. Without a degree of confidence, it will be difficult to demonstrate the facilitator's qualification to work with learners. At the same time, it is equally important to possess a degree of *humility*. Humility means modesty or down-to-earthness. In other words, the humble facilitator is one who knows "their stuff and they let their actions work for them without the need to prove anything or convince others of their importance" (R. G. Brockett, 2015, p.13). Taken together, a balance between confidence and humility is vital to demonstrating a caring relationship with the learner. This relationship, in turn, is necessary for helping learners feel both safe and ready to exercise control of their own learning context. They are therefore essential to the person and context dimension of the model described earlier in this chapter.

It should go without saying that demonstrating *enthusiasm* is a must in effective facilitation. Learners can tell whether someone is interested in the topic or in them. Quite simply, it is not possible to hide a lack of enthusiasm. On the other hand, an enthusiastic facilitator is most likely to do things that will increase the individual's motivation to learn and to therefore increase the likelihood of demonstrating self-motivating behaviors.

Finally, it is essential to demonstrate *respect* for the learner. Working with self-directed learners is, by necessity, a very close personal experience. Sometimes instructors and learners may find that they have differences in values, attitudes, and beliefs. In such cases, it is important to be nonjudgmental and accept that they may not always see things the same way. It is this acceptance that makes it possible for the facilitator–learner relationship to move forward and grow in spite of different ways of looking at things.

It is worth stating again that while the TEACHER acronym was developed as a heuristic for effective teaching–learning interactions in general, it is particularly applicable to facilitators of SDL because these qualities are vital to creating the effective one-to-one helping relationship needed to support this approach. Self-directed learners have made a conscious choice to learn about something that matters to them. The better facilitators are able to tap into this desire to learn, the more likely they are to help create a successful learning outcome. The seven qualities discussed here can truly help instructors become more effective facilitators of SDL.

Trends and Issues in SDL

SDL is one of the most studied topics in the literature of adult education. However, there is less scholarship in the area today than there was in the 1970s through the

1990s. Perhaps this is due to a greater focus on more recently emerging areas of study, such as transformative learning, postmodernism, and critical adult education. Yet there are examples of the scholarship continuing to evolve. The International Society for Self-Directed Learning has hosted an annual symposium since 1987. The society also publishes an online, open-access journal, the *International Journal of Self-Directed Learning*, which addresses current state-of-the-art studies on SDL.

Developments in SDL are not limited to North America. As one example, in South Africa, the Self-Directed Learning Research Focus Area at North-West University is a group of more than 50 researchers and postgraduate staff who are currently conducting research on SDL. Their work focuses on such areas as problem-based learning, assessment, blended learning, cognition and metacognition, cooperative learning, and Indigenous knowledge and contextualized learning (North-West University SDL Research Focus Area, n.d.). This group has begun to hold conferences on SDL for which open-access books have been published. The continued research in this area suggests that, despite the fact that scholarship in SDL may not be as prevalent now as it was in the 1980s and 1990s, it is still alive and well in the world of adult education. It also suggests that there is still much for us to learn about self-direction and new avenues of practice to explore.

Despite this continued presence, SDL is at an important crossroads as an area of research. Most of the researchers who have established and solidified the importance of SDL research to date through their own scholarship and mentoring of others have since retired or passed away. Research on SDL continues to be published, but it is important to create a cadre of new scholars who will take up the mantle of earlier generations and make SDL a priority in their own work. If this happens, the opportunities to expand understanding of SDL even further will be unlimited. This will have clear implications for improving practice through new understandings of SDL. Though much is known about SDL, there is still much to be learned. Three examples are presented in the following sections.

Self-Directed Learning and Positive Psychology

In the 1990s, positive psychology emerged as an area of specialization in the field of psychology. Positive psychology involves understanding human strengths. For example, Peterson and Seligman (2004) identified 24 human strengths. They proposed that all people score high on several of these strengths and low on several others. Teal et al. (2015) created the self-directed wellness model to look at intersections between these human strengths and concepts related to self-directedness. This model compares, contrasts, and synthesizes concepts discussed in SDL in relation to the 24 human strengths Peterson and Seligman identified. By showing the connections between elements of SDL and positive psychology, the authors made a convincing case that SDL plays an important role in positive psychology.

Several other studies have also looked at self-directedness in relation to different human strengths. These include hope in the workplace (Dieffenderfer, 2014), gratitude (Vess, 2015), grit (Ruttencutter, 2018), and resilience (Beeler, 2018). The positive relationships found in these studies are promising because they present evidence of connections to SDL and suggest that it may be productive to study additional human strengths in relation to SDL. There are clear practical implications for understanding and implementing these strengths to promote effective SDL strategies. For example, one strategy to enhance self-directedness might be for practitioners to learn about the various human strengths so that they can help learners develop strategies to address resilience, hope, gratitude, grit, and other strengths. There are instruments that facilitators can take themselves or administer to learners to assess these strengths. Many of these are available online.

Lessons From the Coronavirus Pandemic

In early 2020, the world was thrown into great upheaval due to the coronavirus pandemic, which has impacted millions of people and shut down economies throughout the world for a time. "Social distancing" entered the lexicon of everyday life as people were urged or mandated by law to stay at home and keep a safe distance from others in order to minimize the risk of spreading the virus. Colleges and universities moved from face-to-face to online learning with little advance preparation. Many K–12 schools adopted online approaches to teaching and learning. As a result, the pandemic had unforeseen consequences for the world of education. For instance, teachers and learners who were unfamiliar with distance education technologies had to be self-directed in learning new ways of working with students via online platforms. In fact, while it is still too early to tell for sure, it has been argued that the pandemic has led to a growth in online learning, particularly in higher education.

But the world health crisis also left many people with ample time to do things within the boundaries of their homes. This provided a previously unknown opportunity for individuals to engage in a whole range of SDL projects. An interesting question for the future would be to consider whether people used this period of relative isolation to learn new things and, if so, how did they go about this learning? Clearly, the pandemic has had an impact on how people learn in order to negotiate their lives, health, employment, and schooling. And it will continue to have an impact in the future as the world resumes a new normal.

Technology and Self-Directed Learning

Technology has long been an essential aspect of SDL. As previously noted, technology was—and still is—a mediating force in education during the pandemic. Whether it be motion pictures (Adam, 1940) in the 1940s, educational broadcasting (Blakely, 1979) in the 1950s, or programmed instruction in the 1960s and 1970s, technology has played an important role in adult learning, and specifically in SDL.

Today, technology for learning can be used in a variety of formats, including synchronous and asynchronous online learning, social networking, and open-access resources. And as previously mentioned, the pandemic has done much to transform the nature of online learning and technology use. Opportunities abound for the self-directed learner who wishes to access knowledge and information to assist them with their learning projects. For example, someone who wishes to learn about gardening can go to Wikipedia for general information and social networks to connect with others interested in gardening. For more specific knowledge, the person can enroll in a noncredit online learning course from a university, an agriculture extension program, a community college, a public school, or a nonprofit agency. This perspective of developing strong networks of self-directed individuals through technology is echoed in Rita Kop's chapter (chapter 13) on connectivism in this volume.

The difficulty in discussing technology is that it is constantly evolving. Modes of technology that are popular at present will inevitably be replaced by newer forms of technology in the future. Nonetheless, it is almost certain that the self-directed learner who can tap into current forms of technology will be in a position to learn in a more proactive and proficient way. Facilitators can play an important role in making this happen.

Conclusion

Although it has been studied only for about the past 5 decades, SDL has existed throughout history. For purposes of this chapter, the topic of SDL focuses on an interface among personal characteristics of learners; the process of engaging in SDL, whether in an instructional setting or on one's own; and the social and political context in which learning takes place. An optimal situation for SDL to occur is when there is a balance among these three components.

There are many trends and issues in SDL. A potential linkage between positive psychology and SDL can help provide a greater understanding of what learner characteristics enhance or restrict self-directedness. The coronavirus pandemic has presented challenges and opportunities for SDL that may have long-term implications for how SDL is viewed in the future. Technology has a clear and essential role to play in the future of SDL. And, finally, there is a need for further research on SDL in order to ensure that knowledge remains ahead of the practice.

SDL, regardless of the name that is used to describe it, is essential for success in today's world. With the rapid rate of change, one who is not proactive in taking responsibility for learning will readily become lost in the sea of information and ideas now available. SDL is truly an imperative for the 21st century.

References

Adam, T. R. (1940). *Motion pictures in adult education*. American Association for Adult Education.

Andruske, C. L. (2003). Self-directed learning projects of women on welfare as political acts. *Adult Learning, 14*(4), 13–16. https://doi.org/10.1177/104515950301400404

Beeler, L. M. (2018). *An investigation of the relationships between self-directedness in learning and resilience among undergraduate nursing students* [Unpublished doctoral dissertation]. University of Tennessee, Knoxville.

Blakely, R. (1979). *To serve the public interest: Educational broadcasting in the United States.* Syracuse University Press.

Brockett, M. R., & Brockett, R. G. (2020). Lincoln as learner: Three scenarios of successful self-directed learning. *International Journal of Self-Directed Learning, 17*(2), 1–9.

Brockett, R. G. (1985). The relationship between self-directed learning readiness and life satisfaction among older adults. *Adult Education Quarterly, 34*(4), 210–219. https://doi.org/10.1177/0001848185035004003

Brockett, R. G. (2015). *Teaching adults: A practical guide for new teachers.* Jossey-Bass.

Brockett, R. G. (2019). John Steinbeck and *The Grapes of Wrath:* A writer and his self-directed learning process. *International Journal of Self-Directed Learning, 16*(1), 1–11.

Brockett, R. G., & Hiemstra, R. (2019). *Self-direction in adult learning: Perspectives on theory, research and practice.* Routledge. (Original work published 1991)

Brookfield, S. (1993). Self-directed learning, political clarity, and the critical practice of adult education. *Adult Education Quarterly, 43*(4), 227–242. https://doi.org/10.1177/0741713693043004002

Caffarella, R. S., & Caffarella, E. P. (1986). Self-directedness and learning contracts in adult education. *Adult Education Quarterly, 36*(4), 226–234. https://doi.org/10.1177/0001848186036004004

Cavaliere, L. A. (1989). *A case study of the self-directed learning processes and network patterns utilized by the Wright brothers which led to their invention of flight* [Doctoral dissertation, Rutgers—The State University of New Jersey, 1988]. Dissertation Abstracts International, 49, 2894A.

Chuprina, L., & Durr, R. (2006). Self-directed learners' readiness and cultural adaptability in expatriate managers. *International Journal of Self-Directed Learning, 3*, 13–24.

Conner, T. R. (2012). *The relationship between self-directed learning and information literacy among adult learners in higher education* [Doctoral dissertation, University of Tennessee, Knoxville]. https://trace.tennessee.edu/cgi/viewcontent.cgi?article=2689&context=utk_graddiss&httpsredir=1&referer=

Cox, B. F. (2002). *The relationship between creativity and self-directed learning among adult community college students* [Unpublished doctoral dissertation]. University of Tennessee, Knoxville.

Dieffenderfer, V. M. (2014). *The relationship between hope and self-directedness in the workplace* [Unpublished doctoral dissertation]. University of Tennessee, Knoxville.

Findley, B. W., & Bulik, R. J. (2011). The relationship of self-directed learning readiness to knowledge-based and performance-based measures of success in medical students. *International Journal of Self-Directed Learning, 8*(2), 28–43.

Fogerson, D. L. (2005). *Readiness factors contributing to participant satisfaction in online higher education courses* [Doctoral dissertation, University of Tennessee, Knoxville]. https://trace.tennessee.edu/utk_graddiss/1952

Frambach, J. K., Driessen, E. W., Chan, L.-C., & van der Vlueten, C. P. M. (2012). Rethinking the globalization of problem-based learning: How culture challenges self-directed learning. *Medical Education, 46*(8), 738–747. https://doi.org/10.1111/j.1365-2923.2012.04290.x

Gibbons, M., Bailey, A., Comeau, P., Schmuck, J., Seymour, S., & Wallace, D. (1980). Toward a theory of self-directed learning: A study of experts without formal training. *Journal of Humanistic Psychology, 20*(2), 41–56. https://doi.org/10.1177/002216788002000205

Grover, K. S. & Miller, M. T. (2014). Gender differences in self-directed learning practices among community members. *PAACE Journal of Lifelong Learning, 23*(1), 19–31.

Grow, G. O. (1991). Teaching learners to be self-directed. *Adult Education Quarterly, 41*(3), 125–149. https://doi.org/10.1177/0001848191041003001

Guglielmino, L. M. (1977). *Development of the Self-Directed Learning Readiness Scale* [Unpublished doctoral dissertation]. University of Georgia.

Guglielmino, L. M., & Guglielmino, P. J. (2004). Becoming a more self-directed learner: Why and how. In G. M. Piskurich (Ed.), *Getting the most from online learning* (pp. 25–38). Jossey-Bass.

Guglielmino, L. M., Long, H. B., & Hiemstra, R. (2004). Historical perspectives series: Self-direction in learning in the United States. *International Journal of Self-Directed Learning, 1*(1), 1–17.

Guglielmino, P. J., Guglielmino, L. M., & Long, H. B. (1987). Self-directed learning readiness and performance in the workplace. *Higher Education, 16,* 303–317. https://doi.org/10.1007/BF00148972

Hall, J. (2018). *Relationships of self-direction and attitudes toward continuing education in community college allied health programs* [Unpublished doctoral dissertation]. University of Tennessee, Knoxville.

Harvey, B. J., Rothman, A. I., & Frecker, R. C. (2006). A confirmatory factor analysis of the Oddi Continuing Learning Inventory (OCLI). *Adult Education Quarterly, 56*(3), 188–200. https://doi.org/10.1177/0741713605286167

Hiemstra, R. (1996). *What's in a word? Changes in self-directed learning language over a decade* [Paper presentation]. Annual International Self-Directed Learning Symposium, West Palm Beach, FL, United States.

Hiemstra, R. (2004). Self-directed learning lexicon. *International Journal of Self-Directed Learning, 1*(2), 1–6.

Hiemstra, R., & Brockett, R. G. (2012). Reframing the meaning of self-directed learning: An updated model. In *Proceedings of the annual Adult Education Research Conference.* https://newprairiepress.org/aerc/2012/papers/22/

Hiemstra, R., & Sisco, B. (1990). *Individualizing instruction: Making learning personal, empowering, and successful.* Jossey-Bass.

Holt, L. L. (2011). *Self-direction and technology use among new workforce entrants* [Doctoral dissertation, University of Tennessee, Knoxville]. https://trace.tennessee.edu/utk_graddiss/1191

International Society for Self-Directed Learning. (2020). *ISSDL adopts a definition of SDL.* https://www.sdlglobal.com/single-post/2020/02/16/issdl-adopts-a-definition-of-sdl#:~:text=Self%2Ddirected%20learning%20is%20an,a%20better%20sense%20of%20SDL

Knowles, M. S. (1970). *The modern practice of adult education: Andragogy versus pedagogy.* Association Press.

Knowles, M. S. (1973). *The adult learner: A neglected species.* American Society of Training and Development.

Knowles, M. S. (1975). *Self-directed learning: A guide for learners and teachers.* Association Press.

Kulich, J. (1970, February 23–24). *An historical overview of the adult self-learner* [Paper]. Northwest Institute Conference on Independent Study: The Adult as a Self-Directed Learner, University of British Columbia, Vancouver, British Columbia, Canada.

Leeb, J. (1985). *Self-directed learning and growth toward personal responsibility: Implications for a framework for health promotion* [Doctoral dissertation, Syracuse University]. Dissertation Abstracts International, 45, 724A.

North-West University SDL Research Focus Area. (n.d.). *Self-directed learning: Putting the "self" in learning.*

Oddi, L. F. (1986). Development and validation of an instrument to identify self-directed continuing learners. *Adult Education Quarterly, 36*(2), 97–107. https://doi.org/10.1177/0001848186036002004

Owenby, P. H. (1996). *Robert A. Heinlein: Popular adult educator and philosopher of education* [Unpublished doctoral dissertation]. University of Tennessee, Knoxville.

Peterson, C., & Seligman, M. E. P. (2004). *Character strengths and virtues: A handbook and classification.* American Psychological Association/Oxford University Press.

Roberson, D. N., Jr., & Merriam, S. B. (2005). The self-directed learning process of older, rural adults. *Adult Education Quarterly, 55*(4), 269–287. https://doi.org/10.1177/0741713605277372

Rogers, C. R. (1961). *On becoming a person.* Houghton Mifflin.

Ruttencutter, G. S. (2018). *Getting gritty with it: An examination of self-directed learning and grit among doctoral students* [Unpublished doctoral dissertation]. University of Tennessee, Knoxville.

Sabbaghian, Z. S. (1980). *Adult self-directedness and self-concept: An exploration of relationships* [Doctoral dissertation, Iowa State University]. Dissertation Abstracts International, 40, 3701A.

Smith, E. A., Grover, K. S., Miller, M. T., & Nadler, D. P. (2013). Self-directed learning practices of Caucasian and African-American community members: Do races differ? *Eastern Education Journal, 42*(1), 30–44.

Stockdale, S. L. (2003). *Development of an instrument to measure self-directedness* [Doctoral dissertation, University of Tennessee, Knoxville]. Dissertation Abstracts International, A64/06, AAT 3092836.

Stockdale, S. L., & Brockett, R. G. (2011). Development of the PRO-SDLS: A measure of self-direction in learning based on the Personal Responsibility Orientation Model. *Adult Education Quarterly, 61*(2), 161–180. https://doi.org/10.1177/07471713610380447

Teal, C., Vess, K. R., & Ambrose, V. K. (2015). Linking positive psychology with self-directed learning: A model of self-directed wellness. *International Journal of Self-Directed Learning, 15*(1), 16–28.

Tough, A. M. (1979). *The adults' learning projects.* Learning Concepts. (Original work published 1971)

Vess, K. R. (2015). *Examining the relationships between gratitude and readiness for self-directed learning in undergraduate nursing students* [Unpublished doctoral dissertation]. University of Tennessee, Knoxville.

Wagner, S. R. (2018). The self-directed learning practices of elementary teachers. *International Journal of Self-Directed Learning, 15*(2), 18–33.

Editors' Key Seminal and Supplemental Text Suggestions

Brockett, R. G., & Hiemstra, R. (2011). *Self-direction in adult learning: Perspectives on theory, research and practice.* Routledge.

Garrison, D. R. (1997). Self-directed learning: Towards a comprehensive model. *Adult Education Quarterly, 48*(1), 18–33.

Grow, G. O. (1991). Teaching learners to be self-directed. *Adult Education Quarterly, 41*(3), 125–149.

11

EXPERIENTIAL LEARNING

Defining Parameters, Contextual Foundations, and Influential Contributions

Colin Beard

There are many ways that people might learn from their experiences, for example, through everyday life, social interaction, or by going to a conference or other event. But are all these experiences "experiential learning"? After all, they are all potential learning *experiences*. Many experiential learning theorists would say not. Experience alone does not necessarily lead to learning. Something has to happen to these experiences: There has to be an intention, a readiness to grasp and transform the experience in some way and at some point in order to learn from it. One way to do this is by reviewing and reflecting in or on experiences. While this suggests mental processing distinct from experience, this chapter will highlight other interactional processes integral to transformation. As the term *experiential learning* is now commonly used, this raises an important question: What exactly is experiential learning?

This chapter will consider the meaning of the term *experiential learning* and, in doing so, some of its defining parameters, core principles, and significant contextual issues will be outlined. Early notions of experiential learning found in ancient philosophical thought will be briefly outlined and then followed by a consideration of a few of the more significant contributions to our understandings of the term from the 19th, 20th, and 21st centuries. The chapter will also demonstrate how experiential learning has continually developed and evolved in many directions, with new ideas built on preceding ones. With advances in knowledge about learning, more complex modeling of experiential learning is developing in the 21st century, and so the chapter will conclude with an exploration of the implications of this emerging complexity in terms of both theory and practice.

Experiential Learning: Definitions and Core Concepts

Experiential learning is a category or type of learning, and the term implies that the nature of the "experience" of learning has significance. However, *experience* and *learning*—both fundamental to human life—are perhaps two of the most complex and elusive words to define. The word *experience* derives from the Latin *experiri*: to *try*. The term *learning* relates to change, or transformation, in a person, community, or organization, resulting from the acquisition of knowledge, ideas, skills, behaviors, or attitudes derived from experiences. It can be argued that there can be no learning without experience and so they are, to an extent, intimately intertwined. It is in this vein that Fenwick (2003) suggested that "If we include all human experience, then is not every minute of our lives, and every part of our ongoing sense-making, actually experiential learning?" She noted that many writers have grappled with the difficult and not-insignificant problem of where to place the boundaries around experiential learning in adult education. Yet she pointed out that the "distinction between experience and non-experience becomes absurd" (p. ix).

Before considering how the history and evolution of experiential learning contribute to its defining parameters and core principles, it might be helpful to give a very basic understanding of what experiential learning is. A key, foundational principle underpinning experiential learning is to let the learners "do" the learning (Beard & Wilson, 2018). This principle acknowledges that, ideally, learners should explore, discover, and find things out for themselves by doing. It follows, then, that the richest resources for learning reside in the learners themselves. Traditional teaching, teacher-directed knowledge transmission, can be transformed and redesigned to be experiential, to enable learners to be more fully engaged, through active participation, in finding things out for themselves. Learning by "doing" includes exploration, reflection, problem solving, experiencing difficult or challenging tasks that evoke emotional responses, manipulating objects, asking difficult questions, observing the self in action on a video, or intentionally learning about communication through everyday social interactions. The list of possibilities for doing is potentially endless.

There is no one definition of experiential learning, but there have been numerous attempts to create one. The existing definitions can be used to construct additional foundational characteristics of experiential learning. One comprehensive definition, offered by Itin (1999), an outdoor educator, captures some of the practical aspects of experiential learning:

> a holistic philosophy, where carefully chosen experiences supported by reflection, critical analysis, and synthesis, are structured to require the learner to take initiative, make decisions, and be accountable for the results, through actively posing questions, investigating, experimenting, being curious, solving problems, assuming responsibility, being creative, constructing meaning, and integrating previously developed knowledge. (p. 93)

Nearly a decade later, Beard and Wilson (2018) defined experiential learning as

> a sense-making process involving significant experiences that, to varying degrees, act as the source of learning for individuals, groups, and organizations.

These experiences actively immerse and reflectively engage the inner world of learner(s) as whole beings (including physical-bodily, intellectually, emotionally, psychologically, and spiritually) with the intricate "outer world" of the learning environment, in places and spaces, within the social, cultural, and political milieu to create memorable, rich, and effective experiences for, and of learning. (p. 3)

The existence of a rich range of definitions for experiential learning is understandable as experiential learning encompasses a broad field of practice. Nonformal learning contexts, including outdoor education, expeditionary learning, adventure learning, service learning, environmental education, and adventure therapy, represent some of the more popular outdoor activity-based forms of experiential learning. Experiential learning can also be implemented in informal learning contexts or form part of a community change project or a personal development initiative. Experiential learning can also be part of formal learning contexts, such as a workshop session, a classroom lesson, or program design. Because it can be applied in so many different contexts, experiential learning avoids being interpreted as an all-or-nothing concept. Although diversity of practice contexts creates problematic issues for the creation of definitional boundaries, what is common to them is that the experience is regarded as the foundation of, and the stimulus for, learning.

A third definition of experiential learning, created by Boud et al. (1993) in their book *Using Experience for Learning*, further develops these principles:

We found it to be meaningless to talk about learning in isolation from experience. Experience cannot be bypassed; it is the central consideration of all learning. Learning builds on and flows from experience: No matter what external prompts to learning there might be—teachers, materials, interesting opportunities—learning can only occur if the experience of the learner is engaged, at least at some level. These external influences can act only by transforming the experience of the learner. (p. 8)

In this definition the word *experience* is portrayed in two very different but interwoven ways. First, experience is purposefully provided, or pointed to by the teacher, which then becomes the raw material for learning. Second, learners brings their own experience to the table, and so the experience of learning becomes more significant for the learner when it builds on what is already known, that is, there is an element of continuity to any experience (Dewey, 1938). A suitable experience for learning is intentionally planned and designed unless it is informal and emergent (Megginson, 1994). Thus, expert design skills are required on the part of the educator. Experiential learning design involves the art and science of intentionally orchestrating and choreographing learning experiences to provide opportunities for learners to achieve desired outcomes or objectives (see chapter 14 for a general discussion of instructional design). Experience design is not just about the design of things for learners to *do*, or the design of the resources required. There are two other experience design considerations for the teacher or facilitator: (a) the design of an experience *for* learning (e.g., an experience to develop team building or communication) and (b) the design of an experience based on an understanding of *how* people learn, not only with regard to cognitive processes but also the ways in which learning is embodied through movement, spatial perception, and social interaction. The definition by Itin (1999) focuses on the micro layers of experience, such as being curious, creative, and asking questions, while Beard and Wilson (2018) focused on the universal macro layers of experience, referring to cognitive, physical, emotional, and spiritual modes. However, both definitions highlight the special role that the experience plays in learning when it takes center stage. Together these definitions reveal that *experience* engages the whole person.

So far, several foundational concepts have been established from these definitions: (a) experience is important to the learning process, taking center stage in experiential learning design; (b) the experiential dynamic has multiple layers in that the experience of and for learning are both important in the design of experiential learning; (c) learning engages the whole person in terms of their inner experiences (cognitive, affective, etc.) and their outer world experiences (spaces, power, culture, interactions with others and materials, etc.); (d) there should be a certain quality to the experience so as to engage the learner; (e) the experience should be memorable; (f) conditions for learning, and learner motivation, active engagement, and immersion are significant; (g) experience can be generated by an instructor to be experienced by the learner, or drawn on from the student to make use of their existing experience as content; (h) the richest resources originate within the learner as new experience builds on previous experiences, creating continuity; and (i) the experience of learning has potential for transformation of the self and or others.

Early Beginnings: The Contributions of Philosophers From the East and the West

Moon (2004) commented that across many disciplines the "views of experiential learning differ widely" (p. 110), and in this respect any search for unanimity might be impracticable. She did, however, suggest that the core meaning of experiential learning is derived from "all those who have contributed to the literature" (p. 107). Because experiential learning has a long history, there have been many contributions, and only a few of the more prominent contributors can be briefly discussed in this chapter.

An important starting point for understanding the evolution of experiential learning concerns how the term *experience* has been understood over the centuries. The ancient philosophers from both the East and West explored the role that experience plays in terms of how we humans make sense of our world. Some writers even suggest that the term *experiential learning* is descended from the work of Aristotle (Stonehouse et al., 2011), who was regarded as an empiricist in that he argued that we can only know the world through that which is presented to our senses. This is in comparison to Socrates, who focused on learning through the experience of questioning and social interaction, or Plato, the rationalist who used the experience of argument and logic. Although these philosophers had differing views, between them they identified some of the most significant ideas about how humans learn from experience, that is, that we can learn from social interaction and from our embodied sensory and cognitive capacities. However, these early philosophers argued that workers and slaves required only basic training for a job, and Aristotle "explicitly excluded women and slaves from higher stages of education" (Palmer, 2001, p. 18). This is significant as concerns over the need to create a just and democratic society emerge later as an important principle in the evolution of experiential learning.

Eastern philosophy, particularly from Confucian and Taoist traditions, also contributed early foundational concepts. The common Chinese aphorism: "I hear, I forget; I see, I remember; I do, I understand" is derived from Confucian thought. This contributes more concepts to the practice of experiential learning, notably that experiential learning involves actively "doing" for one's self, that is, learning by doing, and that such an approach enhances memory and understanding. The aphorism was first written in the rich pictographic Chinese language, and the Western understanding is reportedly an inadequate translation, particularly in terms of the meaning of the original Chinese notion of *doing*. Confucian philosophers sought rather to capture the broader notion of the role of experience in learning, notably the need for immersion, practice, dedication, and discovery, of an attitude, a skill, or knowledge (see Beard & Wilson, 2018). These early philosophical deliberations, concerning the part played by experience in terms of how we might know the world, continued. However, it was not until the early 19th century that the many foundational concepts related to experiential education were developed, largely due to concerns about the experience of schooling. It is at this point in history that the heritage of experiential learning is significantly rooted in, and intertwined with, experiential learning in formal educational settings.

Nineteenth Century: Inequality and Traditional Educational Methods

Beginning in the late 19th century, an impetus for change grew out of concerns about the experience of schooling. These included the arrangements of "the typical traditional schoolroom, with its fixed rows of desks and its military regimen of pupils who were permitted to move only at certain fixed signals" (Dewey, 1938, p. 61); concerns about the teaching methods of recital and rote learning that prevailed at this time; and elitist and repressive ideas about schooling. The following passage, taken from a UK educational pamphlet in 1867, illustrates an elitist mentality that promoted social control:

> The lower classes ought to be educated to discharge the duties cast upon them. They should also be educated that they may appreciate and defer to a higher cultivation when they need it, and the higher classes ought to be educated in a very different manner, in order that they may exhibit to the lower classes that higher education to which, if it was shown to them, they would bow down and defer. (Curtis, 1963, p. 256)

In the 1880s, leading UK educationalists argued that more rigorous, child-centered methods should be introduced, built on "progressive discovery involving observation, experiment, and the use of inference" (Curtis, 1963, p. 295). These ideas developed contemporaneously in both the United States and the United Kingdom, and they were being encouraged by similar-minded theorists. In the United Kingdom, educational progressives proposed the heuristic method (meaning discovery), and these ideas had clear similarities to the "scientific discovery methods" proposed by John Dewey in the United States. Both involved learning experiences that called for the systematic use of observation, hypothesis forming, experimentation, and testing. These "progressive" proposals for schooling advocated for an approach that is regarded as essentially humanist, in that learners' experience of learning, and their own ideas, are respected and given value when teaching methods embrace them discovering things for themselves. This push for progressive educational change, and the impact that John Dewey and others in the United States had in the United Kingdom, is further illustrated by the following comment by Curtis (1963):

> The idea that education means learning from books has given place to a wider interpretation, and the project method and activity methods have replaced the meaningless grind of earlier days. In this respect the ideas of John Dewey have had a strong influence, and the value of practical occupations in the school has become widely recognized. (pp. 369–370)

These progressive ideas about active, learner-centered methods of teaching in schools laid some of the foundations of what was to become known as *experiential education*, a term that was to become regarded at times as synonymous with experiential learning.

The Early 20th Century: The Impact of the Work of John Dewey

John Dewey, like others, built his ideas on the work of peers and predecessors. For example, Jean-Jacques Rousseau published *Emile* (1762), a book that exposed oppressive schooling. It is suggested that his revolutionary ideas about the need for a more "natural," developmental education, are "now strongly associated with the names Piaget, Vygotsky and Dewey," and that "Rousseau's ideas were as much a revolt against Plato as Plato's were against the schooling he sought to replace" (Wilson, 1998, p. 279). Rousseau became famous for his ideas about teaching by using the senses and applying the principles of nature found in the natural environment. His thinking, along with others, relates not just to teaching methods within school classrooms but also to experiential education within nature and the outdoors in general. Thus, we can see the early experiential foundations of outdoor education, adventure education, and environmental education. While the focus of Dewey's work was school education, his thinking continues to inform and underpin the concepts and practices of adult experiential learning in the 21st century. Dewey focused on the nature of the experience of learning in schools. The oppressive school conditions previously highlighted would have been in existence before, during, and after Dewey's own schooling and were influential to his thinking. Likewise, the practice of teacher as strict disciplinarian and the notion of the unquestioned authority transmitting fixed knowledge would have undoubtedly shaped Dewey's reaction against these traditional approaches.

Dewey produced several books that have contributed many foundational concepts underpinning experiential education and experiential learning. His core educational ideas are described in *Experience and Education* (1938), a book based on a series of lectures he gave on the state of the school in 1937 and said to contain the most concise statements of his ideas about the needs, problems, and possibilities in education. It was written after Dewey's direct teaching experiences with progressive schools and because of much criticism of his ideas. Dewey argued that a thorough scientific approach to learning should be adopted in schools, in which children would engage in rigorous investigation that would result in them intelligently exploring lived experiences using observation, reasoning, thinking, testing, reflection, and subsequently would scrupulously test and revise their hypotheses as provisional but not final truths.

Dewey was regarded as one of the most distinguished promoters of the need for more progressive approaches to education. He was, however, critical of both progressive and traditional education, particularly because he saw that both lacked a coherent theory of experience. He sought to advance the intimate relationship between education and experience, though he noted that not all experiences are educative. What Dewey meant by this is that some experiences can distort or arrest development and growth. An experience may be fun, but if it engenders careless attitudes, or callousness, or if future experiences are restricted because of them, then these experiences are miseducative. Dewey also introduced the notions of *continuity*, and *interaction,* that "intercept and unite" experience (Dewey, 1938, p. 44). In this way, he argued that experiences do not occur in isolation: Modes of experiencing interact with and are linked to previous experiences of the learner. Such continuity creates the foundation for ever-expanding possibilities for future experiences.

For Dewey, the problem for traditional education was the nature of the educational experiences, and so he outlined many important features required in the careful design of experiences, a process that he regarded as being more difficult and strenuous for teachers than teaching by rote and drill. Dewey's specific concerns were that significant effort was required to determine the materials, methods, and social relationships needed for experience-based education. He felt that abstract ideas should be translated into concrete, physical, and material form so that the abstract would have practical application. While his ideas continue to influence educational reform efforts in many ways, Palmer (2001) noted that Dewey's ideas never fully permeated the classroom realities of the U.S. educational system.

The Late 20th Century: Other Contributors

From the preceding discussions, it becomes clear that the 19th-century foundational roots of experiential learning came about as a result of concerns about the inadequacy of teaching methods, repressive and inequitable forces, and the use of strict discipline. These roots are considered as being located within progressive, humanistic, and liberatory movements representing additional foundational concepts underpinning experiential learning. Tony Saddington (1999) utilized the metaphor of a tree to highlight the complexity of experiential learning, with the roots being the underpinning theoretical positions and the branches being the different approaches to practice. He explained the importance in adult education of experience within three traditions. The *progressive* tradition, he suggested, utilizes the learner's own experience as an important source of knowledge, whereas traditional didactic approaches present knowledge as given. The *humanist* tradition pursues and values wholeness, self-actualization, and personal growth. The *radical* tradition sees reflection on experience as a means of resisting oppression, encouraging empowerment, and generating social transformation. According to Hager, these traditions explain why experiential learning is an approach that is central to the theory and practice of adult education (Hager, 1999).

While these concerns about schooling gave rise to important underpinning foundations for experiential learning, the term was not specifically used, nor mentioned by Dewey; nor was it generally known. Seaman et al. (2017) tentatively traced the first use of the term *experiential learning* back to human relations training of the 1940s, though it is not clear whether the term may have simply evolved as a shorthand version of what was generally known as experiential and experience-based approaches to adult human relations training, where people reflected on and discussed their community and workplace experiences. These authors suggested that the "phrase itself began to circulate in the 1950s and proliferated in the 1960s and

70s as authors published models based on their involvement in therapeutic and adult education practices" (p. 3). Boydell (1976) referred to a U.S. doctoral thesis (Hughes, 1974) that similarly described experiential learning as the classroom adaptation of 2 decades of research on human relations training that used laboratory education and the T-group method. The term *T-group* is short for *training group*, and the term *laboratory* here refers to workshop-style investigations that were conducted by behavioral scientists on the development of interpersonal skills to help individuals, groups, and communities gain awareness about human relations. This is significant as Kurt Lewin's action research and T-group training methods applied the following sequence: concrete experience, observations and reflections, formation of abstract concepts and generalizations, and, finally, testing the implications of concepts in new situations. It was this approach that was to become the foundational basis of the experiential learning theory developed by cognitive psychologist David Kolb and his colleagues (Kolb et al., 1971).

David Kolb played an important role in popularizing the term *experiential learning* in the late 20th century. His seminal publication, *Experiential Learning: Experience as the Source of Learning and Development* (1984), raised the profile of experiential learning across the globe, an achievement that few if any other experiential learning authors have accomplished. The growing popularity of experiential learning at that time was reflected by the fact that the first major international conference on experiential learning was held in 1987 (see Weil & McGill, 1989), and it is significant that it attracted practitioners from a diverse range of disciplines. Other theorists were also using the term *experiential learning*, such as the management educator and consultant Tom Boydell in 1976. Others have produced important texts with noteworthy titles that use other popular phrases associated with experiential learning. Edward Cell (1984), for example, produced a book on experiential learning at the same time as Kolb (1984) titled *Learning to Learn From Experience*. Kolb's early publications in the 1970s also introduced the Learning Style Inventory in 1976, which he argued would allow learners to recognize their preferred ways of learning and help them gain greater control of their learning abilities. Learner control, as has been highlighted so far, is an important principle for experiential learning.

Kolb (1984) specifically stated that "Learning is a process whereby knowledge is created through the transformation of experience" (p. 38). Kolb acknowledged that he built his theoretical ideas on Dewey's (1938) work as well as nine others within the fields of philosophy and cognitive and developmental psychology, including William James, Jean Piaget, and Kurt Lewin (1946). It was Dewey's ideas about the use of "scientific" methods and reflection on experience, as well as the four-step sequence of Lewin's training group process that were particularly influential to the development of Kolb's experiential learning model. The model incorporates four basic modes of experience that relate to each other in what he called an *experiential learning cycle*: concrete experience, reflection, abstract thinking, and action/testing.

Kolb (1976) referred to the four experiential learning modes as representing four individual abilities. These modes require the learner to be actively involved in a concrete experience; to reflect on this experience; and, using analytical skills, be able to conceptualize and apply solutions to solve problems through a process of testing and experimentation. For Kolb, the experience has to be grasped in order for it to be transformed into learning. He explained that grasping occurs in two ways: (a) through a concrete experience and (b) through the development of abstract concepts or ideas. Transformation of the experience also occurs in two ways: through (a) reflective observation and (b) active experimentation. Assessing the learner's capacity to engage in these four activities formed the basis of his Learning Styles Inventory. When modeled as a cycle, Kolb's theory is easily remembered, and along with its relative simplicity, this may be one reason why it has gained considerable influence.

The 21st Century: Learning and Experience as Complex Concepts

While circular models like Kolb's reached a peak of popularity in the 1970s, they began to lose prominence by the early 1990s (Boydell, 1976; Seaman, 2008; Taylor, 1991). Although the learning cycle, as a visual representation of Kolb's (1976) theory, continues to be remarkably influential, it is not without criticism. It is regarded by some as being overly mechanistic and formulaic (see Moon, 2004; Rowland, 2000; Seaman, 2008). Other criticisms include (a) its undue focus on cognition in a way that downplays the importance of other modes of experiencing, including the role of the body, emotions, and the influence of social and cultural contexts; (b) the view of the learner as an isolated individual working alone to make sense of experiences; and (c) the lack of recognition that other modes of experiencing, beyond the four highlighted in the model, also play a role in learning. That Kolb's theory is overly individualistic is a critique put forward by Holman et al. (1997). These authors suggested that, although extremely influential, the learning cycle is located within the cognitive psychology tradition and mechanically explains learning as divorced from social, historical, and cultural contexts. They argued that social interaction in learning is important and that the idea of a learner mentally (cognitively) reflecting on learning events as an isolated individual suggests an intellectual Robinson Crusoe, as if the experiential interaction with others and the world out there somehow does not exist.

From a critical feminist perspective, Michelson (1998) questioned the privileging of mind over body and the lack of recognition of the role of the body as a site of knowledge in the experiential learning theory articulated by Kolb (1976). Fenwick (2003) critiqued Kolb's experiential learning theory because it suggests that "knowledge is extracted and abstracted from experience by the processing mind" (p. 21), as if learning is something concrete and knowable rather than in a permanent fluid state of construction. She suggested that experiential learning should be understood as involving the whole person, "physically, emotionally, sensually, mentally and perhaps spiritually" (p. 13). *Learning Through Experience: Troubling Orthodoxies and*

Intersecting Questions is an influential text in which Fenwick explored four theoretical orientations toward experiential learning in addition to the experience–reflect–learn constructivist theory that Kolb's work is orientated toward. The three other orientations are *situative* theories (place, participating communities of practice), *psychoanalytic* theories (unconscious desires, ego, etc.), and *complexity* theories (exploring complexity, systems, ecological relationships). Roberts, who similarly offered alternative theoretical perspectives in his text *Beyond Learning by Doing* (2012), argued that "constructivist models reduce the highly interactive and bodily qualities of outdoor and adventure experiences to secondary elements in an individual's experience" (Seaman, 2008, p. 14). While there is not the space here to explore the orientations that Fenwick pointed to, they underline the importance of the calls for theories that broaden the notion of experiential learning.

These criticisms warrant further exploration as they signpost areas for the further advancement of experiential learning in the 21st century. The theoretical trajectory outlined so far, from ancient Confucian sayings and other philosophical roots; to the work of Dewey and Kolb; and on to the work of Fenwick, Michelson, Roberts, and other contemporary writers, illustrates that the understanding of experiential learning has become more discerning and complex. Long ago, Dewey advised that there was a need to create a sound and substantive *philosophy of experience*. Any philosophy of experience, Dewey argued, should investigate the complexity of life as humans experience it. According to Crosby (1995), Dewey maintained that, as humans, "We find ourselves in continual transaction with the physical, psychological, mental, spiritual world, and philosophy should be a systematic investigation into the nature of this experience" (p. 11). This reference to the need to investigate all these modes of experience becomes significant to the creation of additional foundations on which to build new theories of experiential learning in the 21st century in which many interacting modes of experience are assumed to be in constant flux. Similarly, the interactional processes involved in learning are neither static nor confined to a few experiencing modes, because, as Davis and Sumara (1997) suggested, any inquiry into the experience of learning should not focus "on the components of experience but, rather, on the relations that bind these elements together in action" (p. 108). Feeling or sensing and thinking, body and mind, culture and politics, individual and group, nature and nurture represent some of the components of experience that continually interact and overlap. Like Fenwick, Davis and Sumara suggested that cognition does not reside solely in the mind of the individual, and they questioned what might happen if learning is considered in ways other than from a constructivist orientation:

> [What would happen] if we were to reject the self-evident axiom that cognition is located within cognitive agents who are cast as isolated from one another and distinct from the world, and insist instead that all cognition exists in the interstices of a complex ecology of organismic relationality? (p. 110)

Fenwick (2003) positioned this work by Davis and Sumara (1997) within the theoretical orientation of *complexity theories*. In this orientation there is a recognition that humans continually act and interact within a fluid, overlapping, and interconnected ecology of experiences. Interactions occur between psychological, biological, personal, social, and cultural selves. She noted that this orientation focuses on coemergence of all the systems (e.g., learners, settings). From this perspective, thinking does not occur separately from our sense of belonging, being, or acting in the world. Humans operate within large social networks where we negotiate norms and values and attend to relationships, involving power and politics, within complex societal, historical, and environmental frames. Thus, experience is jointly constructed through interactions with others, including the nonhuman world. Contemporary theories and modeling of experiential learning would ideally reflect this complex, experiential ecology in a way that has applications for educational practice.

An illustration of an approach that embraces complexity can be found in the work of Beard and Wilson (2018). In this work, a model based on seven overarching modes of experiencing is offered to acknowledge the complex interactions occurring between belonging, doing, sensing, feeling, knowing, and being in the world. They also differentiated and subdivided layers of experiencing: Sensing, for example, incorporates the sublevel modes of visual, haptic, auditory, kinesthetic, olfactory, spatial awareness, and other modes of sensing. Their multidisciplinary approach adopts an ecological, holistic modeling of experiencing, as shown in Figure 11.1. The basic interpretation of their model is a simple linear representation, offered as an introduction only for ease of understanding because these foundational components are, in fact, not separate; instead, they are in a constant state of interactive flux. The model in Figure 11.1 positions the sensing body as an interface between the internal and external world modes of experiencing.

This model, and the theorizing that accompanies it, unlike most other experiential learning models does not neglect the extra-human (physical, natural world

Figure 11.1. A simple linear representation of the foundational dimensions or modes of experiencing.

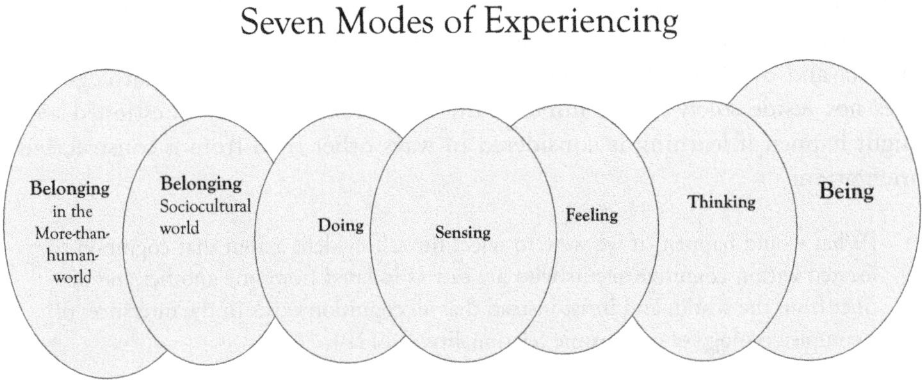

Seven Modes of Experiencing

of living species, and spiritual aspects). What is suggested in this new model is that experiential learning should move beyond simplistic approaches to experience design by giving design attention to the holistic breadth and depth of experience. In the design process, the questions of where, when, with whom, by doing what, and why and how, of the experience all require consideration. All these interacting modes of experiencing contribute to the potential for change and transformation of our being (ontological/self/who we are/identity/values/beliefs, etc.), and these in turn can result in learning, change, and/or action (e.g., behaviors, skills, and agency) or an intention to act, in individuals, organizations, and groups. Beard and Wilson (2018) argued that individuals, organizations, and groups exist in a state of *becoming*, always changing, always in an interactional process of remaking the self and/or the world. To an extent, this ecological approach to experience can be seen to build on Dewey's (1938) broad philosophy of experience, as previously outlined, where he suggests that we humans are in a continual transaction with the physical, psychological, mental, and spiritual world and that philosophy should systematically investigate the nature of these experiences.

Complex Models and Complex Experience Designs

Theory and practice should inform each other. Indeed, Lewin suggested that there is nothing so practical as a good theory. Here, I provide a design that illustrates this theory–practice relationship is one that is used within a higher education setting called "Walk the Talk." The context in this case is learning about the evolution of the environmental movement in an experiential learning-by-doing design that includes, for example, understanding the evolving environmental tactics, laws, significant events and milestones, extinctions, environmental disasters, significant individuals, and the private and public organizations involved. The design includes relationship building and active and creative engagement by the learners in the process of finding out by doing. It also includes the cocreation and continuous development of learning materials and other resources by students across several cohorts. The following description highlights how this was done.

The design was first conceived and developed for adult evening classes delivered for the local community on behalf of the UK Workers Education Association. The community wanted to be more actively involved in environmental issues, including local planning, and so a learning experience was designed to utilize their existing experience, to facilitate active engagement, involvement, participation, and discovery. The design was further developed over a period of 3 years of evening class delivery to community groups. It was eventually utilized with mature students studying for an environmental master of arts degree, and it is this higher education design that is described here.

There are three distinct phases to this design solution, with each involving a very different experience in terms of the interactions with knowledge, objects, materials, and peers. Each of the adult students contributes to the experience by utilizing their own existing life experiences and expertise. First, the students work together in small groups to acquire information about a topic they select from a list that includes identifying when certain organizations were established; which government bodies were set up, when, and why; and the impact that specific environmental events had on development and change. This fact-finding phase is simply termed the *informational* phase. The substantial amount of foundational information acquired is shared among groups and discussed before progressing to the next stage. The students also documented this work, creating booklets and databases. These documents also formed foundational learning material for future cohorts who inherited them and then further develop and update them each year. Over several years, a complex database covering over 350 years of the evolution of the environmental movement was coconstructed in an electronic format. However, knowledge acquisition on its own generates only a limited understanding that has been referred to as *surface learning* (Marton & Säljö, 1976). In this phase of experience design, the production of foundational teaching materials was carried out by the students. This serves additional purposes, such as to develop a sense of confidence; responsibility for their learning; a sense of belonging to, and interdependence with, other students; and as a preparation and a prerequisite to the next, more complex design phase.

This second phase experience is called the *relational* phase of learning as it explores connections and relationships between events. During this phase, students are required to develop a greater depth of understanding beyond knowledge acquisition by considering how the facts, figures, and other information are related to the broader evolutionary narrative. To do this, the students are asked to design a representation to show the spatial relational complexity, that is, how one set of events or facts is related to (many) others. Their representation took the form of a large floor map not unlike the now-iconic cartographic design of a subway or underground map. Each group lays out their own specific key data on the floor, using color-coded laminated cards with dates and basic information on them. These cards, consisting of an initial set created by the instructor and further added to by students over many years, are utilized by students to construct a representation of their group data. When the other groups add theirs, a collective visual representation is developed that is required to fit in terms of the spatial (in relation to) and temporal (time) elements of other group data (see Kirsh, 2010). This skeletal but complex representation acts as a visual tool (see Verschaffel et al., 2010) to be explored and further developed in a process that can enhance thinking and reasoning by making visible what they were beginning to understand in terms of the complex evolution. Students interact by, for example, walking among the cards (embodied), examining the map from different (spatial and temporal) perspectives, and articulating (oral) and sharing (social) what they see (sensory/observation/thinking aloud). As the relational complexity emerges, the reflective conversations generate a deeper understanding (higher abstract conceptualization) of the evolution of the environmental movement. This phase also generates further queries and questions. The Walk-the-Talk experience can also be recorded, captured, and posted online to be shared and further analyzed. The recording can also be enhanced with facilitator and instructor comments and challenging questions.

The third and final phase is termed the *transformational* phase, involving a level of critical reflection, dissonance, and discomfort, where values, beliefs, views, and existing interpretations are challenged and questioned. In this case, for example, questions included:

> Why are the leading characters mostly men?
> In what ways has the voluntary movement developed or been thwarted in terms of their changes in tactics over periods of time?
> What is the political story behind this spatially expanded timeline?
> What is your own personal contribution to environmental change?
> Where and in what way does equality fit into this storyline?
> What role do the public, private, and voluntary sectors play?

This pedagogic example briefly illustrates an experiential design that embraces the holistic ecological complexity of experiencing that has been alluded to earlier in this chapter (for a full account see Beard, 2018).

Implications for Practice

This Walk-the-Talk example outlines several important aspects of experiential learning, including valuing the learners as a source of knowledge, as whole persons able to think for themselves and take responsibility for their learning. The students are required to develop a deep level of understanding about how a substantial number of interrelated events contributed to the development of the environmental movement, and they do this by being actively involved in several modes of experiencing. While the full extent of the design format cannot be presented here, this approach involves the intentional design of active doing (e.g., producing databases, booklets, and fact sheets), sensing (e.g., moving color-coded cards containing key facts with their hands to place them in the correct spatial and temporal relationship in a way that produces a pictorial and textual representation of the evolutionary narratives), thinking (e.g., developing abstract reasoning through discussion), and belonging (e.g., engaging in a variety of peer interactions). The students also experience a range of feelings during the three phases (the joys of sharing and self-discovery, the unsettling feelings that are the result of dissonance created by the design of difficult questioning that challenges the assumptions held by a group or an individual).

The implications for experiential learning are that the seven core modes of experiencing (Figure 11.1) offer a design framework that promotes the inclusion of a wide range of experiential activities. Within each mode, it is the active verbs that point to the experience designs. Doing might, for example, involve undertaking an expedition, the design and implementation of an experiment, the production of databases, creating a reflective photo log (see Beard & Rhodes, 2002), a video diary, a radio program, or the choreography of a dance routine. A sensing experience might involve the experience of manipulating objects (touching, rotating, handling) or other materials (to create new thinking), or the observation (seeing) of a presentation or event, or listening to (hearing) a recording and taking notes. Social interaction might involve group conversations (social belonging mode of experiencing) that can also generate new abstract concepts (thinking mode of experiencing), and difficult questioning and dissonance might challenge assumptions held by a group, or an individual, leading to unsettling feelings (feelings mode of experiencing). In practice, all these core modes are interactively intertwined in a complex experiential fluidity. An important design skill is the ability to understand how the experiences are put together, to create the overarching shape and flow of the whole experience (Beard, 2022).

Conclusion

This chapter has described the evolutionary roots of experiential learning, though only the more prominent contributions are outlined due to space limitations (for a more extensive coverage, see, e.g., Smith & Knapp, 2011). What has been revealed is that *experiential learning* is a contested term, often with contradictory meanings. Long ago, philosophers noted the importance of learning by doing, and they debated how we can know and make meaning of the world. Late 19th-century educational concerns about the need for more rigorous, scientific, child-centered teaching methods within school classrooms contributed to new thinking about experiential education. Outside the classroom there were calls for more holistic approaches to education grounded in adventure and environmental education (Veevers & Allison, 2011). In addition, conversational reflection on past experiences in adult group learning processes within organizational and management workshops in the 20th century gave rise to a focus on experiential learning in adult education. More recently, there have been calls for a broadening of understanding of experiential learning. Fenwick (2003), for example, suggested the adoption of a more diverse range of theoretical orientations, while Roberts (2012) outlined the diverse currents that exist in the flowing river of experiential education. Over time, new contributions have led to an increasingly complex conceptualization of experiential learning in terms of both the theoretical foundations and the design of effective practice. To return to Saddington's (1999) tree metaphor, the full extent of the ever-changing mass of entangled roots of experiential learning may never be fully exposed. This abbreviated introduction to experiential learning has necessarily omitted a great deal of detail. Indeed, *experience* is a term that, as historian Martin Jay (2005) suggested in his book *Songs of Experience,* "exceeds concepts and even language itself" (p. 5). The more we know about experiential learning, the more we recognize that there is much more still to understand, and the more we participate in experiential learning, the more we learn about it by experiencing it for ourselves.

References

Beard, C. (2018). Learning experience designs (LEDs) in an age of complexity: Time to replace the lightbulb. *Reflective Practice, 19*(6), 736–748. https://doi.org/10.1080/14623943.2018.1538962

Beard, C. (2023). *Experiential learning design: Theoretical foundations and effective principles.* Routledge.

Beard, C., & Rhodes, T. (2002). Experiential learning: Using comic strips as "reflective tools" in adult learning. *Australian Journal of Outdoor Education, 6*(2), 58–65. https://doi.org/10.1007/BF03400756

Beard, C., & Wilson, J. P. (2018). *Experiential learning: A practical guide for training, coaching and education* (4th ed.). Kogan Page.

Boud, D., Cohen, R., & Walker, D. (1993). *Using experience for learning.* Open University Press.

Boydell, T. (1976). *Experiential learning* (Manchester Monograph No. 5). Department of Adult Education, University of Manchester.

Cell, E. (1984). *Learning to learn from experience.* State University of New York Press.

Crosby, A. (1995). A critical look: The philosophical foundations of experiential education. In K. Warren, M. S. Sakofs, & J. S. Hunt (Eds.), *The theory of experiential education* (pp. 3–13). Kendal Hunt.

Curtis, S. J. (1963). *History of education in Great Britain.* University Tutorial Press.

Davis, B., & Sumara, D. J. (1997). Cognition, complexity and teacher education. *Harvard Educational Review, 67*(1), 105–125. https://doi.org/10.17763/haer.67.1.160w00j113t78042

Dewey, J. (1938). *Experience and education.* Touchstone.

Fenwick, T. J. (2003). *Learning through experience: Troubling orthodoxies and intersecting questions.* Krieger.

Hager, P. (1999). Robin Usher on experience. *Educational Philosophy and Theory, 31*(1), 63–75. https://doi.org/10.1111/j.1469-5812.1999.tb00374.x

Holman, D., Pavlica, K., & Thorpe, R. (1997). Rethinking Kolb's theory of experiential learning in management education. *Management Learning, 28*(2), 135–148. https://doi.org/10.1177/1350507697282003

Hughes, J. C. (1974). *Experiential learning in management education* [Unpublished doctoral dissertation]. Texas Technical University.

Itin, C. (1999). Reasserting the philosophy of experiential education as a vehicle for change in the 21st century. *The Journal of Experiential Education, 22*(2), 91–98. https://doi.org/10.1177/105382599902200206

Jay, M. (2005). *Songs of experience: Modern American and European variations on a universal theme.* University of California Press.

Kirsh, D. (2010). Thinking with external representations. *Artificial Intelligence and Society, 25*, 441–454. https://doi.org/10.1007/s00146-010-0272-8

Kolb, D. (1976). *The Learning Styles Inventory: Technical manual.* McBer & Company.

Kolb, D. (1984). *Experiential learning: Experience as the source of learning and development.* Prentice Hall.

Kolb, D., Rubin, I., & McIntyre, J. (1971). *Organisational psychology: An experiential approach.* Prentice Hall.

Lewin, K. (1946). Action research and minority problems. *Journal of Social Issues, 2*(4), 34–46. https://doi.org/10.1111/j.1540-4560.1946.tb02295.x

Marton, F., & Säljö, R. (1976). On the qualitative difference in learning: I—Outcome and process. *British Journal of Educational Psychology, 46*, 4–11. https://doi .org/10.1111/j.2044-8279.1976.tb02980.x

Megginson, D. (1994). Planned and emergent learning. *Executive Development, 7*(6), 29–32. https://doi.org/10.1177/1350507696274002

Michelson, E. (1998). Re-remembering: The return of the body to experiential learning. *Studies in Continuing Education, 20*(2), 217–233. https://doi.org/10.1080/0158037980200208

Moon, J. (2004). *A handbook of reflective and experiential learning: Theory and practice.* Routledge/Falmer.

Palmer, J. (Ed.). (2001). *Fifty major thinkers on education: From Confucius to Dewey.* Routledge.

Roberts, J. (2012). *Beyond learning by doing: Theoretical currents in experiential education.* Routledge.

Rowland, S. (2000). *The enquiring university teacher.* Open University Press and Society for Research in Higher Education.

Saddington, T. (1999, July 5–6). *The roots and branches of experiential development* [Paper]. The Brathay Youth Conference: Experiencing the Difference: The Role of Experiential Learning in Youth Development, Ambleside, England.

Seaman, J. (2008). Experience, reflect, critique: The end of the "learning cycles" era. *Journal of Experiential Education, 31*(1), 3–18. https://doi.org/10.1177/105382590803100103

Seaman, J., Brown, M., & Quay, J. (2017). The evolution of experiential learning: Tracing lines of research in the JEE. *Journal of Experiential Education, 40*, 1–20. https://doi .org/10.1177/1053825916689268

Smith, T. E., & Knapp, C. E. (2011). *Sourcebook of experiential education: Key thinkers and contributions.* Routledge.

Stonehouse, P., Allison, P., & Carr, D. (2011). Aristotle, Plato, and Socrates: Ancient Greek perspectives on experiential learning. In T. Smith & C. Knapp (Eds.), *Sourcebook of experiential education* (pp. 18–31). Routledge.

Taylor, H. (1991). The systematic training model: Corn circles in search of a spaceship? *Journal of the Association for Management Education and Development, 22*(4), 258–278. https:// doi.org/10.1177/135050769102200401

Veevers, N., & Allison, P. (2011). *Kurt Hahn: Inspirational, visionary, outdoor and experiential educator.* Sense.

Verschaffel, L., De Corte, E., De Jong, T., & Elen, J. (Eds.). (2010). *Use of representations in reasoning and problem solving: Analysis and improvement.* Routledge.

Weil, S., & McGill, I. (Eds.). (1989). *Making sense of experiential learning.* Open University Press and Society for Research in Higher Education.

Wilson, F. R. (1998). *The hand: How its use shapes the brain, language, and culture.* Pantheon.

Editors' Key Seminal and Supplemental Text Suggestions

Boud, D., Keogh, R., & Walker, D. (1985). What is reflection in learning? In D. Boud, R. Keogh, & D. Walker (Eds.), *Reflection: Turning experience into learning* (pp. 7–17). Routledge.

Dewey, J. (1938). *Experience and education.* MacMillan.

Kolb, D. (1984). *Experiential learning: Experience as the source of learning and development.* Prentice Hall.

- Chapter 7: Adult Education and Reconstruction of Experience

Michelson, E. (1998). Re-remembering: The return of the body to experiential learning. *Studies in Continuing Education, 20*(2), 217–233.

Rousseau, J. J. (1762). *Émile, Book 1.* http://www.iltcolumbia.edu/pedagogies/rousseau/emengbk1.html.

Schon, D. A. (1983). *The reflective practitioner: How professionals think in action.* Basic Books.

- Chapter 2: From Technical Rationality to Reflection in Action
- Chapter 5: The Structure of Reflection-in-Action

Tennant, M., & Pogson, P. (1995). *Learning and change in the adult years: A developmental perspective.* Jossey-Bass.

12

TRANSFORMATIVE LEARNING

Evolving Theory for Understanding Change

Chad Hoggan and Elizabeth Kasl

Education changes people. Or, at least, educators hope that the education they provide changes the lives of their students for the better. But what does it mean that people change—especially if we mean that they change in dramatic and significant ways? How are learners different after this process of change? What processes lead to significant changes? What environmental factors contribute to or inhibit these changes? Many scholars interested in these questions have, for the past several decades, developed theories of *transformative learning* to describe this phenomenon of dramatic change. A contemporary definition states that transformative learning "refers to processes that result in significant and irreversible changes in the way a person experiences, conceptualizes, and interacts with the world" (Hoggan, 2016, p. 71).

Although originating in the discipline of adult education with a very specific meaning, the term *transformative learning* is increasingly being used more broadly. It is used so frequently, in such varied ways, that some adult education scholars argue the term lacks any distinctive meaning (Brookfield, 2003; Newman, 2012). Perhaps a better way to describe the evolution of the term is to say that it originated with a very specific meaning, but its meaning has become diffuse through popular use. This is not uncommon with popular ideas: The idea attracts people with diverse interests who then apply the idea in diverse ways.

This chapter traces the evolution of scholarship associated with transformative learning theory. We begin with an overview of the theory as originated by Jack Mezirow, followed by an explanation of his theory's key concepts and a summary of how early critiques and Mezirow's responses clarified his thinking. We then outline several approaches to transformative learning that are different from Mezirow's and explain that these variations lead some scholars to assert that the idea of transformative learning is best considered a metatheory (i.e., a collection of theories and ideas around a common topic rather than a single coherent theory). Finally, we provide guidance to practitioners regarding implementation.

Overview of Mezirow's Theory and Its Origins

Transformative learning theory made its debut in 1978 with two publications— an evaluation report on programs designed for women who wanted to reenter the workforce after an employment gap (Mezirow, 1978a) and a journal article describing the type of learning engendered in these programs (Mezirow, 1978b).

The evaluation research took place in 12 community colleges, with populations diverse in race and class, located in the New York/New Jersey and San Francisco metropolitan areas and the state of Washington. Across the country in the 1970s, community colleges and universities were creating programs designed to assist women preparing for new or resumed careers, often by pursuing additional education. Although these reentry programs were not designed as consciousness-raising vehicles, they emerged during the second-wave feminist movement, when traditional gender roles were being contested and many women wanted change after spending several years as stay-at-home wives and mothers. This social–historical context is relevant to understanding how Mezirow interpreted the women's experiences.

Mezirow (1978a) was intrigued by the changes women experienced as they engaged the challenges of contesting long-standing social norms related to women and work. He called this change *perspective transformation* and published a journal article (Mezirow, 1978b) that presented perspective transformation as a learning theory. (The term *transformative learning* was introduced later and became the de facto name for Mezirow's work.)

Taking off from this initial work, Mezirow eventually developed what he perceived to be a comprehensive theory of adult learning, which included but was not limited to the idea of transformative learning. His theory and its terminology evolved over the years (see Kitchenham, 2008, for an overview of these changes), but its essence remained the same. It focuses on how people use *meaning perspectives* to make meaning—first, to select which sensory impressions in their environment (sights, sounds, smells, etc.) receive their attention and, second, to make sense out of those impressions. Meaning perspectives are developed throughout life, but the most fundamental and important ones, the meaning perspectives that are deeply engrained and that operate behind the scenes of our thinking, are developed in childhood as a result of interaction with and observation of significant authority figures, such as parents and society.

> A meaning perspective is the structure of psychocultural assumptions within which new experience is assimilated to past experience. It is a way of seeing yourself and your relationships. More than that, it establishes the criteria that determine what you will experience—criteria for identifying what you will find interesting, for deciding which problems are of concern to you, for determining what you are prepared to learn and from whom, for determining values, for setting priorities for action, and for defining the meaning and direction of self-fulfillment and personal success. (Mezirow, 1978a, p. 11)

A person's most influential meaning perspectives generally operate outside conscious awareness; if they are conscious, they are often perceived as *common sense*, rather than only one of many possible ways to see the world. Because meaning perspectives determine how we make sense of everything that we see, hear, and read, these deeply embedded "cultural and psychological assumptions" cause us to be "caught in our own history" and "reliving it" (Mezirow, 1978b, p. 101).

For Mezirow (1978a), becoming aware of these powerful influencers and deciding for ourselves whether we will continue to believe in them constitutes the process of maturation as it occurs in adulthood (an important distinction, since theories until that time conceptualized development as a phenomenon limited to childhood and adolescence).

> In childhood, maturity is a *formative* process—one of socialization, of learning adult roles. In adulthood the process is *transformative*—involving alienation from those roles, reframing new perspectives, and reengaging life with a greater degree of self-determination. Perspective transformation is a generic process of adult development; it is a kind of learning—perhaps the most important kind—that enables us to move through the critical transitional periods of adulthood. (p. 12)

Mezirow's goal was to create a theory that would explain both the similarities and differences between learning in childhood and adulthood. In formulating this goal, he was acting in response to three topics that, at the time, dominated adult education research and guidance for practice. These topics were (a) adult motivation to participate in education, (b) andragogy, and (c) self-directed learning. Mezirow believed that these topics were descriptions of factors affecting practice, not conceptualizations of theory about learning. From his perspective, principles for guiding adult education practice ought to be based on knowledge about how adults learn, yet a theory describing the process of adult learning had yet to be developed.

During this same time, a new field of inquiry was emerging in the discipline of developmental psychology. In this field of study about childhood and adolescence, research and theory about adulthood suddenly proliferated. Of special interest to Mezirow were the psychosocial stage theorists, especially psychoanalyst Roger Gould (1972), and the constructivists, such as Kitchener and King (1990) and Daloz (1988). As Mezirow's theory generated attention among adult educators, they began to link transformative learning to another constructivist, Robert Kegan (1998).

In this context of aroused interest about adult learning and adult development, Mezirow plunged into a quest that would occupy the rest of his life—to describe and explain the distinctive nature of adult learning. The nature of his quest and the theory it produced evolved from his determination to escape the limits of any single academic discipline by creating a synthesis of ideas drawn from multiple perspectives.

In the preface to his book that provides the first comprehensive description of his adult learning theory, he explained,

> A disturbing fault line separates theories of adult learning from the practice of those who try to help adults learn. Psychologists interested in adult learning often find themselves trapped within the framework of particular theories and paradigms, such as the behaviorist or psychoanalytic; they seldom communicate with each other, let alone with educators. Philosophers, linguists, sociologists, and political scientists also have legitimate interests in adult learning, but each group has a different frame of reference and a different vocabulary for interpreting the phenomenon. Few efforts have been made to develop a synthesis of the different theories that educators of adults can use. (Mezirow, 1991a, p. xi)

The following section provides an overview of the most salient features of Mezirow's theoretical work and the vocabulary that it generated.

Key Concepts in Mezirow's Theory

Mezirow based his theory on *social constructivism*—the premise that humans are, by nature, meaning-making creatures (i.e., we interpret our sensory impressions of sight, sound, etc., in order to make sense of our experiences and provide a coherent understanding of ourselves and the world around us). Social constructivism asserts that these processes of interpretation are learned from our social surroundings. An important presupposition for his theory is that truth exists, but nobody can ever claim to know it completely (Mezirow, 1996). The only way to gauge whether one's beliefs are valid is to compare them with the beliefs of others, each sharing justification for their beliefs: "As there are no fixed truths or totally definitive knowledge, and because circumstances change, the human condition may be best understood as a continuous effort to negotiate contested meanings" (Mezirow, 2000, p. 3).

Based on these two foundational assumptions, Mezirow's (1996) theory begins with the assertion that we make meaning by "filtering" our sense perceptions through a "frame of reference" (p. 163); these frames of reference comprise meaning schemes and meaning perspectives. A *meaning scheme* is a particular way of thinking about something; it is a "cluster of specific beliefs, feelings, attitudes, and value judgments" (p. 163) that shapes a person's thinking. One example of a meaning scheme would be homophobia, with the particular stereotypes, biases, and condemnations believed by an individual person (Mezirow, 1997). In contrast, a *meaning perspective* is more foundational; it is the basis upon which meaning schemes are built. Mezirow (1996) described a meaning perspective as a "broad, generalized, and orienting predisposition" (p. 163). In the example of homophobia, Mezirow suggested that the underlying meaning perspective is ethnocentrism, "the predisposition to regard others outside one's own group as inferior" (Mezirow, 1997, p. 6).

According to Mezirow's theory, learning involves the following possibilities, which represent a continuum of complexity:

- elaborate existing meaning schemes
- learn new meaning schemes
- transform meaning schemes
- transform meaning perspectives

All four types of learning may be valuable depending on one's learning needs in a given situation, but the last type is relatively rare and particularly impactful (i.e., transformative). Because they operate behind the scenes of one's thinking, meaning perspectives are especially influential to a person's meaning making. In 2000, Mezirow changed terminology, converting *meaning schemes* to *points of view* and *meaning perspectives* to *habits of mind*, but their meanings are the same.

Mezirow (2000) defined the process of transformation as "becoming critically aware of one's own tacit assumptions and expectations and those of others and assessing their relevance for making an interpretation" (p. 4). This critical reflection is best accomplished, he argued, by engaging in critical discourse, or dialogue with others, where the purpose is to seek to understand each other's views, test the evidence or other rationale underlying those views, and work together to develop more comprehensive ones. It is important to recognize that Mezirow was not advocating for debate but rather for sincere efforts to understand how others may see the world differently as well as willingness to question one's own views rather than justify or defend them. Establishing a tone of solidarity and mutual searching in an environment of respect and safety is a necessary prerequisite for this open-minded interaction between critical discourse and critical reflection.

While some have described Mezirow's theory as being too individualistic, this claim does not match what he actually wrote. The process is individual only in the sense that each person considers his or her own problematic meaning perspectives, but learners work together to name assumptions, envision alternatives, "try on" different perspectives, and so forth. According to Mezirow, it is through critical discourse and critical reflection that meaning perspectives are most likely to change in positive, developmental ways, that is, meaning perspectives that are more "inclusive, differentiating, permeable, critically reflective, and integrative of experience" (Mezirow, 1996, p. 163).

One of the most oft-cited aspects of Mezirow's theory is his explanation of 10 phases that describe the perspective transformation process (Mezirow, 1978a):

A disorienting dilemma. Mezirow coined this term to describe how the process begins. When one's meaning perspectives are contradicted or otherwise begin to seem inadequate because of life events or exposure to new ideas, a sense of discomfort and/or confusion can arise. As Mezirow's theory evolved, he noted that this process could be epochal (brought about by a powerful event) or incremental (growing discomfort or realization over time). (See Ensign, 2019, for an expanded typology for how the transformation process begins.)

Self-examination with feelings of guilt or shame. If a disorientating dilemma becomes strong enough, people may begin to ask themselves how they, or their way of understanding the world, may be the cause of problems. Because meaning perspectives are deeply embedded and learned from influential authority figures during childhood, questioning them can feel like an act of betrayal and often brings feelings of guilt or shame.

Critical assessment of assumptions. As people become consciously aware of assumptions embedded in meaning perspectives they have tacitly assumed to be true since childhood, they have the opportunity to assess them and to evaluate how they might be distorted, incomplete, or perhaps wrong. Mezirow (1991a) described three types of reflection involved in this critical assessment: (a) *content reflection* (questioning facts used to frame a problem), (b) *process reflection* (questioning processes used to try to solve a problem), and (c) *premise reflection* (questioning underlying assumptions that led to a problem in the first place); it is the last one that is most likely to lead to perspective transformation. Mezirow initially identified three types of assumptions (epistemic, sociocultural, and psychological) and later expanded his list with another three (moral–ethical, philosophical, and aesthetic). (See Mezirow, 2000, for brief descriptions of each type of assumption.)

Recognition that one's discontent and the process of transformation are shared and that others have negotiated a similar change. Because meaning perspectives are shaped and formed by a person's most influential childhood authority figures, growing disorientation can feel isolating, as if rejecting one's meaning perspectives is abnormal. Therefore, recognizing that other people have shared similar concerns is an important part of the overall process because it allows the meaning perspectives developed in one's childhood to move from being normal and common sense to being just one way among many of seeing the world.

Exploration of options for new roles, relationships, and actions. People can make purposeful change only when they have viable options from which to choose. Thus, becoming aware of new options for thinking, feeling, and acting is a necessary step when going through transformative change.

Planning a course of action. Habits built over a lifetime do not go away easily, and life trajectories do not change automatically. Therefore, learners must think about and plan their future, especially their initial steps into unknown territory.

Acquisition of knowledge and skills for implementing one's plan. In order for people to accomplish the plan they create for their future, they must acquire the knowledge and skills necessary to enact it. For instance, if a learner wants to develop the habit of healthy eating, she or he might first need to learn about nutrition, cooking, and food shopping.

Provisional trying of new roles. Transformation often involves a change in one's social roles, whether that is a stay-at-home-mom returning to the workforce (as in Mezirow's [1978b] study) or a low-income adult deciding to attend college. A tentative trying of these new roles may initiate this change.

Building of competence and self-confidence in new roles and relationships. Having learned new knowledge and skills and then foraying into a new social role can create a sense of foreignness, perhaps even impostership. Over time, one becomes better at inhabiting the new role and therefore also more confident.

Reintegration into one's life on the basis of conditions dictated by a new perspective. Over time, all the intentional effort invested into change begins to feel more normal. Changes in thinking and acting in one of life's contexts (e.g., work) begin to affect other contexts (e.g., home, community).

Mezirow (1978a) was clear that these phases do not occur in a neat, orderly, or even sequential process:

> While it is useful to analyze the process in terms of phases, it should be clear that the phases do not follow an invariant sequence. . . . [I]t is true that one can never return to an old perspective once a transformation has occurred, [but] the process is seldom one of consistent forward movement. [One] can get stalled— temporarily or permanently—at any phase; typically, difficult negotiation and compromise, backsliding and self-deception occur. (pp. 15–16)

Although Mezirow presented these 10 phases as a general descriptor of the process inherent in perspective transformation, he consistently emphasized that the core facilitator of perspective transformation is the interaction between critical reflection and critical discourse.

Critiques of Mezirow's Theory of Transformative Learning

A ubiquitous critique of Mezirow is that he emphasized cognitive, rational thinking as the primary facilitator of perspective transformation. This critique is justifiable in the sense that Mezirow's publications tend to focus on rational activities such as critical dialogue and critical reflection. However, the critique ignores the fact that he emphasized the social and lived nature of the process (e.g., recognition of shared experiences, trying on of roles, developing competence and self-confidence, reintegration into one's life).

Another strand of critique arose because Mezirow framed his theory of transformation as being intrinsically emancipatory, that is, as providing guidance for educators to help people free themselves from social norms that are somehow hurtful or restrictive. These critiques claim that he focused too much on individual transformation, seeming to assume that it would inevitably lead to collective, social transformation (Cunningham, 1992; Inglis, 1997). Mezirow countered that his intent was not to create a theory focused exclusively on emancipatory education but rather a comprehensive theory of adult learning that included an explanation of how transformative learning was possible (1992, 1998). For him, emancipatory learning was only one form that transformative learning could take (Mezirow, 1994; Newman, 1994). Equally relevant is his response to critics who asserted inadequacy of his thinking about emancipatory learning (Collard & Law, 1989; M. Hart, 1990). Mezirow (1989) was adamant that collective social action must include dialogue and deliberation to create individual learning. Without self-determined self-reflection carried out by individuals in a social setting, agendas for social change would resemble indoctrination rather than emancipatory education (Mezirow, 1989).

Another oft-cited criticism applies a postmodern critique to Mezirow's theory. The argument is that the theory assumes a unified self (as opposed to a constantly shifting, situation-dependent self), treats Western concepts as if they are universal (e.g., it presents self-direction as a universal aspect of human development rather than a Western value), and assumes a universal form of rationality rather than thought that differs based on context (Clark & Wilson, 1991). It is important to note that Mezirow (1996) purposefully designed his theory as an alternative to postmodernist thinking, so he likely did not feel the need to justify his theory to that line of thought. Nevertheless, Mezirow (1991b) responded that, rather than ignoring context, his writings consistently say that cultural context is the primary shaper of all meaning perspectives.

Tennant (1993) argued that Mezirow committed an error that is common among all adult educators—misperceiving "the tension between the individual and the social: between individual psychological development and social development and transformation" (p. 35). Based on a substantial literature that documents the interplay between social structures and human development, Tennant argued that what Mezirow described as transformation in meaning schemes is more appropriately perceived as "normative life cycle changes" (p. 39). Mezirow (1994) countered:

> I see no good reason to differentiate between transformative adult learning and adult development. . . . In my view, meaning perspectives and meaning schemes are two dimensions of the same learning process, and the process through which adults learn—through the elaboration, acquisition, and transformation of meaning schemes and perspectives—is the same as the process of adult development. Perspective transformation is the engine of adult development. (p. 228)

Recent critiques of transformative learning tend to focus on the general body of scholarship that refers to this topic, rather than on Mezirow's articulation of his theory. The most common critical assessment is that scholars and practitioners use the term *transformative learning* too loosely, as a catchall referring to any type of learning. Newman (2012) articulated this critique most cogently by identifying several research articles where, he argued, the authors' examples of transformative learning are actually not transformation. Based on inferential analysis of these examples, he conceptualizes six fatal flaws of transformative learning theory and concluded, therefore, that transformative learning must not exist. In its place, he suggested that learning should be considered either good or not good. Cranton and Kasl (2012) and Dirkx (2012) responded, mostly agreeing with Newman's first assertion that many scholars misuse the term but disagreeing with his other conclusions.

Taylor and Cranton (2012) critiqued the transformative learning research literature for being redundant and deterministic. They argued that scholars need to engage in greater theoretical analysis and work more with original sources rather than relying on literature reviews. (Interestingly, Taylor, who made this critique, wrote the reviews most often "relied upon.")

Different Theoretical Approaches to Transformative Learning

It could be argued that the transformative potential of learning has been written about for centuries, if not millennia, using vastly different terms, and by scholars across the globe. Because this chapter is necessarily limited to the small part of this scholarship that has coalesced under the term *transformative learning*, much of our focus is on scholarship primarily from North America published during the past 30 years. Although Mezirow's publications catalyzed discourse about transformative learning among adult educators, many approaches to transformation have their own, separate theoretical origins. As attention to transformative learning expands among adult educators, they increasingly turn attention to other theoretical approaches.

It is common in the literature for scholars to talk about different *approaches* to transformative learning. The phrase actually means that different *theoretical perspectives* guide thinking about what transformation looks like, what prompts it, how best to support it, and so forth. Clark (1993) was first to suggest a classification system for transformational learning when she described three strands of thought common in the literature, naming them by their most visible proponent: (a) Mezirow (perspective transformation), (b) Freire (critical pedagogy), and (c) Daloz (adult development). In Taylor's (1998) monograph, which provides a definitive review of research related to Mezirow's theory, he begins by acknowledging two important approaches to transformation that are different from Mezirow's: (a) Boyd's concept of individuation and (b) Freire's view of social transformation. Perhaps the most complete classification system is Taylor's (2008), wherein he identified eight categories of transformative learning

scholarship that he labeled cultural/spiritual, neurobiological, planetary, psychoanalytic, psychocritical, psychodevelopmental, race centric, and social–emancipatory.

The following is a partial accounting of several approaches to transformative
learning. To create this overview, we began with Taylor's (2008) list and then modified it based on our reading of the literature; specifically, we omitted neurobiological
because (to our knowledge) there have not been enough publications to justify naming it as a general approach. We added *identity* because it is increasingly used and has
a distinct theoretical base. To better reflect the literature, we changed Taylor's *cultural/
spiritual* to *spiritual/transpersonal*. Last, we reordered the list to reflect, in descend-
ing order, the preponderance of each approach. These categories are not discrete;
differing approaches as they appear in literature or in practice are often blended.
The psychocritical category is not discussed because it refers to Mezirow's approach,
already described in detail. Each of these approaches has generated a body of scholarly
literature, but we name only a few sources that can serve readers as a beginning point
for further exploration.

Psychoanalytic

Perhaps the most popular approach, apart from Mezirow's, is from the perspective
of *depth psychology*, which draws on Jungian theory. It views transformation as an
internal process of self-discovery, paying particular attention to emotions, images,
fantasies, and other messages from one's inner self (see chapter 6 for more on the
role of emotions and the self in learning). Boyd and Myers (1988) were the first to
connect Jungian psychology to transformative learning. Dirkx (1997) continued this
approach, becoming the most visible scholar writing from this perspective, which he
often refers to as "soul work":

> Learning through soul calls for a more central role of imagination and fantasy in
> our instructional methods and content. Stories, narratives, myths, tales, and ritual
> capture aspects of this world in ways not readily available through more traditional
> instructional methods. . . . Rigid adherence to an agenda or curriculum mitigates
> against expression of soul. . . . We need to make room for grief work, for passions of
> fear and sorrow, for dreams and desires. . . . In nurturing soul, we do not try to solve
> problems for ourselves or for our learners, or move learners toward more rational,
> enlightened ways of being. Rather, we seek to cultivate the presence of soul, watch it
> gain expression, and participate in its unfolding. . . . We focus on helping individu-
> als and groups own what it is they are rejecting of themselves and to see what they
> are projecting onto others. (p. 85)

Emancipatory

A long tradition of scholarship examines emancipatory education, most of which
does not draw on Mezirow's theory. Much of this scholarship is based on Freire's
(1970/2005) *Pedagogy of the Oppressed* (see chapter 1 for more on Freire's emancipatory approach), as well as others in the tradition of critical theory (e.g., Adorno,

Habermas, Honneth). This tradition did not historically use the word *transformation*, but emancipatory education is considered inherently transformative, and many adult education scholars have made this connection explicit. Although Mezirow built on ideas from Freire and Habermas, and considered his theory emancipatory, scholars who explicitly adopt a social emancipatory perspective (Brookfield, 2003; M. Hart, 1990; Schugurensky, 2002) distinguished their work from Mezirow's.

Psychodevelopmental

Grounded in theories from developmental psychology, this approach defines transformation as developing more complex cognitive and psychosocial capacities. The book by Mezirow and Associates (2000) includes three chapters written by scholars who are prominent voices within developmental psychology. Kegan (1982, 1998) used his constructive–developmental model as a lens for explaining "the form that transforms." By this, he means that transformation is manifested as change in a person's epistemology or the way a person constructs knowledge. Adult educators frequently connect Kegan's model to transformative learning (see chapter 7 for detailed discussion of the constructive-developmental theory). Belenky et al. (1986) also wrote about epistemology, applying to transformative learning a model derived from groundbreaking research on women's epistemological development. Daloz (1986, 2012) explored transformational development for "the common good," which reflects his long-standing attention to both epistemological and psychosocial development. In addition to the three chapters written by prominent developmental theorists, the book also includes a chapter with concrete examples of how to teach with developmental intention, based on interviews with adult education practitioners around the globe (Taylor et al., 2000).

Spiritual/Transpersonal

Some scholars have explored how a sense of connection with something larger than the self promotes transformation. For instance, T. Hart (2000) saw transformation as the transpersonal evolution of consciousness and learning as a process of going deeper into one's experiences. Ferrer et al. (2005) described how "cocreative participation of . . . body, vital, heart, mind, and consciousness . . . naturally enhances the transformative, healing, and spiritual power of education" (pp. 313, 321). Shahjahan (2004) examined the possibilities and challenges encountered in formal learning settings when engaging with and promoting the spiritual. Similarly, Tolliver and Tisdell (2006) described connections between spirituality and transformative learning, as well as the challenges of fostering spirituality in higher education.

Identity

In this approach, identity is considered the central factor that differentiates transformation from other forms of learning. In an extensive elaboration of this idea, Illeris (2014) defined transformative learning as any process that changes one's identity (how we experience ourselves and how we want to be experienced by others). He pointed to constituent components such as identity development and defense, personality, and changing life conditions as influencing this process. Tennant (2005) similarly defined transformative learning as revolving primarily around identity. He advocated four practices ("technologies of the self") that are useful for people to shape their own formation and change: (a) knowing oneself, (b) controlling oneself, (c) caring for oneself, and (d) re-creating oneself.

Planetary

Some scholars focus on transformations inherent in coming to a lived sense of connection with (rather than domination over) the world. O'Sullivan et al. (2002) asserted that transformative learning is the experience of a deeper appreciation for the interconnectedness of all life on earth. Their approach is possibly prescriptive, as they seem to advocate that the outcome of transformative learning is a specific worldview:

> Transformative learning . . . involves our understanding of ourselves and our self-locations; our relationships with other humans and with the natural world; our understanding of relations of power in interlocking structures of class, race, and gender; our body awarenesses; our visions of alternative approaches to living; and our sense of possibilities for social justice and peace and personal joy. (p. xvii)

Lange (2018) asserted that the planetary perspective, which is necessary for social and environmental sustainability, requires *relational ontology*. Drawing on diverse traditions ranging from quantum physics to North American Indigenous philosophies, Lange explained that relationality requires ethical, ontological (i.e., ways of being), and epistemological (i.e., ways of knowing) transformation. Hathaway's (2018) review of literature on ecological wisdom and his analysis of its relationship to transformative learning paid special attention to emotions, reason, imagination, and empathy.

Race Centric

An expanding discourse in education explores how the social positioning of learners impacts their learning experiences. Within adult education, most of this scholarship does not refer to transformative learning. However, discourse that challenges the norm of white hegemony as a dominating force in education is inherently calling for paradigm shifts and therefore is about transformation. Sheared (1994) is frequently cited for her explanation of how learners' views are ignored or devalued, often based on race. She advocated moving marginalized voices to the center of the classroom environment so that new realities emerge (see chapter 2 for a further discussion of centering marginalized voices). Williams (2003) and Johnson-Bailey and

Alfred (2006) wrote about power in educational contexts and the implications for transformative learning. *The Handbook of Race and Adult Education: A Resource for Dialogue on Racism* (Sheared et al., 2010) explores issues of race from a variety of perspectives with an eye to transformation.

Moving Beyond Approaches Into Metatheory

Seeking to move beyond *approaches* as an organizing strategy, Gunnlaugson (2008) was the first to provide a fundamentally different classification system. Advocating for *metatheoretical discourse* (i.e., dialogue across different theories), he suggested the existing literature be characterized as first- or second-wave theories. *First-wave* theories offer specific perspectives on what transformation is and how it happens (e.g., the work of Mezirow, Kegan, or Dirkx). Gunnlaugson (2008) recommended that scholars begin offering *second-wave* theories, which are integrated conceptions melded from multiple specific perspectives (e.g., he suggested, Wilber's [2006] integral theory).

Hoggan (2016) provided a rationale for thinking of transformative learning as a metatheory. He begins by explaining uses and forms of the concept:

> A metatheory is an overarching paradigm relative to a particular phenomenon or range of phenomena. As Aldridge, Kuby, and Strevy (1992) describe, it is "the umbrella under which several theories of development or learning are classified together based on their commonalities regarding human nature" (p. 683). There are two types of metatheory in the social sciences: synthetic metatheory sorts underlying theories into categories; analytic metatheory seeks to provide categorizations of components that are common among all the underlying theories (Wallace, 1992). Taylor's (1998, 2007) categorization of approaches to transformative learning is an example of synthetic metatheory. (p. 63)

Hoggan (2016) then stepped toward creating an analytic metatheory. Based on a comprehensive literature review, he suggested criteria by which to determine whether any particular phenomenon should or should not be considered an example of transformative learning, which he defined as "processes that result in significant and irreversible changes in the way a person experiences, conceptualizes, and interacts with the world" (p. 71). To be described as transformative, a learning experience must lead to change that has depth, breadth, and relative stability. *Depth* refers to the significance of the change; *breadth* means that a change applies to many, if not all, contexts of a person's life; and *relative stability* means that change is irreversible. These parameters are intended to be broad enough to capture diverse ways that transformation might happen but narrow enough to delimit which learning experiences can rightly be described as transformative. As the purpose of analytic metatheory is to provide conceptual tools that are useful across all underlying theories, Hoggan offered a typology of transformative learning outcomes that can be used to describe specific ways people can or may change.

Implementing Transformative Learning

Obviously, guidance about how best to implement transformative learning depends on the educator's theoretical approach to defining goals. With that caveat, we suggest two general guidelines for practitioners wanting to implement transformative learning regardless of approach.

Attending to Four Elements

When implementing processes for transformative learning, we recommend that practitioners strive with disciplined clarity to define their goals and strategies for actualizing these goals. To this end, we recommend that educators distinguish four elements: (a) what they hope to accomplish (learning outcome), (b) what learners need to experience in order to accomplish this outcome (learning process), (c) what the educator needs to do in order to facilitate this process (pedagogical strategy) and, finally, (d) specific activities that implement this pedagogical strategy (pedagogical activity).

The following examples illustrate the nature of these four elements.

Example 1: Psychocritical Approach

This approach is grounded in Mezirow's conception of transformational learning theory.

> **Context.** A work-based course to help people become better at working in diverse groups, such as teams with members from across job functions or from different countries.
>
> **Learning outcome.** Learners develop better meaning perspectives. *Better* is defined as more inclusive of diverse views, differentiating (based on evidence and reason rather than personal or cultural bias), permeable (open to change), and critically reflective (thoughtfully examined rather than unconsciously accepted as "how things have always been done").
>
> **Learning process.** Learners develop the skills and habits of being critically aware of their own tacit assumptions and expectations as well as those of others in order to evaluate the relevance, accuracy, and/or usefulness of these assumptions for understanding and acting in the world.
>
> **Pedagogical strategy.** Educators facilitate interaction between critical reflection and critical discourse.
>
> **Pedagogical activity.** Educators create learning environments that foster solidarity for mutual searching rather than competition and debate. They present and model practices of active listening, naming underlying assumptions in their own and others' perspectives, examining evidence

and rationale, and exploring alternative possibilities. Learners gain experience with these skills through activities such as small group discussions, case study analysis, role play, reflection papers, or action learning interventions.

Example 2: Psychodevelopmental Approach

This approach is grounded in developmental psychology. As explained earlier, psychosocial or epistemological development are the theory types most often used. The example in our illustration is grounded in epistemological development, or the way people know.

> **Context.** A management development program to support new and mid-level managers in their ability to manage complex projects and diverse work teams.
>
> **Learning outcome.** Learners inhabit a more complex way of knowing, that is, their personal epistemology progresses to a more advanced form.
>
> **Learning process.** Learners become conscious of how they decide what knowledge they accept as true, relevant, or valuable and become open to new possibilities in how to make this judgment. (Note the contrast to psychocritical, in which learners evaluate the content of their beliefs, rather than the process by which they form their beliefs.)
>
> **Pedagogical strategy.** Educators provide support, understanding, and validation for learners' current ways of thinking and acting but do not justify them as being the best possible alternative. Educators model openness to differing viewpoints and challenge learners to be similarly receptive. They teach skills of evidence assessment.
>
> **Pedagogical activity.** Learners engage in a social forum, such as with a mentor or action learning group, where they participate in ongoing reflective assessments of their accomplishments, challenges, and performance. Educators model effective self-critique and open-mindedness. Learners gain experience with these skills through activities such as mentoring, small group discussions, teams composed of learners who inhabit differing developmental stages, action learning teams, case study analysis, personal learning journals, or educational life histories.

These two examples are intended to illustrate that the same type of learning activity (e.g., small group discussion or case study analysis) will be designed differently, depending on the practitioner's intentions about learning outcomes and processes.

Ethical Considerations: Three Orientations Toward Implementing Transformative Learning

Hoggan and Kloubert (2020) described three orientations toward implementing transformative learning. Practitioners should be aware of their orientation, so their practice does not unfairly abuse their inherent power.

Prescriptive

In the prescriptive orientation educators decide how learners need to transform, including the specific worldview they should have, and design pedagogy accordingly. Hoggan and Kloubert (2020) warned that a prescriptive approach is often problematic because it focuses too much on what the educator decides is important for learners, which is understandable when planning for knowledge and skill acquisition but is fraught with ethical challenges when planning for ways to change learners in dramatic ways. This orientation can too easily manifest as indoctrination rather than emancipatory or developmental education.

Process Oriented

A second orientation is to teach skills and habits that are helpful for learning and life, knowing that these skills and habits may (and should) have long-term, transformative effects. One example of a transformation-promoting *skill* is capacity to discern one's worldview with increasing complexity; an example of a transformational *habit* is to be ever alert for unexamined assumptions so they can be examined and challenged when problematic. The process-oriented educator does not seek to instill learners with particular worldviews or to advocate that particular assumptions be challenged. As exemplified in Example 1, Mezirow never advocated a specific worldview but rather for developing a better worldview (meaning perspective). If critical discourse based on a shared sense of solidarity and critical reflection are believed to lead to better perspectives, then a process-oriented pedagogy that teaches those skills and fosters a predisposition to use them can be said to promote transformative learning.

Adaptive

The third orientation toward implementing transformative learning is to recognize that in certain situations, learners might reasonably be expected already to be wrestling with challenges conducive to transformative learning. For instance, Hoggan and Browning (2019) illustrated the profound social and emotional challenges faced by nontraditional (historically underserved) students when they enter community college. These challenges, when understood as transformative learning needs that exist on top of normal, curricular learning needs, put these students at a severe disadvantage and help explain disparities in degree completion rates. When understood this way, educators can design supports and pedagogies that help learners effectively navigate the challenges of transformative learning.

Conclusion

This chapter has sketched the broad outlines of transformative learning. We believe its popularity in scholarly literature is likely because the idea of transformational change resonates with people, whether they are teachers, counselors, professors, clergy, or simply observers of life. People can—and often do—experience transformative change throughout their entire lives. The literature around transformative learning provides a structure of scholarship for those interested in studying these processes of change and guideposts for practitioners who seek to support that change.

References

Belenky, M. F., Clinchy, B. M., Goldberger, N. R., & Tarule, J. M. (1986). *Women's ways of knowing: The development of self, voice, and mind*. Basic Books.

Boyd, R. D., & Myers, J. G. (1988). Transformative education. *International Journal of Lifelong Education, 7*(4), 261–284. https://doi.org/10.1080/0260137880070403

Brookfield, S. (2003). Putting the critical back into critical pedagogy: A commentary on the path of dissent. *Journal of Transformative Education, 1*, 141–149. https://doi.org/10.1177/1541344603001002007

Clark, M. C. (1993). Transformational learning. In S. B. Merriam (Ed.), *Best Practices Teaching ESL: A Lifelong Learning Approach* (New Directions for Adult and Continuing Education, no. 57, pp. 47–56). Jossey-Bass. https://doi.org/10.1002/ace.36719935707

Clark, M. C., & Wilson, A. L. (1991). Context and rationality in Mezirow's theory of transformational learning. *Adult Education Quarterly, 41*(2), 75–91. https://doi.org/10.1177/0001848191041002002

Collard, S., & Law, M. (1989). The limits of perspective transformation: A critique of Mezirow's theory. *Adult Education Quarterly, 39*(2), 99–107. https://doi.org/10.1177/0001848189039002004

Cranton, P., & Kasl, E. (2012). A response to Michael Newman's "Calling Transformative Learning Into Question: Some Mutinous Thoughts." *Adult Education Quarterly, 62*(4), 393–398. https://doi.org/10.1177/0741713612456418

Cunningham, P. M. (1992). From Freire to feminism: The North American experience with critical pedagogy. *Adult Education Quarterly, 42*(3), 180–191. https://doi.org/10.1177/074171369204200306

Daloz, L. (1986). *Effective teaching and mentoring*. Jossey-Bass.

Daloz, L. (1988). The story of Gladys who refused to grow: A morality tale for mentors. *Lifelong Learning, 2*, 4–7.

Daloz, L. (2012). *Mentor: Guiding the journey of adult learners*. Wiley.

Dirkx, J. M. (1997). Nurturing soul in adult learning. In P. Cranton (Ed.), *Best Practices Teaching ESL: A Lifelong Learning Approach* (New Directions for Adult and Continuing Education, no. 74, pp. 79–88). Jossey-Bass. https://doi.org/10.1002/ace.7409

Dirkx, J. M. (2012). Self-formation and transformative learning: A response to "Calling Transformative Learning Into Question: Some Mutinous Thoughts," by Michael Newman. *Adult Education Quarterly, 62*(4), 399–405. https://doi.org/10.1177/0741713612456420

Ensign, T. (2019). *The seed of transformation: A disorientation index*. Pepperdine University.

Ferrer, J. N., Romero, M. T., & Albareda, R. V. (2005). Integral transformative education: A participatory proposal. *Journal of Transformative Education, 3*(4), 306–330. https://doi.org/10.1177/1541344605279175

Freire, P. (2005). *Pedagogy of the oppressed*. Continuum. (Original work published 1970)

Gould, R. L. (1972). The phases of adult life: A study in developmental psychology. *American Journal of Psychiatry, 129*(5), 521–531. https://doi.org/10.1176/ajp.129.5.521

Gunnlaugson, O. (2008). Metatheoretical prospects for the field of transformative learning. *Journal of Transformative Education, 6*(2), 124–135. https://doi.org/10.1177/1541344608323387

Hart, M. (1990). Critical theory and beyond: Further perspectives on emancipatory education. *Adult Education Quarterly, 40*(3), 125–138. https://doi.org/10.1177/0001848190040003001

Hart, T. (2000). *From information to transformation: Education for the evolution of consciousness*. Peter Lang.

Hathaway, M. D. (2018). *Cultivating ecological wisdom: Worldviews, transformative learning, and engagement for sustainability*. [Doctoral dissertation, University of Toronto]. ProQuest Dissertation & Theses Global. Publication No. 10687583.

Hoggan, C. (2016). Transformative learning as a metatheory: Definition, criteria, and typology. *Adult Education Quarterly, 66*(1), 57–75. https://doi.org/10.1177/0741713615611216

Hoggan, C. D., & Browning, B. (2019). *Transformational learning in community colleges: Charting a course for academic and personal success*. Harvard Education Press.

Hoggan, C., & Kloubert, T. (2020). Transformative learning in theory and practice. *Adult Education Quarterly, 70*(3), 295–307. https://doi.org/10.1177/0741713620918510

Illeris, K. (2014). Transformative learning and identity. *Journal of Transformative Education, 12*(2), 148–163. https://doi.org/10.1177/1541344614548423

Inglis, T. (1997). Empowerment and emancipation. *Adult Education Quarterly, 48*(1), 3–17. https://doi.org/10.1177/074171369704800102

Johnson-Bailey, J., & Alfred, M. V. (2006). Transformational teaching and the practices of black women adult educators. In E. W. Taylor (Ed.), *Teaching for Change: Fostering Transformative Learning in the Classroom* (New Directions for Adult and Continuing Education, no. 109, pp. 49–58). Jossey-Bass. https://doi.org/10.1002/ace.207

Kegan, R. (1982). *The evolving self: Problem and process in human development*. Harvard University Press.

Kegan, R. (1998). *In over our heads: The mental demands of modern life*. Harvard University Press.

Kitchener, K. S., & King, P. M. (1990). The reflective judgment model: Transforming assumptions about knowing. In J. D. Mezirow & Associates (Eds.), *Fostering critical reflection in adulthood: A guide to transformative and emancipatory learning* (pp. 159–176). Jossey-Bass.

Kitchenham, A. (2008). The evolution of John Mezirow's transformative learning theory. *Journal of Transformative Education, 6*(2), 104–123. https://doi.org/10.1177/1541344608322678

Lange, E. A. (2018). Transforming transformative education through ontologies of relationality. *Journal of Transformative Education, 16*(4), 280–301. https://doi.org/10.1177/1541344618786452

Mezirow, J. D. (1978a). *Education for perspective transformation: Women's re-entry programs in community colleges*. Center for Adult Education, Teachers College, Columbia University.

Mezirow, J. D. (1978b). Perspective transformation. *Adult Education, 28*(2), 100–110. https://doi.org/10.1177/074171367802800202

Mezirow, J. D. (1989). Transformation theory and social action: A response to Collard and Law. *Adult Education Quarterly, 39*(3), 169–175. https://doi.org/10.1177/0001848189039003005

Mezirow, J. D. (1991a). *Transformative dimensions of adult learning.* Jossey-Bass.

Mezirow, J. D. (1991b). Transformation theory and cultural context: A reply to Clark and Wilson. *Adult Education Quarterly, 41*(3), 188–192. https://doi.org/10.1177/0001848191041003004

Mezirow, J. D. (1992). Transformation theory: Critique and confusion. *Adult Education Quarterly, 42*(4), 250–252. https://doi.org/10.1177/074171369204200404

Mezirow, J. D. (1994). Understanding transformation theory. *Adult Education Quarterly, 44*(4), 222–232. https://doi.org/10.1177/074171369404400403

Mezirow, J. D. (1996). Contemporary paradigms of learning. *Adult Education Quarterly, 46*(3), 158–172. https://doi.org/10.1177/074171369604600303

Mezirow, J. D. (1997). Transformative learning: Theory to practice. In P. Cranton (Ed.), *Best Practices Teaching ESL: A Lifelong Learning Approach* (New Directions for Adult and Continuing Education, no. 74, pp. 5–12). Jossey-Bass. https://doi.org/10.1002/ace.7401

Mezirow, J. D. (1998). Transformative learning and social action: A response to Inglis. *Adult Education Quarterly, 49*(1), 70–72. https://doi.org/10.1177/074171369804900109

Mezirow, J. D. (2000). Learning to think like an adult. In J. D. Mezirow & Associates (Eds.), *Learning as transformation: Critical perspectives on a theory in progress* (pp. 3–33). Jossey-Bass.

Mezirow, J. D., & Associates. (Eds.). (2000). *Learning as transformation: Critical perspectives on a theory in progress.* Jossey-Bass.

Newman, M. (1994). Response to "Understanding Transformation Theory." *Adult Education Quarterly, 44*(4), 236–242. https://doi.org/10.1177/074171369404400405

Newman, M. (2012). Calling transformative learning into question: Some mutinous thoughts. *Adult Education Quarterly, 62*(1), 36–55. https://doi.org/10.1177/0741713610392768

O'Sullivan, E., Morrell, A., & O'Connor, M. (2002). *Expanding the boundaries of transformative learning: Essays on theory and praxis.* Palgrave Macmillan.

Schugurensky, D. (2002). Transformative learning and transformative politics. In E. O'Sullivan, A. Morrell, & M. A. O'Connor (Eds.), *Expanding the boundaries of transformative learning* (pp. 59–76). Palgrave Macmillan.

Shahjahan, R. A. (2004). Centering spirituality in the academy: Toward a transformative way of teaching and learning. *Journal of Transformative Education, 2*(4), 294–312. https://doi.org/10.1177/1541344604268330

Sheared, V. (1994). Giving voice: An inclusive model of instruction—A womanist perspective. In E. R. Hayes & S. A. J. Colin III (Eds.), *Confronting Racism and Sexism in Adult Education* (New Directions in Adult and Continuing Education, no. 61, pp. 27–37). Jossey-Bass. https://doi.org/10.1002/ace.36719946105

Sheared, V., Johnson-Bailey, J., Colin, S. A. J., III, Peterson, E., & Brookfield, S. (Eds.). (2010). *The handbook of race and adult education: A resource for dialogue on racism.* Jossey-Bass.

Taylor, E. W. (1998). *The theory and practice of transformative learning: A critical review.* (ED423427). ERIC. https://files.eric.ed.gov/fulltext/ED423422.pdf

Taylor, E. W. (2008). Transformative learning theory. In S. B. Merriam (Ed.), *Third Update on Adult Learning Theory* (New Directions for Adult and Continuing Education, no. 119, pp. 5–15). Jossey-Bass. https://doi.org/10.1002/ace.301

Taylor, E. W., & Cranton, P. (Eds.). (2012). *The handbook of transformative learning: Theory, research, and practice.* Jossey-Bass.

Taylor, K., Marienau, C., & Fiddler, M. (2000). *Developing adult learners: Strategies for teachers and trainers.* Jossey-Bass.

Tennant, M. (1993). Perspective transformation and adult development. *Adult Education Quarterly, 44*(1), 34–42. https://doi.org/10.1177/0741713693044001003

Tennant, M. (2005). Transforming selves. *Journal of Transformative Education, 3*(2), 102–115. https://doi.org/10.1177/1541344604273421

Tolliver, D. E., & Tisdell, E. J. (2006). Engaging spirituality in the transformative higher education classroom. In E. W. Taylor (Ed.), *Teaching for Change: Fostering Transformative Learning in the Classroom* (New Directions for Adult and Continuing Education, no. 109, pp. 37–47). Jossey-Bass. https://doi.org/10.1002/ace.206

Wilber, K. (2006). *Integral spirituality.* Shambhala.

Williams, S. H. (2003). Black Mama Sauce: Integrating the theatre of the oppressed and afro-centricity in transformative learning. In C. A. Wiessner, S. R. Meyer, N. L. Pfhal, & P. G. Neaman (Eds.), *Proceedings of the Fifth International Conference on Transformative Learning* (pp. 479–484). Columbia University Teachers College.

Authors' Notes

There are several helpful reviews of research on transformative learning in Taylor (1997, 1998, 2007) and Taylor and Snyder (2012).

Mezirow and Associates (2000) is an overview of viewpoints that influenced early development of transformative learning theory. Taylor and Cranton's (2012) *Handbook of Transformative Learning* (34 chapters) and Nicolaides et al.'s (2021) *The Palgrave Handbook of Learning for Transformation* (51 chapters) showcase a range of contemporary perspectives on theory and practice.

Editors' Key Seminal and Supplemental Text Suggestions

Charaniya, N. D. (2012). Cultural–spiritual perspective of transformative learning. In E. Taylor & P. Cranton (Eds.), *Handbook of transformative learning: Theory, research, and practice* (pp. 231–244). Wiley.

Clark, M. C., & Wilson, A. L. (1991). Context and rationality in Mezirow's theory of transformational learning. *Adult Education Quarterly, 41*(2), 75–91. https://doi.org/10.1177/0001848191041002002

Cranton, P. (2016). *Understanding and promoting transformative learning: A guide to theory and practice.* Stylus.

Dirkx, J. M. (2012). Nurturing soul work: A Jungian approach to transformative learning. In E. Taylor & P. Cranton (Eds.), *Handbook of transformative learning: Theory, research, and practice* (pp. 116–130). Wiley.

Mezirow, J. D. (1991). Transformation theory and cultural context: A reply to Clark and Wilson. *Adult Education Quarterly, 41*(3), 188–192. https://doi.org/10.1177/0001848191041003004

Mezirow, J. (2012). Learning to think like an adult: Core concepts of transformation theory. In E. Taylor and P. Cranton (Eds.), *Handbook of transformative learning: Theory, research, and practice* (pp. 73–95). John Wiley and Sons.

13

DIGITAL LEARNING AND THE PROMISE OF CONNECTIVISM FOR ADULT EDUCATION

Rita Kop

> The question persists and indeed grows whether the computer will make it easier or harder for human beings to know who they really are, to identify their real problems, to respond more fully to beauty, to place adequate value on life, and to make their world safer than it now is. (Cousins, 1966, p. 535)

There has been much discussion about the impact of virtual learning on adult education. It has been spurred, in part, by the potential of technology in education to change the dynamics of control in education and, to a certain extent, the control of knowledge creation traditionally held by academics in universities. Such promise is aligned with the social traditions of equity and emancipatory goals embedded in the discourse of adult education. This is exemplified, for example, by Paulo Freire and Ivan Illich, two authors who envisioned radical approaches to education. In the 1970s, for example, Illich wrote about the importance of an educational revolution, one in which learners were liberated by the constraints of traditional educational institutions and were instead freed to take ownership over their educational values, knowledge sharing, and collaborative knowledge generation (Kop, 2008). This discourse of liberation is further emphasized in adult education through the work of Freire (1970), whose own work highlighted the need for learner control and discourse as mechanisms for achieving the democratic and emancipatory goals of education. Technology has the potential to enable these ideals. Yet despite this potential, adult educators have, for a long time, been very reluctant to engage with emerging technological developments and have more often than not seen such developments as undermining these emancipatory social traditions (Martin, 2006). Some have criticized technology for the stifling influence it can have on institutional systems (Foucault, 1977; Illich, 1971). This strengthening of institutional authority over learning has further led to technology being widely promoted by politicians using economic discourse with an agenda of upskilling the workforce through a vocationalization of the curriculum (Blair, 2000; Leitch, 2006). Moreover, the naïve enthusiasm of learning technologists and the failure of initial high-profile and high-funding e-learning programs (Bacsich & Bristow, 2004) also have contributed to a skepticism among adult educators about what technology could offer adult learners.

For some, the changed position of educational institutions due to the altered sense of space, place, and identity in a virtual learning environment has been lamented as a loss. Educational institutions have been seen as places where people came together; where minds met; and where new ideas were conceived, criticized and tested, and provisionally accepted if they were found to stand up sufficiently under robust criticism. Some academics have expressed reservations about the online alternatives (Greener & Perriton, 2005) suggesting, for example, that Learning Management Systems (LMSs) have neither managed to support communication and engagement among students nor be an effective alternative to the actual classroom. Peters (1999) compared classroom rituals that are lost in online environments to rites with religious undertones:

> Learning and teaching might be based on unconscious, but at the same time "deep-seated" patterns of behavior, not only of students but also of the teachers. Their ritualization lends solidity and permanence to the actions taking place in the teaching space. (p. 1)

These patterns can make it difficult for educators to want to challenge the orthodoxy of traditional paradigms, even as our understanding of learners and learning evolves.

However, changes in technology and in patterns of technology use over the past several decades, in addition to the emergency use of technology in education during the COVID-19 pandemic, have led some to suggest that changes to educational paradigms generally and academic technology specifically are needed. In particular, the use and proliferation of social networks for communication and networking have led proponents of peer-to-peer technology in education to argue for social media and related applications to be used as an alternative to face-to-face teaching (Bates, 2019; Blessinger & Bliss, 2016; Bouchard, 2009). The openness of these media, and the willingness of people to share in experiences in online contexts, encourage the discussion of ideas and collaborative development of thoughts and knowledge that traditionally formed part of a quality educational experience. The added advantage of these online tools lies in their global availability as knowledge-constructing forums, which provide immediate responses and options for informal self-directed learning and information retrieval on a scale unimaginable in the traditional classroom (Bates, 2019). Moreover, current technologies make it easy to link to any information available online, which is especially useful as everyone with a mobile phone in their pocket also has an enormous library at their fingertips. In addition, although informal teaching had taken place earlier, it is only since the 1970s that serious suggestions have been made, first through the radical perspectives of Freire and Illich, and more contemporaneously under the influence of developing technologies, to deschool society and leave the traditional classroom behind.

Instructional designers, teachers, and learners have started to question the effectiveness of traditional classroom-based teaching strategies developed over generations (Illich, 1971; Peters, 1999; Tularam, 2018).

The theory of *connectivism* is at the center of new thinking about networked approaches to education that speaks to the change occurring in education made possible by the growth of technology and access to broadband. As a theory, connectivism emerged in 2004, which is the time that social media were also first becoming available in the form of Web 2.0 applications. This led to educators starting to experiment with social, creative, and communicative technologies in learning and education, which in turn led to thinking about new theories of knowledge and learning, such as connectivism. According to Siemens (2005), connectivism is a learning theory that integrates "principles of chaos, network, complexity, and self-organization theories" (p. 5). Contrary to theories of learning that focus on how individuals make meaning, connectivism recognizes that

> learning is a process that occurs within nebulous environments of shifting core elements—not entirely under the control of the individual. Learning (defined as actionable knowledge) can reside outside of ourselves (within an organization or a database), is focused on connecting specialized information sets, and the connections that enable us to learn more are more important than our current state of knowing. (p. 5)

In this chapter, I explore what connectivism is, how it has evolved to its current form of hyperconnectivism, if it is a good fit with the purposes of adult education, and how and if adult educators can embrace the opportunities for openness and creative activity it makes available to ensure these purposes remain firmly in place. I will discuss the role of the teacher with regard to information and communication, and I finish the chapter with some final thoughts on knowledge and human learning in the era of hyperconnectivism. Many different terms related to learning while using technology are used by authors cited in this chapter. These include *online learning, virtual learning, networked learning, peer-to-peer learning*, and *technology-based learning*. These terms are related, but each means something slightly different; thus, they will be explained as they are used throughout the chapter when they are most appropriate.

Connectivism

The term *connectivism* was first coined by George Siemens (Siemens, 2005), then an instructor at University of Manitoba in Canada. Siemens further developed the term through his work on the earliest connectivist activities, the massive open online courses (MOOCs), which he developed in collaboration with Stephen Downes, from the National Research Council of Canada (Kop & Hill, 2008). Siemens (2005) defined connectivism as "a learning theory that explains how internet technologies have created new opportunities for people to learn and share information across the World Wide Web and among themselves" (p. 1). Siemens and Downes, together with some other network enthusiasts, started an online movement in the early 2000s, a time that coincided with the rise of individual blogging and an expansion of broadband services. This confluence led to new ideals and excitement about the potential of the technologies available at that time for learning development. People driving this connectivist movement could see how the emerging technologies shaping the internet (the underpinning technologies) and the Web (the software applications) could provide access to information and the ability to work, communicate, and learn with others in new, creative, global collaborations outside the educational structures that had been the norm for centuries (Downes, 2019).

The earliest MOOCs were distinct from institutional and commercial products that emerged later (Downes, 2019). These early connectivist networking events occurred before Facebook, MySpace, Twitter, Instagram, and TikTok, although the photo-sharing site Flickr was operational and widely used to store images and photos produced by participants in the MOOCs. This meant that writing blog posts and producing images were at the heart of the sharing and learning activities, and RSS technology (Really Simple Syndication technology that aggregates information related to particular hashtags) provided the opportunity to easily collect and share the posts and images relevant to the MOOCs with participants. The first MOOC was called "Connectivism and Connective Knowledge" (CCK2008); it was 10 weeks long. Each week had a different topic as the focus of the discussion, all supported by a new, weekly lecture from a different expert, activities on the course wikis, and extensive blogging by participants. Additionally, Stephen Downes developed a daily newsletter (named *Daily*) that used RSS technology to aggregate these blogposts and other artefacts that had been created and made these resources available to all course participants, which in turn created additional engagement on the discussion board. Several MOOCs followed in the same vein, becoming more and more sophisticated in their technology use, although they did not use a single institutional platform (after CCK2009, no institutional LMS was used). Instead, they used distributed technologies under the control of learners. Hashtags and a daily newsletter that collected what was to be found on the Web through these hashtags were at the heart of the course network. Experiments to see what was possible with such large MOOC participant numbers meant that these courses grew from 600 to 1,600 during this time. These experimental courses were sometimes hosted by the National Research Council of Canada and sometimes by University of Manitoba (CCK2009, CCK2011, CCK2012, PLENK2010; Kop & Fournier, 2011). Importantly, they also provided the context for early research on connectivism that underscored the humanist (Kop, Fournier, & Mak, 2011), self-directed (Kop & Fournier, 2011), and data-driven (Kop, Fournier, & Sitlia, 2011) potential of this emerging practice.

Instead of institutional control, MOOC participants were in control of their own learning and knowledge creation. The main assumptions underpinning these early connectivist experiments and that were later widely accepted by practitioners and participants are that individuals should be in charge of their learning and that engaging with personal networks fosters learning. Connectivism advocates for the active engagement of people with resources in communication with others, rather than the transfer of knowledge from educator to learner. Moreover, connectivists promote a learning organization whereby there is no body of knowledge to be transferred from educator to learner, and learning does not take place in a single environment. Instead, knowledge is distributed across the Web, and people's engagement with it constitutes learning (Downes, 2019). As Bouchard (2011) explained:

> Many-to-many communication and zero-cost publishing have created a world where fluid knowledge is collectively built and deconstructed on a daily basis. It is no longer sufficient to "know" something (or learn something); one must keep track of ideas in constant motion, and ideally participate in their generation in order to fully grasp the evolution of their bases. (p. 290)

If learning is viewed this way, it means changes in the nature of knowledge and a reconceptualization of what teaching and learning are.

Two Positions in E-Learning

In online learning research over the past decades, two positions on learning have developed (Weller, 2007). In the first view, information and resources are seen to be at the center of the learning environment; in the second, communication among teachers and learners is seen to be the most important factor in developing an effective learning environment. Some argue that an emphasis on resources has led e-learning to frame education as a commodity. This suggests that technology would not be suitable for enacting the transformational learning ideas such as those of Illich and Freire that became prominent in the 1970s. Gur and Wiley (2007), for instance, discussed the concept of *objectification* in relation to online learning and concluded that when the first position is dominant, "education is often reduced to the packaging and delivery of information, in which the process of teaching is reduced to the transmission of information and courses are transformed into courseware" (p. 1). The development of early LMSs facilitated this depersonalization. Despite their capacity to facilitate communication, in traditional brick-and-mortar universities the use of LMSs was initially mainly limited to transfer of information or for storage of resources (Dron & Anderson, 2009). In the context of these systems, the communication position can be deemphasized when teaching is turned into delivery in which the instructional transaction consists simply of the transmission of information. Such an approach explains why institutions promote the use of behavioral objectives and see the LMS as a content repository, even as some educators and educational theorists move toward more communicative, holistic, and individualized approaches to learning. Biesta (2015) observed, however, that the "learnification" of education, the takeover of education by administrators who want to package learning into nicely formulated learning outcomes, has caused many teachers' transformation from creative professionals into technicians involved in the delivery of information packages.

Weller (2007) and others (Stone & Springer, 2019) have highlighted that online adult education can be organized in quite a different way. In the second position, which emphasizes interaction, information is mediated by two-way communication. In this view of e-learning, "The internet encourages discussion, dialogue and community that is not limited by time or place. The role of educators in this world is to facilitate dialogue and support students in their understanding of resources" (Weller, 2007, p. 6). This suggests that simply packaging and introducing information online is not enough; rather, learning can be enhanced by communication and active engagement in sharing and analysis and reflection within a community of learners. Researchers at Athabasca University and the University of Alberta and their development of the community-of-inquiry model have shown the importance of social, teaching, and cognitive presence in how online groups-based communication developed (Garrison et al., 2000). They suggested that if people are clearly socially present in an online learning group, it fosters trust and a level of comfort that will support the learning process and the learning experience.

The communication position has had a place in distance education since the 1970s, when Turoff introduced and developed the first conferencing system, which then evolved over time to more fully synchronous and asynchronous interaction in the online learning space (Harasim et al., 1995). In the late 1980s, distance education institutions started developing what would become LMSs, a natural progression from the early conferencing systems, such as First Class (Mason & Bacsich, 1998). The LMS combines the potential for communication with the distribution of resources and information.

In more recent years, new developments in technology related to now-ubiquitous social media have encouraged a higher level of communication in technology-based learning (Bates, 2019). The first discussions about their possibilities for education and learning started in the early 2000s, and research on the learning opportunities they can provide began a few years later (Conole et al., 2006; Downes, 2004; Gulati, 2006). In particular, some saw social media as expanding the potential for lifelong and lifewide learning with possibilities to facilitate informal and self-directed learning as well as enhancing opportunities for communication in the online learning environment, for instance, through video conferencing platforms (Anderson & Dron, 2011; Bates, 2019; Blessinger & Bliss, 2016; Downes, 2019).

Connectivism emerged as a developing theory in this period, and many ideas were formed around it related to concepts of knowledge, learning, and pedagogy. Social media were seen to be important in its development as the potential for communication on a global scale was now a reality. This also meant the learning context had changed considerably. Downes (2019) suggested, while citing AlDahdouh et al. (2015), that it no longer makes sense to consider knowledge to be something transferred and "worked with" in the head, as the context in which knowledge is created also plays an important role. This assertion resonates with the early development of social constructivism and situated cognition that emerged from cognitive learning theory, and—finally—aligns educational technology use with the critical, emancipatory purposes of education suggested earlier in this chapter. After all, these theoretical constructs also started by moving away from the idea that learning takes place solely in the mind. In everyday practice, according to the tenets of situated cognition, learning is more likely to be situated in a context in which authentic practice takes place; a person learns not only in the head, but rather the whole human—body and mind—is engaged in the learning and its context. In contrast to cognitive theory, the brain is no longer seen as a symbol-processing machine, a popular metaphor from this theory, and learning is no longer seen as solely a processing of language symbols in the mind. Instead, the learner is actively engaged in activities with all their human characteristics and emotions (Bredo, 1994); the importance of the relationship between emotions and cognition is also highlighted in chapters 5 and 6 of this volume. In this respect, connectivism can be seen as a theoretical construct that extends the ideas of situated cognition. It extends not only the perception of what knowledge is but also what learning is. Learning is framed to involve cognition but also with regard to how it relates to the learning context. The learning context could be constituted of the personal real and wider network, such as a face-to-face or online classroom or a professional community of practice. It allows for self-directed and autonomous learning, where it is not the teacher in control of what happens but rather the learner and the network of learners (although this process may be facilitated or supported by a teacher). If one thinks of approaches to learning as existing along a continuum, from strictly controlled by instructors to no instructor control at all, connectivism extends and expands this continuum by giving a prominent place to the network in learning and extends the classroom to include a much wider context.

The Promise of Connectivism

Since the development of the first MOOC, much has changed in the use of information communication technology in education. Educationalists and learning technologists (Lankshear & Knobel, 2006; Latour, 2005; Wilson et al., 2007) philosophized over how the second wave of internet technologies could be instrumental in moving from a hierarchical, institutionally based teaching approach to a peer-to-peer networked approach. Technology moved from email and basic LMSs to incorporate social network technology, data, and more advanced creative technologies for photography and video. This showed the potential to radically transform the nature of education and what it meant to teach and learn. Social media could facilitate the transformation from an educational model that is structured in courses, controlled by the institution using a broadcasting model in an enclosed environment, to becoming a model adaptive to learners' needs, controlled by individuals, using a sharing and aggregation model in a personalized open learning environment, and a fluid extension of the wider informal personal space.

The essence and early promise of connectivism is the suggestion that the social networks it engenders can help people in a wide range of academic and nonacademic aspects of learning. For example, informally engaging with other learners can be motivating and help with critical analysis and validation of information and knowledge, support self-direction as learners, and contribute to the formation of future networks (Littlejohn et al., 2016). From an adult education perspective, one of the most exciting aspects of these affordances is that a wide variety of people can come together easily to pursue self-directed learning activities in a way that would not have been possible in the past, when the emphasis on learning was on formal education within a classroom. People can self-organize their learning based on their own needs in an enormous variety of online, networked learning contexts (for more information on self-directed learning, see chapter 10).

The networked open environment of connectivism exemplified in, for instance, the MOOC concept seemed promising for creating virtual communities of people learning from each other and at the same time contributing to a "knowledge commons," a common area accessible to all where people not only consume information and knowledge passively but also contribute to its development and creation and share it with others. It offers the possibility for a democratization of content creation and access. This comes close to the early ideas of Illich (1992), who perceived that the alternative to "scholastic funnels," as he called educational institutions, would be true communication and community webs. In his work, Illich discussed the restriction on freedom, the "enclosure of the commons," the increased policing, the surveillance of everyday life that is perpetrated by traditional educational institutions (Illich, 1992, p. 51), and the stifling effect all this has on people's creativity. His idea was to foster open education in a "common" area. Others have advocated for similar ideas by promoting and developing the affordances of MOOCs. In the words of Willis et al. (2013):

> MOOCs tread on the utopia of education, the promise of knowledge, power, and social mobility vis-à-vis traditional or even online platforms, thereby marking out space that undermines the monetary value of education all the while elevating the value of disseminating the potentiality of knowledge for those who otherwise may not be participants. (p. 2)

New technologies make it possible to connect with other people and exchange information and create knowledge on an unprecedented scale; they facilitate the creation of an open knowledge commons. Learners and educators alike can use and reuse open educational resources that suit their needs in their particular context. However, not all researchers agreed with this utopian idea of how new technologies could support adult education. To name a few issues, there are imbalances in power relations online, just as there are in face-to-face interactions; access to technology is not evenly distributed; the dominant language online is English. Kop and

Bouchard (2011) also questioned whether all adult learners could thrive in the semi-autonomous and self-directed learning environment of connectivism.

The Current State of Connectivism: Opportunities and Tensions

As interest in connectivism grew, so too did interest in using MOOCs to drive enrollments or building MOOCware that emphasized the importance of "massive" over the promise of "open." This corporatization of the MOOC and other learning technology has challenged the initial promise of connectivist pedagogies. The promise of connectivism to open up self-directed and self-regulated learning in connection with others in a form of creative and active learning in open networks and in an open learning environment has not quite worked out in the way that its early adopters envisioned. For example, even though most people now own a mobile telephone, this does not necessarily imply access to online learning opportunities. Additionally, the developments have led to the adoption of MOOCs for commercial gains. Not only are there MOOCS that have a (sometimes significant) cost, but the commercial power of big data in open online environments and the co-opting of these approaches and the influence of modern technology have led to a problematic tension. The history and promise of connectivism may be lost as the potential to make money from data. In addition, the network structure itself can cause ethical challenges and can erode democratic values upon which adult education is based. If developments in educational technology generally, and connectivism more specifically, are not carefully monitored, its promise will not be met.

The first tension is the power of commercial interests in networks, which is unmistakable as companies use their algorithms to make decisions on what information learners do and do not get to see (Goldman, 2010; Grimmelmann, 2010). Second, critics of social networks have pointed out the problem of these commercial interests encouraging the creation of "echo-chambers" of particular opinions and ideologies that get distributed on the networks that largely serve to reinforce user opinions rather than challenging them with new information and ideas. They can also amplify digital disinformation and propaganda (Karpf, 2019). Both of these processes can contribute to a lack of criticality (Norris, 2011). This may be due to the temptation to connect with like-minded people, but even more fundamentally because of how networks form (Barabási, 2003; Schreurs et al., 2019). In other words, despite its initial development as a means of fostering democratic discourse, educational technology use may instead inhibit independent thought. Researchers have shown that network formation itself has inherent problems because the process is not conducive to equal distribution of resources and information as it operates on the principle of preferential attachment. *Preferential attachment* means that people (the nodes on the network) get attached to a certain other node (usually a person writing or producing a digital artefact) on a network where they like the ideas, as well as the group that forms around that person. Additionally, they have found that the earlier the node got engaged in the network, the more people will attach. This does not necessarily mean that their ideas are better, but because people prefer to attach to an established network, built around a particular node, it will grow more than a newer network with less established members, which in its turn will attract additional new people (Barabási, 2003). The current challenges in relation to disinformation and "fake news" are examples of negative outcomes caused by this phenomenon. This shows the importance of the presence of knowledgeable others (i.e., adult educators) nearby who can help learners make sense of the information and opinions expressed on online networks. Initially, connectivists thought that the networks could help with this, for example, by encouraging selective Twitter contacts for learners to follow (Stewart, 2015), but the current barrage of disinformation on the Web suggests that the teacher role in adult education is invaluable to ensure that the underpinning values of adult education will not be lost within a large networked learning community. Adult educators have seen it as a part of their role to help establish critical engagement with topics relevant to society, but on an online network people rely on their peers for their dialogue, which means that without these knowledgeable others the danger exists of echo chambers with the same opinion or misinformation being repeatedly amplified, rather than engagement happening at a more critical level. Therefore, as technology is forever changing, it seems the adult educator role needs to change with the changing technology to ensure learners develop skills to critically question information on the networks; adult educators can also help to curate information relevant to learners' needs.

It is clear when analyzing the current state of social media networks that the cautions heard in the early days of connectivism regarding the challenges of learning outside an institution were justified. Some theorists have assessed these by looking critically at what technology does in and to society. They do not emphasize the connections on networks per se but critically assess their underlying structures and assumptions to a connected society and adult education. In this chapter there is not enough room to detail all of these challenges, but I will at least mention the work on materiality that technology has added, especially the ethical issues related to the use of data and analytics in the educational landscape (Fenwick, 2015; Selwyn, 2019). On the plus side, it is now possible to use the digital traces that users leave behind when learning online, together with algorithms making choices of resources, for instance, to help shape what a learner actually experiences and what kinds of supports they might receive. This could be in the form of information or resource recommender systems or scaffolding in the form of providing a choice of useful apps to carry out a certain project based on earlier learning projects (Fournier et al., 2019; Verbert et al., 2012). However, on the negative side, there are clear ethical issues when the educational field moves in a direction where personal data are being used for educational prediction based on mathematical constructions such as algorithms, especially if these are based on demographic information of users (Boyd & Crawford, 2012; Fenwick, 2015; Paul, 2019). One example where this type of data-driven prediction has gone spectacularly wrong was during the COVID-19 pandemic in the final grades predictions in the United Kingdom in 2020. Algorithms replaced teacher judgment, and students ended up with unexpected grades (Duncan et al., 2020). This also means that careful consideration needs to be given by adult education leaders to the division of teaching between humans and machines and the degree to which machine learning should be allowed in education (Boyd & Crawford, 2012; Selwyn et al., 2020). One might question how teachers will be involved in aspects of these new developments or whether these changes will be part of institutional technologies outside the control of the teachers. With that in mind, it is important to move back to how connectivism relates to adult education.

Realizing the Potential of Connectivism in Adult Education

As an adult educator, it is my first impulse to question and critique how and what the current form of connectivism offers. I do this with regard to the social and personal purposes of adult education, which have historically revolved around social change, humanism, and transformative learning. I think it will be difficult to achieve the original connective and human components of these purposes in the current climate of commercial connectivism, data management, and hyperindividualism. There are major challenges in reconciling these with meaningful human learning and the social justice and democratic principles of adult education. Even though information might be available openly, and it seems that authentic interaction in groups is possible in online learning contexts, underlying challenges, including the extended spread of misinformation, must be addressed. What follows are two key ways that adult educators may support connectivism in ways that help to do this.

Curating Information and Supporting Critical Evaluation of Resources by Knowledgeable Others

Adult educators in the past have emphasized the desirability of moving control over the educational experience from the institution to the learner (Illich, 1971, 1972). Illich's ideas of "community webs" seem to be an especially strong precursor to the online networks envisioned by Siemens and Downes that could break the institutional grip and foster the development of personal learning environments with the learner firmly in control. However, Freire and Macedo (1999) emphasized the need for teachers to help people develop conscientization, becoming aware of the unequal power relations in society and how to teach and learn in ways that help people work toward achieving more just outcomes. This involves being a teacher in the sense that Palmer (1998) described—being present with heart and soul. This is a very different role than that associated with a facilitator in an online environment or as a node on a network. The role is not simply to transfer knowledge or facilitate information sharing but rather to engage in dialogical interaction with learners to reach an awareness of the power structures in society. Power structures are everywhere in society; they exist not only in educational institutions but also in open online networks. However, connectivism has mainly ignored these and has not shown any thought about the traditional values of adult education.

Of course, decisions can be made to choose particular aspects of technology in support of adult education values and purposes; some technologies are better than others at helping learners connect and critically engage. Discussion and chat forums can be used in combination with creative tools and applications. For example, Lawrence and Cranton (2015) carried out research on transformative learning using a variety of media, such as novels and films, to help learners understand perspective transformation and to reflect on their own experiences. This activity could easily be adapted to an online environment by using Web-based artifacts and tools; the Web offers many high-quality options for creative expression that can be applied in adult education contexts. These can be used as stimulating resources in connectivist learning outside the classroom or as discussion starters within formal online learning contexts.

However, the recent development of an "unfactual" Web is anathema to adult education, has social justice implications, and requires a high level of critical analysis by users to distinguish between information and misinformation. This challenge calls out for adult educators and knowledgeable others on the connectivist network to support learners in developing their digital and media literacy and helping learners curate information and develop criticality when it comes to evaluating online resources. If connectivism is to further evolve in the direction taken as it was conceived in early 2004, as a way to conceptualize educational engagement in online networks, this lack of criticality and teacher support will be a great challenge for the future. To realize the potential of new technologies, helping adult learners develop skills to be able to curate information and be critical about the information found needs to be achieved by engaging with knowledgeable others or, in the adult education context, adult educators.

Use of Data and Information

As mentioned before, there are major challenges in the underlying data structures and networks forming on the Web. However, data can also be used to the advantage of users of the Web and adult learners in their quest to filter information and for educational institutions to receive early signals when online learners are struggling and need additional support. Educational institutions are already using data to do this. For example, artificial intelligence tools are increasingly being used to provide "smart" tutoring in adult education settings. Research groups are working on the development of information recommender systems and others are working on retention and early signaling systems that can indicate to learners that particular support should be considered (Fournier et al., 2019; Verbert et al., 2012). These are only at an early development and research stage, and it will take some time before these can be integrated in LMSs, but they could do a great deal toward using data for helpful learning purposes and provide important support structures for student learning in online learning. However, these tools also have the potential to collect intrusive levels of information about students and, like other aspects of connectivist learning, have the potential to supplant meaningful human interaction.

Conclusions: Challenges for the Future

I have used this chapter to lead readers through some of the history of connectivism and educational technology development. It seems that we are at the cusp of new developments on how the Web is developing and what this might mean for adult education. On the one hand, the information and knowledge landscape is changing dramatically because of the emerging technological networked developments that cause an openness and abundance of information. On the other hand, there is the widespread use of dehumanization, surveillance, and disinformation. This opportunity and challenge mean that learners will need to learn to seek filter information effectively using critical analysis skills, and online networks are one option for doing so. The online networks also foster a different sense of autonomy in the learner as they no longer need to use an institution to be involved in adult education; they can make their own choices, depending on their engagement with technologies and their own needs. However, there is still an important role to play for the adult educator.

These are contextual factors in adult education that have instigated a discussion about the development and the human involvement in being connected in online networks, in addition to in classroom groups. I would suggest that this has led to shifts in how adult educators and learners engage in the learning process. The premises of connectivism are correct in that it is possible to use the Web to build networks to share information, create resources, and build knowledge through interaction on a global scale. However, a good teacher or knowledgeable other who can help learners find and critically analyze information, and foster the development of trusted groups to engage the self in learning, will still be indispensable. The human connection, the close relationships and camaraderie that can emerge, are still at the heart of helping people learn and stay motivated and engaged. The adult educator is critical to cultivating, nurturing, and sustaining them as they support critical Web-oriented skill development as part of the online learning experience.

References

AlDahdouh, A. A., Osório, A. J., & Caires, S. (2015). Understanding knowledge network, learning and connectivism. *International Journal of Instructional Technology and Distance Learning, 12*(10), 3–21. http://www.itdl.org/Journal/Oct_15/Oct15.pdf#page=7

Anderson, T., & Dron, J. (2011). Three generations of distance education pedagogy. *The International Review of Research in Open and Distance Learning, 12*(3), 80–97. https://doi.org/10.19173/irrodl.v12i3.890

Bacsich, P., & Bristow, S. (2004). *The e-university compendium: Volume one.* Higher Education Academy.

Barabási, A. L. (2003). *Linked: How everything is connected to everything else and what it means.* Penguin Books.

Bates, A. W. (2019). *Teaching in a digital age: Guidelines for designing teaching and learning* (2nd ed). Tony Bates Associates. https://pressbooks.bccampus.ca/teachinginadigitalagev2/

Biesta, G. (2015). What is education for? On good education, teacher judgement, and educational professionalism. *European Journal of Education, 50*(1), 75–87. https://doi.org/10.1111/ejed.12109

Blair, T. (2000, March 7). *Tony Blair's full speech: 'The e-generation is with us' Tony Blair proclaimed at the Knowledge 2000 conference* [Speech transcript]. The Guardian. https://www.theguardian.com/uk/2000/mar/07/tonyblair

Blessinger, P., & Bliss, T. J. (2016). *Open education: International perspectives in higher education.* Open Book. https://www.openbookpublishers.com/product/531/open-education-international-perspectives-in-higher-education

Bouchard, P. (2009). Pedagogy without a teacher: What are the limits? *International Journal of Self-Directed Learning, 6*(2), 13–22.

Bouchard, P. (2011). Network promises and their implications. In the impact of social network on teaching and learning. *Revista de Universidad y Sociedad del Conocimiento, 8*(1), 288–302. https://doi.org/10.7238/rusc.v8i1.960

Boyd, D., & Crawford, K. (2012). Critical questions for Big Data. *Information, Communication & Society, 15*(5), 662–679. https://doi.org/10.1080/1369118X.2012.678878

Bredo, E. (1994). Reconstructing educational psychology: Situated cognition and Deweyian pragmatism. *Educational Psychologist, 29*(1), 23–35. https://doi.org/10.1207/s15326985ep2901_3

Conole, G., de Laat, M., Dillon, T., & Darby, G. (2006). An in-depth case study of students' experiences of e-Learning—How is learning changing? In L. Markauskaite, P. Goodyear, & P. Reimann (Eds.), *Proceedings of the 23rd annual Ascilite Conference: Who's learning? Whose technology?* (pp. 153–161). University of Sydney.

Cousins, N. (1966). The poet and the computer. In Z. W. Pylyshyn & L. J. Bannon (Eds.), *Perspectives on the computer revolution* (pp. 535–536). Ablex.

Downes, S. (2004). Educational blogging. *EDUCAUSE Review, 39*(5), 14–26.

Downes, S. (2019). Recent work in connectivism. *European Journal of Open, Distance and E-Learning, 22*(2), 113–132. https://doi.org/ 10.2478/eurodl-2019-0014

Dron, J., & Anderson, T. (2009). *On the design of collective applications.* In *IEEE International Conference 2009 on Computational Science and Engineering* (pp. 368–374).Vancouver, British Columbia, Canada.

Duncan, P., McIntyre, N., Storer, R., & Levett, C. (2020, August 13). Who won and who lost: When A-levels meet the algorithm. *The Guardian.* https://www.theguardian.com/education/2020/aug/13/who-won-and-who-lost-when-a-levels-meet-the-algorithm

Fenwick, T. (2015). Professional responsibility in a future of data analytics. In B. Williamson (Ed.), *Coding/learning: Software and digital data in education* (pp. 68–72). University of Stirling.

Foucault, M. (1977). *Discipline and punish: The birth of the prison.* London.

Fournier, H., Kop, R., & Molyneux, H. (2019). New personal learning ecosystems: A decade of research in review. In K. Becnel (Ed.), *Emerging technologies in virtual learning environments* (pp. 1–19). IGI.

Freire, P. (1970). *Pedagogy of the oppressed.* Herder and Herder.

Freire, P., & Macedo, D. (1999). Pedagogy, culture, language and race: A dialogue. In J. Leach & B. Moon (Eds.), *Learners and pedagogy* (pp. 46–58). Open University Press.

Garrison, D. R., Anderson, T., & Archer, W. (2000). Critical inquiry in a text-based environment: Computer conferencing in higher education model. *The Internet and Higher Education, 2*(2–3), 87–105. https://doi.org/10.1016/S1096-7516(00)00016-6

Goldman, E. (2010). Search engine bias and the demise of search engine utopianism. In B. Szoka & A. Marcus (Eds.), *The next digital decade: Essays on the future of the Internet* (pp. 461–474). TechFreedom.

Greener, I., & Perriton, L. (2005). The political economy of networked learning communities in higher education. *Studies in Higher Education, 30*(1), 67–79. https://doi.org/10.1080/0307507052000307803

Grimmelmann, J. (2010). Some skepticism about search neutrality. In B. Szoka & A. Marcus (Eds.), *The next digital decade: Essays on the future of the Internet* (pp. 435–460). TechFreedom.

Gulati, S. (2006). Application of new technologies: Nurse education. In P. Moule & S. Glen (Eds.), *E-learning in nursing* (pp. 20–37). Macmillan Education. https://doi.org/10.1007/978-1-137-08846-8_2

Gur, B., & Wiley, D. (2007). Instructional technology and objectification. *Canadian Journal of Learning and Technology, 33*(3), 1–13. https://doi.org/10.21432/T2PW2X

Harasim, L., Hiltz, S. R., Teles, L., & Turoff, M. (1995). *Learning networks: A field guide to teaching and learning online.* MIT Press.

Illich, I. (1971). *Deschooling society.* Marion Boyars.

Illich, I. (1992). *In the mirror of the past.* Marion Boyars.

Karpf, D. (2019, December 10). *On digital disinformation and democratic myths.* Social Science Research Council, MediaWell. https://doi.org/10.35650/MD.2012.d.2019

Kop, R. (2008, June 5–7). *Web 2.0 technologies: Disruptive or liberating for adult education?* [Paper presentation]. Adult Education Research Conference, St. Louis, MO, United States. https://newprairiepress.org/aerc/2008/papers/37/

Kop, R., & Bouchard, P. (2011). The role of adult educators in the age of social media. In M. Thomas (Ed.), *Digital education: Opportunities for social collaboration* (pp. 61–80). Palgrave Macmillan.

Kop, R., & Fournier, H. (2011). New dimensions to self-directed learning in an open networked learning environment. *International Journal of Self-Directed Learning, 7*(2), 1–20. https://nrc-publications.canada.ca/eng/view/object/?id=c4dc46c9-ef59-46b8-af01-4a7fec44b023

Kop, R., Fournier, H., & Mak, J. S. F. (2011). A pedagogy of abundance or a pedagogy to support human beings? Participant support on massive open online courses. *International Review of Research in Open and Distributed Learning, 12*(7), 74–93. https://doi.org/10.19173/irrodl.v12i7.1041

Kop, R., Fournier, H., & Sitlia, H. (2011, February 27). *The value of learning analytics to networked learning on a personal learning environment* [Paper presentation]. First International Conference on Learning Analytics and Knowledge, Banff, AL, Canada. https://doi.org/10.1145/2090116.2090131

Kop, R., & Hill, A. (2008). Connectivism: Learning theory of the future or vestige of the past? *The International Review of Research in Open and Distance Learning, 9*(3), 1–13. http://www.irrodl.org/index.php/irrodl/article/view/523/1103

Lankshear, C., & Knobel, M. (2006, April). *Blogging as participation: The active sociality of a new literacy* [Paper presentation]. American Educational Research Association Conference, San Francisco, CA, United States.

Latour, B. (2005). *Reassembling the social: An introduction to actor–network theory.* Oxford University Press.

Lawrence, R. L., & Cranton, P. (2015). *A novel idea: Researching transformative learning in fiction.* Sense.

Leitch Review of Skills. (2006). *Prosperity for all in the global economy: World class skills.* Her Majesty's Treasury.

Littlejohn, A., Hood, N., Milligan, C., & Mustain, P. (2016). Learning in MOOCs: Motivations and self-regulated learning in MOOCs. *Internet and Higher Education, 29*, 40–48. https://doi.org/10.1016/j.iheduc.2015.12.003

Martin, I. (2006). In whose interest? Interrogating the metamorphosis of adult education. In A. Antikainen, P. Harinen, & C. A. Torres (Eds.), *In from the margins: Adult education, work and civil society* (pp. 11–26). Sense.

Mason, R., & Bacisch, P. (1998). Embedding computer conferencing into university teaching. *Computers & Education, 30*(3–4), 249–258. https://doi.org/10.1016/S0360-1315(97)00068-7

Norris, P. (2011). *Democratic deficit, critical citizens revisited.* Cambridge University Press.

Palmer, P. (1998). *The courage to teach: Exploring the inner landscape of a teacher's life.* Jossey-Bass.

Paul, K. (2019, April 17). "Disastrous" lack of diversity in AI industry perpetuates bias, study finds. *The Guardian International Edition.* https://www.theguardian.com/technology/2019/apr/16/artificial-intelligence-lack-diversity-new-york-university-study

Peters, O. (1999). *New learning spaces: A pedagogical model for new learning spaces.* FernUniveritaet. https://www.ucviden.dk/ws/portalfiles/portal/124754617/peters_new_learning_spaces.pdf

Schreurs, B., Cornelissen, F., & de Laat, M. (2019). How do online learning networks emerge? A review study of self-organizing network effects in the field of networked learning. *Education Sciences, 9*(4), 289–289. https://doi.org/10.3390/educsci9040289

Selwyn, N. (2019). What's the problem with learning analytics? *Journal of Learning Analytics, 6*(3), 11–19. http://dx.doi.org/10.18608/jla.2019.63.3

Selwyn, S., Hillman, T., Eynon, R., Ferreira, G., Knox, J., Macgilchrist, F., & Sancho-Gil, J. M. (2020). What's next for ed-tech? Critical hopes and concerns for the 2020s. *Learning, Media and Technology, 45*(1), 1–6. https://doi.org/10.1080/17439884.2020.1694945

Siemens, G. (2005). Connectivism: A learning theory for the digital age. *International Journal of Instructional Technology and Distance Learning, 2*(1), 3–10. http://www.itdl.org/Journal/Jan_05/article01.htm

Stewart, B. (2015). Open to influence: What counts as academic influence in scholarly networked Twitter participation. *Learning, Media and Technology, 40*(3), 287–309. https://doi.org/10.1080/17439884.2015.1015547

Stone, C., & Springer, M. (2019). Interactivity, connectedness and "teacher-presence": Engaging and retaining students online. *Australian Journal of Adult Learning, 59*(2), 146–169. https://doi.org/10.3316/aeipt.224048

Tularam, G. A. (2018). Traditional vs. non-traditional teaching and learning strategies—The case of e-learning! *International journal of Mathematics Teaching and Learning, 19*(1), 129–158.

Verbert, K., Manouselis, N., Ochoa, X., Wolpers, M., Drachsler, H., Bosnic, I., & Duval, E. (2012). Context-aware recommender systems for learning: A survey and future challenges. *IEEE Transactions on Learning Technologies*, 5(4), 318–335. https://doi.org/ 10.1109/ TLT.2012.11.

Weller, M. (2007). *Virtual learning environments: Using, choosing and developing your VLE*. Routledge.

Willis, J. E., Spiers, E. L., & Gettings, P. (2013, June 16–19). *MOOCs and Foucault's heterotopia: On community and self-efficacy* [Paper presentation]. 2013 Conference of MITs Learning International Network Consortium, Cambridge, MA, United States. https://linc.mit .edu/linc2013/proceedings/Session3/Session3Willis.pdf

Wilson, S., Liber, O., Johnson, M., Beauvoir, P., Sharples, P., & Miigan, C. (2007). Personal learning environments: Challenging the dominant design of educational systems. *Journal of e-Learning and Knowledge Society*, 3(2), 27–38.

Editors' Key Seminal and Supplemental Text Suggestions

Brown, J. S., & Duguid, P. (1991). Organizational learning and communities-of-practice: Towards a unified vision of working, learning, and innovation. *Organization Science*, 2(1), 40–57.

Garrison, D. R. (2017). *eLearning in the 21st century: A community of inquiry framework for research and practice* (3rd ed.). Routledge.

Lave, J., & Wenger, E. (1991). *Situated learning: Legitimate peripheral participation*. Cambridge University Press.

  • Chapter 1: Legitimate Peripheral Participation

Siemens, G. (2005). Connectivism: A learning theory for the digital age. *International Journal of Instructional Technology and Distance Learning*, 2(1), 3–10.

PART FOUR

Conclusions

14

INSTRUCTIONAL DESIGN

Applying Principles of Adult Education

Brian Dashew and Diane Gayeski

As explored throughout this text, the field of adult education has cultivated a number of representations and explanations for why and how adults learn. Our understanding of the adult brain, of motivation, of identity formation, and emotional development—all have evolved to deepen our understanding of learners and learning. Adult educators attempting to put this new knowledge into practice, however, may find that they encounter barriers. This includes the difficulty of implementing specific theories to address the practicalities of instruction that meets specific learning and performance goals within a given organizational context. The study of how our understanding of adult learning can be routinely and systematically applied within our practices for teaching and facilitation is the field of instructional design. Since its inception as an area of practice and scholarship, models of instructional design have emerged from academic research, practitioner experience, and even efforts to sell new services and technology. Though they are often discussed interchangeably, these many models can actually be viewed as representing two distinct perspectives of instructional design that serve very different purposes. Instructional design *processes*—or design models—provide systematic sets of operations by which a training, course, or program is developed. This can be contrasted with instructional design *theories*, which are concerned with the content and format of instruction rather than how it is built (Reigeluth, 1999). In this chapter, we will explain these two types of perspectives, and we will demonstrate how understandings of instructional design have paralleled the rich tapestry of learning theories that have evolved to inform adult education.

A certain degree of confusion may be anticipated in reviewing the parallel histories of these two views of instructional design, because most professional adult educators likely see learning theories and instructional design theories as two sides of the same coin. While instructional designer is a distinct job in some organizations, it is also the case that adult educators take responsibility for the development, facilitation, and management of programs, courses, or training at some point in their careers, and must recognize that applying an understanding of adult learners to the creation of these programs requires a distinct set of skills and knowledge. New adult educators, then, should have a basic understanding of the work and history of instructional design as a discipline distinct from yet connected to adult education.

Knowledge of and experience with ADDIE (see p. 258 if this is an unfamiliar term) is often a job qualification for adult educators. The assumption is that it and other instructional design models provide prescribed steps that are effective in meeting individual and organizational goals for learning. However, many experienced instructional designers interpret the theories of design presented in the following section more as recommended guidelines rather than as recipes to be strictly followed. It is our contention that successful adult instruction is informed by both a systematic application of adult learning theories as well as an understanding of instructional design models. Because of the sheer volume of available process models and theories, successful adult educators must understand these concepts and strategies and make decisions about their use that fits the specific problem and design context they are facing. We provide more details in our discussion of design in the following section.

What Is Instructional Design?

In discussing the relationship between instructional design and adult education, it is important to offer a definition of *instructional design* first. This can be a somewhat contentious task, and it is necessary to discuss it in relationship to two disciplinary histories.

Arguably the most common definition views instructional design as being part of the discipline of instruction, as described in the early work of John Dewey. This term, in contrast to its usual denotation, focuses on how to teach instead of what to teach or the actual implementation of instruction in the classroom (Reigeluth, 1983). Dewey (1901) distinguished between existing studies of specific curriculum (specializing in content knowledge) and educational theory (concerned with studying how people learn) and their respective related roles of teacher and researcher. He proposed the need for a new "linking science" (p. 16) that could serve as a conduit between them. He suggested that this field would create a bridge between our evolving understanding of learning and the instructional methods used to teach learners across diverse contexts. This bridge became the field known at that time as instruction, and early definitions of instructional design (e.g., Morrison et al., 2013; Reigeluth, 1983; Snellbecker, 1974) positioned it as a part of this linking science.

As a field of practice and research, the linking science of instruction itself contained a number of subdisciplines: design, development, implementation (or utilization), management, and evaluation (Reigeluth, 1983; Reiser, 2001). From this perspective, instructional design is deployed when a learning problem is identified and the designer's knowledge of learning sciences and learners is combined to generate the best-fit set of methods for solving it (Morrison et al., 2013). As defined by Reigeluth (1983), instructional design is both the professional practice of defining an "architect's blueprint" for instruction (process), and the discipline of studying how to optimize these blueprints (theory), combining "knowledge about diverse methods of instruction, optimal combinations of methods (i.e. whole models), and situations in which each of these models is optimal" (p. 7). Over time, the distinctions among these subdisciplines have blurred, and instructional design is frequently thought of as the systematic process of instruction, from design through evaluation.

An alternate definition of instructional design does not view design as a subdiscipline of instruction but, rather, positions instruction as a subdiscipline of design (Rowland, 1993). It is interesting to note that—like the discipline of instruction—the discipline of design may also have emerged from the work of John Dewey. As Buchanan (1992) noted, Dewey articulated a new orientation toward liberal arts education in the early 20th century that moved from "specialization in the facts of a subject matter [to] the use of new disciplines of integrative thinking" (p. 6). In reviewing Dewey's effort to provide an alternate perspective on the liberal arts, Buchanan interpreted Dewey's definition of technology as "an art of experimental thinking" (p. 8) and suggested that both art and science—together—are required for productive problem solving. Dewey's integrative and experimental perspective—a technology for problem solving—became a central tenet of design thinking. The emergent discipline focused on inquiry, empathy, and problem solving (Rowland, 1993), with a practical emphasis on both user and utility (Norman, 2016). This focus on use means that design is not, strictly, an artistic endeavor. At the same time, design is not strictly a science, because artistry and ingenuity are required to engage in design. Design therefore represents a unique disciplinary perspective. As an alternative to the paradigm of a linking science, instructional design can therefore be seen as the application of this design perspective to the resolution of instructional problems.

Both of these perspectives recognize the important relationship between adult learning and instructional design. The definition of design as a subdiscipline of instruction suggests that separating curricular studies from instructional studies enables educators to have a fuller focus on general learner development. If designers are focused on the development of effective instructional resources, then teachers can focus their efforts on implementing curriculum in ways that attend to the social and emotional well-being and growth of learners. For adult educators, this distinction between design and teaching can be seen as a challenge to the more traditional role of instructor, echoing new roles as emphasized in asynchronous and autonomous e-learning, self-directed learning (facilitating learner-driven instructional plans), experiential learning (encouraging reflection and active learning), or connectivism (promoting nondirected engagement across a network) as discussed in chapters 10, 11, and 13 (respectively) in this volume. At the same time, such a distinction between design and instruction may ring false—and not only because, as explained at the outset of this chapter, many educators are themselves responsible for the design of their own programs and classrooms. Experienced instructional designers recognize that design and facilitation of learning must be considered together. Imagine a participatory workshop designed to engage community leaders and police officers in dialogue to build relationships that can improve public safety. It would be a mistake for designers not to consider the implications for facilitation in light of the emotional elements of this program goal. Thus, even from the perspective of design as a subdiscipline of instruction, instructional design is not necessarily mechanistic and antihumanist (Morrison et al., 2013). The perspective of instructional design as a subdiscipline of design, meanwhile, more explicitly engages a holistic approach that considers learner, learning, environment, and instructional problem. As a discipline, design is an inherently human-focused and empathic function, and so the learner and their specific needs must be considered in decisions about solutions to instructional problems. In practice, then, both perspectives—design as a subset of instruction and instruction as a subset of design—emphasize the importance of understanding learners and learning in instructional design.

Adult educators who engage in design should understand that concepts of instructional design have been built on the foundation of competing histories that can be categorized into the two distinct types: (a) process models and (b) design theories. Each has its own relationships to adult education theory and implications for practice.

Instructional Design Process Models

Efforts to codify the professional practice of instructional design started in the 1970s. Glaser (1976) built on the concept of a linking science proposed by Dewey (1901) in an effort to develop what he saw as a comprehensive theory of instructional design. He felt that instructional design should be similar to other disciplines that used "optimization methods" (Glaser, 1976, p. 6) that identify a gap between a current and desired state (in this case articulated as program learning goals) and then defined the specific instructional actions necessary to meet these goals. This led him to define a set of four components for an emergent psychology of instruction: (a) an analysis of the desired performance, (b) a description of the initial state, (c) an exploration and implementation of the conditions necessary to attain desired performance, and (d) an assessment to establish whether these conditions have led to the intended outcomes.

This work has led to the emergence of models that view instructional design as a structured process. The most prominent process models serve as project management tools, meaning they are focused more on the steps to completing process tasks than they are on any specific instructional outcome. This task orientation is also known as *instructional systems design* (ISD). ISD models are defined by a linear progression of steps in which each step must be completed in order to inform the next step in the process.

The most well-known ISD model is called ADDIE. ADDIE is an acronym for the design steps of Analysis, Design, Development, Implementation, and Evaluation. The call for a systematic model for instructional design emerged during the U.S. military and industrial responses to World War II. War efforts required new recruits to be trained quickly on equipment and tactics. Weapons manufacturers needed to provide consistent training to ensure that workers filling positions vacated by the growing number of people entering the war would be speedy, consistent, and accurate. This precipitated a significant emphasis on behaviorism (a theory defined in chapter 1).

Though ADDIE emerged out of work that took place in the 1940s, it was only codified as a model by the U.S. Army in 1975 (Kurt, 2018). As the Vietnam War came to a close, the U.S. military began to reflect on the difficulties it had experienced in systematically training new soldiers across their various military and civilian operations. Their analysis concluded that while "there are outstanding examples of well-conceived and delivered instruction available within the interservice training community . . . these efforts do not represent a very large fraction of the total interservice training establishment" (Branson et al., 1975, p. 6). The report suggested a new model called the *interservice process for instructional systems development* (IPISD). The model had five steps: Analyze, Design, Develop, Implement, and Control. Later, *Control* was switched to *Evaluation*, and the acronym ADDIE was created.

As understanding of adult learners and learning has evolved, so too have the models on which ISD is based. Several years after the publication of the IPISD report, Dick and Carey (1978) elaborated on this model with their own process of systematic design that provided additional detail to the ADDIE model. For example, analysis in this new model consisted of three steps—(a) assessing need to determine the goals of the learning event, (b) conducting an instructional analysis to determine skills needed by learners, and (c) analyzing learners and their contexts—while design and development were more concretely structured into four steps: (a) writing performance objectives, (b) development of assessment instruments, (c) creation of instructional strategy, and (d) selection of instructional content. In another example of an ISD model, the Morrison, Ross, and Kemp model (Kemp, 1985; Morrison et al., 2013) emphasized the importance of design as a mechanism for solving an instructional problem. The nine-step design model begins with the identification of an instructional problem, followed by an analysis of the learner and of the content. Content and strategies are designed and planned, and evaluation instruments are created. Finally, support resources are identified.

Despite the theory-driven differences in approach and nomenclature, both the Dick and Carey and the Morrison, Ross, and Kemp models follow the pattern established by the original IPISD report and have prompted some to suggest that, however design is defined, the basic structure of Analysis, Design, Development, Implementation, and Evaluation is both a logical and practical methodology (Zemke & Rossett, 2002).

Since the 1990s, however, one of the most significant debates in instructional design has been whether the linear progression embedded in early ISD models is reflective of the real contexts in which the models are put into practice. ADDIE, it is said, "fails to recognize the necessary creativeness and inventiveness of the work, to allow for and support exploration and changing ideas that need to arise within and as part of the process" (Allen & Sites, 2012, p. ix). For example, the ubiquity of technology at the turn of the 21st century has transformed our understanding of information and of how adults gather and share knowledge. The transition of knowledge management from cataloguing and taxonomies to communities of practice and network development challenged preconceived relationships between learners and content, educators, and other learners. The 1990s saw an emphasis on harvesting and indexing the knowledge that existed within individuals and communities in organizations and promoting knowledge sharing and informal learning as critical to the success of organizational learning. Such learning is iterative and collaborative, not linear, and so it necessitated an approach to design that was similarly nonlinear. Perhaps because it was also becoming more prevalent during this time that design products were created for digital platforms, designers found inspiration for these new models for design by adopting practices from software product development that emphasize iteration and rapid prototyping.

The successive approximation model (SAM) replaced the linear model of ISD with iterative design phases that contain formative testing and collaborative review (Allen & Sites, 2012). In traditional ISD models, analysis is a process of information gathering. Several ISD models end analysis with the development of clear instructional learning objectives (Dick & Carey, 1978; Kurt, 2018). The SAM instead begins with what its authors refer to as a "savvy start," a collaborative, performance-based brainstorming event. By emphasizing performance change over content goals, SAM can ensure a deeper focus on performance improvement as a goal of learning events. The design and development phases of SAM are iterative, and prototyping and review can lead designers to reexamine any prior step of the process; it is this recognition that design is not simply over because a project has moved to development that differentiates this type of process model from ISD approaches.

The LLAMA model follows a similar iterative approach, and is so named because it is a "Lot Like an Agile Management Approach." Like the SAM, LLAMA recognizes that no phase of the design process can ever be considered complete. Here, the assumption is that learning events should be developed for an ever-changing context. This changing context means that a rapid, responsive approach to design is necessary. To address this, LLAMA builds the steps of a traditional ADDIE model into a set of successive loops, where implementation and evaluation lead, by necessity, to design and development revisions. Each version of the design is a completed and usable product, meaning that instruction can get in front of learners faster, and then ongoing evaluation is faster and more actionable.

While these models are positioned as an alternative to traditional ISD models, their proponents have sometimes mischaracterized elements of these approaches. For example, the developers of SAM suggested their model emphasizes performance improvement as the goal of learning, which they contrast to more cognitive-focused approaches of ADDIE. However, learning objectives derived in an ISD model need not be exclusively oriented to cognitive goals. As noted, in fact, the earliest ISD models emerged out of a behaviorist tradition, and nearly all ISD models are performance-based models concerned with behavioral objectives and behavioral change.

A final approach that addresses criticisms of ISD has been the *design thinking approach*, most closely associated with the work of Stanford University's d.school. Design thinking is described as a human-centered, empathic approach to design. Rather than opening with a standard analysis phase, the first phase in design thinking is "empathize." Design thinking suggests that it is impossible to understand the needs of the learner until there is understanding of the learner. A second major shift in the design process is the addition of an ideation phase. Where ISD suggests a more linear and concrete connection between the analysis phase and design solutions, design thinking promotes brainstorming, creative game play, and an open-minded approach to building solutions that are defined through a deep understanding of the learner as a user. It is only after this ideation phase is complete that projects are prototyped and refined. Distinct from rapid prototyping models, design thinking may include prototypes for multiple solutions, indicating that the end product can be built from a combination of approaches rather than from one single solution. Proponents of design thinking suggest it is optimal for addressing so-called "wicked" problems that are particularly ill structured, where information and context are confusing, and for which previously used strategies that provide a direct link between analysis and solution do not seem to work (Buchanan, 1992). It is also seen as more learner centered than traditional ISD because it is centered on the user rather than the content.

For novice designers, process models for design provide a systematic approach to the development of trainings, courses, and programs. At the same time, none of these approaches is directly tied to any understanding and application of adult learning theory. In fact, some early theorists felt these process models served as guidance for the management of a design project but offered little in the way of a linking science to connect learning theory to instructional practice. A second branch of instructional design, however, has concerned itself more with the relationship between learning and design.

Instructional Design Theories

In contemporaneous research first published 2 years after Glaser's (1976) work, Reigeluth and Merrill (1978) drew a contrast to the process approach. Rather than focus on the specific procedure for design, Reigeluth and Merrill were concerned with developing a *theory of instruction* that accounted for how specific instructional methods could be applied in specific contexts (conditions); in addition to methods and conditions, a third component of theory (outcomes) identified both the actual and anticipated impacts of utilizing a method under given conditions. Furthermore, Reigeluth and Merrill contended that fixed and universal principles of learning and instruction should dictate the method or methods applied under given conditions in order to achieve intended outcomes.

Reigeluth's (1999) paradigm identifies several requirements that he believed all instructional design theories should address. First, he noted, all design theories must be focused on the "means to attain given goals for learning or development" (p. 6), meaning that an instructional design theory is meant to assist a designer in making decisions about what methods are the best fit for reaching specific goals rather than to explain descriptively why such a theory works. This is connected to a second requirement, which is that design theories must identify both situations and methods. For Reigeluth, the situation includes both desired learning outcomes and the learning conditions, such as prior knowledge of learners and constraints of the development process. Methods are those environmental factors that can be manipulated, such as teaching strategies. A third requirement is that methods of instruction can be broken up into detailed component methods for more detailed instructor guidance. Finally, Reigeluth noted that sound instructional design theories should be probabilistic, meaning that following the theory increases the likelihood of, but does not guarantee, learning. These elements are focal in the following examples of design theory. Although we have attempted to avoid a lengthy listing of competing theories in favor of more detailed explorations that describe the major distinctions between and within families of theory, we describe four distinct theories in the following to explore the parallel development of instructional design theory and adult learning theory. Merrill's work—as an analysis of design theories—is introduced first as something of a précis for those new to instructional design. The other three theories are presented in chronological order.

Merrill's First Principles of Instruction

The impetus for Merrill's First Principles stems directly from Reigeluth's exploration of instructional theory. Merrill (2002) noted Reigeluth's (1999) definition of an instructional principle as a "relationship that is always true under appropriate conditions regardless of program or practice" (p. 43), where a *program* is a prescribed set of practices and a *practice* is a specific activity. In other words, practices and programs succeed or fail based on their fidelity to underlying principles. Merrill—through an exploration of existing instructional design theories—sought to understand the most common underlying principles that related to the predictive success of instructional methods.

The conclusion of Merrill's analysis was a description of what he called "First Principles" that he believed were central to effective instruction. These are that learning is promoted through (a) engagement in real world problems, (b) activation of prior knowledge, (c) demonstration of new knowledge relevant to the problem-solving task, (d) opportunities to practice newly learned material, and (e) integration of material into the learner's own context. Merrill further suggested that the applicability of this model is in its generalizability. For example, the term *problem* is used to represent a range of activities from involvement in real world tasks to simulations and role plays. While Merrill found that some models for design used principles that were not included in this list, there were none that excluded his First Principles. In other words, though certain conditions may necessitate more specific methods, the theory's broad scope and applied focus improved the likelihood of success in all situations.

Gagne's Nine Events

Another prominent instructional design theory is the *nine events model* developed by Robert Gagne (1977). The development of Gagne's model intersects with a period of time when learning theory was moving from a strict behavioral model into more cognitivist approaches. Gagne's work appears in parallel with a developing focus on information processing in the learning sciences and the understanding that effective teaching and environment-setting could promote sensory information (new knowledge) being moved to short-term memory and then eventually to long-term memory.

Gagne developed a set of nine "events," or instructional steps, that would encourage information processing and behavioral response:

1. Gain attention and emotional buy-in
2. Establish expectations, objectives, and criteria
3. Simulate recall of prior knowledge
4. Present new material
5. Provide guidance on expected performance
6. Challenge the learner to perform the anticipated outcomes
7. Provide immediate feedback
8. Assess learner performance against established criteria
9. Provide opportunities and suggestions for transfer and application

Gagne's model has been widely used as an assessment for the quality and comprehensiveness of learning events, in particular for behavior-oriented training for adults. It should be noted that Merrill's First Principles are included in Steps 1, 3, 4, 6, and 9. However, Gagne's model provides additional, more specific methodology that focuses on the emotional connection to relevant case studies or examples, clarity around the expectations for the educational program, and the importance of guidance and feedback; each element provides evidence of the behaviorist orientation of its author that are missing from the cognitivist and constructivist orientations in later theories. This is, therefore, a demonstration of the historical and theoretical context impacting the construction of instructional design theory.

Keller's Attention, Relevance, Confidence, and Satisfaction Model

At the end of the 1970s, Keller began work on the Attention, Relevance, Confidence, and Satisfaction (ARCS) model, which emphasized strategies for building motivation for learning. Keller noted that there was no prior theory of design pertaining to learner motivation. The 1960s and 1970s saw the study of motivation in education transition from the behaviorist-based study of classroom control to the study of human psychology. Keller (1987) believed that early efforts to expand the applicability of emergent theories of motivation "did not help the designer or teacher know how many or what types of strategies to use with a given audience, and they did not incorporate important principles" of motivation and design (p. 2).

Keller drew on existing psychological research to formulate a set of predictive conditions for improving and sustaining learner motivation. To Keller, *attention* means establishing a reason to both attract and sustain attention by attending to learners' sense of curiosity. *Relevance* refers to both content and instructional process. For example, a learner may require knowledge of a particular system in order to solve a problem at work. Alternatively, they may demonstrate a high need for affiliation, and that may mean that activities promoting social presence are more relevant to the learner. As noted in chapter 4 of this volume, directing attention by providing appropriate goals is a predictor of performance. *Confidence* refers to self-efficacy and addresses the degree to which a learner's fear of failure is minimized and self-confidence is strengthened. This is reflective of self-efficacy as described by Bergin et al. in chapter 4 of this volume, which focuses on learners' perceptions of their own cognitive and performative potential. Strategies to foster confidence include self-evaluation tools to help learners assess their own learning, scaffolded materials that help learners gain mastery, and promoting independent learning and self-sufficiency. Deci and Ryan's (2000) self-determination theory (also discussed in detail in chapter 4) also describes a model for improving motivation by developing autonomy, relatedness, and competence (it is worth noting that although self-determination theory refers to these psychological conditions as ARC, this is different from the acronym ARCS as defined by Keller). Finally, *satisfaction* addresses efforts to define rewards and schedule reinforcements. This means attending to both the intrinsic and extrinsic interests of learners and fulfilling those needs in a timely fashion.

Reigeluth's Elaboration Theory

A final design theory is Reigeluth's (1979, 1999) elaboration theory. Elaboration theory recognized the importance of sequencing and structure in learning processes and concepts of moderate to high complexity. Reigeluth actually suggested three distinct instructional methods depending on whether the instructional goal was the attainment of multiple related concepts (a conceptual elaboration sequence), related principles (theoretical elaboration sequence), or tasks (simplifying conditions sequence). For each of these sequences, Reigeluth said that instruction must be structured for increased orders of complexity over time, although he noted that these sequences might be *topical*—meaning that they moved directly from simple to increased complexity for each of the topics included—or *spiraled*, in which a learner passes across the least complex version of each topic prior to adding additional complexity in successive passes. The groups of sequenced steps and their supporting concepts are organized into learning episodes that account for both the needs of the learners and the content. For example, Reigeluth said that designers should consider what the optimal length of a learning episode is given the conditions under which the learners will operate, whether outside work would be necessary, and whether there is sufficient payoff at the conclusion of each episode to keep learners motivated. Finally, Reigeluth promoted the idea that learner choice in the order and approach to episodes was important where appropriate. For example, one suggested approach is a problem-based learning model in which learners are responsible for identifying the learning episodes they feel would best serve their ability to address the problem and develop a solution.

Though Reigeluth believed the major contribution of his approach was guidance for the design of holistic sequences for both task-based and concept-based instruction, we have highlighted the elaboration model here because it emphasizes principles important in both self-directed learning and experiential learning models that were gaining in prominence during the late 1970s and early 1980s, when elaboration theory was being developed. That learners should have the authority and autonomy to make scoping and sequencing decisions during the learning process was one of the principal values on which elaboration theory was based. As discussed in chapter 10 in this volume, self-direction and planning as both a need of learners and as a goal for instruction has long been associated with adult education. Furthermore, Reigeluth offered that this self-direction might come in the context of problem-based or project-based learning events, in which the selection of content and sequence was determined by learners as their understanding of the problem or project becomes successively more complex.

Like the design theories promoted by Merrill, Gagne, and Keller previously presented, Reigeluth's model is just one of many approaches. Reigeluth's assertion that these theories draw on principles that express the relationship between method and outcome suggests a connection between these theories and the theories of adult learning presented elsewhere in this text. Whether the relationship between learning theory and design theory is causal or representative of two parallel evolutions, it should now be clear that learning theory, design process, and design theory have all undergone significant and shared changes over time. These theories are examples of how our understanding of adult learning is put into practice through instructional design and of how our knowledge of learners and learning has evolved in concert with our understanding of design.

Models and Theories-in-Use

The historical context in which design has emerged as a discipline, the two disciplinary tracks it has followed, and divergent perspectives on what it means to have a comprehensive theory of design have led to a degree of confusion about what constitutes instructional design. The fact that process, theory, and model have all been used interchangeably in both practice and scholarship has served to deepen that confusion. We have attempted to untangle these threads in the prior sections by separately defining process models and theories of design. For practitioners, this distinction is important. Process tells you how to design, and theories explain what to design; but one without the other provides an incomplete perspective.

What follows are two stories of design. To more concretely demonstrate how an adult educator might employ various ISD theories and models, we will discuss two examples with similar content but different contexts.

Example 1

A large manufacturing company is developing diversity training that will be required of all supervisors across four different sites in the United States, emphasizing the avoidance of legal issues. The training will be conducted by six trainers from head-quarters over a 6-month period. In this situation, it will be essential to gain explicit guidance from the company's legal team and to identify specific learning objectives related to areas in which they feel their supervisors are most at risk of creating legal actions. This action may be the result of violations of various laws that protect specific classes of employees, specifically, racial and ethnic minorities, employees over the age of 50, LGBTQ employees, women, and employees with disabilities. As designers, we would recognize the experiences and expertise that supervisors already hold and expect that they would be applying the training content directly in their work. We would draw on Merrill's principles and design a lesson plan that would include:

- activating learners' prior knowledge with a warm-up discussion; engagement in case studies that relate to the learners' work situations, and the presentation of concepts, approaches, and laws that relate to those cases; role plays that would allow them to demonstrate and practice the techniques presented; and an activity during which learners create specific plans about how they intend to implement some changes in the way that they interact with their subordinates

Gagne's work would remind us to get emotional buy-in—perhaps by starting with a dramatic video—and to provide explicit criteria and feedback for the student plans—perhaps by giving them a checklist. Reigeluth's work advises us to view this as a conceptual elaboration sequence, so starting out with more obvious and simple cases would lead to discussing complex cases that require learners to apply a variety of concepts. Finally, a fairly traditional ADDIE process would be used to create design documents so that all trainers had access to the analysis and design decisions and so that the training could easily be updated by designers in the future.

Example 2

An urban church's pastors and lay leadership decide that they will offer a series of antiracism workshops for their congregation focused on creating dialogue between people to uncover hidden biases and how they play out in personal and professional contexts. As designers, we would begin with the understanding that while there will certainly be some specific concepts included, these workshops will be informed by the experience of the learners themselves, not merely by subject matter experts. Keller's theory informs our design because motivation, relevance, and confidence are major outcomes that are expected. We would expect that learners may lack confidence in navigating this challenging territory, and they may fear failure or embarrassment. The instructional aim of these workshops is to promote further independent learning and self-sufficiency. Because these workshops are meant to leverage the lived experiences of the learners and to be responsive to their emerging needs and interests, the SAM is the most appropriate process model. We would expect that the design of the workshops might emerge or evolve based on the initial rollouts and a participatory approach to developing the content is essential in order to honor the various ideas and personal expertise of the participants.

These two examples demonstrate how experienced designers approach different design situations by employing a range of processes and theories. The relevant factors that influence the choice of approaches include whether the subject matter is mostly stable facts or if various interpretations and experiences need to be incorporated, the goals of the instruction in terms of what learners will be expected to do both immediately and in the future, and the need to achieve consistency and documentation of design choices for more than one trainer and/or designer. Experienced designers are familiar and comfortable with drawing from a menu of different strategies depending on the situation rather than having preferred theories or processes.

Further Considerations for Design

As explored in these examples, questions remain about how adult educators can put these models into practice. How does a designer or educator decide which process model or theory to implement in a given situation? That the models are related by learning theory means that they are in some ways bound by the same limitations for practice explored elsewhere in this chapter. Reigeluth (1999) noted that elaboration theory, for example, is not intended for affective learning. Given what we know about the important role of emotion in learning, can elaboration theory be seen as a comprehensive model for design? ISD models are intended to bring individuals to a level of predetermined mastery; in an environment that is increasingly emphasizing a growth mentality over deficits-based approaches, is this still appropriate? What do we make of an individual's self-defined goals in the context of set performance-based goals? And how do we consider all of these models in the context of learning environments that are increasingly diverse with respect to setting, content, and learner demographics?

The answers to these questions may be related to the nature of models and maps. In the literature on systems thinking, a map is a representation of a system, but it is understood to be distinct from the system itself. Such may be the nature of the design models explored in this chapter: They represent what design might look like under certain conditions but are not in and of themselves sufficient as instructions for how to "do design." In asking novice and expert designers to engage in think-aloud analysis and solution development of a design problem, Rowland (1993) found that expert designers were more likely to engage in creative solution-seeking based on their prior design experience and relied on design principles only to self-assess the quality of decisions, not to inform their design process. For novice designers, the primary goal of design models may be to serve as a substitute for experience by providing a set of heuristics on which context-specific design approaches can be designed. Some expert designers feel that these models are useful for teaching new designers and may be thought of like the kind of specific sequential moves that one is taught when learning a new dance. Once dancers become more expert, they do not need to follow these exact routines and will combine them in creative ways.

The knowledge that design theories are heuristics—and not necessarily road maps—is important for adult educators because it suggests that while instructional design is informed by process models and theories, it should also be uniquely shaped by the specific instructional problem and context. Three specific challenges related to the implementation of these theories are discussed in the following sections: (a) the organizational context, (b) the role of learner participation, and (c) the future of technology and artificial intelligence–informed design.

Organizational Context

All instruction is provided within some kind of context and setting: for example, an undergraduate liberal arts college degree, professional certification as part of a graduate degree, training for specific military roles, public health education to change attitudes that impact behavior choices, or corporate training to enhance the skills and performance of employees. Most instructional design models begin with objectives that specify what learners must be able to do in order to demonstrate mastery of the material.

In more formal K–12 and higher education settings, it is not clear how or when learners will actually be able to make use of their new knowledge, skills, or attitudes, and thus the design and assessment of the learning materials are much more general. These contexts also may be much more instructor centered. For example, while university professors are expected to teach a shared body of discipline-specific knowledge (especially in foundational courses), they also select specific examples and teaching methods that align with their own expertise, research interests, and styles, and students are expected to demonstrate that they have grasped taught concepts and can think creatively and critically based on those concepts. Professors are not only allowed, but even encouraged, to develop unique and personalized approaches that may only be able to be carried off by themselves; an example is a professor known to come to class dressed in character as a famous person in history, or others who have rather iconoclastic viewpoints or interaction styles with students.

In stark contrast are military and corporate training situations, where a very specific set of behaviors and opinions are expected of learners, and the role of instructors and designers is to create standardization. The instruction that is designed for these settings is generally meant to be carried out by many different trainers in different locations, so the delivery of the instruction must be much more standardized, while the content is much more specific. Learners are often expected to put the new skills and knowledge into practice almost immediately, and they are assessed not only on what they learned but how they actually perform on the job.

Adult educators need to be aware of the needs and expectations of their specific settings, because ISD models are employed differently depending on the context. For example, while nearly every ISD model involves the development of specific learning objectives, the objectives for a university course on leadership would look quite different from a corporate or military training course on leadership because in the latter case, learners would be expected to adopt specific leadership practices and theories and apply them immediately on the job. Additionally, when adult educators are engaged in instructional design that produces materials that will be used by other trainers over time, when the training must be approved by others, and when the material will likely also be revised over time, the specific parts of the design process will need to be fully documented. In many cases, designers need to submit each step of the design process (e.g., learner analysis or the list of behavioral objectives) to subject matter experts or supervisors for approval before moving on to the next steps. In situations where the designer is also the person who will deliver the material, the formal documentation of all of the steps is not necessary, and approvals may not be needed.

Learner and Subject Matter Expert Roles in Design

The importance of understanding the learner leads to questions about prospective or former learners' participation in the design process. Almost all models emphasize the need to analyze prospective learners' knowledge and skill gaps, previous knowledge, and motivation for learning. However, they do not speak to how that input should be gained. In linear models, it might be assumed that interviews and/or observations take place in the early stages of the design process. In actual practice, knowledge of the learner may come from a subject matter expert or manager who has some insights about the learners and who is available to participate in the design process. However, there are valid questions about whether a subject matter expert actually can be a good proxy for actual learner input, since many subject matter experts cannot really put themselves in the shoes of a novice, and many experts have actually never taught the material.

Another missing piece of most existing models is what the source of the content should be and how designers should identify those sources. Given the typical design and development situations encountered by instructional designers, it might be assumed that there is one "correct" set of facts or procedures to be taught and that these can be found in existing texts or identified by subject matter experts. However, in many applied adult learning settings there may indeed be different ideas about what content is valid. For example, if manufacturing technicians are to be trained on maintenance procedures for a factory line, various engineers may have differing and equally effective approaches for ascertaining when maintenance is needed or how exactly to perform a repair procedure. Likewise, techniques for selling that are effective in one location or culture may be ineffective or even inappropriate in other performance settings.

Even more significant critiques about the source of valid content are being raised in the current environment in which diversity and inclusion practices are being examined. In formal education, the lack of BIPOC (Black, Indigenous, people of color) and LGBTQ (lesbian, gay, bisexual, transsexual, and queer) authors and examples in textbooks and traditional curricula that draw on the experiences of these populations has become increasingly clear, and newer resources (as noted in chapter 2 of this volume) are beginning to reflect much more diverse perspectives and examples. In many adult learning contexts, it is common to identify only one subject matter expert, who may not be prepared to provide the perspectives or address the needs of a diverse body of learners and practitioners. Indeed, critics of traditional approaches to instructional design point out that its systems engineering, positivist, and rational foundations do not promote critical perspectives or help designers challenge traditional Western, white, and patriarchal belief and power structures (Carr-Chellman & Reigeluth, 2002; Nilikanta, 2006). Vargas Ramos (2021) suggest three fundamental ways that instructional designers can leverage design to address inequity. First, designers must use learning experiences to generate a safe space for discussions of inequalities and their impacts on individuals within our community. Secondly, they can develop intentional mechanisms for participants to connect with others in the broader community. Finally, they should intentionally and explicitly build efforts to address inequality directly in the learning experiences.

The literature on general systems design includes participatory design perspectives that became prevalent in the early 1990s, especially in Scandinavia (Muller, 1991; Schuler & Namioka, 1993). Trials of participatory design that included students in the design process indicated that there was increased satisfaction among students when their perspectives were included (Könings et al., 2010) and that significant improvements in student participation, project performance, and deep learning were observed among minority students in engineering (Dong et al., 2015). Beyond incorporating learners in the design process, Gayeski (1979, 1981) developed a participatory design model that includes as its third step "determine constituency," which includes not only learners but also communities impacted by the learners and content experts drawn from a variety of backgrounds, including communities represented by the content and academic experts in the subject matter. This model, first developed in the process of creating ethnic studies curricula, was extended by the emerging ability of end-user learners to actually contribute to the content and flow of interactive multimedia learning and to corporate training contexts where regional and cultural variations of content and regulations made it imperative to incorporate a wide range of principles and examples. In order to develop instruction that is more inclusive and relevant to diverse populations of adult learners, adult educators must develop facility with these more participatory approaches to design.

Artificial Intelligence and Future Systems

A final consideration for design practice is the role of artificial intelligence in the design process. There were several attempts to automate or at least support novices in the instructional design process in the 1990s, but they proved to be more cumbersome than helpful and never got traction (Dodge, 1994; Gayeski, 1991; Gros & Spector, 1994; Halff, 1993; Merrill, 1993, 1998; Spector et al., 1993; Tennyson, 1994). However, there is currently much activity in the development of intelligent tutoring systems that can be very laborious to develop, requiring about 200 hours of coding to develop each hour of instruction. New processes using machine learning enable teachers to create a 30-minute lesson in about 30 minutes, including having the development software not only learn solutions that the teacher provides but also generalize and provide solutions and examples in ways that might differ from those of the teacher (Spice, 2020). These considerations highlight the complexity of the design process and emphasize the point raised earlier in this chapter that instructional design may be neither exclusively an art nor a science. Adult educators can expect that artificial intelligence will have significant impacts on the production of content (e.g., automating animation or synthesizing transcripts of interviews of content experts), but the creativity of the designer will likely never be replaced by algorithms.

Conclusion

This chapter began by defining instructional design as a subdiscipline of both instruction and design. This foundation led to a discussion of two approaches to defining design models that emerged out of research in the 1970s. In the first, design process models—be they linear, iterative, or creative—all provide guidance for designers on how to assess and resolve an instructional problem. In contrast, design theories focus on principles that inform the appropriate application of instructional methods in a given context. In both approaches, we connected the evolution of adult learning theory to the practice of instructional design, emphasizing how topics raised elsewhere in this book are represented in the effective design of instruction for adult learning. We ended by providing two examples to demonstrate the application of models and theory in practice, and we described conditions that further inform how adult learning principles inform the practice of design. In so doing, we hope to reemphasize the complexity in defining design that opened our chapter. Recognizing the relationship between theory and design is important for the practice of adult educators, but equally important is recognizing the gaps in how this theory has been applied. Learning theory, combined with a deep understanding of organizational context, learner involvement, and emerging technical capabilities, will all inform the exercise of design principles and the improvement of adult education practice.

References

Allen, M., & Sites, R. (2012). *Leaving ADDIE for SAM: An agile model for developing the best learning experiences.* American Society for Training and Development Press.

Branson, R. K., Rayner, G. T., Cox, J. L., Furman, J. P., King, F. J., & Hannum, W. H. (1975). *Interservice procedures for instructional systems development* (5 vols.; TRADOC Pam 350–30 NAVEDTRA 106A). U.S. Army Training and Doctrine Command.

Buchanan, R. (1992). Wicked problems in design thinking. *Design Issues, 8*(2), 5–21.

Carr-Chellman, A., & Reigeluth, C. M. (2002). Whistling in the dark? Instructional design and technology in the schools. In R. A. Reiser & R. A. Dempsey (Eds.), *Trends and issues in instructional design technology* (pp. 239–255). Merrill/Prentice Hall.

Deci, E. L., & Ryan, R. M. (2000). The "what" and "why" of goal pursuits: Human needs and the self-determination of behavior. *Psychological Inquiry, 11*(4), 227–268. https://doi .org/10.1207/S15327965PLI1104_01

Dewey, J. (1901). *Psychology and social practice.* University of Chicago Press. https://www .gutenberg.org/files/40744/40744-h/40744-h.htm

Dick, W., & Carey, L. (1978). *The systematic design of instruction.* Scott Foresman.

Dodge, B. J. (1994, February). *Design and formative evaluation of PLANalyst: A lesson design tool* [Paper]. Association for Educational Communications and Technology Conference, Nashville, TN, United States.

Dong, J., Cheng, P., & Hernandez, A. (2015, June 14). *Designing effective project-based learning experience using participatory design approach* [Paper]. American Society for Engineering Education Conference, Seattle, WA, United States.

Gagne, R. M. (1977). *The conditions of learning* (3rd ed.). Holt, Rinehart and Winston.

Gayeski, D. (1979). *An ethnic studies curriculum: The development of a curriculum model through the production and evaluation of community-based materials* [Unpublished doctoral dissertation]. University of Maryland.

Gayeski, D. (1981). When the audience becomes the producer: A model for participatory media design. *Educational Technology, 21*(6), 11–14. http://www.jstor.org/stable/ 44422584

Gayeski, D. (1991). Software tools for empowering instructional developers. *Performance Improvement Quarterly, 4*(4), 21–36. https://doi.org/10.1111/j.1937-8327.1991. tb00521.x

Glaser, R. (1976). Components of a psychology for instruction: Toward a science of design. *Review of Educational Research, 46*(1), 1–24. https://doi.org/10.3102/00346543046001001

Gros, B., & Spector, J. M. (1994). Evaluating automated instructional design systems: A complex problem. *Educational Technology, 34*(5), 37–46.

Halff, H. M. (1993). Prospects for automating instructional design. In J. M. Spector, M. C. Polson, & D. J. Muraida (Eds.), *Automating instructional design: Concepts and issues* (pp. 67–132). Educational Technology.

Keller, J. M. (1987). Development and use of the ARCS modes of instructional design. *Journal of Instructional Development, 10*(3), 2–10. https://doi.org/10.1007/BF02905780

Kemp, J. E. (1985). *The instructional design process.* Harper & Row.

Könings, K. D., Brand-Gruwel, S., & van Merriënboer, J. J. G. (2010). An approach to participatory instructional design in secondary education: An exploratory study. *Educational Research, 52*(1), 45–59. https://doi.org/10.1080/00131881003588204

Kurt, S. (2018, December 16). *ADDIE model: Instructional design.* Educational Technology. https://educationaltechnology.net/the-addie-model-instructional-design/

Merrill, M. D. (1993). An integrated model for automating instructional design and delivery. In J. M. Spector, M. C. Polson, & D. J. Muraida (Eds.), *Automating instructional design: Concepts and issues* (pp. 147–190). Educational Technology.

Merrill, M. D. (1998). ID expert: A second generation instructional development system. *Instructional Science, 26,* 243–262. https://doi.org/10.1023/A:1003011431677

Merrill, M. D. (2002). First principles of instruction. *Educational Technology Research and Development, 50*(3), 43–59. mdavidmerrill.com/Papers/firstprinciplesbymerril.pdf

Morrison, G. R., Ross, S. M., Kalman, H. K., & Kemp, J. E. (2013). *Designing effective instruction* (7th ed.). Wiley.

Muller, M. J. (1991). PICTIVE—an exploration in participatory design. In S. P. Robertson, G. M. Olson, & J. S. Olson (Eds.), *Proceedings of the SIGCHI Conference on Human Factors in Computing Systems* (pp. 225–231). SIGCHI.

Nilakanta, R. (2006). *Participatory instructional design: A contradiction in terms?* [Unpublished doctoral dissertation]. Iowa State University.

Norman, D. A. (2016). When you come to a fork in the road, take it: The future of design. *She Ji: The Journal of Design, Economics, and Innovation, 2,* 343–348. https://doi.org/10.1016/j.sheji.2017.07.003

Reigeluth, C. M. (1979). In search of a better way to organize instruction: The elaboration theory. *Journal of Instructional Development, 2*(3), 8–15. https://doi.org/10.1007/BF02984374

Reigeluth, C. M. (1983). *Instructional-design theories and models: An overview of their current status.* Erlbaum.

Reigeluth, C. M. (Ed.). (1999). *Instructional-design theories and models: A new paradigm of instructional theory* (Vol. II). Erlbaum.

Reigeluth, C. M., & Merrill, M. D. (1978). A knowledge base for improving methods of instruction. *Educational Psychologist, 13*(1), 57–70.

Reiser, R. A. (2001). A history of instructional design and technology: Part 1. A history of instructional media. *Educational Technology Research and Development, 49*(1), 53–64. https://doi.org/10.1007/BF02504506

Rowland, G. (1993). Designing and instructional design. *Educational Technology Research and Development, 41*(1), 79–91. https://doi.org/10.1007/BF02297094

Schuler, D., & Namioka, A. (Eds.). (1993). *Participatory design.* CRC Press.

Snellbecker, G. E. (1974). *Learning theory, instructional theory, and psychoeducational design.* McGraw-Hill.

Spector, J. M., Polson, M. C., & Muraida, D. J. (Eds.). (1993). *Automating instructional design: Concepts and issues.* Educational Technology.

Spice, B. (2020, May 6). New AI enables teachers to rapidly develop intelligent tutoring systems. https://www.cmu.edu/news/stories/archives/2020/may/intelligent-tutors.html

Tennyson, R. D. (Ed.). (1994). *Automating instructional design, development, and delivery.* NATO Advanced Science Institutes Series.

Vargas Ramos, G. E. (2021). Decentralizing whiteness. In J. Quinn (Ed.), *The learning-centered instructional designer: Purposes, processes, and practicalities of creating online courses in higher education* (pp. 107–115). Stylus.

Zemke, R., & Rossett, A. (2002). A hard look at ISD. *Training, 39*(2), 26–34.

Editors' Key Seminal and Supplemental Text Suggestions

Dick, W., & Carey, L. (1978). *The systematic design of instruction*. Scott Foresman.

Fink, L. D. (2013). *Creating significant learning experiences: An integrated approach to designing college courses* (2nd ed.). Jossey-Bass.

Gagne, R. M. (1977). *The conditions of learning* (3rd ed.). Holt, Rinehart and Winston.

Merrill, M. D. (2002). First principles of instruction. *Educational Technology Research and Development, 50*(3), 43–59. mdavidmerrill.com/Papers/firstprinciplesbymerril.pdf

Reigeluth, C. M. (Ed.). (1999). *Instructional-design theories and models: A new paradigm of instructional theory* (Vol. II). Erlbaum.

Silberman, M., & Beich, E. (2015). *Active training: A handbook of techniques, designs, case examples, and tips* (4th ed.). Wiley.

15

NEXT STEPS

Interrogating and Using Theory

Alisa Belzer and Brian Dashew

As we conclude this book, we offer some of our own reflections on learning in adulthood, on the connections between theory and practice, and on the experience of editing this volume. We hope that these reflections will serve as both a model and a prompt. We will end with some suggestions for continuing your own reflective practice as a developing adult educational professional in this field.

Gnanadass and Merriweather (chapter 8) point out that practitioners may not always take up theory in a conscious way. Although adult education practice is always driven by theory, in that it is shaped by the educator's interpretation of learning, learners, and context, this may be done without intentionality. One critical gap in practice that this can produce is found in considerations of what it means to engage in equitable, just, and inclusive teaching. Without a theoretical lens to guide them, some educators may fail to consider the ways in which learners' voices and experiences are valued or silenced in an evolving understanding of "why we do what we do, why we think what we think, and why we value what we value" (p. 138). There are multiple reasons why educators may fail to draw on theory. Some adult educators do not have the training that would inform them of key theories. Others may have drifted away from the theories they once knew as the years since entering the classroom or training room begin to outnumber those spent in graduate courses. They may not know, or no longer draw on, how theory drives decisions about lesson planning, instructional design, or in the moment-to-moment interactions that take place in learning contexts. Other practitioners would say they actively avoid theory, instead preferring to draw exclusively on a set of practices forged through years of experience. And still others may disregard it, believing it to be something static and ignoring the ways in which an ever-changing context necessitates a constantly evolving base of theory.

This book has presented a number of theories for adult learning, each developed to explore questions about the purposes of adult education, the roles and responsibilities of the adult educator, or the nature of adult learning and learners. However, adult education theorists have not always been as intentional as they could be about how context and culture matter to the many variables of practice. Yet theories always offer implications for practice, and we argue that when educators understand and are reflective about theory and intentionally consider how it can inform their practice, they are more effective. This is precipitated by an intentional investigation of the theory and a reflection on how it can inform and is informed by—or silences—the voices and experiences of learners and educators. This last chapter addresses essential reflective actions for adult educators. First, we consider approaches to interrogating theory by doing what Brookfield (1995) called "hunting assumptions." Although he suggested engaging in this as a way of critically reflecting on practice, we find it similarly useful for considerations of theory. Next, we highlight specific ways that theory can be a value-added part of reflective practice. Although presented as a linear process here, analyzing theory for what it does and does not explain and considering its utility in practice is more of an iterative, circular, back-and-forth process. The relationship between theory and practice should be a dynamic one that is continuously modified by the learning purpose and context and by who the learners are and what it means to meet their needs. Finally, we provide a description of our own students' work demonstrating the integration of theory and practice in their capstone projects.

Strategies for Interrogating Adult Learning Theory

As readers think across the theories discussed in this book, it is important to have strategies to critically assess them as part of the process of deciding how and under what circumstances to integrate them with practice. In becoming a critically reflective practitioner, Brookfield (1995) pointed to the importance of "hunting assumptions." He identified three types of assumptions: (a) paradigmatic, (b) prescriptive, and (c) causal. These taken-for-granted beliefs include the ways in which we think about how our outer world is categorized and ordered; how we believe the world should operate and how we believe individuals should relate to one another; and what causes and effects can be expected. Typically, our own assumptions seem normal, while others may seem strange and inextricable. Without "hunting" for them we cannot be conscious of how our assumptions guide our actions and interpretations.

We believe this same hunting approach can also promote critical reflection on theory. Brookfield (1995) suggested asking four different kinds of questions of theory that can promote this type of quest. Epistemological questions delve into the paradigmatic or evidentiary grounds on which a theory is demonstrated to be true. Questions aimed at interrogating a theory with regard to epistemology could include the following: *What does this theory establish as known? What is taken for granted as given? What evidence is offered for what is assumed to be known? What cultural assumptions seem to be present in this knowledge? What are the key intellectual influences for the theorist?* Experiential questions seek to interrogate the ways in which a theory is aligned with educator, learner, and collective experiences.

Questions aimed at interrogating a theory with regard to experience could include the following: *In what ways does this theory resonate with my experiences as an adult learner and adult educator? In what ways does this theory resonate with the range of what I understand to be learners' experiences? How does this theory help widen my understanding of diverse experiences? What gaps and omissions are present in theory that relate to the lived experiences of educators and learners?* Communicative questions look at how and where theory is explicated and in what formats and voices. Questions aimed at interrogating a theory with regard to its communicative properties could include the following: *Where was this theory first published, and what does that say about how it was valued by the field? What meanings do the format, language choice, and style of the writing convey? What adult education conversation (or debate) is this theory a part of?* Political questions get at whose interests are served, whose voices are heard, and what is subjugated and silenced. Questions aimed at interrogating a theory with regard to its political properties could include the following: *How does this theory maintain or disrupt the status quo with regard to hegemony? Whose interests are represented in this theory? In what ways does the theory create a sense of belonging for all learners?* Overall, the goal is to interrogate the substance and the form of theories for the ways in which they do and do not create spaces, interrupt silences, and disrupt hegemonies in ways that encourage all learners to feel they have a rightful place in the learning context and all practitioners to feel they can effectively meet them where they are and help them move forward on their own terms. We encourage readers to use these questions as grounds for engaging in reflection and interrogating theory, practice, and the role of adult educators in adopting and challenging these canonical theories.

In our opening chapter, we reviewed three commitments in the field of adult learning that we believe are shared by and reflected across many adult learning theories: (a) humanism, (b) critical pedagogy, and (c) reflection. By revisiting them here, we offer a reminder of some of the critiques that have been raised by chapter authors in relation to the theories they explicate. In this way, we begin to hunt some of the assumptions (and problematics) that evolve over time, and we encourage all adult educators to continue down that path in ways that are specific to their learners and learning contexts.

Humanism puts an emphasis on the growth and development of the whole person. Its theoretical basis is explored in Dirkx and Schlegel's discussion of the self (chapter 6) and is also explored in the discussions of experiential learning (chapter 11), transformative learning (chapter 12), and in constructive–development theory (chapter 7). It is interesting to note that the commitment to humanism not only undergirds key adult education theory but also provides a lens for critique. For example, in challenging the interpretation of Mezirow's work (1978) as overly focused on rational thinking (e.g. Clark and Wilson, 1991), the field has come to recognize versions of transformative learning that acknowledge the importance of imagination, emotion, and spirituality in learning.

A second commitment we identified at the beginning of this text was a focus on critical pedagogy, or a commitment to identify teaching practices that advance justice and equity, both within the classroom and across external social and political contexts. In his chapter on the democratic impulse of adult education (chapter 3), Brookfield points to the many ways that democratic practice can redistribute power in the classroom and help adults work toward a more just society. Critical pedagogy is recognized as both an instructional approach and a contributing factor in learning outcomes related to equity and justice. Andragogy (chapter 9), self-directed learning (chapter 10), and connectivism (chapter 13), for example, are all presented with an understanding that decentering the role of the educator and providing additional learner control is necessary for creating more democratic adult learning spaces; both transformative learning (chapter 12) and constructive–development theory (chapter 7) posit that a central goal of learning should be surfacing and challenging previously unconscious frameworks and habits of mind in order to foster more open and inclusive engagement with the world.

In discussing structured silences embedded in adult education theory (chapter 8), however, Gnanadass and Merriweather highlighted that both humanism and critical perspectives on adult education focus on Western conceptions of self that promote an ideal of individuality. This critique is certainly acknowledged in many theories of adult learning. For example, in chapter 9, St. Clair noted that, in analyses of andragogy, it has "proven difficult to peel the core of andragogical values away from the notion of the rational, self-diagnosing, individualistic actor who views increased actualization as the purpose of learning" (p. 168). Hoggan and Kasl point to the perceived value of individual emancipation as one of the most significant critiques levied against transformative learning (chapter 12). We argue that this recognition is part of the evolution of theory. Theories of learning and teaching that are more inclusive of new lenses and worldviews (chapter 2, chapter 8); emotional and postrational perspectives (chapter 6, chapter 12); and embedded, social learning contexts (chapter 13) have emerged as critical voices and structures in the 21st century. We expect this evolution will continue as adult educators reflect on the intersections of theory and practice, identity, and equity.

Although reflection is obviously key to interrogating adult learning theory, Brookfield (1995) offered some cautions about this process that take us back to the importance and challenge of hunting personal assumptions. We need to stay alert to the ways in which personal experience can obscure the experiences of others, make other selves seem abnormal or deficient, and create boundaries and limitations on the exploration of other contexts. This makes interactions with others whose experiences and contexts diverge from our own critical to providing additional lenses for seeing what is present and missing from theories. Thus, as Brookfield suggested for critical practice, but is also relevant to critical interrogation of theory, we must use alternative lenses—our learners, our colleagues, and theoretical literature—that stretches us beyond the canonical body of work captured in this book.

Using Theory in Practice

Although we have noted that there is an inherent connection between theory and practice, there are a number of ways in which a conscious and intentional use of theory can improve adult education practice. These include viewing theories as

A set of tools that can inform design decisions. The theories presented in this book can broaden a practitioner's repertoire of approaches, enabling them to be responsive to a range of tasks, learners, and contexts. Consider, for example, the ways in which Dashew and Gayeski (chapter 14) identify the connections between learning theory and the evolution of instructional design practice. But also consider the ways in which individual authors have identified instructional practices that emerge from the theories they describe. In fact, explicitly connecting theory to practice was a part of our request to each of the chapter authors when we invited them to participate in this project. The tools are too plentiful to name here, but each author responded with a unique set of strategies connected to their own theoretical stance on learning in adulthood. We hope that readers will consider the theories they have learned about in this book as a set of tools in a toolbox from which they can choose. The correct tool for the job depends on the learning task, context, and learners. At times, one tool will be just the right fit; at other times, multiple tools will be needed to create a rich array of solutions to learning and teaching challenges.

A set of analytic lenses that can be used to interpret classroom interactions around the material, the activities, and the people. Theory is useful as a way of interpreting complex phenomena; viewing how students respond to learning tasks and processes through theoretical lenses can improve practitioners' ability to respond appropriately to them—their cultural identities, their goals, their fears and hopes, and their enthusiasms and resistances. For example, consider the way that Sheared responded to students in her class who challenged the way she taught about race (chapter 2). Applying her own theoretical lens allowed her to understand their responses from the perspective of voice and positionality, and the dialogues that emerged as a result were transformative for her and her learners. Dirkx and Schlegel (chapter 6) draw on the imaginal method as a way to learn from and reengage learners whose enthusiasm for coursework had flagged.

A part of professional identity. The theories presented in this text represent many of the shared discourses of adult education. Knowledge of these theories not only reflects a personal relationship to the field but also is part of what defines adult education as a field in and of itself. When adult education was still an emerging discipline, one of the concerns was that a theoretical core that could serve as the basis for engaging in the study of adult education was lacking (Plecas & Sork, 1986). Centering adult education's theoretical core around andragogy, self-directed learning, experiential learning, and transformative learning has given a vernacular for describing and exploring learning in adulthood. As such, they have provided adult educators, researchers, and theorists an educational arena that is distinct. However, as previously discussed, every practitioner is responsible for reflecting on these theories and posing questions about their relevance and significance for the learners and the learning context within which they work. Theories are incomplete and contested. While shared knowledge and understanding can help create a professional identity, they should not circumscribe a unitary way of thinking about and using them.

These three uses of theory are modeled by practitioners in all facets of adult education. Here we highlight what this looks like with our own students, emerging leaders in the field of adult education. Toward the end of their time in our graduate program in adult and continuing education, our students engage in a two-course capstone experience in which they develop a learning intervention for adults. Frequently, they begin this project by exploring some sort of problem of practice or performance in their own organizational contexts. For example, this could be a team that uses a system improperly or perceptions that an organization has a noncollegial culture or low morale. Yet, as they explore these problems and develop deeper insights into the organizational and social contexts in which they exist, they come to recognize the complexity of adult learning, and the multiplicity of spaces and structures in which adult education takes place. From our role as program faculty, it always serves as an important reminder about how embedded adult education is in addressing issues of varying scales within so many different types of institutional contexts. Over the past 3 years, a sampling of our student work has included

- plans for the launch of a new program designed as an alternative for emerging adults who had left formal schooling early in a large city in New Jersey
- an approach to design and evaluation of informal professional development networks for new minority educators
- a community-based intervention for medical students at an area teaching hospital
- a program for onboarding jail administrators to a program that uses service animal training as a reform mechanism for reducing recidivism
- initiatives for improving technology use among educators and nontraditional adult learners in a community college setting

That these projects represent ways in which adult education intersects with different contexts, problems, and audiences may be immediately clear. But it has also been powerful to read student reflections on their projects and to learn about the different ways in which they have drawn on the theories discussed in this volume. For some, their perceptions of adult learning have been shaped by principles of andragogy, and their solutions to problems of practice in adult education are guided by a need to develop problem-focused orientations to their training. For others, they recognize a capacity for adult learners to engage in transformation. One student, for example, began her project focused on the fact that staff at a recently acquired subsidiary were not able to use the parent company's software systems, only to discover midway through her project that the training actually required a shift in habits of mind and new frameworks related to the nature of their work and the importance of communicating across the new business. She moved from seeing the problem as a simple behavioral training task to a need for transformative learning. Still others emphasize the importance of learning from experience—either through rational, critical discourse or through reflecting on emotional responses to a learning event.

Over the years, several patterns have emerged. The design of each student's project is informed by their understanding of theories of adult learning. This aligns with the first use of theory in practice previously explained, as a tool. This understanding is typically informed not by a single theory but based on the student's understanding of various points of intersection across multiple theories. In other words, an understanding of the theories of adult learning, both broadly and specifically, inform the design of these projects. But these projects are also informed by their context, and a student's ability to leverage theory to explain how learning occurs within that context; this is the second use of theory we have described, as an analytic lens. When we talk about context, we are speaking of three layers of context. Most narrowly, we mean the general type of learning context: formal, informal, or nonformal. We also mean the larger organizational context in which these learning interventions take place. Students come to find that adult learning is not only about helping individuals succeed but also about improving organizational capacity. This requires an understanding of adult education as a social, embedded process that connects to the final layer of context. The student projects are informed by a specific social and culture framework that guides their interpretation of the theory and the problem. A deep understanding of self and positionality is required in order to recognize this third layer and its impact on the work of each adult educator. This, then, speaks to a final theme that emerges from student reflections on their projects. Students report that their understanding of the theories exists in a reflexive relationship with their own personal and professional identities. The theory helps them to understand who they are as adult educators but also informs the way they perceive themselves as learners and as adults. This evolving sense of self informs new interpretations of the theory, and so on. In other words, our students come to see themselves as adult educators by gaining an understanding of adult education theory, but they recognize that adult learning theories—like nearly all theories—are incomplete. As they come to see themselves as part of this field, they question whether theory reflects their own experiences as learners as well as what they know from practice as educators and from the learners with whom they work. Their intentional attempts to answer these questions lead to new interpretations and ways of thinking about the field.

As we conclude this text, we wish to note that it is both critical and inevitable that today's emerging adult educators will continue to advance the theory base for tomorrow in ways that are more inclusive, just, and reflective of the global contexts of adult learning. Yet it is also important to recognize that doing so requires a knowledge of our existing theory base and a set of tools for engaging in a critical, reflective analysis of these theories.

Conclusion

When we began working on this book in 2019, we engaged in the usual editor tasks of identifying chapter topics and brainstorming potential authors. Although it should not have surprised us, because they did their work decades ago, many of the topic experts who we turned to were retired or had moved on to writing about other topics. This should have been an indicator that we were, in some ways, treading on old (but hallowed) ground in the field. Although we felt committed to presenting canonical theories, we also felt committed to finding new ways to present them. We believe we have succeeded by inviting authors to share critiques and evolving understandings of theories, by including new topics from inside and somewhat outside the field and by juxtaposing them in new and elucidating ways.

However, the world is different now than when we started the project. The ensuing years have brought events that have radically transformed life in the United States and around the world. The global COVID-19 pandemic has altered the way we live, work, and learn. It has accelerated changes in our relationships with truth, science, and knowledge; it has introduced new ways of and new capacities for using technologies that connect us across the globe and change the ways we can think about formal, nonformal, and informal learning contexts. The murders of Breonna Taylor and George Floyd widely altered our national conversations about race and identity. In the field of adult education, these discussions amplified calls for disrupting hegemonic structures that silence Black and Brown voices. To be clear, the need for dismantling these structures has always been present, but the recent shift in discourse has signaled a growing recognition of the gaps present in our field. These gaps are the structured silence discussed in chapter 8 by Gnanadass and Merriweather. Given that this text was conceived of as a reflection of the state of our field, we suddenly saw these same structural issues present in our choice of chapter topics and in the tasks we set (and did not set) for our authors. This recognition has encouraged us to hunt our own assumptions in our teaching and our research as we move forward in our work. Recognizing gaps and silences this reveals is a necessary first step to addressing them.

As we move forward through the uncertain waters of the 21st century, we suggest that adult education theory—with its commitments to humanism, critical pedagogy, and reflection—still provides tools that help educators meet learners where they are and helps them move forward in their knowledge, understanding, analytic abilities, and skills. But we also recognize that they go only so far in helping individuals engage with their world and develop new structures that promote equity, access, and justice. Knowledge of the theory base in adult education, and of the factors that make each adult learner unique, as well as how they are generally different from younger learners, is essential for our changing world. We believe the questions used to hunt assumptions within these theories can help practitioners make deliberative decisions about when and how to use theories while simultaneously wrestling with the silences and gaps that are present within them. Doing so will make for more effective practitioners and will help the theory base presented in this volume to evolve. In this way, our understanding of the adult learner can be more reflective of our current realities and a catalyst for systemic change. Emerging adult educators reading this text should play a critical role in drawing on and participating in this evolution.

References

Brookfield, S. D. (1995). *Becoming a critically reflective teacher*. Jossey-Bass.

Clark, M. C., & Wilson, A. L. (1991). Context and rationality in Mezirow's theory of transformational learning. *Adult Education Quarterly, 41*(2), 75–91.

Mezirow, J. D. (1978). *Education for perspective transformation.: Women's re-entry programs in community colleges*. Center for Adult Education, Teachers College, Columbia University.

Plecas, D. B., & Sork, T. J. (1986). Adult education: Curing the ills of an undisciplined discipline. *Adult Education Quarterly, 37*(1), 48–62. https://doi.org/10.1177/0001848186037001005

EDITORS AND CONTRIBUTORS

Colin Beard is a professor of experiential learning at Sheffield Hallam University. He is a UK National Teaching Fellow, recognized for his excellence in teaching and learning. He is the owner of Experience the Difference consulting, working with leading global public and private organizations on learning and development. He specializes in human learning and has substantial experience in both theory and practice.

Hal Beder, EdD, is an emeritus professor at the Rutgers University Graduate School of Education. His many scholarly achievements are based in his research on adult literacy. His work is grounded in practice and in the context of the limited funding and fragile operational environments of adult literacy programs. His most recent projects prior to retiring focused on learner engagement and classroom dynamics. His scholarly prominence was recognized by the Imogene Okes Award for outstanding research by the American Association for Adult and Continuing Education for his book, *Adult Literacy: Implications for Policy and Practice* (Krieger, 1991). He has also served in many leadership roles, including for the Commission of Professors of Adult Education, the New Jersey Association for Lifelong Learning, and the New Jersey State Council for Adult Literacy Services.

Alisa Belzer is a professor at the Rutgers University Graduate School of Education and program coordinator for the online EdM in adult and continuing education. She coedits *Adult Literacy Education: The International Journal of Literacy, Language, and Numeracy*. Widely published in peer-reviewed journals and edited books, the research topics she investigates focus on adult literacy education policy, professional development, and adult learner experiences. Funded by the Dollar General Foundation, she is currently developing a mobile app for adult developing readers called URead.

Christi A. Bergin is associate dean of research and innovation in the College of Education and Human Development at the University of Missouri. She is an applied developmental psychologist with an EdS and PhD from Stanford. Her research focuses on prosocial behavior—or helping children become kind, trustworthy, and cooperative—as well as teaching effectiveness. She has recently published a book titled *Designing a Prosocial Classroom* (Norton, 2018). She is coauthor of *Child and Adolescent Development in Your Classroom* (Cengage, 2017), a university-level textbook that helps teachers promote the cognitive and socioemotional well-being of diverse children in their classrooms. She consults with many teachers and schools on promoting prosocial behavior in students.

David A. Bergin, PhD (Stanford), is professor of educational psychology at the University of Missouri. He studies motivation and has researched topics such as classroom engagement, academic interest, and motivation for low-stakes tests. His research focuses on motivation in formal and informal settings. He was a Fulbright Scholar to Chile, where he taught a course on motivation in Spanish. He has been an instructional designer and Silicon Valley consultant on instructional topics.

Ralph G. Brockett, PhD, is professor emeritus at the University of Tennessee, Knoxville. His major scholarly interests are in the areas of self-directed learning, ethics in adult education, and the study of the adult education field. He is the author, coauthor, or editor of 10 books, including *Teaching Adults: A Practical Guide for New Teachers* (Jossey-Bass, 2015). Ralph is on the board of the International Society for Self-Directed Learning, is past chair of the Commission of Professors of Adult Education, and has served on the board of the American Association for Adult and Continuing Education. Ralph received the Malcolm Knowles Memorial Self-Directed Learning Award in 2004 and is a member of the International Adult and Continuing Education Hall of Fame.

Stephen Brookfield has worked in England, Canada, and the United States, teaching and consulting in a variety of adult, community, organizational, and higher education settings since beginning his educational career in 1970. His overall project is to help people learn to think critically about the dominant ideologies they have internalized and how these can be challenged. He is particularly interested in methodologies of critical thinking; discussion and dialogue; critical reflection; leadership; and the exploration of power dynamics, particularly around racial identity and white supremacy. To that end, he has written, cowritten, or edited 20 books on adult learning, teaching, critical thinking, discussion methods, critical theory, leadership, and teaching race, six of which have won the Cyril O. Houle World Award for Literature in Adult Education (in 1986, 1989, 1996, 2005, 2011, and 2012). His academic appointments have included positions at the University of British Columbia, Teachers College Columbia University (New York), Harvard University, and the University of St. Thomas in Minneapolis–St. Paul. He has consulted with numerous organizations and institutions across the world and delivered multiple workshops and conference keynotes. He is currently part-time Antioch University Distinguished Scholar, Adjunct Professor at Teachers College, Columbia University and emeritus professor at the University of St. Thomas.

Brian Dashew is a leader in adult education, program and curriculum design, and learning strategy. He is currently the head of learning for GroupM North America. Previously, he was an assistant professor of practice in adult and continuing education at Rutgers University, teaching coursework in adult learning theory and applied research. He has more than a decade of prior administrative appointments in the areas of professional studies, academic administration, faculty development, and course design. He received his EdD in adult learning and leadership from Teachers College, Columbia University.

John Dirkx is a professor and Mildred B. Erickson Distinguished Chair (emeritus) in higher and adult education at Michigan State University. He received his doctorate from the University of Wisconsin–Madison in 1987 with a focus on transformative learning. He is a former editor of the *Journal of Transformative Education* and author of *A Guide to Planning and Implementing Instruction for Adults* (Wiley, 1997), and numerous book chapters and journal articles on adult learning.

Diane Gayeski, PhD, is professor of strategic communication at the Roy H. Park School of Communications at Ithaca College, where she also served as dean for 11 years. Her areas of research and consulting are emerging technologies and practice models for organizational communication and learning; the management and valuation of intangible assets; and cocreation models for strategic planning, collaboration, and organizational knowledge. She has led more than 300 engagements for clients worldwide through Gayeski Analytics, is the author of 14 books and scores of academic and professional articles, and has been recognized for her leadership by the International Society for Performance & Instruction and the International Association of Business Communicators.

Edith Gnanadass is an assistant professor of higher and adult education at the University of Memphis. Her research interests are at the intersection of race and learning in adult education, DesiCrit (theorizing the racialized experiences of South Asian Americans using Critical Race Theory), cultural–historical activity theory as a framework to analyze learning, using Black texts in adult and higher education, and racialized and gendered immigrant narratives. She is the coeditor of the upcoming "Being Black in the U.S."–themed issue of *Dialogues in Social Justice: An Adult Education Journal* and serves on the board for the Commission of Professors of Adult Education, the Adult Higher Education Alliance, and Literacy Mid-South.

Deborah Helsing, EdD, is the director of Minds at Work, where she coaches, consults, and provides training on applications of adult development theories and the immunity-to-change approach. She designs leadership development programs and learning experiences that are "deliberately developmental," going beyond technical or informational approaches to engage transformational or adaptive learning and change. Deb is also a lecturer at Harvard University's Graduate School of Education, teaching courses in adult development and immunity to change. She has coauthored several articles, chapters, and books, including *An Everyone Culture: Becoming a Deliberately Developmental Organization* (Harvard Business Review Press, 2016, with Robert Kegan, Lisa Lahey, Andy Fleming, and Matt Miller); *Right Weight, Right Mind: The ITC Approach to Permanent Weight Loss* (Minds at Work, 2014, with Robert Kegan and Lisa Lahey); *The Immunity to Change Coach's Guide* (Harvard

Business Review Press, 2011, with Lisa Lahey and Robert Kegan); and "Unlocking Leadership Potential: Overcoming Immunities to Change" (with Lisa Lahey) in the edited volume *Extraordinary Leadership: Addressing the Gaps in Senior Executive Development* (Jossey-Bass, 2010).

Chad Hoggan is an associate professor of adult and lifelong education at North Carolina State University and coeditor of the *Journal of Transformative Education*. Chad's research addresses significant learning experiences in adulthood. One branch of research explores the learning and change required during major life transitions. This research has addressed such diverse groups as college students, breast cancer survivors, military veterans, and migrants. Another important area of scholarship deals with the learning necessary for a free and democratic society.

Elizabeth Kasl, PhD, is an independent scholar who served as faculty in the adult education program at Teachers College, Columbia University, before moving to San Francisco to help create a doctoral program in transformative learning at the California Institute of Integral Studies. She retired in 2005. Over the course of her teaching career, she focused on collaborative learning, participatory inquiry, the role of diversity in knowledge construction, and holism in learning process and pedagogical practice. She helped create and participated actively in three small group learning collaboratives: Group for Collaborative Inquiry, Transformative Learning Collaborative, and European-American Collaborative Challenging Whiteness. This last group was founded in 1997 and continues today.

Rita Kop works as a core member of faculty in the Department of Education at Yorkville University. She has a PhD in adult continuing education. After a career in teaching, higher education administration, research, and development activities related to education and technology in Canada, the United Kingdom and the Netherlands, she currently researches advanced educational technologies, such as personal learning ecosystems and massive open online courses and how best to support the human in learning. She worked as researcher for the National Research Council of Canada and as professor in adult education and higher education in the United Kingdom and is an advocate for open learning and widening access. Her research interests include adult education, ethics of artificial intelligence and analytics, online learning and teaching, widening access, and the design of learning experiences.

Catherine Marienau, PhD, is professor emerita, DePaul University, where she served on the full-time faculty in the School for New Learning for more than 3 decades. She mentored and taught adult learners, founded and directed innovative graduate programs, and created cross-sector forums for community engagement. Currently, she consults, teaches, and writes in the areas of adult learning and neuroscience, women and aging, and women and holistic health. She is coauthor of *Facilitating Learning With the Adult Brain in Mind* (Jossey-Bass, 2016) and *Developing Adult Learners: Strategies for Teachers and Trainers* (Wiley, 2000).

Lisa R. Merriweather is a professor of adult education at the University of North Carolina at Charlotte. She has a PhD in adult education from the University of Georgia and is cofounder and coeditor of *Dialogues in Social Justice: An Adult Education Journal* and an aspiring writer of historical science fiction centering issues of race and racism. Employing the art of story and dialogic engagement, complete with creativity and innovativeness, emotionality and theorizing, and historical and contemporary cultural and political critique informed by Africana philosophy and Critical Race Theory, Lisa invites readers and interlocutors to a space of reflection through (re)presenting and (re)languaging racialized experiences. Her research interests include culturally liberative mentoring, critical race pedagogy, STEM doctoral mentoring, and race and racism in non/informal adult education.

Sarah L. Prewett, PhD, is an educational psychologist and research consultant. Her expertise focuses on K–12 students' academic and social–emotional well-being. She studies the mechanisms that promote forming high quality teacher–student relationships, particularly among adolescent youth. Much of her work is with teacher professional development and training in methods that support positive school and classroom climates.

Steven Schlegel is an independent scholar and teaching and learning consultant specializing in adult education. He received his PhD from Michigan State University in 2021. His scholarship occupies an interdisciplinary space between intellectual history and the study of higher and adult education that considers changes in the scholarly record as a subject of inquiry.

Vanessa Sheared, EdD, has more than 30 years of experience in the field of adult education as an administrator, counselor, and faculty member in public and private universities and vocational and technical colleges and has served as a board member on foundations and community-based and nonprofit organizations. She has given presentations at international, national, state, and local conferences and conducted research and taught in the areas of race, class, language and gender, policy and leadership, instructional and funding strategies, and Africentric womanist perspectives. Her publications include *Welfare Reform, Race, Class, and Gender: The Elusive Quest for Self-Determination* (Routledge, 1998); *Making Space: Merging Theory to Practice* (Bergin & Garvey, 2001, coedited with P. Sissel); *The Handbook on Race in Adult Education: A Resource for Dialogue on Racism* (Jossey-Bass, 2010, coedited with J. Johnson-Bailey, S. A. J. Colin III, E. Peterson, and S. Brookfield), and a special issue of *Educational and Urban Society* focused on Adult Basic Education in the Urban Community (SAGE, 2000, coeditor, Donna Amstutz). She is currently board president (2021–2022) of the American Association for Adult Continuing Education and board president, Executive Director for Closing the Gap.

Ralf St. Clair works at the University of Victoria in Canada, where he was dean from 2014 to 2022. He has written widely in adult and higher education, including a review of 50 years of andragogy with Bernd Kåpplinger published in *Adult Education Quarterly* in 2021. Ralf has been involved in adult education, most often around literacy, for several decades and deeply values all he has learned from the field. Ralf's most recent books are *Creating Courses for Adults*, published by Wiley in 2015, *Learning-Centred Leadership* (Palgrave Macmillan, 2020), and *Researching Learning and Teaching With Adults* (Stylus, 2023).

Kathleen Taylor, PhD, is professor, doctoral program in educational leadership, Saint Mary's College of California. Her research focuses on how affective neuroscience informs best practices in facilitating adult development and learning. For 3 decades, her emphasis has been on learning that enhances human flourishing. She is coauthor of *Facilitating Learning With the Adult Brain in Mind* (Jossey-Bass, 2016) and *Developing Adult Learners: Strategies for Teachers and Trainers* (Jossey-Bass, 2000). A former Fulbright scholar, she presents professional development workshops and keynotes on adult learning and brain science in international educational and organizational settings.

access, 42, 47
accommodation, 9
achievement goal theory, 60–61. *See also*
    goals
active imagination, 108
adaptive orientation for transformative
    learning, 228
ADDIE (Analysis, Design, Development,
    Implementation, and Evaluation)
    model, 258–259, 266
adult development
    application regarding, 130–132
    constructive-development theory,
        118–127
    critiques and responses regarding,
        128–130
    distribution of, 129–130
    evolution of, 117–118
    Immunity to Change approach regarding,
        131–132
    Imperial Mind stage of, 122–123, 131
    relevance of, 130
    Self-Authoring Mind stage of, 121,
        124–125, 126, 131
    Self-Transforming Mind stage of, 121,
        126–127
    Socializing Mind stage of, 121, 131
adult education
    adult-to-adult relationships within, 170
    affective neuroscience and, 88–90
    barriers to, 255
    contexts for, 12–13
    examples of, 59
    foundational commitments in, 13–17
    growth of, 158
    personal stories regarding, 99, 105, 108,
        110–111
    purpose of, 88–89
    as recursive process, 163

social movements and, 15–16, 143
    20th century goal of, 39
adult educators. *See* educators, adult
adulthood
    arrival as journey into, 6
    defined, 4–6
    delineations of, 5
    expectations within, 130
    Imperial Mind stage of, 122–123, 131
    maturation to, 215
    responsibilities of, 5
    Self-Authoring Mind stage of, 121,
        124–125, 126, 131
    self-perception of, 6
    Self-Transforming Mind stage of, 121,
        126–127
    Socializing Mind stage of, 121, 131
adult learners
    defining, 4–6
    descriptions of, 3–4
    diversity of, 6–8, 131
    learning styles of, 166–167
    states of mind of, 81–82
    strategies regarding, 7–8
    as whole person, 94–95
adult learning theory
    benefits of, 282–283
    bifurcated taxonomy of, 143
    brave spaces and, 150
    building on, 148–149
    commitments within, 140–141
    development of, 143–144
    formal, 143
    missed opportunities regarding, 143–144
    personhood within, 143
    questioning within, 142–143
    as race-based, 142
    reimagining commitment through,
        146–151

strategies for interrogating, 276–278
structured silences within, 140–144, 278
See also theories; *specific theories*
The Adults' Learning Projects (Tough),
    174–175
adult-to-adult relationships, 170
affective neuroscience, 79, 82–90, 94–95
African Americans, 25, 26, 27, 42–43
African-centered feminist perspective, 29
African-centered perspective, 29
African diaspora, 30
Afrocentric feminist epistemology, 27–28
Afrocentricity, 26, 27
after-hours group, 51
age, as goal influencer, 60
Alexander the Great, 173
Amplification step of imaginal method,
    109–110
analytic metatheory, 225–226
andragogy
  applications in practice of, 160–166
  assumptions regarding, 159
  challenges to, 166–169
  diversity and, 167–168
  educator role within, 161, 162–163
  empirical foundation building and,
    168–169
  evaluation within, 163
  focus of, 161
  implications for practice of, 163–164
  incentives regarding, 169–170
  influences on theory and, 160–166
  instruments regarding, 168
  overview of, 44, 157–160, 278
  participation role within, 163
  pedagogy *versus,* 158
  potential regarding, 169–170
  as process model, 160
  self-directed learning and, 45
  stages of, 161–163
  structure within, 162
  study regarding, 168–169
  survival of, 169
  theoretical influence of, 164–166
Animation step of imaginal method,
    110–111
antiracism training, 266–267

antiracist education, 50
anxious brain, 81–82. *See also* brain
Aristotle, 197
artificial intelligence, 246, 271
assimilation, 9
Association step of imaginal method, 109
assumptions, 142, 218, 276
attention, 264
Attention, Relevance, Confidence, and
    Satisfaction (ARCS) model, 263–264
authenticity, 184–185
autonomy, 68–69

baggage to learning, 91
banking model of teaching, 15
barriers, 63–64, 91
Basic American Negro Creed (Du Bois),
    42–43
becoming, 151, 205
behaviorism, 8–9, 82
belongingness, 68, 148
Black church, 30
body-brain, 83, 87
Bohm, David, 49
Bohmian dialogues, 49
brain
  alteration of, 84–85
  anxious, 81–82
  basics of, 80–81
  body-brain, 83, 87
  categorization by, 86
  curious, 81–82
  defined, 83
  emotion of, 80–81, 84–85, 86, 241
  hemisphere role within, 93
  information processing of, 82
brave space, 150
breadth, 225

call and response communication, 30
canon, whitewashing of, 147–148
cardboard box analogy, 119–120
Cartesian mind-body dualism, 83–84
centering identity, 25–29
Chalk Talk, 51
childhood, maturity within, 215
Chinese students, 70

circle of voices exercise, 45
circular response activity, 49
classical conditioning, 8–9
classroom
    democracy within, 41, 51
    discussion within, 49
    inclusive, 36
    learner diversity within, 131
coauthorship of knowledge, 22–23
cognition, 84, 241
cognitive dimension of learning, 138
cognitive neuroscience, 82–88
cognitive science, 9
cognitivism, 9–10
collective signification of theory, 145–146
collective unconscious, 107
commitment
    of adult learning, 277
    to critical pedagogy, 278
    to goals, 63
    intentionality of, 147, 148
    reimagining, 146–151
    self-efficacy and, 66
common sense, 215
communication, 30, 90, 240
community, growth cultures and, 128
community webs, 245
competence, 68
competition, 61
complexity theory, 203, 204
concrete experience, 28
concrete operational intellectual capacities, 122
confidence, 185, 264
connecting, thread of understanding through, 32–33
connectivism
    challenges regarding, 247
    opportunities regarding, 243–245
    overview of, 237–243, 278
    potential of, 245–247
    promise of, 241–243
    within social media, 240–242
    tensions regarding, 243–245
"Connectivism and Connective Knowledge," 238
conscientization, 245

conscious mind, 104–105
consciousness, 108
constructive-development theory, 118–127
constructivism, 9–10, 22, 118
content dimension of learning, 138
content reflection, 218
continued learning, 173–174
continuity, within experiential learning, 199–200
conversations, uncomfortable, 144–145
coronavirus pandemic, 13, 187, 236, 244–245, 282
corporate training, instructional design for, 268–269
counseling, client-centered approaches to, 160–161
counterstories, 145
critical awareness of assumptions, 142
Critical Incident Questionnaire, 45
critical pedagogy, 14–16, 140, 278
critical race theory (CRT), 149
Crowded Brain activity, 91–92
cultural lens, 30
culture, 70, 180
curious brain, 81–82. *See also* brain

Damasio, Antonio, 80, 83, 84–85, 86–87, 89–90
data-driven prediction, 244–245
decolonizing theory, 146
deconstructive stance, 126
degree of cognitive openness, 179
degree of learner commitment, 179
democracy/democratic impulse in adult education
    andragogy and, 163
    changes within, 50
    within the classroom, 41, 51
    as decentering power, 49–51
    defined, 41–43
    as dialogue, 47–49
    as economic equity, 42–43
    experiential, 43–45
    frameworks regarding, 43–51
    as ongoing conversation, 41–42
    overview of, 39–41, 52
    as premature ultimate, 41

as self-directed control, 45–47
socialism and, 42
as struggle against ideological
    manipulation, 43
depth, 225
depth psychology, 222
Descartes, 83
Description step of imaginal method, 109
design, 256–258, 259. *See also* instructional
    design
design processes, 255
design theories, 255
design thinking approach, 261
development, adult
    application regarding, 130–132
    constructive-development theory,
        118–127
    critiques and responses regarding,
        128–130
    distribution of, 129–130
    evolution of, 117–118
    Immunity to Change approach regarding,
        131–132
    Imperial Mind stage of, 122–123, 131
    relevance of, 130
    Self-Authoring Mind stage of, 121,
        124–125, 126, 131
    Self-Transforming Mind stage of, 121,
        126–127
    Socializing Mind stage of, 121, 131
Dewey, John, 39–40, 48, 198, 199–200,
    203, 256, 257
dialogue
    Bohmian, 49
    democracy as, 47–49
    within imaginal method, 111
    importance of, 33
    knowledge structure challenge and, 32
    meaning making and, 28
    spaces for, 33
disorienting dilemma, 217–218
distance education, communication within,
    240. *See also* online learning/online
    adult education
diversity, 142, 167–168, 270
diversity of learners, 6–8
diversity training, 266
Du Bois, W. E. B., 42–43

educational theory, 138–139. *See also* adult
    learning theory; theories; *specific
    theories*
educators, adult
    within andragogy, 161, 162–163
    antiracist practices of, 51
    change modeling by, 132
    characteristics of, 4
    data collection from, 45
    democratic political projects of, 46
    developmental considerations by,
        131–132
    emotion-laden experiences of, 113
    equity commitment of, 147–148
    expert role of, 70
    giving voice by, 24, 28, 35–36
    goal of, 35
    incentives of, 169–170
    learner relationships with, 69
    literature exposure by, 149–150
    lived experience reflection by, 32
    mastery goal approach of, 64–65
    personal reflection of, 113
    relatedness fostering by, 71–72
    role of, 14
    self-determination theory (SDT) practices
        of, 69–72
    self-efficacy practice of, 66–67
    technology change role of, 244
    theory engagement by, 147
    theory failures by, 275
ego, 104
ego consciousness, 107
elaboration theory, 264–265, 267
e-learning. *See* online learning/online adult
    education
Elliot, case of, 84–85
emancipatory learning, 220, 222–223
embodiment, 83
Emile (Rousseau), 199
emotional brain, 84–85, 241. *See also* brain
emotional buy-in, 266
emotional intelligence, 103–104
emotion-laden experiences
    defined, 100
    of educators, 113
    imaginal approach to, 106–112,
        108–111

overview of, 100–106, 112–113
unconscious messages from, 107
emotion management, 106
emotions
    brain and, 80–81
    cliché descriptions of, 87
    cognition and, 84, 241
    cycle of, 85
    defined, 85
    Extra-Rational era of, 104–106
    Humanistic era of, 102–104, 106
    influence of, 102
    within life regulation, 85
    memory and, 80
    motivation and, 80–81
    neuroscience of, 85–88
    Pre-Rational era of, 100–101, 106
    primary, 85
    purpose of, 80
    Rational era of, 101–102, 106
    state of, 86
    study of, 83
    up-hierarchy and, 89–90
    verbalization of, 94
empathy, 184
enthusiasm, 185
ethic of caring, 28
ethic of personal accountability, 28
ethnicity, as goal influencer, 60
evaluation, within andragogy, 163
Evocative Images activity, 93–94
experience
    analyzing, 44
    within andragogy, 162
    defined, 193–194
    emotion and, 86
    emotion-laden, 100–106
    historical understanding regarding, 197
    intellectualizing of, 90
    learning role of, 102–103
    mastery, 66
    obscurities from, 278
    overview of, 159, 193
    theories of learning and, 141
    value of, 44
    vicarious, 66
Experience and Education (Dewey), 199
experience design, 196, 205–207

experiential democracy, 43–45. *See also*
    democracy/democratic impulse in
    adult education
experiential education, 198
experiential learning
    becoming within, 205
    complexities of, 202–205
    complexity theory within, 203, 204
    complex models within, 205–207
    core concepts regarding, 193–196
    criticism regarding, 202
    definitions regarding, 193–196
    design within, 196, 205–207
    early beginnings of, 196–197
    within the early twentieth century,
        199–200
    implications for practice of, 207–208
    inequality within, 197–198
    John Dewey's work regarding, 199–200
    laboratory within, 201
    within late twentieth century, 200–202
    modes of, 201–202
    within the nineteenth century, 197–198
    overview of, 193, 208
    psychoanalytic theory within, 203
    reflect-learn constructivist theory
        regarding, 203
    senses within, 203
    seven modes of experiencing within,
        204–205
    situative theory within, 203
    T-group (training group) within, 201
    traditional education models regarding,
        197–198
    within the twenty-first century, 202–205
    Walk-the-Talk regarding, 205–206
    within whole person, 202–203
experiential learning model, 89
Extra-Rational era, 104–106, 107

facism, 39
feedback, 45, 63
feelings, 85, 86. *See also* emotions
fee paying institutions, democracy within,
    42
First Principles of Instruction, 262–263
Follett, Mary Parker, 49–50
formal learning, 12

formal theories, 137. *See also* theories
formation of self, 100–106
free-writing, 111–112
Freire, Paulo, 15, 40, 49
From Pedagogy to Andragogy (Knowles), 158

Gagne, Robert, 263
gender, as goal influencer, 60
genuineness, 184–185
giving voice
  ambiguity within, 35–36
  connecting through thread of
    understanding within, 32–33
  dialogue importance within, 33
  hub for learning within, 34–35
  naming within, 23–24
  overview of, 22–24
  paradigm shift and, 29, 30
  polyrhythmic realities reflection within,
    31–32
  resources and materials for, 33–34
goals
  achievement, 60–61
  barrier plan regarding, 63–64
  challenge of, 63
  commitment to, 63
  competition and, 61
  concrete, 122
  defined, 59
  demographics and, 60
  effectiveness regarding, 62
  feedback and, 63
  growth mindset and, 64
  "if-then" plan for, 63–64
  immediate, 122
  implications for practice regarding,
    64–65
  instruction regarding, 65
  mastery, 60, 61
  monitoring, 65
  multiple related concepts, 264
  networks of people and, 60
  performance, 60, 61
  related principles, 264
  response to, 70–71
  self-directed learning (SDL) as, 180–181
  self-efficacy and, 66
  setting of, 61–64
  sources of, 60
  specificity of, 62
  subgoals, 63
  tasks, 264
goal theory, 59–65
governance, shared, 51
growth cultures, 127–128
growth mindset, 64

habits of mind, 217
hashtags, 238
hegemonic signification, 140–141, 144
Heron, John, 88–90, 94–95
heterogeneity, 130
heteropatriarchal capitalism, 148
Highlander Folk School, 44
holding environment, 128
holistic health practices, 47
Horton, Myles, 44
human flourishing, 94–95
humanism, 14, 140, 142, 277
Humanistic era, 102–104, 106
humanist tradition, of adult education of
  experience, 200
humanization, 146
humility, 185
hunting assumptions, 276

iceberg metaphor, 174
identity, centering, 25–30
identity approach to transformative
  learning, 223–224
ideologies, democracy as struggle against, 43
"if-then" plan, 63–64
Illich, Ivan, 235
images, Evocative Images activity and,
  93–94
imaginal approach, 100, 106–112
imaginal method, 94, 106, 108–112
imagination, 103, 108
Immunity to Change approach,
  131–132
Imperial Mind, 122–123, 131
incentive dimension of learning, 138
inclusion, 142, 148, 270
inclusive classroom, 36

inclusive spaces, 30–36
individualism, 140–141
individualizing instruction, 181
individuation, 107–108, 129
informal learning, 12–13
informal theories, 137. *See also* theories
information, gathering and sharing of, 260
informational phase, within Walk-the-Talk, 206
information processing, 82
inner self, 104, 111, 222
In Search of Our Mothers' Gardens (Walker), 27–28
instructional design
    ADDIE, 258–259
    artificial intelligence and, 271
    Attention, Relevance, Confidence, and Satisfaction (ARCS) model, 263–264
    components of, 258
    considerations regarding, 267–271
    debates regarding, 259–260
    design and instruction distinction within, 257–258
    design thinking approach, 261
    elaboration theory, 264–265
    First Principles of Instruction, 262–263
    future systems for, 271
    interservice process for instructional systems development (IPISD), 259
    learner roles within, 269–270
    LLAMA (Lot Like an Agile Management Approach) model, 260
    map for, 267–268
    models regarding, 265–267
    nine events model, 263
    organizational context regarding, 268–269
    overview of, 256–258, 271
    participatory design model within, 270
    process models of, 258–261
    subject matter expert roles within, 269–270
    successive approximation model (SAM) for, 260
    theories regarding, 261–267
instructional principle, 262
instructional systems design (ISD), 258–259, 260–261, 267, 269

intentionality, 147, 148
interaction, within experiential learning, 199–200
interests, response to, 70
interservice process for instructional systems development (IPISD), 259
invisibility, recognizing, 145

journaling, 111–112
Jung, Carl, 107
Jungian, defined, 107

Kegan, Robert, 118–127, 128
Keller, J. M., 263–264
knowledge, 22–23, 28, 90, 260
Knowles, Malcolm, 43–44, 157–160, 161–162, 163–165, 166, 173, 175, 178, 181
Kolb, David, 201–202

laboratory, within experiential learning, 201
labor market, 13
learner control, 45–47
learner proactivity, 179
learners, adult
    defining, 4–6
    descriptions of, 3–4
    diversity of, 6–8, 131
    learning styles of, 166–167
    states of mind of, 81–82
    strategies regarding, 7–8
    as whole person, 94–95
learning
    as active mental work, 9
    baggage to, 91
    barriers to, 91
    defined, 8, 194
    dimensions of, 138
    evolution of, 11
    hub for, creating, 34–35
    overview of, 194
    possibilities regarding, 217
    preferences regarding, 7
    process of, 255
    purpose of, 95
    as recursive process, 163
    See also adult education

learning contracts, 40, 47, 164

learning management system (LMS), 239–240

learning theories, 8–12. *See also* adult learning theory; theories; *specific theories*

liberal arts, orientation to, 257

Lindeman, Eduard, 39–40, 48, 49

linking science of instruction, 256, 258

literacy, 49

lived experience, 32

LLAMA (Lot Like an Agile Management Approach) model, 260

machine learning, 271

manufacturing, instructional design within, 269–270

map, function of, 267

marginalized people groups, 25, 30

Maslow, Abraham, 14

massive open online courses (MOOCs), 238–239, 242, 243

mastery approach goals, 60, 61. *See also* goals

mastery experience, 66

maturation, 215

meaning making, 22, 28, 216

meaning-making development, 120–127

The Meaning of Adult Education (Lindeman), 48

meaning perspectives, 214, 216

meaning scheme, 216

memory, 80

Merrill, M. D., 261, 262–263

metacognition, 10

metatheory/metatheoretical discourse, 225–226

Mezirow, Jack, 213–221

microaggression, 72

military training, instructional design for, 268–269

mind, 83

The Mis-Education of the Negro (Woodson), 25–26

The Modern Practice of Adult Education (Knowles), 157, 158–159, 165

motivation
attention and, 80–81
defined, 59
emotion and, 80–81
goal theory and, 59–65
increase of, 71
for learning, 159
overview of, 59
self-determination theory (SDT) and, 67–72
self-efficacy and, 65–67

multiple intelligences, 7

multiple related concepts goal, 264

mutually reinforcing cycle, 120

myth making/mythopoetic, 108

myths, regarding African Americans, 26

naming, within giving voice, 23–24

need to know, 159

negativity bias, 81

nine events model, 263

non-formal learning, 12

nontraditional students, 5

Nussbaum, Martha, 104

Obama, Michelle, 151

object, 119

objectification, 239

Oddi Continuing Learning Inventory (OCLI), 179

online learning/online adult education
challenges regarding, 247
communication position within, 239–240
connectivism and, 237–243, 245–247
coronavirus pandemic and, 187, 236
criticism regarding, 236
data and information usage within, 246–247
democracy within, 42
digital traces and, 244
massive open online courses (MOOCs) within, 238–239, 242, 243
organization of, 240
positions regarding, 239–241
power structures within, 245–246
self-directed learning (SDL) within, 242

two-way communication within, 240
  unfactual Web and, 246
operant conditioning, 9
optimization methods, 258
orientation to learning, 159

participation, learning, 163, 164
participatory design, 270
participatory economics (parecon), 42
Pavlov, Ivan, 9
pedagogy, andragogy *versus,* 158
performance approach goals, 60, 61. *See also*
  goals
performance avoidance goals, 60. *See also*
  goals
personal responsibility orientation (PRO)
  model, 176–178
Personal Responsibility Orientation to Self-
  Direction in Learning Scale (PRO-
  SDLS), 179
personal unconscious, 107
person process context (PPC) model,
  176–184
perspective, 28–30
perspective transformation, 214. *See also*
  transformative learning
persuasion, 66
physiological states, 66
Piaget, Jean, 9, 117–118
planetary approach to transformative
  learning, 224
Plato, 173, 197
points of view, 217
polyrhythmic communication, 30
polyrhythmic realities, 22, 29, 30–33
polyrhythmic structures, 30–31
pose questions, 35
positionality, 22
postcolonial theory, 146
post-Jungian, defined, 107
power, decentering, 49–51
power-over decision-making processes,
  49–50
power structures, within online networks,
  245–246
power-with decision-making processes,
  49–50

practice, defined, 262
preferences, 7, 129
preferential attachment, 243–244
premature ultimate, 41
premise reflection, 218
Pre-Rational era, 100–101, 106
prescriptive orientation for transformative
  learning, 228
presentational knowing, 90, 93
priming, 86
problem posing, 49
problem-posing approach, 15
problem-solving approach, 15–16
processes, design, 255
process orientation for transformative
  learning, 228
process reflection, 218
professional identity, 279–280
program, defined, 262
Program for the International Assessment of
  Adult Competencies, 168–169
progressive tradition, of adult education of
  experience, 200
psychoanalytic approach to transformative
  learning, 222
psychoanalytic theory, 203
psychocritical approach to transformative
  learning, 226–227
psychodevelopmental approach to
  transformative learning, 223, 227
psychodynamic thought, 105
psychology, 215

race, 142, 145, 150
race centric approach to transformative
  learning, 224–225
racism, 42–43, 282
radical tradition, of adult education of
  experience, 200
Rational era, 101–102, 106
rationality, 84
readiness to learn, 159
Really Simple Syndication (RSS)
  technology, 238
reflection, 16–17, 110, 140–141, 218, 278
reflect-learn constructivist theory, 203
Reigeluth, C. M., 261–262, 264–265

relatedness, 68, 69, 71–72
related principles goal, 264
relational ontology, 224
relational phase, within Walk-the-Talk, 206–207
relationships, of Self-Transformed leaders, 127
relative stability, 225
relativism, 126
relevance, defined, 264
repressive tolerance, 146
resistance, 148
respect, 185
Rogers, Carl, 14, 160–161, 178
Romanticism, 102
Rousseau, Jean-Jacques, 199

safe space, 150
satisfaction, 264
schema, defined, 9
scientific discovery methods, 198
self-actualization, 14, 161
Self-Authoring Mind, 121, 124–125, 126, 131
self-concept, 159, 178, 180
self-determination theory (SDT), 67–72
Self-Directed Learning (Knowles), 181
self-directed learning (SDL)
    assumptions regarding, 179
    authenticity within, 184–185
    characteristics of, 40, 176
    confidence within, 185
    contextual dimension of, 182–184
    control and power within, 183
    coronavirus pandemic and, 187
    defined, 175
    degree of cognitive openness within, 179
    degree of learner commitment within, 179
    divergent perspectives regarding, 175–176
    within elaboration theory, 265
    empathy within, 184
    enthusiasm within, 185
    evolving model of, 176–178
    facilitating of, 184–185
    genuineness within, 184–185
    as goal, 180–181

historical perspectives regarding, 173–175
human strengths and, 186–187
humility within, 185
implications of the personal dimension within, 179–181
individualizing instruction and, 181
learner characteristics within, 182
learner proactivity within, 179
learner *versus* learning within, 176
within medical education, 180
Oddi Continuing Learning Inventory (OCLI) for, 179
within online learning, 242
overview of, 188, 278
personal responsibility orientation model of, 176–178
Personal Responsibility Orientation to Self-Direction in Learning Scale (PRO-SDLS) within, 179
person dimension within, 178–181
person process context (PPC) model of, 176–184
political conditions for, 183
positive psychology and, 186–187
prediction of, 179–180
process dimension of, 181–182
psychological traits regarding, 179
qualities within, 184
research regarding, 186
respect within, 185
Self-Directed Learning Readiness Scale (SDLRS) for, 178–179
skills for, 174
social context and, 183
staged self-directed learning model within, 182
steps regarding, 181
TEACHER acronym for, 184–185
technology and, 187–188
tendency assessing toward, 178–179
trends and issues regarding, 185–188
trust within, 184
value of, 169
Self-Directed Learning Readiness Scale (SDLRS), 178–179
Self-Directed Learning Research Focus Area (North-West University), 186

self-directedness, 180
self-direction, 45–47
self-efficacy, 65–67, 264
self/self-formation
    complexity of, 103, 105
    emotion-laden experience and, 100–106
    Extra-Rational era of, 106, 107
    Humanistic era of, 106
    imaginal approach to, 106–112
    inner, giving voice to, 104, 111, 222
    Pre-Rational era and, 106
    Rational era of, 106
Self-Transforming Mind, 121, 126–127
sensibility, 87
Siemens, George, 237–238
signification, 139, 145–146
silence, structured, 141–144
situated learning, 11
situative theory, 203
Skinner, B. F., 9
slower process of education, 50
social class, as goal influencer, 60
social comparisons, 64
social constructivism, 11, 22, 216
socialism, 42–43
socialization, 125
Socializing Mind, 123–124, 129, 131
social learning, 10–11
social media, 40, 240–242
social movements, 15–16
social networks, 243
Socrates, 197
soul work, 222
spiraled sequence, within elaboration theory, 264
spiritual/transpersonal approach to transformative learning, 223
staged self-directed learning model, 182
stances, self-authored, 126
state of emotions, 86. *See also* emotions
state of feeling, 86. *See also* emotions
state of feeling made conscious, 86–87
state of mind, 87
stereotypes, as goal influencer, 60
stimulus-response, 82
storytelling, within imaginal method, 111–112

structured silence, 141–144, 278
subgoals, 63. *See also* goals
subject, 119
subject matter expert, within instructional design, 269–270
The Subject-Object Interview, 122
subject-object relationship, 119–120, 129
subject/object shift, 119
successive approximation model (SAM), 260, 267
surface learning, 206
survival, body-brain connection and, 81, 83
symbolizing, before verbalizing, 90–91

tasks goal, 264
TEACHER acronym, for self-directed learning (SDL), 184–185
teaching, art and science of, 21, 35
technology
    artificial intelligence, 246, 271
    benefits of, 236
    challenges regarding, 247
    changes within, 241
    choosing, 246
    defined, 257
    within education, 235–236
    experimentation of, 237
    machine learning, 271
    materiality and, 244
    self-directed learning (SDL) and, 187–188
    within social media, 240
T-group (training group), 201
theories
    collective signification of, 145–146
    consequences of, 139
    criticality of, 137–140
    design, 255
    dismissing, 138
    educational, 138
    engagement through, 147
    espoused, 139
    expansion of, 149–150
    failures regarding, 275
    fault within, 216
    formal, 137, 141
    in-use, 139

as part of professional identity,
     279–280, 281–282
practice and, 138–139
representation within, 150–151
as set of analytic lenses, 279, 281
as set of tools, 279, 281
signification and, 139
strategies for interrogating, 276–278
studies following, 165
using, 275–283, 279–282
whitewashing of, 147–148
See also adult learning theory; *specific*
     theories
theory of instruction, 261–262
tolerance, repressive, 146
topical sequence, within elaboration theory,
     264
Tough, Allen, 174–175
transformation, 127–128, 217
transformational phase, within
     Walk-the-Talk, 207
transformative learning
  adaptive orientation regarding, 228
  classification system for, 221–222
  critiques of, 219–221
  ethical considerations regarding, 228
  identity approach to, 223–224
  implementation of, 226–227
  key concepts within, 216–219
  metatheory/metatheoretical discourse
       and, 225–226
  origins of, 213–216
  overview of, 213–216
  phases of, 217–219
  planetary approach to, 224
  prescriptive orientation regarding, 228
  process orientation regarding, 228
  psychoanalytic approach to, 222
  psychocritical approach to, 226–227

psychodevelopmental approach to, 223,
     227
  race centric approach to, 224–225
  spiritual/transpersonal approach to, 223
  theoretical approaches to, 221–225
  theory of, 41
  tools within, 246
tree metaphor, regarding experiential
     learning, 200
trichotomous goal model, 60
trust, 184
tutoring, 271
two-way communication, 240

uncomfortable conversations, 144–145
unconscious mind, 104–105
understanding, emphasis on, 11
unfactual Web, 246
up-hierarchy, 89–90
U.S. Military, ADDIE usage by, 258–259
utility-value interventions, 71

verbalization of emotion, 94
vicarious experience, 66
Vietnam War, 259
Vygotsky, Lev, 11

Walker, Alice, 27–28
Walk-the-Talk, 205–206
wandering, 109
white supremacy, 50
whitewashing, of canon, 147–148
Wiltshire, Harold, 41
wisdom, knowledge *versus,* 28
womanist perspective, 24, 26–28
women, African American, 26–27,
     30–31
Woodson, Carter G., 25–26
workplace, learning contracts within, 164